Comparative Education:
The Construction of a Field

CERC Studies in Comparative Education

29. Maria Manzon (2011): *Comparative Education: The Construction of a Field*. ISBN 978-988-17852-6-8. 295pp. HK$200/US$32.

28. Kerry J. Kennedy, Wing On Lee & David L. Grossman (eds.) (2010): *Citizenship Pedagogies in Asia and the Pacific*. ISBN 978-988-17852-2-0. 407pp. HK$250/US$38.

27. David Chapman, William K. Cummings & Gerard A. Postiglione (eds.) (2010): *Crossing Borders in East Asian Higher Education*. ISBN 978-962-8093-98-4. 388pp. HK$250/US$38.

26. Ora Kwo (ed.) (2010): *Teachers as Learners: Critical Discourse on Challenges and Opportunities*. ISBN 978-962-8093-55-7. 349pp. HK$250/US$38.

25. Carol K.K. Chan & Nirmala Rao (eds.) (2009): *Revisiting the Chinese Learner: Changing Contexts, Changing Education*. ISBN 978-962-8093-16-8. 360pp. HK$250/US$38.

24. Donald B. Holsinger & W. James Jacob (eds.) (2008): *Inequality in Education: Comparative and International Perspectives*. ISBN 978-962-8093-14-4. 584pp. HK$300/US$45.

23. Nancy Law, Willem J Pelgrum & Tjeerd Plomp (eds.) (2008): *Pedagogy and ICT Use in Schools around the World: Findings from the IEA SITES 2006 Study*. ISBN 978-962-8093-65-6. 296pp. HK$250/US$38.

22. David L. Grossman, Wing On Lee & Kerry J. Kennedy (eds.) (2008): *Citizenship Curriculum in Asia and the Pacific*. ISBN 978-962-8093-69-4. 268pp. HK$200/US$32.

21. Vandra Masemann, Mark Bray & Maria Manzon (eds.) (2007): *Common Interests, Uncommon Goals: Histories of the World Council of Comparative Education Societies and its Members*. ISBN 978-962-8093-10-6. 384pp. HK$250/US$38.

20. Peter D. Hershock, Mark Mason & John N. Hawkins (eds.) (2007): *Changing Education: Leadership, Innovation and Development in a Globalizing Asia Pacific*. ISBN 978-962-8093-54-0. 348pp. HK$200/US$32.

19. Mark Bray, Bob Adamson & Mark Mason (eds.) (2007): *Comparative Education Research: Approaches and Methods*. ISBN 978-962-8093-53-3. 444pp. HK$250/US$38.

18. Aaron Benavot & Cecilia Braslavsky (eds.) (2006): *School Knowledge in Comparative and Historical Perspective: Changing Curricula in Primary and Secondary Education*. ISBN 978-962-8093-52-6. 315pp. HK$200/US$32.

17. Ruth Hayhoe (2006): *Portraits of Influential Chinese Educators*. ISBN 978-962-8093-40-3. 398pp. HK$250/US$38.

16. Peter Ninnes & Meeri Hellstén (eds.) (2005): *Internationalizing Higher Education: Critical Explorations of Pedagogy and Policy*. ISBN 978-962-8093-37-3. 231pp. HK$200/US$32.

15. Alan Rogers (2004): *Non-Formal Education: Flexible Schooling or Participatory Education?* ISBN 978-962-8093-30-4. 316pp. HK$200/US$32.

14. W.O. Lee, David L. Grossman, Kerry J. Kennedy & Gregory P. Fairbrother (eds.) (2004): *Citizenship Education in Asia and the Pacific: Concepts and Issues*. ISBN 978-962-8093-59-5. 313pp. HK$200/US$32.

13. Mok Ka-Ho (ed.) (2003): *Centralization and Decentralization: Educational Reforms and Changing Governance in Chinese Societies*. ISBN 978-962-8093-58-8. 230pp. HK$200/ US$32.

Earlier titles in the series are listed on the back page of the book.

CERC Studies in Comparative Education 29

Maria MANZON

Comparative Education: The Construction of a Field

 Springer

Comparative Education Research Centre
The University of Hong Kong

Comparative Education Research Centre
Faculty of Education, The University of Hong Kong,
Pokfulam Road, Hong Kong, China
© Comparative Education Research Centre

First published 2011
ISBN 978-988-17852-6-8 Paperback

Printed and bound by The Central Printing Press Ltd. in Hong Kong, China

Contents

List of Figures   vi

List of Tables   vi

List of Appendices   vi

Abbreviations   vii

Acknowledgments   ix

Series Editor's Foreword   xi
   Mark Bray

Foreword   xiii
   Robert Cowen

1. **Introduction: Deconstructing Comparative Education**   1

2. **Disciplines and Fields in Academic Discourse**   13

3. **The Empirical Substance and Mass that Constitute the Field of Comparative Education**   37

4. **Intellectual Histories of Comparative Education**   127

5. **Mapping the Intellectual Discourse on 'Comparative Education'**   153

6. **Reconstructing Comparative Education**   217

Appendices   231

References   251

Notes on the Author   285

Index   287

List of Figures

2.1   A Preliminary Mapping of Disciplinary Change   21
3.1   Typology of Comparative Education Textbooks   69
3.2   Typology of Comparative and International Education Organisations   102
5.1   A Classification of the Educational Sciences   192
5.2   Halls's Typology of Comparative Education   196
5.3   Schema for the Field of Comparative and International Education   197
6.1   Intellectual and Institutional Construction of Comparative Educations   222

List of Tables

2.1   Epistemological and Sociological Features of Academic Disciplines   17
3.1   Models of Teaching Comparative Education, by Levels   40
3.2   Comparative Education Taught as a BEd. Lecture Course (2008)   61
3.3   Comparative Education Taught as a Master's Lecture Course (2008)   62
3.4   Member Societies of the WCCES (2010)   75
4.1   Paulston's Taxonomy of Root Paradigms and Branching Theories in   135
        Comparative Education
4.2   Paradigmatic Themes in Comparative Education (Cowen, 2003a)   141
5.1   A Comparison of Typological Definitions of Comparative Education   207

List of Appendices

1   List of Key Informants Interviewed   231
2   A Chronology of the Institutionalisation of Comparative Education   233
        World Wide (North America)
3   A Chronology of the Institutionalisation of Comparative Education   234
        World Wide (Europe)
4   A Chronology of the Institutionalisation of Comparative Education   237
        World Wide (Africa)
5   A Chronology of the Institutionalisation of Comparative Education   238
        World Wide (Asia and Australasia)
6   A Chronology of the Institutionalisation of Comparative Education   240
        World Wide (Latin America and the Caribbean)
7   Number of Universities where Comparative Education is Taught,   241
        June 2008
8   Key Data on WCCES Member Societies   243
9   Citation and Content Analysis of Comparative Education Journals   246
10   Attitudinal & Demographic Surveys of the Field of Comparative   249
        Education

Abbreviations

ADB	Asian Development Bank
AFDECE	Association française pour le développement de l'éducation comparée et des échanges
AFEC	Association francophone d'éducation comparée
ANZCIES	Australian and New Zealand Comparative and International Education Society
APC-SEC	Asociación de Pedagogos de Cuba (Sección de Educación Comparada)
BAICE	British Association for International and Comparative Education
BCES	Bulgarian Comparative Education Society
BEd	Bachelor of Education
BID	Banco Interamericano de Desarrollo
CCEK	Council on Comparative Education of Kazakhstan
CCES	Chinese Comparative Education Society
CCES-T	Chinese Comparative Education Society-Taipei
CEDE	Centro Europeo dell'Educazione
CE	*Comparative Education*
CER	*Comparative Education Review*
CERI	Center for Educational Research and Innovation
CERC	Comparative Education Research Centre, The University of Hong Kong
CESA	Comparative Education Society of Asia
CES-CPS	Comparative Education Section - Czech Pedagogical Society
CESE	Comparative Education Society in Europe
CESHK	Comparative Education Society of Hong Kong
CESI	Comparative Education Society of India
CESP	Comparative Education Society of the Philippines
CIECAP	Comparative and International Education Course Archive Project
CIEP	Centre international d'études pédagogiques
CIES	Comparative and International Education Society
CIESC	Comparative and International Education Society of Canada
CNIER	China National Institute of Educational Research
CUSO	Canadian University Service Overseas
EC	European Community
ECEEAS	Egyptian Comparative Education and Educational Administration Society
EU	European Union
GCES	Greek Comparative Education Society
HKIEd	Hong Kong Institute of Education
HPS-CES	Hungarian Pedagogical Society (Comparative Education Section)
IB	International Baccalaureate
IBE	UNESCO International Bureau of Education
IBRD	International Bank for Reconstruction and Development
ICES	Israel Comparative Education Society
IDA	International Development Association
IEA	International Association for the Evaluation of Educational Achievement
IER	*International Education Review*
IIEP	International Institute for Educational Planning
IJED	*International Journal of Educational Development*
IRE	*International Review of Education*

JCES	Japan Comparative Education Society
KCES	Korean Comparative Education Society
LACE	London Association of Comparative Educationists
LOGSE	General Law of the Educational System
MA	Master of Arts
MEd	Master of Education
MESCE	Mediterranean Society of Comparative Education
MPhil	Master of Philosophy
NGO	Non-governmental Organisation
NGVO	Nederlandstalig Genootschap voor Vergelijkende Studie van Opvoeding en Onderwijs
NIER	National Institute for Educational Research (Japan)
NOCIES	Nordic Comparative and International Education Society
OECD	Organisation for Economic Co-operation and Development
OEI	Organización de Estados Iberoamericanos
OISE	Ontario Institute for Studies in Education
PCEd	Postgraduate Certificate in Education
PCES	Polish Comparative Education Society
PhD	Doctor of Philosophy
PISA	Programme of International Student Assessment
PRC	People's Republic of China
RCCE	Russian Council of Comparative Education
REEC	*Revista Española de Educación Comparada*
ROC	Republic of China
SACHES	Southern African Comparative & History of Education Society
SAECE	Sociedad Argentina de Estudios Comparados en Educación
SBEC	Sociedade Brasileira de Educação Comparada
SEEC	Sociedad Española de Educación Comparada
SICESE	Sezione Italiana della CESE
SIIVEDGE	Sektion International und Interkulturell Vergleichende Erziehungswissenschaft in der Deutschen Gesellschaft für Erziehungswissenschaft
SOMEC	Sociedad Mexicana de Educación Comparada
TÜKED	Turkish Comparative Education Society
TIMSS	Third International Mathematics and Science Study
UBA	Universidad de Buenos Aires
UCES	Ukrainian Comparative Education Society
UIE	UNESCO Institute for Education
UK	United Kingdom
UN	United Nations
UNESCO	United Nations Educational, Scientific and Cultural Organization
US / USA	United States of America
USSR	Union of Soviet Socialist Republics
WB	World Bank, The
WCCES	World Council of Comparative Education Societies

Acknowledgments

I am sincerely grateful to my intellectual mentors: to Mark Bray, for guiding my initial research work and immersing me in the international scholarly community and literature of the field of comparative education; and to Mark Mason, for steering me wisely through the winding and laborious thought processes that went into this work.

I am indebted also to the international comparative education scholars, whose names are too many to list here, who have generously given their time to be interviewed at major conferences and shared valuable insights into the field. These interviews would also not have been possible if not for the financial support extended by the Comparative Education Research Centre (CERC) and the Faculty Research Fund/Sik Sik Yuen Fund of the Faculty of Education, the University of Hong Kong.

Special thanks go to Vandra Masemann for her timely words of wisdom, to Erwin H. Epstein for his constant encouragement and interest in my work, and to Robert Cowen for challenging me to think beyond my limits.

Series Editor's Foreword

It is a particular pleasure to welcome this book to the series, not only because it is a profound volume which will long stand as a milestone in the field, but also because it emerged over a period of years within the Comparative Education Research Centre (CERC) at the University of Hong Kong. Its author first studied for the Postgraduate Certificate in Chinese Language and then in the Master of Education programme at the University. From the latter she produced an excellent dissertation which was later published by CERC (Manzon 2004). She then registered for the PhD programme, producing a thesis which won the distinguished Li Ka Shing Prize for excellence. This book is a revised version of that thesis.

In between her first book and the present volume, Maria Manzon generated much additional scholarship. It included co-editorship of the book of histories of the World Council of Comparative Education Societies (WCCES) and its members (Masemann et al. 2007) and a book supported by the WCCES entitled *Comparative Education at Universities World Wide* (Wolhuter et al. 2008).

Li Ka Shing Prizes are highly competitive, and the University of Hong Kong describes the winners as "the best of our elite students". Only two prizes are awarded each year among all PhD students in the Faculties of Architecture, Arts, Business & Economics, Education, Law, and Social Sciences. The prizes are awarded at a special ceremony, and are accompanied by personal citations.

For Maria Manzon, the ceremony was held in December 2010. The citation was delivered by Mark Mason, a previous Director of CERC and now Professor of Comparative and International Education and Development at the Hong Kong Institute of Education (HKIEd). Mark Mason referred to Maria Manzon's intelligence and skill in writing a thesis that had been deemed worthy of the prize. He also recognised her bravery in tackling fundamental questions. The work, he added, is the result not only of great vision and tenacity but also of considerable travel as Maria Manzon flew off to distant corners of the world to interview presidents and past-presidents of comparative education societies, "gathering masses of narrative data about the history and constitution of the field".

CERC sincerely congratulates Maria Manzon on her accomplishment. And we much look forward to hearing and further debating the reactions that this book will provoke.

Mark Bray
Chair Professor of Comparative Education
Director, Comparative Education Research Centre

References

Manzon, Maria (2004): *Building Alliances: Schools, Parents and Communities in Hong Kong and Singapore*. CERC Monograph Series 3, Hong Kong: Comparative Education Research Centre, The University of Hong Kong.

Masemann, Vandra; Bray, Mark & Manzon, Maria (eds.) (2007): *Common Interests, Uncommon Goals: Histories of the World Council of Comparative Education Societies and its Members*. CERC Studies in Comparative Education 21, Hong Kong: Comparative Education Research Centre, The University of Hong Kong and Dordrecht: Springer.

Wolhuter, Charl; Popov, Nikolay; Manzon, Maria & Leutwyler, Bruno (eds.) (2008): *Comparative Education at Universities World Wide*. Sophia: Bureau for Educational Services.

Foreword

I remember I once grumbled (gently of course) that "we did not know very much about ourselves". I was referring to comparative educationists and I particularly had in mind the professional networks and professional societies of comparative education scholars (such as the CIES or CESE or WCCES). That was 20 years ago, and off and on since then I have grumbled (gently of course) that we do not know very much about ourselves in another sense: our histories have been so linear, so simple, so teleological, that they reassure only beginners in the study of 'comparative education' that the field is making progress; just as 'the histories' had reassured me too as a student, once upon a time. Now I will have to stop grumbling. Maria Manzon enforces a certain stunned silence.

Of course she does this quite unintentionally. She is too kind and forgiving a person and too good an academic to wish for silences in our collective conversation. However the quality of her work implies the need for a small, and respectful, silence amid our professional chatter. She is creating some freedoms for us, for we can now understand ourselves better.

The work she has done is thorough and detailed. Her theoretical imagination is a pleasure to watch as it melds with, and works through, complex material. Her scholarship is of the highest order. The sweep of her analysis and the clarity of her stated arguments move us forward not merely in terms of an improved sense of how we network in our professional infrastructures, but also in terms of how we might start thinking about our identity (in the sense of our accumulated and contemporary 'history', our historically-formed academic-selves).

Dr. Manzon provides such 'a history'. It is complex. It links biography and social structures and historical forces. It is not merely 'a history' of a field of study, a linear narrative spaced through time. It is also a complex sociological analysis. It traces tensions and contradictions between the intellectual corpus and the institutional embodiments of academic comparative education, as conflicting markers of its identity. It is a history and it is also not a history: it is a canny analysis in the sociology of knowledge. It shows a variety of forms of comparative education which alter over time and in different places for 'reasons' which Manzon makes explicit – though her 'history' has no simple causes and offers no simple 'reasons'; the difficult and ambiguous concept of 'fields of influence' might do more justice to her narrative subtleties within which she locates the political economy of knowledge of academic comparative education. Similarly her history – this version of our history – has no certain future. The present does not arise linearly out of the past. Specific forms of comparative education disappear. Academic comparative education is always being refreshed intellectually from unexpected perspectives; and parts of it are always being institutionally rescripted by political and economic forces, and by the energy of new scholars. Of course the devil is in the detail, and the manuscript of this remarkable book contains a lot of it. The detail is among the delights of the book – Maria Manzon has an almost anthropological sense of the intimacy and significance of detail.

The book also creates a powerful set of interpretations to assist us to understand academic comparative education, as it was and as it is. In understanding those interpretations, we probably come to this Manzon manuscript with different forms of comparative education in mind. Even those of us deeply immersed in academic comparative education probably practise different branches of its arcane arts. I personally came to this manuscript with memories of some other brilliant accounts, recently read, of the 'identity' (within and outside of educational studies) of sociology and philosophy and history. Partly because of this, I suspect I was particularly sensitive to three motifs in Manzon's work, as I watched her inspect some of our traditional assumptions and old ideologies before moving on to state new coherences.

First, I was fascinated by the way in which she moved out of the trap provided by the old question of how far comparative education is a discipline or a field of study. The problem is not to note the ideological bias in the original question, within educational studies, about what is a 'discipline' and what is a 'field of study'. The problem is not to arrive, fairly rapidly, at the proposition that academic comparative education is a 'field of study'. The problem is the next step: to avoid tipping into one or another of our compulsive professional disorders: that comparative education is 'really' sociology, or history, or postmodern or post-structural or multi-or-interdisciplinary or a branch of policy studies; or that it should, as an act of faith, become one of those things; or maybe all of them at once. In other words, because our 'history' is confusing, the escape from that tension and from those ambiguities sometimes means a rush to certainty, a set of strident counter-claims, about our true identity.

The claims come and go, while the comparative academic procession marches on exploring its normal puzzles. Of course this leads to a second question: where is this particular academic procession going, and why it is going there?

Thus, secondly, I was fascinated by the way Dr. Manzon – implicitly confronted by this question – refused to turn inwards, to look for our identity in the magic of our academic name. In other words, there is a trap here too: gazing upon the two words 'comparative education', and insisting on their literal-and-conjoined interpretation, creates an account of the field which emphasises its potentially stable and permanent nature. The implicit argument, in the juxtaposition of the words ('comparative' and 'education'), generates an epistemic position: there is an essential and permanent act of 'comparison' and an essential and permanent institutional entity 'education'. Those words, acted upon together in a certain way, will give us lists of similarities and differences in education-in-context; and, after much work, the identification of the causes of those similarities and differences will become known. Finally there will have been so many 'comparative' investigations done that a 'universal and useful science' of comparative education will have been created, firmly based on fact. Of course this was indeed a historical 'moment' in both applied and theoretical comparative education; this was a comparative education which was hoped for. The problem is not to deny that such a position was once part of our identity nor to refuse to notice that the motif continues in the ideologies of our times (cf. 'robust and relevant research' in comparative education). The academic problem is to refuse those juxtapositions (of two words; of juxtaposed educational systems as the central unit of comparison; and of juxtaposed social contexts as an irritating set of unsolvable puzzles) as the definition of a permanent truth about our field of study. Our field of study responds to many of the social and historical forces it studies – it changes; and Maria Manzon grasps this point and draws it out in great detail and with élan.

The third theme which I was startled to notice Dr. Manzon beginning to take on frontally was the question of the relation of what may be loosely termed 'the base' and 'the superstructure' of comparative education. For example, which comes first, the university department and then the professional comparative education society? Put like that, the answer takes a fast set of empirically based answers. But what about the sociology of the creation, diffusion and use of 'academic comparative education' knowledge? How do the social processes come together, in biographies and higher education institutions of various kinds, research agencies and think tanks and policy-formulating institutions, in journals and in professional societies, in multiple 'foreign' languages, and in multiple social science languages, and in the identities of academic comparative education in university departments? Dr. Manzon does not answer those questions. No one (not even Manzon) could, in the present moment, do the range of research needed to capture all of the 'force-fields' involved in the social construction of this aspect of our academic subject.

However, what did catch my attention is that Maria Manzon is drawing on a conversation which is already well advanced – with much of it currently emanating from Hong Kong, notably the Comparative Education Research Centre (CERC) at the University of Hong Kong and the tradition of work and the questions broached there. Dr. Manzon herself is part of that immediate history, has already written within that conversation, and here she moves the terms of our collective discussion in academic comparative education forwards, and massively so. She sharpens our sense of ourselves in a dangerous world which is making us important commentators on it. We might wish to remember and repeat to ourselves that the world is sometimes dangerous, often unforgiving and occasionally very very unkind to those who comment analytically and act wisely on it.

I personally see her contribution to our academic conversation, via this book, as of historical significance. Indeed, the most difficult single thing involved in writing this Foreword has been to stick to sketching a few things that caught my own imagination – without revealing too much of what follows. The book is too exciting for 'who dunnit' to be revealed in the Foreword. In my view, the book will create a moment of silence as we absorb the analysis and the importance of the new voice – and then the conversation will re-start with renewed vigour, with our imaginations refreshed. I am grateful that this book has been written.

Robert Cowen
Institute of Education, University of London

1

Introduction:
Deconstructing Comparative Education

Despite its history of over a century, questions about the identity and nature of comparative education have been and continue to be raised in the literature, particularly in view of an expansion in the range of activities that have been labelled 'comparative education'.[1] Paradoxically, the field has been established institutionally in university academic courses and professional societies in various parts of the world, and has its own specialist book and journal publications. That the field is institutionalised as a separate area of inquiry in many countries – some stronger than others – does not therefore necessarily imply, much less justify, its intellectual legitimacy as an independent field. Practitioners in the field have debated the issue of whether comparative education is a discipline, a quasi-discipline, a multidisciplinary field, a method, or simply a different perspective in education (e.g., Heath, 1958-59; Broadfoot, 1977; Parkyn, 1977; García Garrido, 1996; Olivera, 1988; Broadfoot, 1999). Farrell (1979, p.3) notes that the debate on these 'grand questions' dwindled as members of the field "became convinced that there neither were, nor had to be, final universal answers to them". The debate nevertheless continues (see e.g., Cowen, 2006; Phillips & Schweisfurth, 2006; Klees, 2008; Mason, 2008a; Olivera, 2009), which, in its time, Kelly and Altbach (1981) sum up into a single question: What is comparative education? From another perspective, critical practitioners in comparative education have also pointed out the field's lack of a substantive institutional and epistemological core, or at least, the lack of clarity about it (e.g., Kazamias & Schwartz, 1977; Cowen, 1990; Cook, Hite & Epstein, 2004). Its academic institutions have had their highs and lows in different places, and its professional societies exhibit varied signs of life and activity. Paradoxically, new professional societies are being formed in

---

[1] Cowen (1982a) distinguished between academic (theoretical) comparative education, professional (teacher training) comparative education and interventionist (policy advice) comparative education, differentiated by their intellectual bases and institutional locations. In this book, I focus mainly on academic comparative education.

1

other parts of the world, despite the absence or fragility of comparative education as a taught course in their universities. Likewise new courses are being institutionally legitimised in some countries, while previously strong programmes are becoming marginalised in other places. The field has no strict gate-keeping rules and is rather inclusive, as seen in its world congresses and other academic forums, where not a few of its participants have only a vague notion of the field or are weakly identified with it (e.g., Epstein, 2004).

This lack of clarity as to the distinctive nature and purposes of comparative education is problematic. How can a field of study survive, develop and perpetuate itself if its scholarly community are unclear, much less unanimous, about their field's identity, aims and contents? More importantly, this raises the question about the relationship between the field's intellectual vis-à-vis institutional legitimacy. Why do the intellectual and the institutional trajectories of this field diverge? In other words, why does comparative education exist and perpetuate itself institutionally (institutional legitimacy) despite the unresolved debates about its intellectual legitimacy? Why is it that comparative education became an institutionally separate field in some places but not in others? These various aspects can be encapsulated into two main questions which I intend to answer in this book:

- Why is comparative education institutionalised as a distinct field when its intellectual distinctiveness seems to be blurred?

- What is comparative education?

The first explores the *institutional* features of comparative education, while the second analyses its *intellectual* substance. Concretely, in the first main question, I explore how and why did comparative education become and continue to be institutionally legitimised as a distinct sub-field of educational studies despite a lack of clarity about its intellectual distinctiveness. Why does it have disciplinary-like infrastructures (e.g., university programmes and centres, professional societies, specialist journals and books, conferences) that make it visible as a field or quasi-discipline? And why is there an uneven development or visibility of comparative education in different places?

On the second main question, I analyse, in the first place, whether comparative education is an academic field or not. What is the nature of a field, in general, and of comparative fields, in particular? What are their necessary or essential features? Does comparative education meet these essential requirements? A cursory survey of the discourse about comparative education reveals the multiple names by which comparativists designate their field of study (e.g., Halls, 1990a). Not only is there no universally consistent definition of comparative education; there have even been moves to widen the scope of the field's work through mergers with allied fields (e.g., Wilson, 1994a; Crossley, 2000). In Cowen's terms, there are multiple comparative educations (2000, p.333). But isn't there a necessary and permanent core in comparative education? If so, how can it be reconciled with its contingent and changing features? Likewise, how can it be substantively distinguished from other comparative fields, in general, and from educational studies, in particular? What distinctive contribution does comparative education make to the study of educational issues otherwise not provided by these other foundation studies?

This work thus essentially revolves around two core themes: the institutional infrastructures of comparative education and its intellectual contours and substance. The relationship between the institutional and intellectual bases of comparative education has been initially addressed by Cowen (1982a). In this book I seek to further elucidate what comparative education is – intellectually and institutionally –, how these two facets relate to each other and, above all, why their trajectories diverge.

Aims of this Book

This book addresses the questions of what comparative education is and how it came to be constructed as a field. Employing sociological analysis and philosophical argumentation, it seeks to elucidate the institutional and intellectual shaping of comparative education by factors associated with epistemology, structure and agency, and discourse.

I contend that comparative education exists and perpetuates itself institutionally as a distinct field despite the continuing debates about its intellectual legitimacy because it is a body of knowledge constructed not purely out of an inner logic based on cognitive criteria, but also as a result of interlocking societal discourses (Foucault) and the interplay of power relations located both in social structures and in human agency (Bourdieu). In the construction of its institutional infrastructures and of its intellectual definitions, power relations embedded in discourses, social structures and human agency intervene conjoined with cognitive principles. I test this argument on the two components of comparative education: the institutional and the intellectual.

In the first place, I examine the institutional infrastructures of comparative education in historical perspective. I argue that comparative education is a field, albeit a constructed field, that initially came to be institutionally legitimised as a distinct subfield of educational studies not only out of an intrinsic logic based on epistemological criteria alone, but also as the result of pragmatic and political reasons working through a complex interplay of discourses, social structures and human agency and their respective power relations. Once institutionally legitimised as a field, comparative education had acquired sufficient (ontological) existence that 'materially' demarcated it from other fields, while subjecting it to further workings of political interests among institutions and individuals who naturally attempted to preserve and increase the field's inertial momentum (Mason, 2008b) and their positions within it. As an institutionally independent field, a distinctive discursive formation had developed and taken the form of disciplinary-like structures and processes, specific discourses on 'canonical' texts, authors and methods. In Chapter 3, I investigate the institutional histories of academic comparative education in the form of taught courses at universities, professional societies and specialist publications, and employ existing surveys to delineate the field's contours. I also examine the empirical substance of interventionist comparative education in the work of national and international agencies. My aim is two-fold: first, to consider the historical contingencies and power relations that led to or furthered the institutionalisation of comparative education as a stable set of heterogeneous discourses in different times and places; and second, to ascertain from an institutional perspective whether comparative education is a distinct field or not, and to offer explanations why this is so in the light of the findings on its institutional construction.

Second, I investigate the intellectual histories and discourses about the epistemological boundaries of comparative education. I contend that, having been institutionally established as a separate field, the intellectual legitimacy of comparative education – of its intellectual corpus/substance – is likewise constructed not only by intellectual traditions and criteria, which endow it with relative intellectual autonomy, but also by the discourses among agents who compete to define the field which, in its turn, is socially located within wider fields of power (academic-institutional, national, international, global). Applying a Bourdieuian field perspective, I propose that theoretical definitions of a field need to be examined in the light of the positions held by those who produce them within the intellectual field, which exhibits homologies with the wider field of power. This implies that theoretical subject definitions are not *a priori* conceptual abstractions by academics based on cognitive criteria alone. Rather they are *a posteriori* definitions based on cumulative work done in the field (which is partly determined by practical developments outside the intellectual field and areas of teaching/research that arise from them, as Anweiler [1977] argues), and on the position and breadth of vision of the academic defining the field in relation to other positions in the field. The intellectual definitions of the field of comparative education are thus constructed partly by discourses and epistemological structures, and partly by the interplay of objective social structures and subjective dispositions of agents and their respective political interests.

In Chapter 4, I trace the intellectual roots – accepted ways of knowing – underlying the work of comparative educationists. This serves as a foundation for understanding the definitions and redefinitions of the field by comparative educationists in the next chapter.

Thus in Chapter 5, I attempt to answer the question – what is comparative education? – based on the intellectual definitions offered by comparativists, analysing them from a realist as well as a constructionist perspective. Not only do I attempt to clarify the debate on whether comparative education is a discipline or a field or a method, but I also seek to establish what makes comparative education distinct from educational studies and related fields. In examining the discourse distinguishing comparative education from related fields, I elucidate some relationships between these intellectual definitions (e.g., between international education and comparative education) and the institutional histories and the covert homologies with the world of power. This penultimate chapter thus leads to the concluding chapter where I pull together the findings of this book.

My aim in this work is to understand how the factors associated with epistemology, structure-agency and discourse construct the field of comparative education. I also seek to offer some critical insights into taken-for-granted notions about comparative education as a field. A particular assumption I seek to critique is the notion that knowledge embodied in the form of academic disciplines or fields – in this case, the field of comparative education – is insulated from power influences. I attempt to achieve this by examining the issue across as diverse cultural contexts as possible and triangulating published accounts with interviews from key informants in order to tease out a wider range of perspectives on the complex factors that impact on the construction of the field. In this way, I also hope to avoid simplistic, partial and ethnocentric explanations.

Attempts to raise questions about power-knowledge relations in comparative education have been frequently rehearsed in its burgeoning literature, and the use of Foucauldian and/or Bourdieuian theoretical lenses is not unprecedented (e.g., Marginson & Mollis, 2002; McGovern, 1999; Ninnes, 2008a). Cowen (2000, 2008) suggests that comparative education should engage with offering a reading of the world by illuminating the interactions among historical forces, social structures and individual biographies and how political and economic power gets compressed into educational forms, in the case of this book, into the forms of comparative educations. The present work may perhaps be the first to address this question in a more sustained, detailed, fairly comprehensive and explicitly comparative manner.

The Theoretical Framework

I draw on the philosophical and sociological literature on education in two domains: first, the discourse about academic disciplines and fields; and second, the discourse on socio-historical explanations of disciplinary change. In the first category, I examine the literature on the substantive, permanent and necessary features of academic disciplines and fields, and in the second, the contingent aspects and forces of change that shape academic knowledge. Echoing the literature, I contend that both epistemological and sociological forms of power interact in dialectic fashion in structuring disciplinary knowledge. I discuss this extensively in Chapter 2 and thus only briefly comment here on pertinent theories to this book.

In the first place, I review the literature on the nature of academic disciplines and fields, categorising it into two main groups based on epistemological stance: first, the theories with a *realist*, essentialist, and objectivist stance on knowledge (e.g., Toulmin, 1972; Hirst, 1974a; Becher & Trowler, 2001), in contrast to the second group, which adopts a *social constructionist*, anti-essentialist, and subjectivist perspective (e.g., Berger & Luckmann, 1966; Young, 1971; Foucault, 1972, 1977). These concepts are useful in understanding the nature of comparative education, which displays both permanent and changing features.

After exploring different perspectives on the essence of disciplines and fields, I explore the issues of change and diversity in the classification of knowledge into disciplines and fields. This issue deals with the social process and context of academic knowledge, that is, with what forces shape the contours and contents of knowledge as institutionalised in disciplines and fields. I draw on the literature on sociology of knowledge, sociology of education and social theories of educational change. The debates in the literature could conceptually be grouped into theories that emphasise *structure* at one end of the spectrum, and human *agency* at the other (with middle ground theories focusing on both structure and agency) and their mutual relationship with knowledge; and those that emphasise *discourse*. Of particular relevance to this book are the critiques offered by Bourdieu (structure-agency) and Foucault (discourse) on fields of knowledge.

Foucault: Genealogies of Academic Fields

Foucault's work on discourse formation sheds a new light on the critical interpretation of meta-narratives on disciplinary histories by highlighting their partly contingent nature and the power-knowledge relations that underlie them. Foucault views academic fields and disciplines as products of historically contingent discourses or as *discursive formations*, understood as "a historically conditioned system of regularity for the co-existence of statements" (1972, p.42). This implies, according to Messer-Davidow et al. (1993, p.3), that academic disciplines give coherence and stability to a set of otherwise heterogeneous statements and practices by bringing them into particular types of knowledge relations with each other.

Furthermore, Foucault's *genealogies* reveal the power-knowledge dialectic in academic disciplines. Academic disciplines are not only a form of 'power-enabled knowledge', but also a 'power-enabling knowledge'. Disciplinary knowledge is both a partial effect of power struggles between and within institutions, fields and disciplines, and among individuals, as it is an enabling force for exercising power.

Bourdieu: Intellectual Field and Distinction

Bourdieu's field theory (1969) is particularly insightful in explaining the interplay between structure and agency in shaping an intellectual field and in clarifying the covert homologies between the field and wider forces of social power. Bourdieu views intellectual fields as a social field which serves as a mediating context for the dynamic interaction of objective social structures and subjective dispositions of agents. An *intellectual field* is dynamically constituted by the encounter between the *habitus* and practices of agents working in the field and the objective, external constraints and opportunities of the social field of power in which the intellectual field is embedded. These external forces of power are refracted within the intellectual field: they empower knowledge formation, but the intellectual field has an autonomous logic of its own. Within the intellectual field, agents – individuals and institutions – occupy hierarchical positions and compete over valued *capital* in order to occupy positions of *distinction* within the field. Bourdieu's metaphor of the intellectual field thus conveys that the political struggle for recognition in the field is inseparable from the cognitive activity of producing authoritative bodies of knowledge.

Bourdieu and Foucault Applied to this Book

I apply these Bourdieuian and Foucauldian conceptual lenses to argue that the construction of the field of comparative education as a distinct subfield of educational studies (institutionally and intellectually) has not solely been the result of a disinterested intellectual endeavour determined by purely cognitive criteria. It has also been intertwined with power relations. Particularly pertinent is Foucault's critique of disciplines/ fields as contingent discursive formations and the power relations working in and through them. Equally insightful is Bourdieu's critique of the intellectual field to analyse the complex interactions among macro-social (national and international agendas), meso-structural (academic/institutional politics), and micro- (human) agency factors in shaping an intellectual field. Concretely, I conceptualise comparative education as an intellectual field dynamically configured by a network of relationships among different agents taking up various intellectual positions and empowered by the different combinations of capital (economic, social, cultural and symbolic) in the field.

The integration of Foucauldian insights into discursive formation with Bourdieuian field theory offers a fairly balanced explanatory framework in order to understand critically the complex and subtle dynamics of the construction of comparative education as a field. This integrated approach addresses the deficiencies of purely internalist/inter-textual analyses of discipline formation, on the one hand, and of purely externalist explanations on the other, as criticised by scholars (e.g., Wagner & Wittrock, 1991a; Lenoir, 1993). Internalist accounts largely view disciplines as the teleological evolution of cognitive content or as the work of foundational geniuses, or also as 'texts within texts', that is, as discourses that move without subjects. Externalist narratives, by contrast, regard disciplines as mere reflections of the economic and political world, as political sites shaped directly by external forces. Integrating Bourdieuian and Foucauldian lenses in this book avoids at one extreme, a reductionism of the field's reality to contingent discourses, and mechanistic determinism of social forces at the other. By drawing on both Bourdieu and Foucault, this critique of comparative education is able to examine the forces of structure and agency, and of discourses intervening in its construction as an 'intellectual field' substantively distinct from educational studies.

Methodological Issues

I employ both philosophical and sociological methods within a comparative framework to achieve the aims of my research. Using a comparative approach, or what might approach Cowen's (2009a) vision for a 'comparative history of comparative education', my investigation of similar phenomena – the institutionalisation of comparative educations – in different geographic spaces and times enables a more nuanced understanding of what comparative education is and why it has come to be as variegated as it is. Through cross-cultural comparison, I hope to elucidate the multiple relationships and directions of relationships between comparative education knowledge and the social world, why the discursive construction of the field has successfully emerged in some countries but not in others, and to what extent the contexts of their production and reception have a role. In other words, I aim to bring to light the diverse factors – geopolitical, institutional, personal – that contribute to shaping a mosaic of comparative educations through the complex interactions of epistemology, structure and agency, and discourse.

Data Collection and Analysis

Given the magnitude of this review of the field of comparative education, I have made use principally of the published literature on the institutional and intellectual histories of comparative education, mainly in English, but also in Spanish, Chinese, and French. In addition, I drew particularly on recently collected data from three globally extensive research projects related to documenting the institutional histories of comparative education, in which I was one of the main researchers/co-editors. They are:

- The WCCES Histories Project (2004-07) which documented the histories of the World Council of Comparative Education Societies (WCCES) and its 36 constituent societies. This culminated in the publication of *Common Interests, Uncommon Goals: Histories of the World Council of Comparative Education Societies and its Members* edited by Vandra Masemann, Mark Bray and Maria Manzon (2007);

- A research project on the histories and current status of comparative education teaching at universities world wide (2007-08). This culminated in the publication of an enlarged 2nd edition of *Comparative Education at Universities World Wide* edited by Charl Wolhuter, Nikolay Popov, Maria Manzon and Bruno Leutwyler (2008a). The volume contained 36 national and regional accounts from five world regions written in English, Spanish and French; and

- A research project for *CIEclopedia*, an online database on Who's Who in Comparative and International Education managed by Teachers College, Columbia University (2006-present). As the project representative for the Comparative Education Research Centre (CERC) of the University of Hong Kong and later as CIEclopedia's Editor (2009-10), I have contributed, and sought the collaboration of others to contribute, personal profiles on comparative education scholars worldwide.

Through these projects, I have collected extensive, cross-cultural data on the histories of the field, its professional societies and on prominent comparative education scholars. In aggregate terms, the geographic contexts I have covered in the first two projects above total over 52 countries. Initial analyses have been published in the editorial conclusions of the first two books mentioned (see Manzon & Bray, 2007; Wolhuter, Popov, Manzon & Leutwyler, 2008b).

Interview Methodology

For the purpose of understanding in-depth and triangulating the institutional histories published in the literature, I conducted 33 semi-structured interviews with current or past presidents/key officers of 16 comparative education societies, achieving a diverse range of geographical origins and field contexts (see Appendix 1). They represented different types of bodies: global (WCCES), regional (3), national (9), and language-based (2). These varied contexts spanned both old and new societies, industrialised and less developed economies, as well as capitalist and socialist systems.

Participant Observation

A further source of material for this book is my work for the WCCES Secretariat from 2004-06, which has given me direct access to the discourse of this world body, the opportunity for participant observation at its meetings and analysis of its documents (e.g., minutes of meetings, bulletins, etc.), and further scholarly interchanges with society leaders from different parts of the world. My participant observations were non-continuous in the form of attendance at some national, regional, and global forums of comparative education (2004-2008). These forums and the chance to interact with comparativists from diverse cultural back-grounds helped me to form a more nuanced perception of the varied forms and qualities of comparative education in other countries. Like-wise, my involvement in the WCCES Secretariat provided me some insights into the political (and sometimes micro-political) issues that intervene in the decisions and discussions of this global scholarly body. In addition, the interaction with comparative education scholars visiting CERC at the University of Hong Kong has also widened my exposure to the field.

The Structure of the Book

The next five chapters will develop the themes introduced above. In Chapter 2, I review the philosophical and sociological literature on the nature of academic disciplines and fields, and the socio-historical theories on disciplinary change. This serves to lay the conceptual foun-dations for the subsequent chapters. Chapters 3 to 5 constitute the substance of this book. I first turn to the institutional histories of the field of comparative education in Chapter 3, followed by an examination of its intellectual histories in Chapter 4. As I present a global picture of com-parative education in these two chapters, I apply the lenses of Foucault on discursive formations and Bourdieu on intellectual fields to under-stand the construction of comparative education as a field. In Chapter 5, I analyse the intellectual substance/nature of comparative education as constructed in the discourses of comparative education scholars. Culmi-nating this study, I recapitulate in Chapter 6 my reflections on the constructed nature of comparative education in the light of the relationships between its epistemological and sociological domains and its implications on the field of comparative education, and on academic fields, in general.

2

Disciplines and Fields in Academic Discourse

Introduction

There has been much scholarly debate on whether comparative education is a discipline, a field, a method, or simply a different perspective in education. Some of its critical practitioners have pointed out the field's lack of a substantive institutional and epistemological core (e.g., Kazamias & Schwartz, 1977; Cowen, 1990). A survey of the comparative education literature reveals that there is no universally consistent definition of comparative education, but that there are instead comparative educations (Cowen, 2000). As a first step to address the above debate adequately, I explore here the literature on the nature of academic disciplines and fields, and the socio-historical explanations of disciplinary change.

The purpose of this chapter is to offer a theoretical framework for this research on the nature of comparative education and the factors of its development. I examine these questions:

- What are the necessary constitutive elements of academic disciplines?
- What are their contingent features?
- And what are the factors – structural, agency-oriented, and discursive – influencing disciplinary changes?

This chapter therefore contains the following content that serves those purposes: first, a review of the literature on the definition and essential nature of academic disciplines and fields; second, a review of relevant socio-historical theories which meaningfully explain the dynamics of disciplinary change; third, the application of Bourdieuian and Foucauldian theoretical frameworks to this book. Since these have been discussed in Manzon (2006), only a brief review of the research literature is presented here.

The literature on academic disciplines and fields can be found in several domains: philosophy of education, sociology of education/ knowledge, social theory, and higher education. Among them, Maton (2000) highlights that two distinct traditions are worth noting: while philosophy of education tends to focus on the logical divisions of knowledge into fields and disciplines (e.g., Hirst, 1974b), the new sociology of education critiques this stance by emphasising the socio-historical contexts underlying knowledge formation (e.g., Young, 1971).

In the first place, I review the literature on the nature of academic disciplines and fields, categorising it into two main groups based on epistemological stance: first, the theories with a *realist*, essentialist, and objectivist view of knowledge, in contrast to the second group which adopts a *social constructionist*, anti-essentialist, and subjectivist perspective. While a realist perspective views disciplinary knowledge as reflecting a discernible and stable reality, or real-world differences in subject matter, a phenomenological perspective takes knowledge as essentially socially constructed.

After exploring different perspectives on the essential nature of disciplines and fields, I explore the issues of change and diversity in the classification of knowledge into disciplines and fields. This issue deals with the social process and context of academic knowledge, that is, with what shapes the contours and contents of knowledge as institutionalised in disciplines and fields, schools and faculties, curricula, programmes. I draw on critical social theories and relate them to disciplinary change. Concretely, I examine the structuration theory of Bourdieu focusing on both structure and agency, and their mutual relationship with knowledge, and the discourse-oriented theory of Foucault. I conclude the chapter with an attempt to integrate Foucauldian and Bourdieuian perspectives into a meaningful conceptual framework for analysing what comparative education is, and the forces that interact in its construction.

On the Nature of Academic Disciplines and Fields
Realist Perspectives
Scholars who address the concept of academic disciplines and fields based on a realist epistemology include Hirst (1974b; 1974c), Heckhausen (1972), Mucklow (1980), and Becher and Trowler (2001). Hirst, in his *Forms of Knowledge Re-visited* (1974b, p.97) distinguishes among three meanings of the term 'discipline': first, as a tightly knit *conceptual and propositional structure* that would seem to apply more readily to a form of knowledge, or a sub-section of a form of knowledge; second, as including *skills and methods, attitudes and values*, related to an understanding and concern for this area of knowledge; and third, as relating to its *use for university and school units* of teaching and research. He suggests that 'discipline' is more aptly applied to a research unit: an area of research and university teaching which professionals recognise as focusing on a

large enough body of *logically inter-related truths*, theories and problems to justify its consideration in relative isolation from other matters. Hirst finally claims that the only relevant dimensions to grouping the disciplines are *truth-criteria, concepts and conceptual structure*.

Mucklow (1980) responds to Hirst with a counter-claim that there are two additional epistemological grounds for disciplinary grouping: argumentation and explanation. He particularly highlights that a discipline is in part a *process*, something its long-time practitioners (and others) engage in, and not just the knowledge products of that process. Mucklow thus introduces the social dimension of institutionalising a discipline.

An earlier work by Heckhausen (1972) offers an expanded conceptual framework for classifying disciplines based on epistemological grounds (albeit referring mainly to the empirical disciplines). He defines 'disciplinarity' as the *specialised* scientific exploration of a given *homogeneous subject matter* producing new knowledge, and identifies seven essential distinguishing criteria of any given discipline: the 'material field' or set of objects of study; the subject matter or point of view; the level of theoretical integration; the methods; the analytical tools; the applications of a discipline in fields of practice; and the historical contingencies of a discipline, referring to interaction between the inner logic of the subject matter and extra-disciplinary and changing forces.

Becher and Trowler (2001) offer a holistic approach to the nature of an academic discipline by noting that both disciplinary epistemology and phenomenology are important. They define disciplinary epistemology as the 'actual' form and focus of knowledge within a discipline, and the phenomenology of that knowledge [as] the ideas and understandings that practitioners have about their discipline (and others). Becher and Trowler argue that disciplinary phenomenology (or academic culture) and disciplinary epistemology are inseparably intertwined and mutually infused. They conceive of an academic discipline as the result of a mutually dependent interplay of the *structural force of the epistemological character* of disciplines that conditions culture, and the *capacity of individuals and groups as agents* of autonomous action, *including interpretive acts* (2001, p.23). Each disciplinary grouping displays distinctive epistemological and sociological features.

Juxtaposing this dyad of epistemological and sociological features with the disciplinary features earlier identified by Hirst, Mucklow and Heckhausen (see Table 2.1) reveals some common elements that enable us to identify the necessary and the contingent features of disciplinary knowledge. Their definitions show overlaps in the conceptualisation of the nature of academic disciplines. The common epistemological features that structure knowledge into a given discipline are six: common object, point of view, truth-criteria, conceptual structure and theoretical integration, methods and skills, and products of knowledge. Common sociological features which group knowledge into one discipline are institutional framework (e.g., departments, research units, etc.), though most authors concur that sociological/institutional divisions do not always dovetail with the epistemological criteria, and that the sociological lags behind the epistemological. The authors also converge in pointing out the social dimension of the disciplines as being a historically contingent process where forces transcending the discipline interact with its inner logic and with its human agents. Thus, the constitutive nature of academic disciplines embraces an epistemological dimension and a socio-historical dimension. The first is concerned with intellectual substance and truth claims, and the latter with the incarnation of that intellectual substance into social and political institutions. The intellectual or epistemological dimension tends to display permanent, universal and necessary characteristics, while the sociological component of disciplines – given its human and cultural component – tends to exhibit changing, particular and contingent characteristics. In the next section, I explore further the issue of the socio-historical contingencies of the disciplines, a key issue tackled in the constructivist literature. But before doing so, I discuss the sociological forms of disciplinary institutionalisation, followed by an explication of the concept of the academic field, distinguishing it from academic disciplines.

Disciplinary Institutionalisation: Forms and Rationales

As discussed in Manzon and Bray (2007, pp.336-338), disciplinary institutionalisation concerns the sociological reality or incarnation of bodies of knowledge. Wagner and Wittrock (1991b, p.3) used it to refer to the creation of a separate sphere of scientific activity in an effort to distinguish the new discipline from amateur or lay explanations of the reality studied, as well as from older, neighbouring disciplines (e.g., Harrison et al., 2004; Lambert, 2003). They added that institutionalisation does not necessarily occur in academic forms alone; does not always, or even often, occur on the basis of having an unequivocal theoretical or methodological baggage; and does not entail complete stability over time or place, but exhibits regional and intellectual variety and transformations.

Table 2.1 Epistemological and Sociological Features of Academic Disciplines

EPISTEMOLOGICAL FEATURES OF A DISCIPLINE			
Becher & Trowler (2001)	*Hirst (1974b)*	*Mucklow (1980)*	*Heckhausen (1972)*
Objects of enquiry			Material field/objects
Relationship between researcher and knowledge	Attitudes and values		Subject matter/ point of view
Extent of truth claims and criteria for making them	Logically inter-related truths	Truth-criteria; explanation	Theoretical integration
Enquiry procedures	Skills and methods		Methods
	Concepts, conceptual and propositional structure	Concepts and conceptual structure; argumentation	Analytical tools
Results of research			Applications – applied disciplines are eclectic. Applications influence the institutionalisation of disciplines in universities.
Nature of knowledge growth			
SOCIOLOGICAL FEATURES OF A DISCIPLINE			
Structural framework – organisational structure in higher education. Disciplines take institutional shape in departments.	University and school teaching units of disciplines are controversial.		Disciplinary knowledge does not always coincide with departmental organisation
Intellectual validity – unchallenged academic credibility			
International currency – freestanding international community (professional journals and societies)			
Tribal identity and tradition which exclude the uninitiated audience (e.g., use of paradigms, disciplinary myths, tribal heroes, and impermeable boundaries).		Process, not product	Historical contingencies – inner logic and extra-disciplinary forces

Institutionalisation of a discipline is not limited to its formal recognition and location within the academic structure of a department or faculty. Institutionalisation also includes the formation of scholarly societies and other forms of academic networking such as scholarly journals, conferences, and invisible colleges (Clark, 1987; Coser, 1965; Crane, 1972; Haskell, 2000; Manicas, 1991).

Different forms of institutionalisation play different roles in academic knowledge production. Institutional support in the form of *academic departments or research centres* ensure the continuity of academic work by providing occupational roles and publication facilities while specialist journals serve as communication networks for the disciplinary community as well as give shape to the discipline's intellectual definition and the legitimation of disciplinary knowledge (e.g., Altbach, 1994; Coser, 1965). *Scholarly societies and other social networks* serve to bring together a community of scholars and practitioners with a common interest and identity, and to further disseminate disciplinary knowledge (Crane, 1972). Clark (1987, p.233) observes that disciplinary associations in higher education have helped "tighten the hold of specialisation upon academic life, a device that would serve externally as a carrying mechanism for a discipline at large, a way of furthering specialties without regard to institutional boundaries". He further remarks that "voluntary associating is a good way to have structure follow knowledge" (p.253). These conceptual tools are useful especially in my analysis of the empirical substance of the field of comparative education (Chapter 3). Since comparative education is more commonly known as an academic field rather than a discipline, I now turn to the concept of a field in both its epistemological and sociological aspects.

The Concept of an Academic Field

Hirst (1974c [original 1965], pp.45-46) defines a 'field' as those organisations of knowledge which are:

> formed by building together round specific *objects*, or *phenomena*, or *practical pursuits*, knowledge that is characteristically *rooted in more than one discipline*. … These organisations are not concerned, as the disciplines are, to validate any one logically distinct form of expression. They are not concerned with developing a particular structuring of experience. They are *held together simply by subject matter, drawing on all forms of knowledge* that can contribute to them. [emphasis added]

Thus, the unifying epistemological element of an academic field is its material object or phenomena of study, or its practical pursuit. The approaches which a field uses to study that object are multiple and are drawn from more than one discipline. Jantsch (1972, pp.106-107) distinguishes among the terms multidisciplinarity, pluridisciplinarity, crossdisciplinarity, interdisciplinarity and transdisciplinarity, depending on the kind of relationship between several disciplines and the hierarchy observed among them. Of relevance to Hirst's definition of a field is the concept of interdisciplinarity, which refers to the cooperation within a group of related disciplines that pursue a common higher purpose. This higher purpose could be synoptic or instrumental (Lynton, 1985, cited in Klein, 1990, p.41). A synoptic justification for interdisciplinarity rests on arguments for unity and synthesis in knowledge, on modern synthetic theories and integrative concepts, and on the work of individual synthesisers, while an instrumental justification arises from the need to solve problems that may be either social or intellectual in origin, but usually practical. These concepts of the field and interdisciplinarity are particularly useful in examining the nature of comparative education, which is often designated by scholars as an interdisciplinary field of study.

In terms of their structural or sociological features, academic fields and 'interdisciplines' are as difficult to delineate as are their epistemological boundaries. According to Klein (1990), a field's presence and importance are largely determined by its relative visibility, which may take at least two forms: (1) the 'overt' form of interdisciplinary institutions (e.g., having a single umbrella organisation or having interdisciplinary graduate programs, or interdisciplinary think tanks); (2) the commonly less overt forums for interdisciplinary dialogue (e.g., study groups, symposia, conferences, publications, and institutes similar or akin to an "invisible college" [Crane, 1972]), which refers to a communication network of productive scientists linking separate groups of collaborators within a research area.

Constructivist Perspectives

Equipped with these provisional definitions of disciplines and fields founded on a realist epistemology, I now explore the constructivist perspectives on the nature of academic knowledge. The constructivist stance views the social world as not having essential, given properties, but only those that become 'objectivated' through social practice. A poststructuralist turn in constructivist theories shifts the emphasis to discourse, where the 'objective world' emerges only in discourse, and where discourses are external to and constituted through individual subjectivity. In the realm of disciplinary knowledge, this means scepticism about the foundations and hierarchies of knowledge leading to, or threatening to lead to, a collapse of disciplinary boundaries. Institutions, including disciplinary knowledge, rather than being understood as reified, are taken as socially constructed practices.

Notions about the nature of academic disciplines and fields thus vary depending on the epistemological lens in use. Whereas realists perceive the universal and necessary epistemological elements of a discipline together with its particular and contingent sociological features, constructivists largely underscore the contingencies and particularities of knowledge. Whereas realists distinguish among the object of knowledge, the knowing subject, and the concept (and the word), constructivists tend to blur the boundaries of object-subject-concept-word, giving primacy to the subject and, in the case of the poststructuralists, to the word. Poststructuralism views the objective foundations and hierarchies of knowledge with scepticism, and instead introduces a sensibility towards perceiving institutions of knowledge as institutions of power. Both perspectives – realist and constructivist – and the theoretical literature which derive from them, enrich our understanding and analysis of the nature of disciplines and fields. I now link this literature with some socio-historical theories of the dynamics of change in the academic disciplines.

Socio-historical Explanations of Disciplinary Change

In this section, I first briefly examine the forms of disciplinary metamorphosis and some reasons that underlie them. As these explanations take a rather functionalist stance, I then turn to review pertinent social theories that examine social change (and *mutatis mutandis*, disciplinary change) from a critical perspective.

Types and Factors of Disciplinary Change

Klein (1990) sees the nature of disciplinary change as a result of either differentiation or integration. Through differentiation or *fission*, existing disciplines split into subdivisions that may become disciplines; while through integration or *fusion*, various disciplines may collaborate with each other, as with the 'interdisciplines'. There is no single pattern of disciplinary interactions, since disciplines are responsive to so many historical, sociological and epistemological variables. I focus on the factors that foster interdisciplinarity because of their relevance to understanding the emergence and development of comparative education as an interdisciplinary field.

Among the epistemological factors, Klein (1990) posits a comprehensive reason for interdisciplinarity in the evolution of knowledge, where new research areas that have emerged fit poorly within the conventional structure of their disciplines. She also cites the influence of synthetic theories (e.g., Marxism, structuralism and general systems theory) and of linguistic models in viewing social reality as discursively constructed and historically contextualised. These theories and paradigms have paved the way for a shift from knowledge fragmentation towards knowledge reintegration and interdisciplinarity. There are also historical and practical factors that catalysed interdisciplinarity in the mid-20th century. Geopolitical factors such as the demands of a post-World War II world (especially in some countries like the United States) for applied research promoted the growth of interdisciplinary work in the sciences in the form of mission-oriented projects funded by governments. Klein notes the prominent influence of these projects on interdisciplinarity: "There was, first of all, considerable financial incentive for universities, in the form of government and foundation grants. There was also the *"inexorable logic that the real problems of society do not come in discipline-shaped blocks"* (1990, p.35) [emphasis added].

Figure 2.1 A Preliminary Mapping of Disciplinary Change

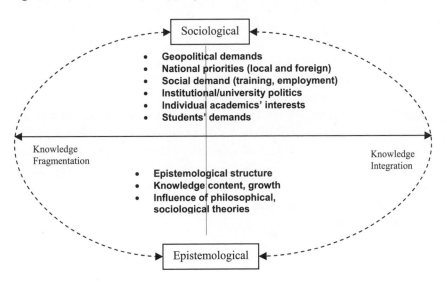

I map these various catalysts and reasons for disciplinary change in Figure 2.1, grouping the epistemological reasons at one end of the y-axis and the multi-level sociological reasons (institutional, socio-political) at the other end. Both epistemological and sociological factors mutually influence each other and are thus connected with two-sided arrows. On the x-axis I plot on a continuum the two directions of disciplinary change: knowledge fragmentation and knowledge integration. Thus we can imagine the dynamics of disciplinary change since the 1970s as moving along the x-axis of interdisciplinarity partly as a result of the dialectic of the sociological and the epistemological forces prevalent at that time.

While the above explanations help clarify the question on why and how disciplines become subdivided into sub-disciplines and fields, they elide the question of power in knowledge construction and how these work through the forces of discourse, structure and agency. It is to these alternative explanatory frameworks to which I now turn.

Critical Social Theories and Disciplinary Change

The interaction between epistemological and sociological factors in influencing disciplinary change can be examined at a deeper level with the aid of those theoretical frameworks which attempt to explain why different types of knowledge emerge, and what reasons, apart from the epistemological, account for the delineation of knowledge boundaries. These theories give a tentative analysis of the complex and dynamic processes by which social factors – structure, agency and discourse – interact with knowledge and its sociological structures. They adopt a critical stance, viewing social institutions and the knowledge they create as sites of political struggle and stratification. Not one single theory is without its limitations and critiques. For this work, I have adopted Foucauldian and Bourdieuian lenses in view of precedent studies that have used either one of them or both in critiquing their own disciplines or fields (e.g., Benson, 1998; García-Villegas, 2006; Messer-Davidow et al., 1993; Sapiro, 2004), including the fields of education (e.g., Ringer, 1992, 2000) and comparative education (e.g., Baeck, 1999; Marginson & Mollis, 2002; McGovern, 1999; Mehta & Ninnes, 2003; Ninnes & Burnett, 2003; Ninnes, 2008a, 2008b). I now turn to a more extensive discussion of Bourdieu's and Foucault's ideas in order to build a conceptual framework for this book.

Foucault and Bourdieu: Critique of Knowledge Fields

Both Foucault and Bourdieu offer pertinent critiques of fields of knowledge. They both seek to unmask the contexts of power in which knowledge is socially embedded. They view disciplines and fields as power struggles over the legitimacy to make truth claims. Foucault's point of departure and emphasis lie in problematising the universal and essential nature of knowledge and truth. He posits that knowledge and truth – embodied in academic fields and disciplines – are the products of historically contingent discourses and are inseparable from institutional power and micro-power. His main unit of analysis is discourse and its associated concepts and analytical tools: discursive formations, episteme, games of truth and dividing practices. I discuss them in the next section. I use Foucault's insights to consider the subtle workings of discursive and institutional power in shaping comparative education as a distinct field.

Bourdieu likewise problematises the issue of knowledge formation and its relation to power. His explanatory framework – field theory – views the *intellectual field* as a mediated effect of complex interactions between objective macro-structures of power and subjective micro-agency *habitus*, these outside influences being 'refracted' by an independent logic of the intellectual field itself (Bourdieu & Wacquant, 1992, p.105). For Bourdieu, the field is a network of relations among agents occupying and competing for positions in the field, such positions being determined by the distribution of power or capital. Bourdieu's field theory offers a structural explanation of the dynamic processes of disciplinary or field construction, which addresses the apparent lacuna in Foucault's approach characterised by contingency in its interlocking of discourses (Lenoir, 1993). Bourdieu's defence of the inner logic that governs the intellectual field remedies the seeming arbitrariness of knowledge boundaries and the apparently direct mutual influence between power and knowledge suggested in Foucauldian thought. I thus employ Bourdieu's theory of the *intellectual field* to argue that the institutionalisation of comparative education as a distinct field is not a pure outcome of intellectual pursuits. Rather, it is partly a result of the complex interplay between macro- and meso-structural conditions and micro-political interests on the part of its practitioners who naturally attempt to preserve and increase the field's inertial momentum and their positions within it.

The integration of Foucauldian insights into discursive formation with Bourdieuian field theory offers a fairly balanced explanatory framework in order to understand critically the dynamics of the construction of comparative education as a field. This integrated approach addresses the deficiencies of purely internalist or externalist explanations of discipline/ field formation identified by some scholars (e.g., Wagner & Wittrock, 1991a; Lenoir, 1993). Internalist accounts largely view disciplines as the teleological evolution of cognitive content – as pure erudition –, or as the sole work of agents or foundational geniuses, or also as 'texts within texts', that is, as discourses that move without subjects. Externalist narratives, by contrast, regard disciplines as mere reflections of the economic and political world, as political sites shaped directly by external forces by way of resource allocation, for example (Lenoir, 1993, p.76). Synthesising Bourdieuian and Foucauldian lenses avoids, on one hand, the reduction of a field's reality to discourse. On the other, it brings to light the crucial role of discourse, partly eclipsed in structurationist theory, which could tend towards mechanistic determinism. Both Bourdieu and Foucault highlight power-knowledge interactions in subtle layers of explanation. Foucault, however, views power and knowledge as directly implicated in each other, while Bourdieu refines the under-standing of this relationship and defends the relative autonomy of the 'field' in reshaping external power. Also, Bourdieu's approach of 'objec-tifying the subjective' (Johnson, 1993, p.4) offers, in my view, a middle-ground explanation that remedies the rather 'internalist' approach and emphasis on historical contingencies suggested in Foucault's discursive formation (taken by some scholars to its extreme form as 'texts within texts') – while also avoiding the mechanistic explanation of externalist accounts by arguing that the field, rather than directly reflecting outside forces, refracts them in terms of its (the field's) own structure and logic. The intellectual field and its 'products' – ideas – enjoy relative autonomy from material conditions.

Foucault: Discursive Formations, Genealogies and Disciplines

Foucault offers critical tools for analysing how specific historical cir-cumstances shape knowledge production. He elucidates the fragility of objects and fields of knowledge, especially in the human/social sciences, which, due to their proximity to social power relations, renders question-able the taken-for-granted assumption that knowledge is independent of power. His critique of 'official' or 'dominant' knowledge in the human and social sciences is particularly pertinent for my argument on how the field of comparative education – likewise associated with these disci-plines and closely linked to social forces – has come to be an officially distinct field.

Foucault, however, seems to conflate truth with knowledge, or at least uses them interchangeably. Moreover, he also seems to associate them inseparably with *discourse, discursive formation* and *disciplines*. A few conceptual clarifications would be apposite here.

Discursive Formations

In Foucauldian terms, a *discourse* is a limited set of statements that establish conditions of truth within a specific historical context. A *discourse* both constrains and enables what can be said, thought, and written about a specific object or practice – what statements come to count as true or false – within a specific historical period or *episteme* (Ball, 1990; Philp, 1990). More broadly, a *discursive formation* can be viewed as "a historically conditioned system of regularity for the coexistence of statements" (Lenoir, 1993, p.74). *Discursive formations* organise ideas or concepts, and produce 'objects of knowledge'. In this respect, we can view academic disciplines and fields as discursive formations, wherein discursive practices constitute or construct a discipline/field's boundaries within a specific historical period or episteme. In other words, fields of knowledge consist of a limited set of historically conditioned statements that establish the conditions of truth within a particular field.

Two related conceptual tools offered by Foucault are *games of truth* and *dividing practices*. By *games of truth*, he refers to the sets of rules within particular institutions by which truth is produced (Rabinow, 1997). Foucault uses this concept to emphasise that truth claims by institutions are dependent on institutional and discursive practices. This is partly achieved through *dividing practices* (Foucault, 1977), which are ways in which disciplinary/authoritative institutions divide individuals or social groups from one another on the basis of judgments made about their actions, classifying them into binary opposites (e.g., scientific from amateurish). The notion of 'dividing practices' is useful for understanding the fragmentation of knowledge into various sub-disciplines or fields and the discourse on disciplinary institutionalisation as a form of 'autonomisation' of academic knowledge from non-scientific discourses.

Foucault's work on genealogy (1980) sought to demonstrate that knowledge and power are implicated in each other. In *Discipline and Punish* (Foucault, 1977, p.27), he posits that "power and knowledge directly imply one another; that there is no power relation without the correlative constitution of a field of knowledge, nor any knowledge that does not presuppose and constitute at the same time power relations". He further argues in *Power/Knowledge* (Foucault, 1980, p.93) that:

> these relations of power cannot themselves be established, consolidated nor implemented without the production, accumulation, circulation and functioning of a discourse. There can be no possible exercise of power without a certain economy of discourses of truth which operates through and on the basis of this association. We are subjected to the production of truth through power and we cannot exercise power except through the production of truth.

Foucault applied his genealogical approach to account for the development of the human sciences, which, in his view, clearly demonstrated a circular relationship between power and knowledge. Concretely, he argues that knowledge and truth produced by the human sciences are tied to power because these truths were used to regulate and normalise individuals. Thus, knowledge legitimises the exercise of power.

At this juncture, I think a distinction should be made between disciplines, knowledge and truth. I agree with Foucault that academic disciplines are, to some extent, socially constructed in the sense of their partly arbitrary and historically contingent grouping as bodies of knowledge having disparate objects, methods and purposes under one institutional department or program and not in another. However, while the institutional form of knowledge – embodied in disciplines/fields – may be contingent and particular, the intellectual substance of knowledge it aims at is essential and universal. I do not agree with the generalisation of such observation – that knowledge disciplines are socially constructed – to the conclusion that *all* truth is socially constructed, a proposition which Foucault seems to suggest. Such a generalisation assumes a conflation of truth with knowledge. However, truth is neither reducible to nor synonymous with knowledge. Paraphrasing Aquinas' classic definition of truth (*De Veritate*, q.1, a.1), it can be understood as "the conformity of the knowing subject with the known thing" (cited in Llano, 2001, p.32). More specifically, logical truth (in contrast to ontological truth) refers to the truth of knowledge insofar as it manifests and declares the being of things, that is, "to the extent that the intellect's judgment refers to the thing as it is in itself" (Aquinas, *De Veritate*, q.1, a.1). Logical truth is given in judgment when the intellect forms a proposition which affirms (or denies) that the thing really has (in the ontological order) the form which is attributed to it in the predicate

(Llano, 2001, p.35; also Bochaca, 2001; Millán-Puelles, 2002). Thus as Aristotle declares: "to say of that which is, that it is not, or of that which is not, that it is, is false; while to say of that which is, that it is, or of that which is not, that it is not, is true" (Aristotle, 1993, *Metaphysics*, IV, 7, 1011b, 26-27). Knowledge may thus be true or false (in which case it is not to know at all) depending on whether it is in conformity with reality or not, where reality serves as an objective criterion outside of the knower. The notion of 'truth', therefore, is distinct from knowledge. Truth adds the element of the 'referentiality' of knowledge to an ontological world, to a realm that transcends our subjective construction. Bhaskar (1986) thus appositely distinguishes between an ontological realm of 'intransitive' objects, processes and events, which exists independently of our knowing them, and an epistemological realm of 'transitive' knowledge-constitutive interests – in whose construction we are involved (Mason, 2000, p.47). Knowledge, and its institutional embodiment into disciplines, may be partly a socially constructed reality. Truth, however, is not socially constructed since it ultimately requires conformity between knowledge and extra-mental reality. Perhaps a more appropriate term to denote knowledge would be truth-claims to allude to the socially constructed and contingent features of human knowledge instituted in the disciplines.

Foucault's genealogies – "counter-history of ideas" – also conceive of history in terms of discontinuity and disjuncture (Danaher et al., 2000, p.100), which put into question the 'official' historical stages of development that disciplines usually offer as a history of ideas. Under this prism, attempts by disciplinary historians to disseminate 'founder narratives' and trace the establishment of their discipline as far back in history as possible are viewed with suspicion as discursive tactics to legitimate political interests in one's discipline (e.g., Fuller, 1993; Graham et al., 1983; Klein, 1993).

In summary, from Foucault we understand by the terms discourse and discursive formations such historically-specific knowledge, produced inseparably from power relations underlying social practices and institutions, which establishes the conditions of truth – official knowledge – within a specific historical period (*episteme*), and maintains the exercise of power relations. Discourses are constituted by knowledge, and knowledge is organised into disciplines. Discourses thus contribute to the construction of academic disciplines (Ninnes, 2004).

A Critique of the 'Discursive Formation' of Comparative Education

These Foucauldian insights are particularly relevant to my critique of the 'development' of comparative education as a distinct body of knowledge, partially as a result of power struggles among fields of knowledge and institutions, and conversely, as a legitimising body of knowledge for the exercise of power. The conceptual tools I take from Foucault in this critique of comparative education as an academic field are:

- That disciplines are historically *contingent discursive formations* of heterogeneous elements;
- That disciplines emerge from *power struggles* and constitute *power relations*; and
- That disciplines and disciplinary institutions are crucial for the *stabilisation* of discourses.

Bourdieu: Field Theory, Intellectual Field and Distinction

Bourdieu offers an alternative critique of social reality in general, and of academic disciplines and fields in particular. He views the social world (and ceteris paribus, any body of knowledge or social practice) as a social construct resulting from a dynamic relationship between objective social structure and the individual's socially constituted mental structures which generate and organise social practice (Johnson, 1993, p.4; Grenfell, 2007, p.54). I will first elucidate his field theory and his critique of intellectual fields, in order to later relate it, in particular, to the field of comparative education.

Theory of a Field

Bourdieu uses the metaphor of the *field* to conceptualise social space as a structured space of objective social forces and struggles among agents/ institutions over specific resources and access to them (Grenfell, 2007; Johnson, 1993). In an interview with Wacquant, Bourdieu defines a *field* as a network or a configuration of objective relations between positions of occupants in the field (Bourdieu & Wacquant, 1992, p.97). It is a *structured space* of unequal social positions. The *occupants* or participants in a field may be agents (individuals) or systems of agents (such as institutions, educational systems, and the like). The *positions* they occupy in a given field are objectively defined by the structure of the distribution of different kinds of power (or *capital*) in the field. Thus, the position of a participant in relation to other participants may be that of domination, subordination or equivalence/homology to each other, by virtue of the access it affords to the relevant form of capital within a field. The occupants' position gives them unequal chances of commanding access to the specific *'profits'* that are at stake in the field. The field is thus a site of struggles in which participants seek to maintain or alter the distribution of the forms of capital valued in the field in order to gain access to the specific 'profits' that are at stake in the field. Agents in the field are "socially constituted as active and acting in the field under consideration by the fact that they possess the necessary properties to be effective ... in this field" (Bourdieu & Wacquant, 1992, p.107). In this sense, an agent (e.g., a particular intellectual) exists per se only because there is an intellectual field within which the value of an intellectual is recognised as such.

Through the concept of *logic of practice,* Bourdieu sought to maintain the relative independence of social fields from political and economic forces. He posits that each field is governed by its *logic of practice* or ruling principles that are considered legitimate ways of working in the field. Through its logic of practice, a field provides some form of sociali-sation for its occupants. It forms dispositions, activated in particular *field* contexts (Grenfell, 2007, p.57), to behave in a certain way within the logic of the particular field – not in a deterministic way, but as "a natural capacity to acquire non-natural, arbitrary capacities" (Bourdieu, 2000/ 1997, p.136).

Bourdieu then offers an explanatory framework for the way agents (individuals or institutions), located in a field of objective social struc-tures, generate practices within a particular field's logic. He introduces the concept of *habitus,* which he defines as:

> systems of durable, transposable dispositions, structured structures predisposed to function as structuring structures, that is, as prin-ciples which generate and organise practices and representations that can be objectively adapted to their outcomes without pre-supposing a conscious aiming at ends or an express mastery of the operations necessary in order to attain them (Bourdieu, 1990/1980, p.53).

Habitus is like a 'practical sense' that inclines agents to act and react in specific situations in a rather unconscious way, as if by a 'second nature' (Johnson, 1993). It is the result of a long process of inculcation since childhood and lasts throughout one's lifetime. It is constituted by a system of 'structured structures' which incorporate the objective social conditions within which an agent's *habitus* is nurtured. It is thus possible to speak not only of *individual habitus* but also of *class habitus*, the latter referring to similarities in the *habitus* of agents belonging say to the same social class. *Habitus* functions as 'structuring structures' or as principles which enable agents to generate and organise practices adapted to specific objective structures. *Habitus* thus mediates pre-consciously between objective structures and practice. To participate in a field, agents must possess the *habitus* that predisposes them to enter that particular field (Johnson, 1993, p.8).

Intellectual Field

Bourdieu's field theory offers a rich explanatory framework for analysing intellectual fields, which is the concern of this book. He conceptualised an *intellectual field* as "like a magnetic field, made up of a system of power lines. ... [T]he constituting agents or systems of agents, may be described as so many forces which by their existence, opposition or combination, determine its specific structure at a given moment in time" (Bourdieu 1969/1966, p.89). The field is thus dynamically constructed by the interactions of occupants within this "system of positions and oppositions" (p.109). Concretely, Bourdieu envisions an *intellectual field* as a "matrix of institutions and markets in which artists, writers, researchers and academics compete over valued resources to obtain legitimate recognition for their artistic, literary, academic or scientific work" (Swartz, 1997, p.226). Structured by hierarchically ordered positions, the *intellectual field* is also governed by the dynamic law of the quest for distinction (Bourdieu, 1977/1972). Thus intellectual interests and products – theories, methods, concepts – that appear to be disinterested contributions to knowledge can also be viewed as 'political' strategies by agents to establish, restore, reinforce, protect or reverse a specific structure of relations of symbolic domination in the field. Actors compete with each other for credit in terms of the socially recognised capacity to speak and act legitimately in the production of scientific goods and the consequent command over resources for the production of more scientific goods (Lenoir, 1993, pp.76-77). In the intellectual field, the

> *political struggle* to dominate resources is *inseparable from the cognitive enterprise* of defining what constitutes legitimate, authorised science. In struggling to gain recognition for their products, scientists are engaged in *legitimating their power to define domains of the scientific field* in which they have interests (Bourdieu, 1975, p.23,

cited by Lenoir, 1993, p.77). [emphasis added]

Bourdieu (1991/1981) thus offers a critique of intellectual practices and institutions, viewing them as struggles for symbolic power – the capacity to name and to categorise, to define the legitimate forms of knowledge production, thereby enhancing one's position in the intellectual field (Swartz, 1997; Delanty, 2001). The 'law of the quest for distinction' suggests that conflict between intellectuals will be more intense for those holding neighbouring positions in the field.

Delanty (2001, p.93) highlights that Bourdieu distinguishes between three types of symbolic capital that are competed for in the university: *academic power, scientific power* and *intellectual power*, described thus:

> (*Academic power* is the) power of control over the administration of academic resources and the means of career influence. It is the power to preside over credentials and allocate status. ... *Scientific power* is ... the power that comes from research reputations based on scholarly publications. *Intellectual power* (or intellectual renown) comes from the ability to influence public opinion. [emphasis added]

All these are relevant to understanding and explaining the contestation among fields and subfields of knowledge, insufficiently accounted for by traditional explanations based on intellectual criteria alone. They are relevant to offering an explanation of why and how a new field of study emerges or not from a contestation with neighbouring fields, carving for itself an institutional niche in some countries but not in others, in some historical periods and not in others; in other words, an explanation of its uneven trajectories.

From another perspective, we can view a new intellectual field as the birth of a new *social practice*. For Bourdieu, practices are generated in and by the encounter between the *habitus* of agents and the constraints, demands and opportunities of the social *field* or market to which their *habitus* is appropriate or within which the agents are moving. Practices come forth – a change in practices comes about – by a less than conscious process of adjustment of the *habitus* and practices of individuals to the objective and external constraints of the social world. The field thus serves as a crucial mediating context wherein external factors of the field of power are brought to bear upon individual practice and institutions (Bourdieu & Wacquant, 1992, p.105). The logic, politics and structure of the field shape the manner in which 'external determinations' affect what goes on in the field (Jenkins, 1992; Johnson, 1993). The field thus enjoys relative autonomy from external fields of power:

> [A]ll influence and constraint exercised by an authority outside the intellectual field is always *refracted* by the structure of the intellectual field. ... Economic and social events can only affect any particular part of that field, whether an individual or an institution, according to a specific logic, because at the same time as it (the field) is re-structured under their influence, the intellectual field obliges them (forces/events) to undergo a conversion of meaning and value by transforming them into objects of reflection or imagination (Bourdieu, 1969, pp.118-119).

External structures of power are refracted, not reflected directly, in the field. Thus, while avoiding one extreme of regarding intellectual fields and practices as autonomous knowledge shaped purely by scholarly reasons, one also avoids the other extreme of treating intellectual knowledge as a simple reflection of the material or social contexts in which it operates (García-Villegas, 2006). The intellectual field enjoys relative autonomy from social forces in external fields of power whose action on the intellectual field is neither direct nor unidirectional. Rather both fields mutually interact and influence each other through subtle processes.

A Critique of the 'Field' of Comparative Education

Bourdieu's insights into the dynamics of an intellectual field are pertinent to my re-examination of how comparative education is shaped and re-shaped by the interaction between macro-/meso-structural forces and the micro-political interests of human agency. In summary, I adopt from Bourdieu the following conceptual tools:

- The intellectual field, while *embedded* in fields of power, *refracts* external forces;
- Agents occupying *positions* – configurations of *capital* – and endowed with *habitus* interact with social structures in shaping the intellectual field; and
- The intellectual field as a *social field/practice* is governed by the quest for *distinction*.

A Working Conceptual Framework

I now integrate Bourdieu's and Foucault's conceptual tools in my critique of comparative education as a distinct subfield of educational studies. I re-examine comparative education from the following critical perspectives.

From a Foucauldian perspective, I view the academic field of comparative education as a historically contingent *discursive formation* comprised of heterogeneous elements – intellectual and institutional – which has emerged partly from *power struggles* while also constituting *power relations*. Its institutionalisation as an independent field has been crucial for the *stabilisation* of otherwise contingent and heterogeneous discourses. Particularly pertinent in this regard is the Foucauldian view of disciplinary truth as a confluence of disciplinary knowledge, commentary and authors, as well as of disciplinary institutions. The intersection of various discourses – intellectual, social, economic, political, cultural, etc. – as well as non-discursive mechanisms and the power relations underlying them – shaped in diverse ways the 'disciplinary' form of comparative education as an independent field/subfield and also contributed to establishing power relations. I argue that the entry of 'comparative education' into the discourse (texts, books, articles, conference papers, policy documents) as a new and distinct field of study – came about partly as a product of historical contingencies and power struggles. In some contexts, proximity to governmental power – those in positions to define university curricula or to advise governments on education issues – played a pivotal role in obtaining distinction for the field. Embracing heterogeneous elements – objects of study, methods, scholars, theoretical frameworks, etc. – it became organised and stabilised as a body of knowledge in the form of an academic field. 'Disciplinary institutions', such as professional societies, scholarly journals, and international education agencies, exerted differentiated influences in 'disciplining' and maintaining comparative education. Academic institutionalisation thus marks a crucial point in a field's establishment as it contributes to the stabilisation of heterogeneous elements into a discursive formation.

While Foucauldian lenses are useful in highlighting the contingencies and heterogeneity of elements that intervene in the discursive construction of the academic field known as 'comparative education', they are inadequate for the task of elucidating the dynamic interaction of objective structural and subjective agency-oriented forces that shape the field. For this reason, I employ Bourdieu's conceptual tool of the *intellectual field*.

From a Bourdieuian perspective, I examine comparative education as an *intellectual field*, that is, as a dynamic network of *positions* among agents – individuals and institutions – configured by the distribution of valued *capital*, over which agents compete to obtain legitimate *distinction* for their work. The intellectual field acts as a mediating context between the external *field of power*, in which it is embedded, and the *habitus* of agents who interact with the field of power in shaping the intellectual field. As a field within fields, comparative education competes for distinction within the field of educational studies. I conceptualise the field of educational studies as a social field configured by relations between actors' positions objectively defined by the structure and distribution of different forms of capital. Actors in this case refer to the existing constituent subfields of educational studies and the individuals and institutions that comprise them, which compete for distinction in the field in order to have the right to define (new) domains of the field, and in so doing, maintain, reinforce, and widen their power and position in the field[1]. Within this social field, comparative education has to compete for legitimacy to exist as a distinct subfield of educational studies. At some point in time, some actors – individuals and institutions – succeeded in leading the institutionalisation of comparative education as a distinct field/subfield of education studies in their respective countries. With the creation of their distinctive 'intellectual field' also follows the 'creation' of the comparative educationist, whose identity and value is recognised within the particular field in which it competes for positions.

Interestingly, the structure and distribution of power in the field of educational studies exhibits homologies with the wider fields of political and economic power, in which it is embedded and whose influences it refracts. Due to its engagement with governments and issues of national educational systems, comparative education's establishment and diffusion worldwide reflects, to some extent, the hierarchical positions of countries in the geopolitical system and thus offers illuminating examples of power-knowledge relations. Nevertheless, the field of comparative education enjoys relative autonomy from fields of economic and political power, since through its inner logic it is able to transform these into objects of reflection and critique. At the same time, the construction of the field of comparative education is also partly due to

---

[1] This is not to say that the power struggle is purely for power's sake. Rather it is to say that academic knowledge is not that disinterested; there is a natural or logical inclination to compete in order to survive according to the logic of practice in one's field. It is to affirm that power-knowledge interactions cannot be ignored, although it is not to affirm that power is reducible to knowledge and vice-versa.

the work of agents endowed with the *habitus* that predisposed them to enter this field and the requisite forms of capital. These include cultural capital (particularly academic and linguistic), social capital (especially international contacts), economic capital (funding support, facility for travel, etc.), and political capital (ability to influence political decisions).

I particularly highlight Marginson and Mollis's (2002) critique of the field of comparative education, which sets a precedent to my research, in its synthesis of Bourdieuian and Foucauldian perspectives. As the authors recognise (p.583), their article does not attempt an exhaustive literature-based study of the field, but only focuses on the 'instrumental' or hegemonic strand of comparative education. In order to address the lacuna in the literature, I take as a point of departure the challenge set by Marginson and Mollis as a neo-comparative agenda (2002, p.602):

> [T]here needs to be independent research dedicated to explanations and interpretations, able to reflect on the *power/knowledge effects of comparative education* itself, strong enough to provide a counterpole to the hitherto dominant instrumental strand in research, and strong enough to affect the content and methods of the latter in the longer term. [emphasis added]

I position this book as an attempt to illuminate how comparative education knowledge is constructed in diverse and differentiated ways by different forms of power. I thus seek to elucidate the heterogeneous *power/knowledge relations in academic comparative education* as a field. I do so following the call of Marginson and Mollis for a multilingual approach (2002, p.615) in order to provide a more balanced reading of the heterogeneous trajectories and shapes of comparative educations. The comparative approach I adopt here enables a finer understanding of the complex interactions among the relatively autonomous theoretical discourses that struggle to appropriate symbolic capital in the field, and the social, political and economic contexts in which these discourses are accepted or rejected. Through cross-cultural comparison, I hope to contribute to a better understanding of why the discourses in the field have successfully emerged in some countries but not in others, and to what extent the contexts of their production and reception have a role. In other words, I aim to elucidate the factors that contribute to shaping a mosaic of comparative educations through the complex interactions of structure, agency and discursive power.

Conclusion

I commenced this chapter with a question whether comparative education is an academic field or not. Some comparative education scholars speak of 'comparative educations' to allude to the diverse particular features exhibited by this 'field'. Does comparative education have a set of necessary and universal elements that constitute it as an academic field? If so, how are these to be explained alongside the field's historically contingent features?

In this chapter, I have explored the epistemological and sociological conceptualisations of academic disciplines and fields. I have also discussed relevant socio-historical theories which throw light on the nature of disciplinary change from the prism of structural, agency-oriented and discursive forces of change. Drawing on the literature, I note that both epistemological and sociological forms of power interact in dialectic fashion in structuring disciplinary knowledge. Scholars suggest a distinction between a *cultural arbitrary* of *habitus* and an *epistemological non-arbitrary* of knowledge, as well as the distinct but intertwined roles of social power and knowledge, of sociological power and epistemological power (Maton, 2000; Moore, 2004). Foucault's work on discourse formation sheds a new light on the role of discourses in knowledge formation and the power-knowledge dialectic underlying disciplinary knowledge. As a counter-weight to the 'subjectivist' stance in Foucauldian thought, Bourdieu's theory of the intellectual field offers a substantially adequate framework to understand the role of agency and structure (sociological) in influencing disciplinary knowledge, while at the same time respecting the inner logic (epistemological) of the intellectual field. The epistemological structure of a field of knowledge exhibits necessary, permanent and universal features while its sociological forms display contingent, changing and particular characteristics. Both interact with external structures and the work of agents who, motivated by intellectual as well as micro-political interests, seek to develop their field and their positions within it. In order to understand the epistemological structuring of intellectual fields, I reviewed realist and constructivist philosophical concepts of academic disciplines and fields. Thus, through the combination of these sociological and epistemological lenses, I hope to contribute to a more comprehensive understanding of the nature of comparative education and the relationships between its institutional and intellectual histories in the construction of the field.

3

The Empirical Substance and Mass that Constitute the Field of Comparative Education

Introduction

In the present chapter, I attempt to present a global and comparative history and current state of comparative education as institutionalised in universities, specialist books and journals, and professional societies from 1900 to 2008. I review earlier surveys of the contours of the field as a critical tool to evaluate the institutional infrastructure of academic comparative education. I also comment on the work of national and international organisations in the field to complete the picture on the empirical mass and substance of comparative education. Finally, I propose three typologies to tease out the processes involved in the institutional construction of the field.

The purpose of this chapter is two-fold: first, to consider – from Foucauldian and Bourdieuian perspectives – the historical contingencies and power relations that led to or furthered the institutionalisation of comparative education as a stable set of heterogeneous discourses in different times and places; and second, to ascertain from an institutional standpoint whether comparative education is a distinct field or not, and if not, to offer explanations why this is so in the light of the findings on its institutional construction.

Presenting a global picture of the field is a daunting task despite the substantial and burgeoning literature available on this theme. This includes general reviews of comparative education teaching and research at a global level (e.g., Arnove & Torres, 2007; Brickman, 1988; Crossley & Watson, 2003; Epstein, 1994, 2008a; García Garrido, 1996; Halls, 1990a; Jones, 1971; McDade, 1982; Noah & Eckstein, 1969; Phillips & Schweisfurth, 2006; Wang, 1999; Wilson, 2003; Wolhuter et al., 2008a) and at a regional/national level (e.g., Bray, 2002; Carry et al., 2005; Fernández Lamarra et al., 2005; García Garrido, 2005a; Harbo & Winther-Jensen, 1993; Leclerq, 1999; Marquina & Lavia, 2006; Wilson, 1994a). There are also histories at an institutional level (e.g., Bray, 2004; Harbo & Jorde, 2000; Lauwerys, 1959, Veikshan, 1959). These, notwithstanding, accurate and comprehensive histories remain to be written. My main focus here is on institutional histories at universities and teacher training colleges, professional societies and specialist publications, specific literature on which I will discuss below. I attempt to expound on alternative inter- pretations and histories from other cultures, in order to widen the discourse and raise awareness that disciplinary histories and snapshot accounts of the institutionalisation of comparative education are complex and far from unitary. As Masemann (2006, p.110) underscores, "[w]e need to search for the pluralistic account, rather than the monolithic account. There are many stories that remain to be heard".

In order to offer a pluralist account of the institutional histories of comparative educations, I build on existing narratives and integrate some untold stories. I take as a starting point the globally comprehensive work of Halls (1990a) and update and enrich it with country reports on com- parative education at universities published in a recent volume which I co-edited (Wolhuter, Popov, Manzon & Leutwyler, 2008a), as well as accounts of the histories of the professional societies (Masemann, Bray & Manzon, 2007). I also draw on other published literature and un- published manuscripts and insights from personal interviews with senior comparative education scholars.

For a conceptual framework, I refer to Epstein (2008a), who distinguished among five benchmarks in the field's organisational tra- jectory. They are the creation of coursework, publication of textbooks and journals, establishment of formal academic programmes at universities, inauguration of professional societies, and more recently, elaboration of databases to document and analyse the field's courses, programmes and development. For the purposes of this chapter, I use the first four categories as a way of surveying the historical development of these institutional forms of comparative education, merging the creation of coursework and of formal academic programmes into one category. As for the databases, rather than viewing them as another organisational benchmark, I utilise them as a tool for a critical analysis of the nature, status and boundaries of the field.

The scope of this institutional narrative is from 1900 to 2008. It commences with the institutionalisation of academic comparative edu- cation as a lecture course pioneered in 1900 by James E. Russell in the USA (Bereday, 1963). I have excluded the 'pre-scientific' phase, generally understood to refer to the period of 'travellers' tales' and cultural bor- rowing by governments (see e.g., Noah & Eckstein, 1969; Phillips & Schweisfurth, 2006). As a separate category, I explore the work of national and international organisations, mainly in 'interventionist' comparative education (otherwise denominated as international education and development education), since these have been influential in the production of comparative education literature outside academia and in engaging the work of comparative education scholars in their projects.

Coursework and Programmes at Academic Institutions
Definitions and Typologies
Several scholars offer various working definitions of comparative education programmes and centres. Bergh et al. (1999, p.8) define a 'programme' as an academic offering that "leads to a degree or a similar qualification" and a 'course' as a "component/building block of a programme". Altbach and Tan (1995, p.vii) define a comparative education 'centre' as having:

- at least one FTE (full-time equivalent) faculty member focusing *mainly* on comparative/international education;
- at least four graduate level courses (master's and/or doctoral) that relate to comparative/international education; and
- a name such as Centre, Institute, or Group.

Bergh et al. (1999, pp.13-14) further distinguish between teaching comparative education as a core course and as a serving course, where serving courses may either be compulsory or optional. As a core course, it is usually found within specialist programmes in comparative education, while as a serving course it is located in programmes in other specialist fields (e.g., adult education, educational management, etc.). Similarly, Walterová (2008) cites three models of teaching comparative education which, while taken from the Czech Republic context, have wider applicability to other countries. They are:

1. Comparative education as a *separate compulsory discipline*. The model is common at faculties where teaching Education (Pedagogy) is a field of training. Comparative education could also be an optional course offered in models (2) or (3).
2. Comparative education as a *compulsory component in the introductory course of General Education*, combined mostly with the History of Education.
3. Comparative education taught as *selected topics spread out among several courses* (e.g., school policy, European studies, methodolo-

gy of educational research).

Manzon (2008a) summarised these various modalities of teaching comparative education as in Table 3.1.

More broadly speaking, Tikly and Crossley (2001) propose three models of approaches to the teaching of comparative and international education. They are specialisation, integration and transformation. *Specialisation* advocates view comparative education as a distinct specialism or separate subfield of education studies, with its distinctive attributes, perspectives and literatures. By contrast, *integration* exponents promote the infusion or integration of comparative perspectives into other courses or programmes of education studies. A third model, *transformation*, seeks to transcend this dichotomous practice of teaching comparative education within the confines of education faculties/ departments, by positioning it within courses offered at the advanced studies level of continuing professional development across departments, disciplines, professional areas, and cultures (p.578).

Table 3.1   Models of Teaching Comparative Education, by Levels

Levels of Education			
BEd		Distinct C.E.	
MEd	**Distinct**	**Subject:**	**Amorphous**
MPhil, PhD	**C.E. Specialism**	a) compulsory	**Subject**
PCEd.	n.a.	b) elective	

Note: n.a. – Not applicable; C.E. – Comparative Education

Epstein (2008a) explains that comparative education programmes and centres developed out of initial coursework, with a view to preparing specialists in the field and to support research. Academic courses and programmes are usually housed at faculties of education at universities, but may also be found at teacher training colleges, depending on the country and historical period in question. This discussion encompasses these two types of academic institutions, but focuses mainly on universities.

Historical Periodisation: A Framework

I discuss the historical trajectory and current state of institutionalisation of academic comparative education which, for analytical purposes, I divide into four periods:

- early establishment (1900-1945)
- expansion and specialisation (1945-1970)
- fragmentation (1970-2000)
- integration and new developments (2000s)

Before proceeding to the empirical data, I address some methodological issues regarding historical periodisation. I concur with Phillips (1994, 2002) that periodisation poses various problems, including selecting the beginning- and end-dates, and adequately encapsulating in period-titles identifiable and meaningful themes (Sweeting, 2007).

With respect to the first problem, I justify the first two periods of 1900-1945 and 1945-1970 by citing two precedents: Epstein (1994) and Bray (2001a). The first period begins in 1900 because of two significant events that were supposedly crucial for the development of academic comparative education: the first lecture course on comparative education taught by J. Russell at Teachers College, Columbia University (Bereday, 1963), and the influential lecture by M. Sadler on the importance of contextual considerations in comparative studies in education (Sadler, 1900). This first period ends around the close of the Second World War, and the second period around 1970. The third period (1970-2000), characterised by uncertainty for and fragmentation of the field in some parts of the world, witnessed the renaissance of academic comparative education in other parts of the world and the establishment of the World Council of Comparative Education Societies (1970), which has been a catalyst of the field's further institutionalisation. Finally, I take 2000 as a symbolic marker of a new era, echoing the discourse in special millennium issues of comparative education journals (e.g., Crossley & Jarvis, 2000).

With respect to the adequacy of the time-words or labels employed for these different periods – early establishment, expansion and specialisation, fragmentation, and integration and new developments – I refer to earlier studies that have taken a similar approach. Larsen et al. (2008) distinguish among three stages in the trajectory of comparative education at universities in Canada: establishment, fragmentation and broadening of comparative education. The establishment phase saw the commencement of comparative education courses and the development of stand-alone specialist programmes. The second phase, fragmentation, witnessed the contraction of course offerings and a reduction in chairs/centres of comparative education. A new phase entailed the broadening or integration of comparative perspectives in educational studies. However, time differentials exist in the start and end of each development phase across countries, and discordant cases as well as opposing trends may also be observed within each qualitative period, since not all countries exhibit the same sequence and direction of development as in the proposed periodisations above. The parallel and simultaneous coexistence of opposite trends (e.g., specialisation and integration) may also be manifested within one country. This echoes the observation of Crossley and Watson (2003, p.21) that historical periodisations oversimplify reality, since they mask the fact that these phases are "not necessarily linear or consistent across time, cultures or individuals". Despite the complexities and limitations of historical periodisations, I use them here for analytical purposes.

Previous Research

Among the major surveys of coursework and programmes of comparative education worldwide are Halls (1990a), Altbach and Tan (1995) and Wolhuter et al. (2008a). Halls' work encompassed both research and teaching of comparative education inside and outside academic institutions, while the latter two surveys focused on universities. Containing seven reports on world regions (Western Europe, The Socialist Countries, North America, Latin America, Asia and the Pacific, Africa, and the Arab States), as well as one chapter on the national and international infrastructures of comparative education, Halls (1990a) gathered important contributions by prominent scholars in the field. More than a survey, it offered insightful analyses and in-depth commentaries on the socio-political and intellectual contexts underlying the development of the field.

Of a rather less analytical but more descriptive nature is the survey by Altbach and Tan (1995), which attempted to offer a global inventory of comparative/international education programmes and centres covering 80 institutions. Some parts of the world, however, were under-represented, including Spain, countries of Eastern Europe, Latin America and Africa.

A more recent survey by Wolhuter, Popov, Manzon and Leutwyler (2008a), expands on the earlier work of Wolhuter and Popov (2007). This new edition explores 47 countries in five world regions: Europe, North America, Latin America, Asia and Africa. Although it is likewise not globally complete (e.g., Australia and many other countries of Europe, Africa and Latin America are absent), it presents an updated and more inclusive picture of the history and status of academic comparative education at the national level (especially in Latin America and post-1989 Eastern Europe) as well as analytical insights, which are both marked improvements on earlier surveys. In the concluding chapter by Wolhuter et al. (2008b), Popov offers a global picture of the historical development of comparative education, and Manzon a perspective on its current status at universities worldwide.

A more regional type of survey is published in French by Leclerq (1999). It features three chapters on the history and current status of comparative education teaching in Francophone countries/regions (e.g., Belgium, Canada, France, Francophone Africa, Switzerland), as well as the USA and some European countries. Carry et al. (2005) further expounded on the Francophone context. In 2006, Wolhuter surveyed universities in the Southern African region, and two other articles analysed the history and institutionalisation of discourses on comparative education in that region, respectively (Bergh & Soudien, 2006; Weeks et al., 2006). Although Senent (2005) examined mainly the state of educational studies in different types of universities in Europe within the context of reforms catalysed by the Bologna Process, he also briefly commented on the position of comparative education at European universities.

In addition to these global/regional surveys, a few other isolated studies have focused on specific countries or country groupings. A series of surveys on teaching comparative education in the UK was conducted by Watson (1982), Schweisfurth (1999) and Wilson (2005). Chen (1992) reviewed comparative education studies in China, while Bray and Gui (2001) and Manzon (2008a) explored patterns in Greater China, encompassing the People's Republic of China, Hong Kong, Macao and Taiwan. A handful of unpublished articles surveyed such countries as Argentina (Marquina & Lavia, 2007), Kenya (Makatiani & Chege, 2008), Poland (Potulicka, 2007) and Senegal (Gomis, 2008).

While the foregoing 'fixed' surveys offer snapshots of coursework and programmes in the field, 'continuing' surveys (a terminology borrowed from Epstein, 2008a, p.19) offer other insights. Possibly a pioneer in this latter category is CIECAP (Comparative and International Education Course Archive Project), a special project launched in 2003 by the Center for Comparative Education and the Comparative and International Education Graduate Students Association at Loyola University of Chicago, USA, under Erwin H. Epstein's direction. "CIECAP is an online database of salient features of introductory courses in comparative education as taught at universities around the world" (CIECAP, 2008). In August 2010, it contained course outlines from over 30 institutions, 22 of which were from American universities and 15 from outside the USA (e.g., Australia, Burundi, Canada, England, Estonia, Finland, Hong Kong, India, Oslo, South Africa and Sweden) (CIECAP, 2010). CIECAP is a laudable initiative that needs to be developed and improved, both in its geographic representation and in its provision of analytical commentaries (e.g., Stone, 2005), if it is to serve as a worthwhile research tool.

A Chronology of Comparative Education at Universities

As the above discussion shows, the literature, though patchy, is abundant. Thus I give here merely a sketch of milestones in the institutionalisation of comparative education in academia and a brief comment on the factors that contributed to the growth or decline of comparative education teaching in each phase. Since most of the empirical data presented below is taken from Wolhuter et al. (2008a), some overlaps will be found between the work presented below and the historical summary in the concluding chapter of that book (Wolhuter et al., 2008b). I have, however, made my own classification of the data from each of the chapters of the aforementioned book, and obtained additional data from other studies and from personal interviews. For ease of reference, the chronology per world region is summarised in Appendices 2 to 6.

Early Establishment (1900-1945)

The first lecture courses on comparative education are attributed to James E. Russell at Teachers College, Columbia University, USA in 1900 (Bereday, 1963) and Isaac Kandel at Manchester University, England in 1905. Soon after, Peter Sandiford initiated a lecture course at the University of Toronto, Canada in 1913. While this was in Anglophone Canada, by 1924, the subject was also taught at Westmount in the Francophone part of the country. Around this time, the first centre for comparative education, the International Institute of Education at Teachers College, Columbia University, was established with seed money from philanthropic sources (Epstein, 2008a). Also in the 1920s, university coursework was reported in Bulgaria, Czechoslovakia, Poland, and Uganda.

In the 1930s, comparative education subjects were also taught at Tokyo University (Japan), Beijing Normal University (China), and the University of Hong Kong (Manzon, 2008a; Takekuma, 2008). Comparative education teaching in China was, however, soon disrupted by political wars, which left the country in isolation until the late 1970s. Early shoots could also be found in Brazil and Cuba. In 1939, comparative education became a compulsory subject in Brazilian Bachelor's degrees in education (Sisson de Castro & Gomes, 2008). By 1944, the subject was also taught at the University of Havana, Cuba (Massón & Torres, 2008), and in 1945, at the University of Sydney (Burns, 1990) and at the National University of Lesotho (Seotsanyana & Ntabeni, 2006). Burns attributes the beginning of the course in Australia to Ivan Turner, who was educated under Isaac L. Kandel. Turner, with his doctoral students and colleagues, who also undertook postgraduate studies in comparative education abroad, in turn developed the field in the country. The case of Australia exemplifies the important role of the leading metropolitan centres of comparative education in the USA and the UK in nurturing 'indigenous' scholars who were later to serve as catalysts of the field in their home countries (e.g., Fox, 2005; Welch, 2005). Lauwerys (1959) already reported on the worldwide contacts and dissemination of comparative education out of the London Institute of Education. This pattern is repeated, in later years, in other countries' historical narratives, such as in Brazil, China, Hong Kong, India, Kenya and Thailand, especially those with strong colonial links or other political and economic ties (Dey-Gupta, 2004; Nogueira, 2004; Rwantabagu, 2006; Thongthew, 2007; also Gu & Gui, 2007; Luk, 2005). This mirrors the catalysing effect of the migration of outstanding scholars, for example, from Europe to the USA, as in the early years in the case of Kandel and several others (Halls, 1990b). More importantly, it signifies that there is a hierarchical structure in the field of knowledge production, wherein some countries occupy a central 'paradigmatic' position for other countries located at the periphery. This phenomenon echoes Bourdieu's notion of the intellectual field as positioned within a wider field of power such that the hierarchical structure of the intellectual field exhibits homologies with the unequal power structure of the geopolitical world. Countries positioned at the centre of world power serve as a 'model' for other countries to imitate and thus as a point of diffusion of educational innovations, in this case, comparative education.

Expansion and Specialisation (1945-1970)

The end of World War II is generally taken by comparative scholars as a watershed for the establishment of the field's legitimacy within universities as a distinct subfield in educational studies (Epstein, 1994; Kelly et al., 1982, p.505). The post-war reconstruction work saw, on one hand, favourable government foreign policies of industrialised countries, particularly the USA, but also Canada, Germany, Great Britain and Japan, to extend aid to the 'developing world', and on the other, nationwide reforms to improve domestic policy encouraged cross-national examination of educational models. In later decades, similar discourses of national reconstruction became salient in Eastern Europe and in other regions emerging from political isolation or colonisation. These macro-level national political factors served as catalysts for comparative education. Availability of funds for foreign study visits and international collaborations opened a new field of work and attracted entrants to meet the demand for new knowledge. The new societal demand after World War II translated into a new phase in the development of the subfield, marked by the expansion of coursework and programmes of study, as well as the formation of its scholarly societies (Manzon & Bray, 2007, p.341). Specialist centres and programmes of comparative education were formed and served in the nurturing of successive generations of scholars in the field. From a Foucauldian lens, a discursive formation was taking shape, that is, even if comparative education had existed in academia in the early 1900s, mostly in the form of isolated lecture courses, it did not have a distinct institutional identity until the 1950s. Through the coalescing of various discourses – political, intellectual – a discourse of 'comparative education' came to be formed around specific institutions, disciplines, commentaries of texts and social practices. A set of statements thus came to be systematically organised to produce the 'objects and practices' of comparative education knowledge.

The 1950s and 1960s were particularly expansionary periods in the field's history in the USA, Canada, England, West Germany, and Japan (Epstein, 2008a; Larsen et al., 2008; Takekuma, 2008; Waterkamp, 2008). Formal academic programmes mushroomed and chairs of comparative education were established in these countries. The pioneer professional societies were formed during this period. In the US, specialist graduate programmes at leading universities, funded by philanthropic donors, attracted people with some international experience gained from internationalist initiatives then in place, such as the Peace Corps and CUSO, among others (Epstein, 2004; Masemann, 2004). From a Foucauldian perspective, this phenomenon shows the historically contingent driving forces, such as practices of patronage by powerful institutions, which made some academic fields triumph over others or at least have the chance to be more distinctly institutionalised from neighbouring fields.

Holmes (1990) takes 1961 as a turning point in the development of comparative education in Western Europe, since during that year a major conference on comparative education was held at London University, which culminated in the formation of the Comparative Education Society in Europe (CESE). By this time, courses in comparative education were already present at various European universities, including in Croatia (then part of Yugoslavia), Flanders, France, Hungary, the Netherlands, and after 1961, also in Belgium, Denmark, Finland, Spain and Sweden, partly catalysed by the CESE gathering (e.g., Bunt-Kokhuis & Van daele, 2007; Winther-Jensen, 2008). Also, in the 1950s/1960s, early forms of comparative education courses were taught at the Chulalongkorn University (Thailand), Ankara University (Turkey), and the Universidad Nacional Autónoma de México (Gök, 2007; Navarro-Leal, 2008; Thongthew, 2008). Nevertheless, the extent of this expansion was fairly moderate. In Scandinavia, for example, the course was found in only one university in each of Denmark, Finland, Norway and Sweden, and did not have much of a following thereafter (Brock-Utne & Skinningsrud, 2008; Raivola, 2008; Winther-Jensen, 2008). In Spain, Juan Tusquets pioneered the Institute of Comparative Pedagogy in Barcelona in 1964 (Vilanou & Valls, 2001), but significant specialisation was not to take place until three decades after Tusquets' foundational work (Naya et al., 2008). Something similar happened in Japan where, after four chairs/institutes of comparative education were established from 1952-1965, no new chair was formed until 30 years later (in Nagoya), that being the last one to date (Takekuma, 2008).

The post-World War II era saw a divided world. Behind the Iron Curtain, a diverse trend in the field could be discerned. This differentiated national response to a single world event and its manifestations in both political and intellectual fields echoes Bourdieu's contention that the intellectual field is a field within fields. Political isolation behind the Iron Curtain logically prevented international contacts. Moreover, a rather ideologically strong form of comparative education operating under Marxist-Leninist principles was taught within the socialist bloc, and comparative education research tended to be politically biased in its aims and objects of study. Walterová (2008, p.43) thus characterised the research prevalent in the then Czechoslovakia as a "one-sided 'criticism of bourgeois education' and (an) overestimation of Soviet education" (also Borevskaya, 2007 on the Soviet Union; Holik, 2008 on Hungary; Waterkamp, 2007 on East Germany). Moreover, the study of Western education systems was considered a potentially criminal act (Popov, 2007; also Walterová, 2007). Thus, comparative education experienced a hiatus, albeit with some limited growth from 1945 to 1989 in such countries as Bulgaria, the former Czechoslovakia, East Germany, Hungary, Poland and Russia (Golz, 2008; Holik, 2008; Popov, 2008; Walterová, 2008; Waterkamp, 2007).

Outside the Soviet bloc, but also upholding socialist and communist doctrines, China was also politically isolated from the rest of the world from 1949 to 1976. Comparative education was abolished as a field of study in the 1950s, after the establishment of the People's Republic of China (PRC) in 1949 (Bray & Gui, 2001). The new government considered comparative education to be "a bourgeois pseudoscience that worshipped and had blind faith in things foreign" (Chen, 1992, p.5).

These discontinuities in the institutionalisation of comparative education illustrate how comparative education is a socially constructed discursive formation wherein political power constrains what could be legitimately said and studied as objects of knowledge in the field. Within that episteme, wherein the dominant paradigm was Marxist-Leninist in orientation, the geographical attraction shifted to 'leading' Soviet models and other socialist countries (Popov, 2007). Thus, diverging from Bourdieu, who contends that the intellectual field has the power to refract the influence of the political field within which it is embedded, the examples in the Socialist bloc demonstrate that the dominant political ideology (discourse and structure) has directly re-shaped, albeit externally and formally, the intellectual field of comparative education by suppressing it or limiting the power of human agency to resist its force, at least externally. This does not, however, mean that human agency is completely deprived of its freedom to resist the dominant ideology internally. The historical narratives written in the post-Iron Curtain era cited here (e.g., Popov, 2007; Borevskaya, 2007, etc.) reflect this spirit.

Although visible at several universities in South Africa and in Chile in the 1960s, course offerings in comparative education were sooner or later disrupted by political upheavals, and became significantly de-institutionalised thereafter. In South Africa, resistance to the apartheid state impacted on the contraction and reshaping of comparative education as a taught course in the 1980s in the major English-speaking universities and in leading black universities, though it remained in some Afrikaans universities (Soudien, 2007). The term 'comparative education' "had fallen into disuse in courses at English universities and had all but disappeared, with much of its impulse subsumed within cognate disciplines such as sociology and development studies" (Bergh & Soudien, 2006, p.44). A parallel political upheaval shook Chile, which fell under military dictatorship in 1973 and was politically isolated until 1990. Within this context, comparative education was discontinued at its universities and later re-emerged only as a perspective infused in educational studies rather than as a stand-alone subject (Rodríguez, 2008). A similar case of fragmentation occurred in Brazil in the 1960s when the subject was removed from the national curriculum for education majors (Sisson de Castro & Gomes, 2008). Subsequently, it was further marginalised in the 1980s due to the prevalent nationalist sentiments that pervaded academia. Comparative education – with its practice of policy borrowing mainly from the West – was seen as an instrument of American imperialism and colonisation (Nogueira 2004; Verhine 2004).

From these and the aforementioned cases in the Soviet bloc as in China, it can be observed that political ideology is a significant factor in deterring the growth of comparative education, particularly if comparative education is viewed as being about 'Western' or 'American' or 'capitalist' education, or other such hegemonic ideologies perceived to undermine the prevailing nationalist ideology. In some cases, the proximity of the intellectual field to the political field is clear and the latter's influence is almost immediate (e.g., Brazil, Chile, China, Soviet bloc). By contrast, in South Africa, the intellectual field of comparative education exhibited a mediating function, a capacity to refract the force of political ideology through the variegated institutional mechanisms of its universities. Thus, depending on the type of university – Afrikaans, English-medium white, historically Black – the shape of comparative education differed. In the end, reforms under a post-apartheid government and shifts in interest toward development issues and less-theoretical content in teacher education saw a contraction of the field's institutional structures. In the competition for institutional space, comparative education lost out to other educational/social science disciplines. Thus, despite the availability of individual and institutional agents who advocate the field, the institutional capital they possessed became devalued in the light of the dominant political environment. The fragmentation and marginalisation of the field in these countries foreshadowed patterns that were to characterise the field in the pioneer countries of the industrialised West in the 1970s and 80s, albeit perhaps owing less to political forces and more to intellectual and economic factors.

Other political transformations, however, served to open up opportunities for comparative education in Africa and parts of Asia, with countries gaining independence or emerging from political wars. In line with the drive for national modernisation, this period witnessed the commencement of comparative education courses at newly-formed African universities (e.g., in Egypt, Kenya, Rwanda, Tanzania and Zimbabwe), as well as in India, Malaysia and South Korea, particularly after the Korean War in 1953 (Anangisye, 2008; Dey-Gupta, 2004; Lee & Kwon, 2007; Machingura & Mutemeri, 2006; Makatiani & Chege, 2008; Megahed & Otaiba, 2008; Mohd. Meerah & Halim, 2008; Nzabalirwa, 2008). The interactions among discourses on political change, educational reforms and the value of learning from foreign educational experiences increased the political capital of comparative education. It is not insignificant that the paradigms of educational innovation came from the industrialised West, concretely the UK and the USA. As in the previous period, most of those who introduced comparative education at universities in these new countries were either indigenous scholars who obtained their scholarly qualifications in major American and British universities, or were foreign scholars from the US and the UK. This shows the importance of human agency moving within a favourable structure for constructing the field of comparative education, as well as the relationships between positions of world power and directions of influence in knowledge production.

Fragmentation (1970-2000)

The decades of the 1970s through the 1990s saw a substantial contraction in both intellectual and institutional legitimacy of academic comparative education at leading centres in the USA, Canada, UK, Germany and Australia (Wolhuter et al., 2008b). Similar patterns of weakening and marginalisation became apparent in South Africa in the 1980s, as discussed above, and even more after 1994 in the post-apartheid era. A confluence of macro-level factors – intellectual, economic, labour – variedly accounted for this phenomenon, in addition to particularities of each national and institutional context. Marked shifts in intellectual topography were provoked by postmodernist challenges to foundationalist theories in the social and human sciences. In time, these eroded the position of educational foundations courses at faculties of education, and within them, comparative education (Epstein, 2004; Larsen et al., 2008; Welch, 1997, p.186). The decline in the dominance of the disciplines and the influence of neo-liberal principles partly exemplified by the accountability movement re-shaped teacher education by introducing externally imposed standards and becoming increasingly focused on measurable skills or competencies rather than on providing an academic grounding in the foundations of education (Kubow & Fossum, 2008; Schweisfurth, 1999; Wolhuter et al., 2008c). The shift of interest to marketable skills, which are in demand in the labour market, made such interdisciplinary fields such as comparative education less attractive to students (e.g., Dey-Gupta, 2004; Ocheng Kagoire, 2008; Raivola, 2008; Sutherland, 2007). In Bourdieuian terms, the logic of the field changed from having a political and intellectual value to an economic value. Where the economic value of comparative education cannot be established, it becomes less attractive to students and it eventually loses out in the competition for distinction and resources within faculties of education. As Wilson (1994b, cited in Larsen et al., 2008, p.148) argues, since

> comparative education has not been 'vested' in curriculum guidelines and was therefore largely absent from teacher preparation programmes[,if] there were comparative courses, they were generally optional; [and] when resources became scarce, as they did throughout the 1980s and 1990s, it was these courses that were often cut back or eliminated entirely from teacher education.

Waterkamp (2005) elaborates on the economic logic of the field in the context of Germany where education is relatively decentralised:

> *Relevance as it is seen by university administration* – that's important – and perhaps politics. But university administration is even more important, because it is up to the university administration to distribute the money within the university ... and their most important criterion is how much money you bring in to the university. [emphasis added]

At the same time, worldwide fiscal crises contributed in part to educational crises and cutbacks in funding for higher education, teacher education and comparative education (Altbach, 1991; Epstein, 2008a; Watson, 1982; Welch, 1997). Faculties or departments of education were streamlined and smaller units were merged into bigger and more economical institutions (e.g., Mochida, 2005; Weeks et al., 2006). These contributed to a wave of pessimism and uncertainty about the academic legitimacy of the field of comparative education then beset by paradigm wars and a lack of commonly agreed theory, methodology and academic priorities (Wolhuter et al., 2008b). Thus, this period witnessed the discontinuance of specialist programmes and centres, sometimes by natural demise with the retirement of university programmes' founders as in Canada, Germany, Switzerland (Larsen et al., 2008; Schüssler & Leutwyler, 2008; Waterkamp, 2008) or the departure of the few qualified lecturers in the field, as was the case in Malaysia (Mohd. Meerah & Halim 2008). This phenomenon is of concern since it implies the failure to recruit and prepare a succeeding generation of scholars equipped with the academic capital and *habitus* to continue the field (Welch, 1997). This is manifest in countries such as Brazil, Ireland, Korea and Russia which report a lack of personnel prepared to teach the subject (e.g., Borevskaya, 2007; Nogueira, 2004; O'Sullivan, 2008; Park & Hyun, 2008). Viewed with Bourdieuian lenses, these discontinuities in the specialist programmes signify that agents in the intellectual field of comparative education no longer considered it 'profitable' to 'play the game' in this field and thus shifted to other more established fields or disciplines. The shifts in dominant political and economic discourses thus reshaped the structures within which the intellectual field of comparative education is embedded. The fragmentation in the institutionalisation of this intellectual field in some parts of the world demonstrates the influence of economic and political power on the field, transforming its dominant logic into an economic one. Human agency either copes and survives within this transformed field or opts out.

Despite this seeming 'dark age' in the field's institutional history, positive developments also took place during the period 1970-2000. The catalysts were similar to the historically contingent factors that intervened in the first wave of expansion, and, to some extent, specialisation, in the 1950s/1960s: emergence from political isolation and national modernisation and democratisation, among them. In this second wave are the newly independent countries of the former Soviet Union, as well as China, which witnessed the re-institutionalisation of comparative education in its universities. In the case of Kazakhstan, the subject became a compulsory component of teacher education (Kussainov & Mussin, 2008). Within similar contexts of political change in Greece, Kenya, Namibia and Spain, the contribution of comparative education became prized in teacher education programmes (Karras, 2008; Likando et al., 2006; Makatiani & Chege, 2008; Naya et al., 2008). The subject was also introduced in Francophone African countries like Burundi and La

Réunion (Lucas et al., 2006; Rwantabagu, 2008). Some common patterns among these countries (e.g., China, Greece, Spain, Kazakhstan) include the strategic positioning of comparative education as a compulsory core subject in degree programmes of teacher education during the process of national education reforms, as governments gave priority to professionalising or upgrading the academic status of teacher education programmes. In China, Kazakhstan and, to some extent, Russia, the subject is compulsory in degree programmes for teaching foreign languages (Golz, 2008; Kussainov & Mussin, 2008; Manzon, 2008a). This is indicative of the international component characteristic of comparative education and the linguistic capital that is valued in the field. The positioning of comparative education in university curricula within this new wave of significant institutionalisation was partly determined by the priorities of national teacher education at that time. In this intertwining of contingent discourses on political priorities and educational reforms, the political capital of comparative education found due recognition, partly through the work of agents who happened to have some knowledge about or interest in comparative education, and who occupied influential positions in education commissions or advisory committees to ministries of education in those countries. To substantiate this claim, I examine some narratives on the institutionalisation of comparative education as a compulsory subject in Spain.

The Spanish case is instructive for elucidating Foucault's and Bourdieu's insights into academic fields. Naya (2004) and Ferrer (2004) posit the role of political changes in the country (structure) and personal biography (agency) of particular individuals who were agents of change in the educational scenario and who played a role in the incorporation of comparative education in 1994 as an obligatory core component of the national curriculum of education degrees in its universities. From a macro-political perspective, Spain was promoting society-wide reforms including of its educational system after emerging from decades of dictatorship. Moreover, in 1992, Spain became incorporated into the European Union. In this historical moment, comparative education entered the discourse on educational innovations in Spain. Ferrer (2004) describes the situation thus:

> The educational reform involved the approval in 1990 of a 'General Law of the Educational System' (LOGSE) after society-wide consultations. In these consultations and debates, the international

element was very salient: 'What is being done in other countries?' ... Often it is a matter of *relations of power*. Logically if in the (Education) Commission there are those who believe that comparative education is important because they have taught it before or they have experience (in the field). ... Perhaps these contributed to the positioning of comparative education in the national curriculum. [emphasis added]

Ferrer (2006) further elaborates on the element of 'personal biography' (agency) and the political (structural) context:

The persons who started to govern Spain in the democratic period (after Franco's dictatorship) were people who had been to foreign universities, whether for reasons of being on exile, or simply for the purpose of study. For example, the first minister of education in the first socialist government of 1982, Maraval, was a professor at LSE (London School of Economics). ... During the consultation period on the new Law of Education in the early 1980s, the White Papers always had a section on international trends in Europe. Thus from the perspective of educational policy in Spain, the international theme was each time gaining importance. The democratic era of Spain was characterised by openness to the outside world at all levels. The international context was becoming ever more important and this logically favoured disciplines of an international nature, and comparative education was one of them.

To this description of a political discourse favouring internationalisation, Naya (2004) adds the interlocking with the discourse on European regionalisation:

At the end of the 1980s and at the beginning of the 1990s, Spain was becoming Europeanised. In 1992, Spain became a member of the European Union. This is an element which to me is crucial to explaining the importance of international programmes within Spanish universities, because it was being seen that the immediate future of Spain was going to be in a much more international context. ... It was the logical consequence of the historical moment that we were living.

The above narration of the Spanish case echoes Foucault's concept of a discursive formation as "a historically conditioned system of regularity for the coexistence of statements" (Lenoir, 1993, p.74). It demonstrates the interaction of historically contingent political and educational discourses, which coalesced into the institutionalisation of a distinctive discursive space for comparative education, by positioning it as a compulsory subject in university curricula. In other words, the compulsory status of comparative education is a contingent and particular, not a necessary and universal phenomenon. The uncertainty as to the sustainability of its status as a core curricular subject suggests that the intellectual legitimacy of comparative education is not self-evident, but requires to be established.

With comparative education becoming an obligatory subject for all students majoring in education, more professors of comparative education were needed, thereby catalysing specialisation in the field and further institutional developments (García Garrido, 2004). As Ferrer (2006) commented: "We, who formed part of this *caldo de cultivo* (literally, a tissue culture, a metaphor to refer to the first/second generation of scholars in the field) could consolidate much more our positions". Thus, according to Naya and Ferrer (2007), after 1994, the Spanish comparative education society saw a significant increase in its membership of professors who were specialists in comparative education. Applying Bourdieu's thought that an agent is socially constituted as such within a particular intellectual field in which its value is recognised (Bourdieu & Wacquant, 1992, p.107), it can be affirmed that the creation of a specialist course or field of comparative education at Spanish universities led to the creation of the 'comparative education specialist'.

Meanwhile, the opposite trend can also be observed: the tardy take-up of comparative education and/or its marginalisation is common among countries where teacher education has (or originally had) a low academic status or a more practical orientation, such as in France and Francophone countries in Europe and Africa, as well as in India, Ireland, Korea, the Netherlands and Flanders, Scandinavia, Switzerland, and Greece until its elevation to a university status in 1984 (Boerma et al., 2008; Carry et al. 2005; Dey-Gupta, 2004; Frenay et al., 1999; Gomis, 2008; Karras, 2008; O'Sullivan, 2008; Park & Hyun, 2008; Senent, 2005; Sutherland, 2007). Historically, teacher education in these places was about pedagogical skills and was less concerned about the 'teacher-researcher' and the place of the social sciences (and, as a corollary, of comparative education) in teacher education. In other words, the 'recipient' structure and the logic of the intellectual field of teacher education were incongruent with the research and theoretical orientations of academic comparative education. Some countries exhibited a fitful growth, such as Argentina and Switzerland. In the case of Argentina, comparative education was taught at the Universidad de Buenos Aires (UBA) in 1976, when the country was under a military dictatorship. The field's positioning changed in the 1990s when the country was democratised. The curriculum for the degree in Educational Sciences at the UBA included a subject entitled: "Comparative Education: Genesis and Current State of an Inexistent Discipline" (Fernández Lamarra et al., 2005, p.165). Yet, a survey in 2007 by Marquina and Lavia reported that the subject is currently taught in education degree programmes at 19 out of 39 Argentinean universities. As for Switzerland, a chair of comparative education was established in 1973 at the University of Geneva held by P. Furter, but his retirement in the 1990s did not have a sustainable succession.

It is paradoxical to find academic comparative education weakly institutionalised at universities in Switzerland, as well as in France and the Francophone region of Belgium, which have high concentrations of international government organisations in their capitals (e.g., the International Bureau of Education in Geneva, UNESCO and the OECD in Paris, the European Union headquarters in Brussels) engaged in international comparative studies of education (Senent, 2005; also Carry et al., 2005). Whereas in the US, the discourse of internationalism advocated by international agencies appeared to have intersected with academic comparative education, such pattern was not repeated in these Francophone contexts. In the case of Switzerland, Schüssler and Leutwyler (2008) attribute the field's paradoxically weak institutionalisation to the restricted framework of educational research that neglects macroapproaches, the small endowment for educational sciences, and provincialism, especially in Germanophone Switzerland. They also claim that Switzerland's non-membership of the EU partly exacerbated this inward-looking attitude. In other words, the discourse on internationalism is not sufficient to catalyse the academic field of comparative education if, by contrast, the academic and scientific power of the field of teacher education is weak, and if there are insufficient agents who are willing to compete for institutional space for the field. The presence of international organisations engaged in comparative studies in education does not necessarily translate to the construction of the field of academic comparative education. These multilateral agencies have a different purpose and clientele from academic institutions.

The patterns of fragmentation and disruption initiated in this era, owing to diverse structural forces in the political, economic and intellectual spheres, as well as the shifting interests and loyalties of the scholars working within the field, seems to indicate the fragility of the field of comparative education despite its world wide dissemination. What we therefore find at the turn of the third millennium is a comparative education that is marginal to educational studies at universities, despite some form of renaissance of the field in some places. Mainly, however, comparative education has been transformed into an 'infused perspective' in educational studies and rarely exists as a stand-alone specialist programme or department.

Integration and New Developments (2000s)

The integration or broadening of comparative and international education teaching, which involves the infusion of comparative perspectives and content into other courses and programmes of study within educational studies (Tikly & Crossley, 2001), marks not so much yet another phase disjointed from the previous phase of specialisation, but a characteristic latent in the previous period that has increasingly become salient in the current state of comparative education world wide. In this phase, comparative education is taught less as an autonomous module entitled as such than as a comparative/international focus of educational issues subsumed under such themes as development, globalisation, higher education, intercultural education, and the like. At the least, comparative education continues to be taught as an independent subject in some countries, though in most cases, as an optional course.

Aside from the reasons cited above for the subject's fragmentation and dilution into a perspective in education, other reasons accounting for the phenomenon of integration include the internationalisation of education studies curricula, partly influenced by the demands of a more internationalised student body, and by the globalisation of education policy (Tikly & Crossley, 2001). This is partly catalysed by geopolitical shifts such as the formation of new supranational groupings and the alignment of their educational systems (e.g., EU integration and the Bologna Process). While these elicit an interest in international themes and consequently attract a wider audience for comparative education, it has not necessarily resulted in the strengthening of comparative education as a *distinct* specialism in education studies, but only as "a subject in the curriculum as well as a method of analysis" for educational issues (Senent, 2005, p.122). A case in point is Walterová's description of the current status of comparative education in the Czech Republic (2007, p.266):

> Comparative education in the Czech Republic has a long history. However, a *diffusion of the comparative education community* and a tendency of fragmentation and isolation have weakened the status of the field. Comparative education is taught in some universities, but it is not a degree specialisation. Comparative research and events are not concentrated at or coordinated by a specific institution. Research topics in the field education are mostly *derived from projects focused on problems in national education or initiated by international projects*. Comparative education is conceived *more as a research method or methodological principle than a special field of study.* [emphasis added]

In these circumstances, and given the inherently weak institutional position of comparative education in academic institutions and the lack of a distinct specialist community, there is the danger of comparative studies being undertaken haphazardly by a wider public who are oblivious of the important methodological and theoretical perspectives from the field of comparative education (Schüssler & Leutwyler, 2008; Sutherland, 2007; Tikly & Crossley, 2001). At the same time, even in places where academic comparative education is significantly well-positioned at universities, its future is insecure. Such is the case of Spain in recent times. Naya et al. (2008) predict an uncertain future for the field, despite the favourable winds of European integration and harmonisation of higher education systems, which initially led to its strong institutionalisation in the 1990s. With expected reforms in the direction of giving Spanish universities greater autonomy, Naya et al. foresee that the positioning of comparative education would depend on competition for 'academic power' (in Bourdieu's sense of power of control over the administration of academic resources within each university). Insights from Naya (2004) and Ferrer (2006) are illustrative:

> Naya (2004): There are discussions of policies ... a new battle is beginning and in this battle, one could be slain (allí pueda haber en esa pelea algún muerto): that status of comparative education may or may not be maintained.

> Ferrer (2006): The battle will be within each university [and] it is the

duty of each professor (of comparative education) to gain the support of colleagues.

In other words, in a new situation wherein the political governing structure is more decentralised, the proximity between the political field and the intellectual field of comparative education – and the intensity of influence of politics on academia – becomes weaker. Instead, a new field gains importance: the universities and their institutional power. The university field comes to mediate between the political field and the intellectual field of comparative education. In this new setting, the logic of the field of comparative education shifts from giving primacy to political capital – power of influencing national educational policies – to other types of capital such as academic capital and social capital with one's colleagues in the faculty or with university administration. Public discourses and societal contexts that foster an international outlook (e.g., on Europeanisation, globalisation, internationalisation) are thus insufficient to catalyse or maintain the institutionalisation of comparative education. These discourses do not *necessarily* result in the institutionalisation of the field as a specialist subfield of educational studies; rather, they are contingent discourses. In some historical circumstances, they may lead to (and have indeed led) to 'disciplinary' specialisation, while in others they may lead (or have led) to its 'disciplinary' integration as a mere perspective infused into educational studies, either purposefully so by scholars who identify with the field or 'accidentally' by persons who are not 'playing the game' inside the intellectual field of comparative education. Disciplinary institutionalisation is, therefore, partly an outcome of historically contingent discursive practices, which interact with objective structural configurations of the political and economic worlds, of teacher education, of academic institutions, intellectual trends, as well as with the subjective dispositions (*habitus*) and backgrounds of individuals (cultural, economic, social, academic and political capital) occupying positions of influence in the intellectual field and the wider field of educational and international politics.

Based on the 2008 survey by Wolhuter et al., encompassing 47 countries/states, and complemented by data on five countries not included in that book, that is, Argentina (Marquina & Lavia, 2007); Australia (Hickling-Hudson, 2004; Welch, 2005; Jones, 2007 cited in Fox, 2007, p.207); Kenya (Makatiani & Chege, 2008); Poland (Potulicka, 2007); Portugal (Senent, 2005), around 30 countries can be said to exhibit a trend of broadening (and less specialisation) of comparative education in the early 21st century. They are Australia, Botswana, Brazil, Canada, Chile, China, Denmark, Egypt, Finland, France, Germany, Hong Kong, Hungary, Japan, Ireland, Italy, Korea, Macao, Malaysia, Mexico, the Netherlands and Flanders, Norway, Oman, Rwanda, South Africa, Sweden, Switzerland, UK, USA, and Zimbabwe (Wolhuter et al., 2008b; also Al-Harthi, 2008; Boerma et al., 2008; Hickling-Hudson, 2004; Larsen et al., 2008; Navarro-Leal, 2008; Palomba & Paolone, 2008; Park & Hyun, 2008; Senent, 2005; Welch, 2005; Wilson, 2005).

Nevertheless, some new programmes of comparative and international education were established during this period. In the early 2000s, Taiwan's National Chi Nan University opened a Department of Comparative Education, and Denmark's Danish University of Education established a Unit of International and Comparative Education. The Danish unit was headed by Thyge Winther-Jensen who, in 2002, received the first Danish professorship in comparative education. However, soon after his retirement in 2004, the Unit was transformed into a research programme of Comparative Educational Policy (Winther-Jensen, 2008). In 2005, scholars in Swaziland and Uruguay also launched modules on comparative education. Uruguay's late entry into the field is due to the tardy development of its higher education system (Martínez, 2008). Furthermore, Thailand seemed to be gearing itself to form a Department of Comparative Education at Chulalongkorn University (Thongthew, 2008). Epstein (2008a) also reported the reincarnation of strong comparative education programmes at Columbia University and Stanford University in the USA. However, the financial tsunami of autumn 2008 that hit worldwide economies, albeit excluding some countries, posed new challenges to academic institutions.

An Inventory of Courses, 2008

Comparative education exists either as a stand-alone programme or as a lecture course at universities world wide in both undergraduate and postgraduate levels. As a lecture course, it may be compulsory or optional, a core course or a serving course. Among the 50 countries surveyed in 2008 (mainly Wolhuter et al., 2008b; also Makatiani & Chege, 2008; Marquina & Lavia, 2007; Potulicka, 2007; Senent, 2005), comparative education is found to exist at universities:

- as a *specialist programme* at the Bachelor's level in 2 countries (4 per cent), namely Norway and Taiwan, and at the Master's level in 14 countries (28 per cent);

- as a *lecture course* entitled 'comparative education' taught at the Bachelor's level as compulsory in 27 countries (60 per cent), and as optional in 18 countries (40 per cent). At the Master's level it is compulsory in 21 countries (42 per cent) and optional in 14 countries (28 per cent). At both levels, around half of the countries surveyed reported the compulsory teaching of comparative education, usually at the university's discretion, except for three countries, where it is nationally mandated as a compulsory core subject at the BEd level (Hungary, Kazakhstan and Spain). These are summarised in Tables 3.2 and 3.3.

The observation of Bergh et al. (1999) that comparative (and international) education is usually a core course in specialist programmes of comparative education and a serving course to programmes in other specialisms, is echoed in this 2008 survey. As a serving course, it may be either compulsory core or optional. Considering that specialist program-

Table 3.2: Comparative Education Taught as a BEd Lecture Course (2008)

Region	Countries	Compulsory	Optional	Total No.	%
Europe	Bulgaria, Croatia, Czech Republic, Denmark, Finland, Flanders, France, Germany, Greece, Hungary, Ireland, Italy, the Netherlands, Norway, Portugal, Russia, Spain, UK	11	7	18	40%
North America	Canada, USA	-	2	2	4%
Latin America	Argentina, Brazil, Cuba, Mexico	-	4	4	9%
Asia	China, Taiwan, Japan, Kazakhstan, Korea, Malaysia, Oman, Thailand	5	3	8	18%
Africa	Botswana, Burundi, Egypt, Kenya, Lesotho, Namibia, Reunion, Rwanda, South Africa, Swaziland, Tanzania, Uganda, Zimbabwe	11	2	13	29%
Total		*27*	*18*	*45*	*100%*
% total surveyed		*54%*	*36%*	*90%*	

Source: Expanded version of Wolhuter et al., 2008b (p.328)

mes in comparative education are less common nowadays, the above inventory suggests that the subject exists mainly as a serving course for other specialisms.

Table 3.3: Comparative Education Taught as a Master's Lecture Course (2008)

Region	Countries	Compul-sory	Optional	Total No.	%
Europe	Bulgaria, Denmark, Finland, Flanders, France, Germany, Greece, Hungary, Italy, Norway, Po-land, Russia, Spain, UK	9	5	14	40%
North America	Canada, USA	-	2	2	6%
Latin America	Argentina, Cuba, Mexico	-	3	3	8%
Asia	China, Hong Kong, Japan, Kazakhstan, Korea, Malaysia, Taiwan, Thailand	5	3	8	23%
Africa	Egypt, Kenya, Lesotho, Namibia, South Africa, Tanzania, Uganda, Zimbabwe	7	1	8	23%
Total		*21*	*14*	*35*	*100%*
% total surveyed		*42%*	*28%*	*70%*	

Source: Expanded version of Wolhuter et al., 2008b (p.328)

These figures should not, however, lead one to conclude that the patterns of compulsory-optional teaching are uniformly present within each country. In the UK, for example, Wilson's survey (2005) reported that at the Bachelor's level, comparative education is a core component in one programme, but is optional in nine other programmes. Similarly, at the Master's level, it is core in nine programmes, but is optional in 18. While such exact figures are available only on a few countries, it is likely that similar patterns may be repeated in most other countries based on the qualitative description in the country reports. Appendix 7 lists the approximate number of institutions per country where comparative education is taught as at June 2008. Despite the limitations in the collection of accurate data, the list reports an estimated total of almost 450 universities where comparative education is taught as a subject at the Bachelor's level and almost 300 universities at the Master's level. Also, despite the limitations of Wolhuter et al.'s survey (2008b) wherein not all countries provided data on the number of institutions where the subject is taught, it is interesting to note that in 20 out of 47 countries (42 per cent), comparative education is taught in at most 5 universities (p.331). For countries in Africa where there is only one university (e.g., Botswana, Namibia and Swaziland), or sub-national regions like Hong Kong, which has fewer than 10 universities, the teaching of comparative education in one institution alone is significant. But in most other countries in the rest of the world which have a bigger university base, comparative education is significantly at the periphery. A case in point is Brazil, where comparative education can be found as a subject in the regular curriculum of undergraduate programmes in only three universities, although it is present as a research area at the graduate level in at least eight other universities around the country (Sisson de Castro & Gomes, 2008, pp.171 & 173). In other words, the institutional foothold of comparative education is generally marginal at universities. Where comparative education had had a traditionally central position as an independent academic subject or specialism, but was later displaced in the context of anti-foreign policies and/or withdrawal of funding support, it has usually been unable to recover its strong institutional presence, unless strong institutional support is given to it, say, by the state, as in the case of post-Mao China. Meanwhile, in some of those locations where it still exists as a specialism, there are signs of decline and unpopularity as a career path among students as in Uganda and South Korea (Ocheng Kagoire, 2008; Park & Hyun, 2008, p.250).

Furthermore, as reported in Wolhuter et al. (2008b, pp.332-334), three broad trends can be discerned in the current state of development of comparative education at universities in the 47 countries surveyed: stability (11 countries or 23 per cent), regression (16 countries or 33 per cent) and revitalisation (10 countries or 21 per cent), with the remaining 10 countries unclassified due to insufficient information or because they were in transition. The authors further remarked that "it can be modestly affirmed that the legitimacy of comparative education as an independent academic field at universities continues to be challenged", and that it is probable that "the revitalised positions of comparative education owe their renaissance to a particularly successful re-definition of their identities" (2008b, pp.339-340) and a demonstration of their usefulness. This is the case in such places as Canada, Hong Kong, Italy, UK and USA (e.g., Kubow & Fossum, 2008; Larsen et al., 2008; Palomba & Paolone, 2008; O'Sullivan, 2008). Thus, the field of comparative education clearly demonstrates the dynamics of an intellectual field whose structure, according to Bourdieu, is defined as a dynamic system of positions and oppositions, where agents in the field compete to define legitimate areas of knowledge with respect to what is valued in the field and, ultimately, in the fields of political and economic power in which the intellectual field is embedded.

On the other hand, regression in the status of comparative education refers to the erosion of its distinct identity as a separate field of educational studies and the incorporation of comparative perspectives in educational curricula, whether by specialists trained in the field or by non-specialists interested in the international aspects of education, the latter phenomenon becoming more likely in the decades to come as specialist programmes in the field become a rarity. It is possible that in future generations, this process of integration and permeation, while making comparative education somewhat omnipresent in educational curricula as a perspective and as a methodology, will eventually blur its distinct academic boundaries for not having scholars trained in its specialist programmes – and therefore possessing the cultural capital in the field – or strongly identifying with its history and aims. In Foucauldian terms, just as a disciplinary programme forms a discursive formation by which distinct disciplines and disciplinary institutions congregate to 'discipline' a scholarly community, the erosion of that discursive formation leads to a blurring of boundaries and specific discourses which construct comparative education as a distinct field of knowledge. This is already partly reflected by the survey of CIES members conducted by Cook et al. (2004), which reported that 70 per cent of respondents received their academic degree in disciplines outside of comparative education, and that 36 per cent had never taken an introductory course on comparative education. This can perhaps partly account for and reflect the field's disciplinary eclecticism and lack of a common understanding of the field's nature and purpose, history and boundaries (Epstein, 2008a). Cook et al. (2004, p.147) thus conclude that comparative education "might be depicted more precisely as a field of study determined by the diversity of its research and interpretive enterprises, rather than one that has any established or consensual agenda".

Specialist Publications

Publications in comparative education represent a second category of the field's empirical substance. As Epstein (2008a, p.10) remarks,

[P]ublications are the lifeblood of all academic fields. Books in comparative education have played an important part in setting the ground for scholarship. Textbooks and encyclopaedias in particular, as they serve to impart accumulated knowledge, have been essential in this regard. Yearbooks and journals have been the principal vehicles for keeping comparativists current on developments in their field.

Although specialist publications in comparative education preceded formal academic programmes, it was through the latter that a discursive formation in the Foucauldian sense of a historically conditioned organisation of concepts into a system of statements which produce objects of knowledge took shape. Through the existence of specialist disciplinary programmes, systematic commentary on specific texts and authors came to be developed. Nevertheless, specialist publications are even more powerful tools for the discursive construction of the field since they have the potential to reach a wider audience and to outlive academic programmes. Epstein (2008a, p.13), speaks of the value of academic journals in "setting scholarly norms and boundaries as well as standards of quality, … [and of giving] a sense of identity about [the] field". By extension, this observation can also be applied to specialist publications in the field. However, there are hierarchies of power and influence in the international knowledge system, wherein those at the centre of power dominate knowledge production while those at the periphery are marginalised (Altbach, 1994) on account of unequal linguistic, economic and/or cultural capital. On the issue of language, English continues to expand its dominant share as the lingua franca in international discourse (Altbach, 2007). The incommunicability of some parts of the world due to language differences is a hindrance to having a comprehensive and globally-inclusive discourse on comparative education (Manzon, 2008a). In this sense, the linguistic barrier contributes to the dominance of some research paradigms simply because divergent paradigms at the periphery are unable to be heard in the international discourse.

In this section, I trace the significant publications that, over time, have given shape and substance to the field worldwide. My aim is not to give an exhaustive list, but to name possibly the earliest known specialist texts at the beginning of comparative education in the countries surveyed or those published in its renaissance. My main sources are the country/ regional reports in Wolhuter et al. (2008a), Masemann et al. (2007), Halls (1990a), as well as Bereday (1964), complemented by other published literature (e.g., Crossley & Watson, 2003; Phillips & Schweisfurth, 2006; Wilson, 2003). For ease of reference, key data are summarised in Appendices 2 to 6.

Textbooks and Encyclopaedias

According to Epstein (2008a, p.12), both textbooks and encyclopaedias aim to transmit systematic and accumulated knowledge to future generations, serving as reference guides, but encyclopaedias do so on a comprehensive range of topics. This section will focus on textbooks, which are more common and abundant, and will only briefly discuss encyclopaedias.

Pre-1945 Period

As coursework and formal academic programmes developed in the field, so did the need for textbooks. Widely considered as the field's first textbook is an edited volume by Sandiford (1918) entitled *Comparative Education: Studies of the Educational Systems of Six Modern Nations*. The book contains country-by-country descriptions of the educational systems in six industrialised countries (Bereday, 1964; Epstein, 2008a). Around the same time, two books were published in Asia, both focusing on national educational systems in industrialised countries: one in Chinese (Yu, 1917) and another in Japanese (Nakajima, 1916). However, those with the title *Comparative Education* were not to appear until 1928, by Higuchi in Japan (Ninomiya, 2007), and 1930 by Chang in China (Bray & Gui, 2001). Nevertheless, it was Kandel's *Comparative Education* (1933) that was regarded as a classic text that contributed substantially to defining comparative education as an academic field during the interwar years (Bereday, 1964, p.225). Plausibly one of the earliest encyclopaedias on national education systems was the *Czech Encyclopedia of Education* (1891-1909) containing 100 monographs on school systems worldwide (Walterová, 2008).

1945-1970

Post-World War II expansion of the field's position in university courses is reflected in the notable increase in local language textbooks published, especially in Western Europe. Bereday (1964, p.227) highlights the work of Friedrich Schneider (1947) as a German classic in the field. The work bears the subtitle 'Introduction to the Discipline of Comparative Education' and discusses the philosophy of comparative education. The first specialist textbooks were published in Bulgaria, France, the Netherlands, Spain and Sweden (Chakarov, 1969; Idenburg, 1959; Sjösted & Sjöstrand, 1952; Tusquets, 1969; Vexliard, 1967). Among the classics in English were the works of E.J. King (1958) and N. Hans (1949), continuing earlier traditions of a historical genre and differing from the more positivist works by Bereday (1964), Holmes (1965) and Noah and Eckstein (1969).

This period also witnessed original works in other parts of the world. In Asia, the first textbooks were published in India, Korea, Taiwan (Lei, 1967; Mukherjee, 1959; Rim, 1961). In Australia, the classic work by P.E. Jones was published in 1971. An early African textbook was written in Egypt by Samaan (1958). Latin America also produced its share of texts, particularly in Brazil, Cuba and Mexico (Filho, 1961; Pérez, 1945; Villalpando, 1961).

1970-2000

This period was generally characterised in the section on coursework as a period of diverse trends, mainly of intellectual and institutional fragmentation in some countries, but also of revitalisation and growth in others. With respect to the latter, textbook production grew in tandem with further expansion of the field, or at least tailed it. This period also saw the publication of important encyclopaedias.

Among the textbooks, new volumes in diverse European languages were published in Eastern Europe before and after the fall of the Iron Curtain. In the former category were works in the former Yugoslavia and USSR (Franković, 1972; Mitrović, 1981; Sokolova et al., 1978). After the dissolution of the Soviet Union, new textbooks were published in Bulgaria, the Czech Republic, Poland and Russia (Bishkov & Popov, 1994; Pachocínski, 1995; Malkova & Wulfson, 1996; Vánova, 1998). In the rest of Europe, non-English classics include Orizio in Italian (1977) and García Garrido in Spanish (1996 [orig. 1986]). Denmark and Finland had their respective textbooks by Glenstrup (1973) and Raivola (1984).

Contributions also came from Asian scholars in Malaysia, post-Mao China and the new Republic of Kazakhstan (Belkanov, 1994; Wang, et al., 1982; Wong, 1973). Original works in South Africa and Kenya included Potgieter (1972) and Rwantabagu (1990), as were Marquez (1972) and Fuentealba (1985) in Argentina and Chile, respectively.

Several encyclopaedias were published in English during this period (Husén & Postlethwaite, 1994; Kurian, 1988; Postlethwaite, 1988a; Taneja, 2000; Wickremasinghe, 1992). Epstein (2008a) highlighted that these works followed the traditional focus of early textbooks on educational systems, with entries usually on a country-by-country basis.

Recent Publications

The continuous stream of new publications of introductory textbooks, though less in volume than in previous decades, suggests signs of revitalisation and reconceptualisation of the field. Expanding the list presented in Wolhuter et al. (2008b, p.336), among the notable works that offer a systematic approach to the introduction of comparative education published in the local languages are:

- *In the UK/USA*: UK (Crossley & Watson, 2003; Phillips & Schweisfurth, 2006; Cowen & Kazamias, 2009); USA (Kubow & Fossum, 2007);
- *In Europe*: Czech Republic (Walterová, 2006); Croatia (Vrcelj, 2005); Denmark (Winther-Jensen, 2004); Germany (Allemann-Ghionda, 2004); Greece (Bouzakis, 2002, 2003, 2005); Hungary (Kozma, 2006); Italy (Gallo, 2006); Norway (Brock-Utne & Bøyesen, 2006); Russia (Wulfson, 2003); Spain (Ferrer, 2002);
- *In Latin America and the Caribbean*: Costa Rica (Olivera, 2009); Cuba (Massón, 2006); Mexico (Villalobos, 2002);
- *In Asia*: Hong Kong (Bray, Adamson & Mason, 2007a); Korea (Chu, 2005); Oman (Issan, 2006).

By way of summary, Manzon's (2008b) typology for categorising textbooks used in teaching comparative and international education courses at universities might be useful here. The textbooks can be classified according to four dimensions along two intersecting continua: the theoretical-practical and the systematic-thematic. Plotted on the horizontal continuum is the 'theoretical' and 'practical' at opposite ends of the axis. Books of a theoretical nature emphasise theoretical and epistemological issues, or analyse educational issues from a particular conceptual thesis in comparative perspective. They serve a more 'advanced' academic audience. Other works, meanwhile, focus on practical methodological applications of comparative education research. Within this genre are more 'user-friendly' books catering to novices in the field and typically used in introductory courses on comparative and international education. On the vertical continuum is the systematic-thematic category. In the systematic approach, books provide an overview of the history, nature and methodology of comparative and international education, whilst works in the thematic or issues-oriented approach explore specific educational topics directly. Combining these two continua into a matrix (see Figure 3.1) some frequently cited contemporary English-medium textbooks (see CIECAP, 2008) can be plotted on the four quadrants. The categorisation is difficult since books may display more than two features, but they are classified according to their two dominant characteristics. Within the theoretical-thematic quadrant would be Arnove and Torres (2007), while the theoretical-systematic would include Crossley and Watson (2003) and Cowen and Kazamias (2009). Textbooks that could be considered thematic-practical include: Alexander, Broadfoot and Phillips (1999); Kubow and Fossum (2007); and Bray, Adamson and Mason (2007a). Finally, Phillips and Schweisfurth (2006) would probably exemplify the systematic-practical genre of textbooks.

Figure 3.1 Typology of Comparative Education Textbooks

	Systematic	
Theoretical	Crossley & Watson (2003) Cowen & Kazamias (2009)	Phillips & Schweisfurth (2006)
	Arnove & Torres (2007)	Alexander, Broadfoot & Phillips (1999) Kubow & Fossum (2007) Bray, Adamson & Mason (2007a)
	Thematic	

(**Practical** appears at the right side of the matrix)

Journals and Yearbooks

In contrast to textbooks and encyclopaedias, journals and yearbooks convey new knowledge and seek to create new knowledge. Moreover, they focus on discrete topics and are less comprehensive in their scope (Epstein, 2008a, p.12). They are published periodically – yearbooks are issued annually, while journals are normally issued at least two or three times a year – which makes the information they offer up-to-date (Bereday, 1964, p.233).

Yearbooks preceded the publication of specialist journals. In the latter category, there are journals sponsored by the professional societies of comparative education, and others independently published by international organisations and other bodies.

Pre-1945 Period

This period saw the founding of three yearbooks of education, which analysed specific educational themes and developments throughout the world. Bereday (1964, pp.232-240) reviewed these works and offered a listing of their contents. First was *The Educational Yearbook* published between 1924 and 1944 by the International Institute of Education at Teachers College, Columbia University. Special themes of selected volumes included: philosophy underlying national systems of education in England, France, Germany, Palestine and the USA (1929); state and religious education in 18 countries and the Latin American region (1932); and the last issue (1944) on post-war educational reconstruction in Western countries as well as China and South Africa. Around the same time, according to Ninomiya (2007, p.130), there were Japanese publications that were almost equivalent to *The Educational Yearbook* of Columbia University. They consisted of three volumes in the series 'Recent Educational Thoughts of European Countries', published between 1921 and 1923, and 46 volumes of 'Studies of Educational Thoughts', published between 1927 and 1948. Another series, the *Year Book of Education*, was founded in 1932 and published in London by the Evans Brothers until 1941; in 1948, it resumed activities, under the sponsorship of the Institute of Education, University of London, and in 1953, became a jointly sponsored publication with Teachers College, Columbia University and continues to be published to the present day. Themes include philosophy and education (1957), higher education (1959), and concepts of excellence in education (1961). A third significant yearbook series is the *International Yearbook of Education* founded in 1933 by the International Bureau of Education in Geneva. In contrast to the previous two series, this yearbook was not university-based and was more encyclopaedic, with brief reports of yearly educational progress supplied by governments participating in the International Conference on Education in Geneva.

As for the journals, the oldest specialist journal devoted to comparative education is the *International Education Review* (IER), founded in 1930 by Friedrich Schneider of Germany, who in 1931 was joined by Paul Monroe (USA) as co-editor. However, the journal came under Nazi control from 1934 to 1945 (Epstein, 2008a). In 1955, the journal acquired its present name, the *International Review of Education* (IRE), when it came under the editorship of the UNESCO Institute for Education in Hamburg (McIntosh, 2002).

1945-1970

For two decades the *IER/IRE* was the only specialist journal in the field, until 1957, when the *Comparative Education Review (CER)*, the second well-established academic journal, was launched by the US-based Comparative Education Society (now Comparative and International Education Society, CIES) and published in Chicago, USA (Sherman Swing, 2007). It was soon followed by a Spanish journal, *Perspectivas Pedagogicas*, under the editorship of Juan Tusquets in Barcelona, published from 1958 to 1984 (Vilanou & Valls, 2001). A Chinese journal, *Foreign Education Conditions* (renamed in 1992 as the *Comparative Education Review* [Beijing]), was launched in 1965 by Beijing Normal University (Bray & Gui, 2001, p.456).

Three other influential journals were launched during this period: *Comparative Education (CE)* (1964), *Compare: A Journal of Comparative Education* (1970) and *Prospects: Quarterly Review of Comparative Education* (1970). The first two journals are UK-based and therefore published in English. *Comparative Education* was founded in the UK by key European comparativists, while *Compare* became the official society journal of the then British Section of the Comparative Education Society in Europe (now the British Association for International and Comparative Education, BAICE) (see Crossley et al., 2007; Higginson, 2001; Sutherland et al., 2007). Meanwhile, *Prospects* is sponsored by UNESCO.

1970-2000

These three decades witnessed a peak in the birth of new journals of comparative education, catering mostly to a rather local readership. Some of these new publications were sponsored by comparative education societies. This phenomenon reflects the growing discursive community and their scholarly activities. At the same time, it reflected a fragmentation of discourses, with some groups excluded from the international discourse on account of language. From a Bourdieuian standpoint, the proliferation of local language journals of comparative education can be interpreted as a quest for distinction. Rather than competing within the intellectual field of comparative education, agents promoting these journals are making discursive moves to seek to propagate and distinguish their field from neighbouring educational or social science disciplines within the national or regional context. Through a journal, a discipline can project its scientific power and its identity as a distinct knowledge domain with specialist literature. At the same time, a journal in itself can be viewed as an intellectual field which is shaped and kept in its inertial momentum by interactions among agents (intellectuals) occupying unequal positions in the field. It provides a forum for agents to further the frontiers of knowledge whether through opposition or contestation of existing positions, while also eclipsing agents' work that do not meet editorial requirements of the journal, or what Bourdieu would term 'the logic of the field'.

Among the five journals founded in the 1970s were three society journals and three in local Asian languages. In chronological order, they were the: *Korean Journal of Education* (1971), the Korean society's journal; the *Journal of Foreign Education Studies* (1972)/*Global Education* (since 2001) published in Shanghai by the East China Normal University; *Canadian and International Education* (1972), the Canadian society's journal; *Comparative Education Studies* (1975), the Japan society's journal; and the well-established *International Journal of Educational Development* (*IJED*) (1979) in the UK.

A second wave of journals was founded in the 1990s. Among them were comparative education society journals: the SEEC's *Revista Española de Educación Comparada* (*REEC*) (1995), SACHES's *Southern African Review of Education* (1995) which later joined with *Education with Production*; the CCES-T's *Journal of Comparative Education* (1997), and the CESHK's *Comparative Education Bulletin* (1998), which, unlike the aforementioned journals, was not peer-reviewed and was fairly inclusive. There were also German journals, *Bildung und Erziehung* and *Tertium Comparationis*, as well as an Italian journal, *Educazione comparata*, which was rather short-lived. *Tertium Comparationis* is the first electronic journal in the field, launched in 1995, principally in German and English (Naya, 2005). Soon after, another online journal, *Current Issues in Comparative Education*, was launched in 1997 by Columbia University's Teachers College.

Various book series in comparative education were also founded. Among them were the *Oxford Studies in Comparative Education*, founded in 1990 with both yearbook and journal characteristics and published twice a year; the *Bristol Papers in Education*, *Monographs in International Education*, and the Hong Kong *CERC Studies in Comparative Education*, launched in 1997 by the Comparative Education Research Centre of the University of Hong Kong. In 2005, the CERC series started to be co-published with Springer (Dordrecht, Netherlands), which publishes the hardback and electronic copy versions. In addition, since 1988, Peter Lang began publishing a *Comparative Studies Series* based in Frankfurt, Germany. In addition, though with less periodicity, some books have been published as a result of conferences organised by societies such as the Comparative Education Society in Europe (e.g., Cavicchi-Broquet & Furter, 1982; Kazamias with Spillane, 1998; Mitter & Swift, 1983); the Chinese Comparative Education Society-Taipei (e.g., CCES-T, 2000), the Association francophone d'éducation comparée (AFEC) (e.g., Leclerq, 1999), and the Bulgarian Comparative Education Society, now on its 8th volume since 2002. For a limited period, the British society had had its annual conference papers published in book form by Croom Helm (1981-87), and in the late 1990s occasionally by Symposium Books in Oxford (e.g., Alexander et al., 1999). Selected papers presented during the World Congress of Comparative Education Societies have also been printed as a special double issue of the *International Review of Education*, and later republished as a book (e.g., Bray, 2003; Zajda et al., 2006).

To some extent, it can be said that book series as well as journals, due to their shared nature of being periodically issued publications, contribute to the discursive construction of comparative education partly drawing on the inertial momentum of their creation. Since they are envisioned to be serial publications, there is somewhat a 'natural' motivation for continuity, for self-perpetuation.

Recent Publications

After 2000, the pace of launching new journals slowed down. Nevertheless, these few years witnessed the birth of *Politiques de éducation et de formation*, a journal launched by the AFEC in 2001 and published in Belgium, but which was discontinued after a few years. On the other hand, there has been a steady stream of books in the series *Collection éducation comparée* published by L'Harmattan in Paris under the editorship of members of the Association française d'éducation comparée et des échanges since 2000 (e.g., Groux & Tutiaux-Guillon, 2000). Other society-sponsored journals include the Greek society's *Comparative and International Education Review*, published in English and Greek since 2002; CESA's *Compare: Journal of the Comparative Education Society of Asia*, with its inaugural issue in 2006 published in English; and a new journal taken over by the Australian and New Zealand society (ANZCIES) in 2007, *The International Education Journal*. Another online journal was launched in 2006, based in Oxford, UK, entitled *Research in Comparative and International Education*.

Professional Societies

The inauguration of scholarly societies is another form of the institutionalisation of a field. Clark (1987, p.233) observes that disciplinary organisations "tighten the hold of specialisation upon academic life, [and serve as] a device that would serve externally as a carrying mechanism for a discipline at large, a way of furthering specialties without regard to institutional boundaries". Professional societies are particularly important for interdisciplinary fields, whose presence and importance are largely determined by their relative visibility in the form of interdisciplinary institutions (Klein, 1990). As Becher and Trowler (2001, p.104) contend, academic networks play a pivotal role in fields of study because they "give shape and substance to the links between knowledge forms and knowledge communities".

Comparative education scholars echo this view on the important role of professional societies. As Epstein (1981, pp.269-271) argues,

> a field's tenability depends on whether the people who run a professional association can capture recognition for their specialisation. … *If comparative education is to succeed as a field, it must gain recognition for its very uniqueness.* … Comparative education is unique inasmuch as its development on a national level is likely to be tied to its growth and strength internationally. The logical conduit for the advancement of comparative education internationally is the World Council of Comparative Education Societies.

Epstein (2004) further elaborates that: "professional organisations (of comparative education) are the backbone of the field. A field cannot exist in the air: there have to be bodies of people who advance it and who talk about and interact about it". From these observations, it can be said that a field, viewed as a discursive formation, requires disciplinary knowledge as well as disciplinary institutions. At the same time, a field's viability depends on its recognition within the educational community. This echoes Bourdieu's view of an intellectual field as governed by the law of the quest for distinction. This quest for distinction takes place within educational and social science circles at both the national and international levels, through the sociological structure of professional societies.

Cowen (1990, p.322) further contends that scholarly networks (journals, centres and societies) are important indicators of the "definition, demand, and supply of comparative education on a world basis". As will be shown in the following paragraphs, the growth of comparative

Table 3.4   Member Societies of the WCCES (2010)

Asociación de Pedagogos de Cuba (Sección de Educación Comparada) (APC-SEC)

Association française pour le développement de l'éducation comparée et des échanges (AFDECE)

Association francophone d'éducation comparée (AFEC)

Australian and New Zealand Comparative and International Education Society (ANZCIES)

British Association for International and Comparative Education (BAICE)

Bulgarian Comparative Education Society (BCES)

Chinese Comparative Education Society (CCES)

Chinese Comparative Education Society-Taipei (CCES-T)

Comparative Education Section of the Czech Pedagogical Society (CES-CPS)

Comparative Education Society of Asia (CESA)

Comparative Education Society in Europe (CESE)

Comparative Education Society of Hong Kong (CESHK)

Comparative Education Society of India (CESI)

Comparative Education Society of the Philippines (CESP)

Comparative and International Education Society (CIES)

Comparative and International Education Society of Canada (CIESC)

Council on Comparative Education of Kazakhstan (CCEK)

Egyptian Comparative Education and Educational Administration Society (ECEEAS)

Greek Comparative Education Society (GCES)

Hungarian Pedagogical Society (Comparative Education Section) (HPS-CES)

Israel Comparative Education Society (ICES)

Japan Comparative Education Society (JCES)

Korean Comparative Education Society (KCES)

Mediterranean Society of Comparative Education (MESCE)

Nederlandstalig Genootschap voor Vergelijkende Studie van Opvoeding en Onderwijs (NGVO)

Nordic Comparative and International Education Society (NOCIES)

Polish Comparative Education Society (PCES)

Russian Council of Comparative Education (RCCE)

Sektion International und Interkulturell Vergleichende Erziehungswissenschaft in der Deutschen Gesellschaft für Erziehungswissenschaft (SIIVEDGE)

Sezione Italiana della CESE (SICESE)

Sociedad Argentina de Estudios Comparados en Educación (SAECE)

Sociedad Española de Educación Comparada (SEEC)

Sociedad Mexicana de Educación Comparada (SOMEC)

Sociedade Brasileira de Educação Comparada (SBEC)

Southern African Comparative & History of Education Society (SACHES)

Turkish Comparative Education Society (TÜKED)

Ukrainian Comparative Education Society (UCES)

Sources: Extracted from Bray, Manzon & Masemann (2007), p.5. and updated from WCCES (2010)

education societies has, despite some exceptions, dovetailed with the growth of specialist programmes and centres, and in most cases, also reflected their internal metamorphosis or decline. From the first professional association formed in 1956 in the USA, the field has undergone substantial growth in half a century with 37 comparative education societies comprising the World Council of Comparative Education Societies (WCCES) in 2010 (see Table 3.4 for a list), in addition to several other societies that are not part of this confederation. This historical development and contemporary status are discussed below, taking as a main source the volume edited by Masemann, Bray and Manzon (2007) documenting the detailed histories of the WCCES and its members. For ease of reference, the chronology is summarised by regions in Appendices 2 to 6.

1945-1970

Unlike the earliest university courses and programmes of comparative education, which were reported to have existed at the beginning of the 20th century, it was not until 1956 when the first comparative education society was inaugurated. The United States was again a pioneer, in its move to establish the Comparative Education Society (renamed in 1968 as the Comparative and International Education Society – CIES) (Sherman Swing, 2007). Being the first society in the world, it did not see the need to use a national qualifier in its name. Moreover, it has the broadest membership of any of the other associations. Later societies were to add qualifiers based on national, regional, and language groupings to their titles to distinguish themselves (Epstein, 2008a).

In the 1960s, eight new societies were formed, the first among them being a regional society: the Comparative Education Society in Europe (CESE) in 1961. There were also the national societies of Japan (1965), Canada (1967) and Korea (1968), and national sections of CESE (British Section, German Section), which later became independent national societies. In Eastern Europe, a Czechoslovakian society was formed in 1964 but was short-lived due to politically disruptive events (Walterová, 2007). A Hungarian society was also established in 1970 (Benedek et al., 2007).

This historical period closes, and a new one begins, with the establishment of the World Council of Comparative Education Societies (WCCES) in 1970, an umbrella body of national, sub-national, regional and language-based comparative education societies founded in Ottawa, Canada under the leadership of Joseph Katz. The five societies that comprised the World Council in 1970 were the national societies of the USA, Canada, Japan, Korea and the regional body of CESE. The two main professional aims of the WCCES are:

- to promote the study of comparative and international education throughout the world and enhance the academic status of this field; and
- to bring comparative education to bear on the major educational problems of the day by fostering cooperative action by specialists from different parts of the world. (WCCES, 1996)

Among the ways the World Council achieves its aims is through fostering the establishment of comparative education societies and the organisation of periodic World Congresses. In 2010, the 14th World Congress was held in Turkey, with over 1,000 participants.

1970-2000

This period witnessed significant expansion in the number of comparative education societies worldwide, which began with seven societies in 1970 and almost quintupled to 32 societies in these three decades (Bray, Manzon & Masemann, 2007). This history of societies demonstrates the 'creative' power of an intellectual field which gains momentum to perpetuate itself through a system of interactions among agents who join the field and seek distinction within it, whether on the basis of national or regional identity or of linguistic identity.

During the 1970s, the first two and so far only language-based societies – Francophone and Dutch-speaking – were inaugurated. National societies were also founded, in chronological order, in Spain, Australia, China, India and Argentina, and, as a 'sub-national grouping', in Taiwan, Republic of China (whose society name was later denominated in English as Chinese-Taipei).

Another wave of new societies came in the 1980s from Latin America, Africa and Asia, in addition to Europe. These included the Venezuelan (though not a member of the WCCES), Colombian and Brazilian societies, an Egyptian and a Nigerian society, as well as societies in Israel and a sub-national grouping in Hong Kong. Also, an Italian section of CESE was formed. The Australian society was joined by New Zealand in 1984, thus becoming a regional body.

In the 1990s, the societies from Argentina, Colombia, Egypt and Nigeria appeared to have become defunct. A new Egyptian society was formed in 1991 (ECEEAS) and, in 2001, a new Argentinean society (SAECE) was established.

Masemann (1994, p.947) captured well the homologies between the political field and the intellectual field, pointing to the impact of external events on society formation: "With the fragmentation of power blocs, there will be a proliferation of national societies". True enough, the newly-formed independent states in Eastern Europe in no time established their own professional societies in the 1990s (Bulgaria, Czech, Poland, Russia, Ukraine). Meanwhile, three new regional associations were also inaugurated in Southern Africa, the Nordic region and Asia. In addition, there were the national societies of Cuba, France, Greece and Portugal, and a revitalised Egyptian society. However, the Ukrainian and Portuguese societies did not last long.

New Developments (2000s)

By the beginning of the 21st century, there were 30 comparative education societies comprising the WCCES. The growth during this first decade has been less dramatic. Six national societies (Argentina, Kazakhstan, Mexico, the Philippines, Turkey and Ukraine) and a regional grouping in the Mediterranean area were established, bringing the total number of WCCES member societies to 37, five times more than the original number in 1970. There were other groupings of comparativists in Albania, the Arab world, Africa, Romania, and Thailand (Bray, 2007a), which were not part of the WCCES. Plans were afoot to form similar groupings in Uruguay and Cambodia (Fernández Lamarra, 2007; Gonzales, 2007).

Comparative Education Societies and the Field: Some Relationships

Correlating the historical development of professional societies with that of the formation of coursework and/or specialist programmes, it can be affirmed that in general, the growth in the establishment of comparative education societies trails behind that of the expansion of university courses in comparative education, plausibly by a decade or so. Except for the USA, this holds true with the pioneering societies formed in the late 1960s in Canada, Western Europe, Japan and Korea where the previous decade had seen the field blossom at universities. As a corollary, the decline in comparative education teaching and the consequent contraction of the community of specialists working in the field has also been reflected in the weakening or discontinuance of some comparative education societies. Thus, the disruptive political events in Brazil, Czechoslovakia, Hungary, and South Africa not only disestablished comparative education in academia but also enfeebled its professional societies (Benedek et al., 2007; Sisson de Castro, 2007; Soudien, 2007; Walterová, 2007).

Paradoxically, the wave of fragmentation and decline in university specialist programmes that swept through North America, UK and Australia in the 1970s and 1980s, and other countries in the 1990s did not, however, deter the formation of new societies in other parts of the world as seen above. I posit that this phenomenon can be explained by the 'centripetal' force of attraction of the WCCES, viewed as an intellectual field where agents – member societies – are attracted to 'play the game' and seek symbolic power (distinction) within the field through their representation as a member society *inter pares* with other comparative education societies from countries with greater political and/or scientific power. The WCCES also offered prospects of increasing the social capital of member societies by enhancing their international scholarly network. These contingent reasons partly account for the multiplication and growth of the field in sociological terms through the formation of professional societies, be they unequal in size and strength. It is a sort of 'bandwagon' effect which keeps the inertial momentum of the WCCES as a living organism that continues to grow. That the World Council has served as a motivating force for some local societies to organise themselves is affirmed by some society leaders [emphases added]:

- *You wouldn't have local organisations without the World Council.* This morning, Lydia Turner (President of the APC-SEC, the Cuban comparative education society), as you saw, came up to me and said: "You are the father of Cuba's comparative education society". Why? Because when I was in Cuba the first time, I was trying to get the Cubans to form together a professional organisation and seek admission into the World Council. Without the World Council, there would not have been *sufficient motivation for them to come together as a group* because what it meant was that when they came together as a group, they came together not simply to talk about comparative education in Cuba, but to project an international identity, *to be part of the global picture.* So the World Council is of enormous, enormous *importance in the organisation of the field.* … In terms of structuring the field, which is essential for fields to be perpetuated worldwide, it's the World Council in its role of enhancing the work of the local organisations. (E.H. Epstein, 2004, WCCES Past President)

- The World Council was a catalyst for the formation of societies because as (Joseph) Katz said to ANZCIES, *"better get yourself organised as a Society so that you can join this world body"*. (C. Fox, 2005, ANZCIES Past President).

- The main driving force that brought the national society (TÜKED) into being was the desire *to form part of an international research and scholarly community.* This desire was specially stimulated by the 12th World Congress at Havana, Cuba in 2004, where 18 Turkish scholars, mainly from Ankara and Istanbul, participated. (F. Gök, 2007, TÜKED President).

- The obvious reason why we (SEEC) joined the WCCES was to initiate and maintain some stable *links with the existing comparative education societies in the world*, for which the WCCES offered an adequate forum. Following SEEC's incorporation to the WCCES, our relations with the other societies became more frequent and fluid. This is why we also got very involved in the very organisation of the WCCES. (J.L. García Garrido, 2005b, SEEC Past President).

The above is corroborated by published literature. For example, Naya et al. (2008, p.122) explained that the *Sociedad Española de Educación Comparada* (SEEC) was formed under the leadership of Juan Tusquets, who urged its creation so as to "avoid the risk of [the Society's] not being represented in the World Council of Comparative Education Societies" (Tusquets, 1979, p.120).

A few other cases serve to buttress the above claim that, as an intellectual field, the WCCES exerts a 'centripetal force' of attraction and somewhat a 'bandwagon' effect that influences groups of scholars to form new discrete societies or to revitalise existing ones. This is achieved with the help of human agency – the advocacy and moral support from WCCES leaders – as well as various contingent factors such as the confluence of international scholars in global forums and/or micro-political interests which fosters the desire to be singled out as a distinct group. As Manzon and Bray (2007, pp.343-344) explain:

The WCCES also catalysed society formation through the *personal networking* of its officers, particularly the President and Secretary

General. ... The *excitement and confluence of international scholars* in World Congresses encouraged the revitalisation of smaller or weaker societies so that they could once more be living members of the global body. Examples from this book [Masemann et al., 2007] include the Brazilian society, which acknowledged the strong impulse it received from WCCES President Michel Debeauvais and Secretary General Raymond Ryba in organising its society and in the preparations for the 1987 World Congress in Rio de Janeiro. The Russian Council pointed to the participation of several Russian scholars in the 1987 Congress as decisive in their foundation as the Soviet Council of Comparative Pedagogics, and the Cuban Congress in the formation of a newly reorganised Russian body. Mochida's chapter on CESA recalled that several Asian scholars started to think seriously about forming their own regional society during the 1992 World Congress in Prague. And SOMEC, which began from a core group of Mexican scholars who assiduously participated in CIES meetings, took shape as a national society with the encouragement of World Council President Mark Bray, who invited them to WCCES meetings.

Furthermore, it is worth noting that the WCCES does not have strict admission criteria for screening new society applications. The minimum requirements are listed in Article 2 of the World Council's By-Laws (WCCES, 2005). They include the submission of a copy of the association's or group's constitution, a list of members or other evidence of size of membership, and evidence of aims and range of activities; as well as the satisfaction of fairly general criteria that the group is duly constituted to pursue comparative education and adheres to the ideals of the UN/UNESCO, among others. Other than a few exceptional situations owing more to political or ideological issues than to intellectual legitimacy, as was the case of SACHES (Soudien, 2007), admissions have been uncontroversial and smooth.

Moreover, once admitted and assuming societies are able to honour annual subscription payments, member societies have a life of their own with little interference or gate-keeping influence from the World Council on intellectual grounds. As Fox (2005) observes: "[f]or emergent societies, it (the WCCES) may be influential, but not to older ones. (The WCCES) could influence [at] the beginning, but after the society is established, the World Council's role is minimal to that society". Within the WCCES, some small (shell) societies have managed to keep themselves on the membership list by paying their dues, perhaps for the perceived benefit of being represented in a global body on equal footing with other member societies, just as the member states of the United Nations have voting rights in the General Assembly and Executive Committee meetings irrespective of differences in their economic or political power. This illustrates the internal dynamism of the intellectual field and the mechanics of the sociological construction of the field of comparative education. Agents are drawn to join the field in order to vie with each other for positions of superiority (or of implicit equivalence with positions of superiority), since they exhibit homologies with the positions of power in the geopolitical world.

To recapitulate, I started with the observation that the establishment of comparative education societies has generally followed the trajectory of the status of comparative education teaching at academic institutions, with a time lag of a decade or so. Nevertheless, discordant cases have shown that even during the lean years of comparative education teaching, new societies continued to be formed. I argued that this is partly explained by the diverse contingent reasons which motivate individuals to establish societies, among them, the attraction of belonging to a global body like the WCCES. The mere fact, however, of existing as a society or as a world body does not represent or justify the intellectual legitimacy of the academic field. I substantiated this claim by pointing out the open admission criteria of the World Council and the contingent, less than intellectual reasons that have motivated society formation. I further support this argument below by discussing the uneven consistency of society membership, weak intellectual cohesiveness and identification with the field of participants in world congresses of comparative education, and the less intellectual and more political/pragmatic reasons that motivate a society's visibility in WCCES activities.

Only a few of the WCCES member societies are big and substantively composed of specialists (Manzon & Bray, 2007). As shown in Appendix 8, the largest societies, having over 300 members, are the USA-based CIES (with over 1,300 individual members, excluding institutional members), and three Asian-based societies: Japan, China and Korea. The next tier comprises seven societies – Asia, Brazil, Chinese-Taipei, Czech, Europe, Spain, UK – endowed with a membership between 101 and 300. The remaining 25 societies have fewer than 100 members, the smallest known membership being that of the Philippine society with only five. A few others may actually also be shell societies that pay their membership fees regularly, either in cash or in kind, or may actually have defaulted on subscription payments but remain on the WCCES members' list. Some such small and troubled societies have also been listed in the table of contents of Masemann et al.'s (2007) compiled histories of the WCCES member societies. A detailed reading of those narratives reveals that a number of them are struggling for survival, if not inactive for years (e.g., CESI, SICESE). This leads one to posit that the institutional mass of the field, as partly represented by the impressive number and geographic spread of professional societies in comparative education, is not a guarantee of the field's intellectual standing or substantive strength and cohesiveness.

I argue this point from another angle by examining the level and quality of member society participation at WCCES forums, starting with its executive committee meetings. As Manzon and Bray (2006) highlight, attendance at WCCES formal meetings has been poor. Most of the active societies were from English-speaking locations: USA, BAICE, Australia and New Zealand, Hong Kong, Canada, Southern Africa. A crucial factor that limited global representation at WCCES meetings was the location of meetings, which meant that financial capacity for travel of society representatives (Bray & Manzon, 2005), and therefore the command over pertinent academic or institutional capital, was important. The fact that a member society is active in these meetings does not, however, necessarily mean that comparative education is extensively developed in that society's country or region of origin. The SBEC and AFEC are two cases in point. Both societies have been rather active in attending WCCES meetings (with an average attendance rate of 60 per cent of a total of 18 meetings, 1995-2007), but academic comparative education is weak in their contexts (Carry, 2004; Sisson de Castro & Gomes, 2008; Verhine, 2004).

Conversely, there are constituent societies that may not have been active in the WCCES forums for various reasons – logistics, language, location of meetings, financial and/or political constraints – but the field of comparative education was highly developed in their respective countries (Bray & Manzon, 2005). This is the case of the SEEC in Spain, especially in the 1990-2000s during the field was blossoming in the country, but the SEEC was not active at WCCES meetings for 5-6 years (Manzon, 2007). García Garrido (2004) attributes this to a linguistic barrier on the part of the then SEEC president: "He never wanted to attend the World Council meetings, except once, because of language difficulties. … So there was a long time without SEEC representation in WCCES". Similarly, China has been absent from WCCES meetings, but the field was robust in its home context. Its abstention was in view of an unresolved political question on the representation of a Taiwanese society (CCES-T) on the WCCES, which China considers incompatible with the one-China policy.

Thus, the level of representation or non-representation of a society in the WCCES does not necessarily mirror the development stage of comparative education in its home country/region. There is no direct relationship between society visibility at the World Council level and the strength of comparative education in the society's home base, although in some cases, they have mirrored each other (e.g., CIES, BAICE). The level of participation and representation at WCCES meetings is more a question of personal agency and possession of various forms of capital: linguistic, economic, social and academic. Moreover, World Council meetings are less concerned with intellectual issues than with organi-sational issues. Therefore, the level of member society activity in the WCCES is not an indication of intellectual legitimacy.

In the same vein, the high profile or worldwide attractiveness and confluence of international scholars in society-sponsored World Con-gresses of Comparative Education Societies do not necessarily guarantee or reflect the strength of the field in the host society's context. Although these activities have seemed to catalyse interest in the field in the host country (Masemann, 2006; see also Hickling-Hudson, 2007; Lee & Kwon, 2007; Sisson, 2007; Walterová, 2007), a sustainable growth in the field was not forthcoming. A few reasons may explain this phenomenon. In the first place, the organisation of a World Congress and which society wins the bid to sponsor it is based more on pragmatic (economic and social capital) and fairly contingent reasons rather than necessary, intellectual principles. ANZCIES' hosting of the 1996 World Congress in Sydney is a case in point. Fox (2005), Secretary-General of the WCCES and long-time member of the WCCES Congress Standing Committee, described the mechanics of Congress sponsorship by member societies:

> The hosting of the Congress was very much the work of the WCCES Secretary-General, President and Congress Chair of invit-ing and motivating persons attending the World Congress [to step forward and propose a bid]. Therefore, it was (1) an issue of the *capacity of the individual societies*; and (2) the *financial capacity* of the

host (society) because the World Council only advances money. [emphasis added]

Likewise, Schriewer (2005), Past Chair of the WCCES Research Standing Committee, also described the more diplomatic and pragmatic (and less intellectual) criteria driving the work of the WCCES and congress organisation:

> This happened by *name-dropping* during World Council meetings, and several people got in touch with these people, and somebody accepted. So it was *not a kind of 'intellectual dictatorship'*, it was really... a kind of looking around [to see] *who can do what...* [emphasis added]

Furthermore, Welch (2005) viewed the ANZCIES's decision to host the World Congress as "just one of those kinds of 'accidental' things", what Foucault would term 'chance encounters'. The historical contingencies by which the field has been constructed through such activities as organising world congresses can be understood better in the explanation by Fox (2005) of the differing motivations and institutional politics of the host societies, which could vary from 'solving' an emergency situation (e.g., CCES pulled out and ANZCIES stepped forward for the 1996 World Congress) to showcasing and putting the local society on the map (e.g., the World Congresses in Brazil [1987]; Czechoslovakia [1992]; South Africa [1998]; Korea [2001]; Cuba [2004]). This phenomenon continues with Congresses held in Bosnia-Herzegovina (2007), Turkey (2010) and, in 2013, in Argentina. Congress hosting was determined less by intellectual reasons as by contingent and, at times, micro-political reasons of who is willing to do what and who has the financial and logistical capacity, as well as the social capital necessary to make the event successful. Hosting the Congress in one's country was thus by no means a 'clean bill of health' for the state of the field – for its intellectual legitimacy – in that country. Soudien (2007, p.290) succinctly depicted this paradoxical situation in Southern Africa: "After the excitement of 1998 (the World Congress hosted by SACHES in Cape Town), SACHES went into a period of stasis" (also Weeks, 2004).

A further case in point is that, despite the high numbers reported of participants in World Congresses – Cuba had nearly 1,000 participants from 68 countries (Hickling-Hudson, 2007, p.79) – plausibly very few had a clear notion about what comparative education is, as Epstein (2004) commented during that World Congress in 2004:

> People had vague notions of it (comparative education). So at that time, and even today, you are dealing with people who have not been prepared sufficiently in the field. For example, in a World Congress like this, 90 per cent of the people don't even know the background of comparative education. That's the problem.

Masemann (2004) echoed this observation with respect to the 1980 World Congress in Japan: "Some [people] wanted to go to Tokyo and take their little paper and read it and the rest of the time, they'd be sight-seeing". Epstein (1981) surveyed that World Congress in Tokyo and reported that the majority of participants were satisfied with "a congress for the *masses*" (p.268) where a wide variety of subject matter prevailed over intellectual rigor. Masemann (1997, pp.133-134) also reviewed the four World Congresses that took place between 1987 and 1996 (Brazil, Canada, Czechoslovakia, and Australia) and pointed out their common denominator:

> There is *no central consensus* about what the World Congress should be focusing on or what its organisation should be like. There was a great diversity of viewpoints, of topics, and of disciplinary back-grounds. ... [T]here was also *no one way of defining comparative education that was being promulgated* as the only way, and the richness of the offerings meant that scholars from many different backgrounds could find panels which suited their interests. [emphasis added]

Thus, even if the WCCES can boast of a dramatic growth in its member-ship over four decades of its existence, one must recognise the diversity in intellectual and institutional strength, stature and specialisation of member societies. This is partly owing to the loose and inclusive admis-sion criteria of the WCCES and its member societies, and the less than intellectual motivations and principles that have contributed to the institutional growth of professional societies. From a Foucauldian per-spective, it can be said that the growth of disciplinary institutions in the form of comparative education societies is not natural and necessary, but contingent and implicated in power relations. By viewing the WCCES as an intellectual field (Bourdieuian sense) dynamically constructed by the interactions of occupants who compete for symbolic capital within this system of positions and oppositions, it becomes clear that having a massive institutional infrastructure does not necessarily mean intellectual legitimacy. This is so because, rather than pure intellectual interests, a confluence of contingent political interests and power relations inhering in institutional structures and human agency have intervened in society formation, and therefore in the construction of the field's institutional infrastructures. The World Council has nevertheless been important, serving at least three roles in society formation and the global dissemination of the field:

- a *political* value (political capital) for nascent societies to organise themselves and form part of a worldwide scholarly body with links to UNESCO;
- a *social networking* value (social capital) to enable member societies to tap an international network of expertise in the field; and
- a *legitimating* value (academic capital) to demonstrate to the academic world that the field has international currency and intellectual legitimacy through high profile activities.

But, in the conduct of its business, the World Council is less concerned with theoretical substance than with organisational issues. Thus, it does not exercise a gate-keeping role with respect to substantive issues such as the nature of comparative education and appropriate methodology. It cannot therefore be taken as a gauge of the intellectual legitimacy of the field.

In summary, I have argued above that the empirical mass of comparative education, partially embodied in the impressive number and worldwide diffusion of its professional societies, is not a guarantee of the field's intellectual standing or substantive cohesiveness. Empirical substance is thus not necessarily equivalent to intellectual validity. If, therefore, one cannot remain with a superficial inventory of the institutional superstructures of the field, what tools can then be used to discern the boundaries and contents of the field? The following section reviews the literature that has surveyed the field's boundaries. I utilise them to ascertain from an institutional perspective whether or not comparative education is a distinct field and why this is so in the light of its institutional construction.

Surveys of the Field's Contours

Epstein (2008a) categorised the databases developed to survey the contours and contents of the field as well as the features of its practitioners into three main types: course and programme surveys; journal content and citation analyses; and attitudinal and demographic surveys. This typology is not mutually exclusive, as some surveys may combine two or three approaches. My purpose in reviewing the existing databases that examine the field of comparative education as such is to arrive, through a 'meta-analysis' of the literature, at a *critical* evaluation of the empirical mass and substance of the field. Does the field have a defining feature that sets it apart from (other fields of) education studies? Does it have a unique content, purpose and method? Do the persons who comprise its professional societies exhibit a unifying characteristic or a strong sense of identity with the field? Ultimately, this is to test the hypothesis that institutional legitimacy – the institutional mass of comparative education – does not necessarily guarantee its intellectual legitimacy as a distinct subfield of educational studies.

I take Epstein (2008a) and Cook et al. (2004) as a starting point in reviewing the surveys of the field conducted in English contexts. I then expand my 'meta-analysis' by including surveys conducted in Chinese, Japanese and Spanish contexts, a few of which have not yet been published. For ease of reference, I summarise the results of this literature review in Appendices 10 and 11. Following the organisation of topics in the preceding sections, I examine the available surveys in this order: course content and programme surveys; journal content analysis; and professional society attitudinal and demographic analysis. Lastly, I discuss Cook et al.'s (2004) demographic and citation analysis, which serves to conclude this section.

Course and Programme Surveys
Epstein (2008a) distinguishes between worldwide surveys and individual country surveys. Among the worldwide surveys, there were the fixed projects and continuing projects, of which the Comparative and International Education Course Archive Project (CIECAP) is probably the only example to date.

Plausibly the first attempt at a world wide survey was by Bereday in 1964 when he examined the centres of comparative education research and teaching in and outside the USA. Soon after, another world wide effort was made in 1970 during the First World Congress of Comparative Education Societies, which took as its theme 'The Place of Comparative and International Education in the Education of Teachers' (WCCE, 1970). Thirty-four scholars representing sixteen countries from Europe, North

America and the Caribbean, Asia Pacific, the Middle East and Africa, mapped out their plans to establish or strengthen the incipient field in their institutions or to share ideas on teaching materials and resources.

In terms of the content of comparative education, the worldwide survey of Halls (1990b) reported that "the content of comparative studies is *as broad as studies of education* itself" (p.42) [emphasis added]. Regional reports conveyed regional peculiarities in terms of the 'ideal' lists of content, with the Soviet bloc countries and Africa converging only on the fact that the topics should be of immediate application, a characteristic that diverged from North American counterparts who were more interested in theoretical issues. Halls attributed such divergences to contextual factors of geography, culture and ideology (p.44). His comment about "the 'unfinished agenda' for comparativists [being] practically limitless and constantly expanding" (p.45) is indicative of the *fluid boundaries* of the field. Furthermore, Halls reported that despite the exceptional dynamism in teaching comparative education in some parts of the world, the 1970s witnessed a dramatic decline in courses, viewing these as "a luxury offering" (Halls, 1990b, p.60) that could *easily be omitted* in teacher training programmes. The decline in clientele brought to light the transient loyalty of so-called 'specialists' in the field, or at least their instinct for survival, and eventually led to further declines in their number. With the contraction of institutional power in the intellectual field of comparative education, occupants in the field saw little value in 'playing this game' (Bourdieuian sense) and in competing with each other for positions within the field.

Bergh et al. (1999) reported the findings of a workshop organised during the 10th World Congress of Comparative Education Societies held in Cape Town, South Africa in 1998. Although it was not a comprehensive survey, a relevant finding is that "the names of themes, programmes and courses workshop participants mentioned confirmed what we already knew: *nomenclature is very diffuse*" (p.17) [emphasis added]. Among the factors that influenced programme contents were institutional specialties and interests, resources, the impact of institutional restructuring on programme restructuring, employer, state and market requirements, as well as student expectations (pp.17-18), or ultimately "institutional politics and which 'master' we are serving, the state or the market" (p.9). This reflects Bourdieu's approach to viewing (academic) texts – in this case, course contents – in their social contexts or intellectual fields, referring to the social conditions of their material and symbolic production, which gives them 'value' based on the defining logic of that field (Johnson, 1993; Ringer, 2000).

In 2008, Wolhuter et al. published a global survey of comparative education courses and programmes in 47 countries. Rather than a mere inventory of coursework at universities, the survey consisted of brief country reports written principally by indigenous authors on the history and current state of teaching comparative education at their universities. In terms of the content of lecture courses on comparative education, almost all of the surveyed universities incorporated a permanent focus on foreign/local educational systems and structures, except for North American, British and German universities which, plausibly owing to the maturity of the field and/or the intellectual traditions in those countries, took a more theoretical and issues-oriented or thematic approach in cross-cultural perspective. Of the 47 countries surveyed, only 11 reported the existence of specialist programmes in the field, principally at the Master's level, including the USA, Canada and the UK, and four countries in Asia. By contrast, an upward trend of integration of the comparative dimension in education curricula was observed. The case of Hong Kong is illustrative of similar patterns of integration elsewhere. Manzon (2008a, p.220) pointed out that in the Faculty of Education of the University of Hong Kong, similar courses with similar names and contents related to comparative education had been taught, even within the same semester and catering to the same audience of postgraduate students, by faculty members not all of whom necessarily identified with or were affiliated with comparative education. Examples of course names include: 'Analysing Educational Reform: Comparative and Sociological Perspectives'; 'School-based Teacher Development in Hong Kong and China'; 'Education in the Context of Globalisation'; 'Global Perspectives on Education in Hong Kong'; and 'Understanding the Hong Kong Education System: Learning from Comparing'. Other country reports in Wolhuter et al. (2008) (e.g., Canada, Hungary, Italy, Korea) listed varied course titles that the authors considered to be a course in comparative education, whose most common elements include a focus on any of the following aspects: the international, development, intercultural, and/or comparative. However, had they not been explicitly singled out by chapter authors as 'comparative education', it would have been difficult to discern their specific nature given the permeation of the 'international' in higher education curricula. This is suggestive of the difficulty in determining what exclusively pertains to the field of comparative education especially when education curricula are becoming more internationalised. What then is the criterion for classifying a course under comparative education and who establishes that criterion? Is it simply a question of the lecturer declaring himself or herself as a member of a professional society or research centre of comparative education? Wolhuter et al. (2008b) thus inferred that the legitimacy of comparative education as an independent academic field remains contested, and the integration of the comparative approach or perspective seems to eclipse past achievements in the area of subject specialisation (p.337). This is indicative of the socially constructed nature of the field's boundaries.

A related survey, though of an ongoing nature, was launched by Loyola University in 2003: the Comparative and International Education Course Archive Project (CIECAP). In August 2010, CIECAP contained course outlines from over 30 institutions. The survey reported 37 topics of course study, of which the two most frequently encountered topics in the course outlines were 'development' and '(comparative education) theory' (Stone, 2005, p.519). The survey also reported a total of 1,031 references used in introductory courses, of which textbooks and textbook chapters comprised less than ten per cent, while journals and other books represented almost one out of four, respectively, of bibliographic references in the course outlines (2005, p.521). Stone concluded that CIECAP data thus far gathered "confirm earlier research that found *little consensus in the field* related to the various aspects of course outline contents. Rather, CIECAP confirms that the field remains *heterogeneous and dynamic*" (p.523). [emphasis added]

The programme surveys reviewed above tend to converge on the following points. First, they indicate an apparently limitless agenda of study, fluid boundaries, a lack of consensus on themes and approaches, heterogeneity, and flexibility in responding to changing institutional (university), national and geopolitical contexts, as well as to market demands. They also reveal an upward trend towards the integration of comparative perspectives in higher education curricula and a downward trend in offering specialist or stand-alone programmes in comparative education.

Journal Content Analyses

Various content and citation analyses have been undertaken of the field's specialist international journals, namely *Comparative Education Review* (CER), *Comparative Education* (CE), *International Journal of Educational*

Development (IJED), and *International Review of Education (IRE)*, all of which are in English except for *IRE*, which in addition to English is published in several languages. Other 'national' journals published in their local languages, including in Chinese, French, Japanese, and Spanish have also been analysed. They are summarised in Appendix 9. Despite the limited value of such surveys in giving a holistic and accurate picture of the state of the field, not only because of methodological constraints (e.g., limited sampling size, superficial classification of articles based on title rather than on content, trivial definition of 'comparative' as binary studies), but also due in part to the differentiated patterns of publishing in different journals, which are in turn determined by a complexity of factors such as authors' underlying motivations, editorial policies, language biases (see e.g., Biraimah, 2006; Bray, Adamson & Mason, 2007b), content analyses nevertheless serve to trace the boundaries and trends of the field as reflected in the literature published in its specialist journals.

A common observation from the content analyses listed in Appendix 9 is that the articles published in comparative education journals are extremely heterogeneous with a *notable plurality of themes, types of studies and units of analysis* (Martínez & Valle, 2005), leading to a dilution and a loss of focus for the field (Little, 2000, p.285). These surveys also converge in concluding the relatively *small proportion of directly/explicitly comparative articles*. Area studies or single-country (unit) studies tend to dominate (e.g., Cheng, 2003; Halls, 1990b; Kitamura, 2005; Little, 2000; Manzon, 2005; Martínez & Valle, 2005; Otsuka, 2005; Rust et al., 1999; Wolhuter, 2008; Yung, 1998). As Martínez and Valle (2005, p.87) comment, the critique of Rosselló (1972, p.54) on the type of studies classified under comparative education still applies today:

> Many of those [studies] do not compare anything. A huge number of studies limit themselves to describing an educational problem as it is found in a specific country .... The research studies that have reached the third stage, 'comparison in the strict sense' ... are still substantially rare exceptions, for reasons that are not very difficult to speculate.

That single-country studies are not comparative in nature is a debated issue. Scholars such as Rust et al. (1999) contend that a single-country study that tests more general theory, or is undertaken by research on a country/system 'foreign' to the researcher qualifies as comparative. But area studies (Bereday, 1964) that principally describe or explain foreign educational phenomena in single countries cannot be categorised as comparative. Epstein (2004) claims that case studies focusing on a particular educational system in a particular country can constitute a comparative study if the study is written within a (comparative) framework that explicitly has theoretical resonance beyond the boundaries of a particular country.

Perhaps the confusion is partly owed to the broader definitions of comparative education, which in some countries is affiliated with international education and, more specifically, development. As Phillips and Schweisfurth (2006, pp.53-57) clarify, international education research is implicitly comparative. This implicit nature can be understood in terms of the relationship between researcher and researched: degree of familiarity with the context, degree of similarity with home culture, degree of culturally comparative perspective, and degree of skill in interculturality. Thus, the greater degree of dissimilarity between the contexts of the researcher and the researched, the more room there is for comparative work.

To this confusion, Cowen (2003a, pp.15-16) would further contend that binary cross-national studies are not sufficient to constitute a comparative study. Rather it should be theory-informed work, paradigmatically framed, and coherent through time, with discernible coherent strategic agendas of attention that build a professional trajectory.

The above discussion indicates that a substantial portion of articles published in the field's specialist journals are area studies or single-country/unit studies. These range from 'foreign education' studies, development-oriented studies and implicitly comparative studies. Authors' purposes – informative, interventionist, theoretical – and the discursive constellations within which they work influence these patterns, as does the specific thrust of each journal. The *IJED*, for example, caters to a development-oriented audience and is less interested in explicitly comparative studies. Whether this finding can be used to argue that comparative education is not distinctively comparative is contentious. While one camp of scholars deplores this lack of explicit comparison as a weakness in the field, another camp defends its acceptability, particularly those coming from a comparative and international education and development background. A third school of thought diagonally critiques these debates and proposes more theoretically substantive work in comparative education literature, transcending the simplistic criterion of explicit or implicit comparison of units of analysis. (More on this in Chapter 5).

Society Attitudinal and Demographic Surveys

Plausibly the first attitudinal and demographic survey ever conducted on World Council participants was by Epstein (1981). He surveyed 62 participants of the General Assembly of the WCCES (equivalent to 13 per cent of total participants) during the 1980 World Congress in Japan, investigating their background characteristics (nationality, membership in a comparative education society, academic qualification, institutional affiliation) and attitudes toward the conduct of the World Congress. Although not a representative sample, the survey nevertheless had revealing results. Of the surveyed respondents, only 13 per cent received their highest degree in comparative education. Also, a large proportion of the UK and US sample were schoolteachers, who were the least committed to furthering the field, and the US participants were much less committed to their professional society – either being non-members or having only newly joined the society – as compared to other participants who were long-standing members of their societies. This is rather indicative of the inclusiveness of World Congresses of Comparative Education Societies.

In 1992, Ross et al. reported on their surveys of the perceptions of comparativists about their field. The surveys, conducted in 1979 and 1988 among participants of the national meetings of the CIES, revealed that the community of comparativists was *highly diverse* and thrived on *methodological eclecticism*. Despite the questionable reliability of the surveys, given their small sample sizes, their findings are coherent with earlier studies cited above.

A more recent survey was undertaken by Cook, Hite and Epstein (2004). It featured a demographic survey component and a bibliometric analysis component. The three abovementioned surveys are summarised in Appendix 10.

In 2007, Masemann, Bray and Manzon published a worldwide 'survey' of the member societies comprising the WCCES. Although not involving a structured quantitative survey but the compilation of historical narratives of these societies, the exercise yielded some valuable data about society profiles. Manzon and Bray (2007, p.356) characterise most WCCES member societies as fairly open groupings, with some being extremely open with no clear admission criteria (e.g. CESA), and/ or not charging membership fees (e.g., RCCE, NGVO). Having an interest in comparative education or its related fields such as international education, development education or cross-cultural studies would suffice for society admission. There are, however, some societies that are closed or fairly elitist networks (e.g., BCES, GCES), requiring members to have at least a Master's degree and research experience in comparative education and publications in the field. The SEEC began as a heterogeneous multidisciplinary group of academics, which later evolved into a specialist group, after comparative education became a compulsory subject in Spanish universities in the 1990s. Most societies have mixed profiles of members integrating personnel from teacher training colleges, university departments of education, international organisations, research institutes, and, sometimes, government bodies. Possibly a common denominator among these individuals is their cultural capital: multidisciplinary origin, interest and experience in a foreign country and linguistic capital. This *inclusive strategy* in society membership may be viewed in two opposite ways: as a positive development to welcome non-specialists in order to attract them to the field, or as a counterproductive strategy since, with the dearth of specialist induction programmes, new entrants will increasingly lack a systematic knowledge about the field and may or may not profess strong loyalty to it, such that when difficult periods come, they may fall back on their major disciplinary specialisations.

Overall, societies admit individual members only, but a few also have institutional members (e.g., CIES, CCES). In the Chinese society (CCES), all scholars working in a research centre or department of comparative education that is an institutional member of the CCES can consider themselves to be CCES members (Gao, 2005). This has contributed to the high number of members of these two societies, each having over 300 members. Yet, these impressive numbers do not necessarily mean a strongly cohesive society and, much less, a substantively distinct field. Gu and Gui (2007, p.237) reflect on the dilution of comparative education's borders even among those who received specialised training in the field:

> [I]t seemed that comparative studies could be conducted by any scholar who knew a *foreign language* or had *foreign education materials*. This dilution created a problem of identity recognition in the field. Many graduates took comparative education as a major, but they did not strongly identify with the field. Most specialised in

other branches of education, such as preschool education, curriculum, management, higher education, and sociology of education, in order to improve their opportunities for employment. [emphasis added]

The foregoing discussion has demonstrated that comparative education societies are varied in size, internal cohesiveness and activity. It is therefore not sufficient to argue that comparative education is a well-established field on the grounds that it has a global network of almost 40 comparative education societies worldwide. A close examination of the nature and internal consistency of these scholarly infrastructures has revealed problems of a dilution of substantive identity as in the case of, and possibly as a consequence of, the status of comparative education teaching and, in the final analysis, of the nature of the field itself.

Demographic and Citation Analyses

The survey undertaken by Cook et al. (2004) is a salient example of demographic and citation analysis and is presented here to pull together the diverse findings discussed above. It combined a demographic survey of background characteristics of CIES individual members and their perspectives on the five major contents of comparative education: important themes, figures, works, universities and organisations. The data gathered on the five major contents were then triangulated with a citation analysis of three leading journals: *CER*, *CE* and *IJED*. The study concluded that

> the demographic composition of the CIES population is predominately North American with distinctive elements of *heterogeneity*. The field, as reflected by CIES, is composed of a membership whose disciplinary lenses, research interests, and academic training are *highly disparate*. ... With a relatively steep membership turnover within the past decade, as well as an age demographic that is conspicuously young, it possibly faces even greater challenges for boundary continuity, the maintenance of cumulative gains in lines of inquiry, and a sustained sense of the field's historical development. These challenges are perhaps evidenced by data that indicate only *weak agreement in the field regarding the most influential themes, works, and figures*. The fact that the vast majority of those figures and works are contemporary reveals a particular epistemological hegemony in and of itself and a weak sense by CIES members of the field's longer history (pp.144-146). [emphasis added]

Evidence of this weak consensus on the 'five major contents' is given below:

- *Important themes*: a total of 550 themes were listed, each cited by at most 7.9 per cent of respondents, which represents a wide information scatter.
- *Important works*: a total of 537 were listed, again with wide information scatter, the top work (Freire, 1970) cited by only 3.6 per cent of respondents.
- *Important figures:* a total of 451 figures were named by respondents, the highest ranked figure (Philip Altbach) garnering only 5.8 per cent of responses.
- *Important universities*: a total of 240 universities with Stanford University ranking at the top with 13.7 per cent of responses.
- *Important organisations*: a total of 188 organisations, of which the World Bank and UNESCO were the most frequently cited (19.7 and 15.8 per cent, respectively).

Thus, unlike other fields which are generally united by a common thematic content and history, "comparative education exhibits little or no consensual references or orientations" on these important indicators such as core themes, specialist literature and leaders in the field (Cook et al., 2004, p.148). The authors posit that this absence of consensus on the content of the field is partly due to the lack of a common induction programme that permits the "cohesive transmission of a particular and identifiable body of knowledge" (p.148). This relates primarily to the open admission criteria for membership in the comparative community. The society is thus a grouping of people with a relatively flexible professional identity and transient loyalty to the society and to the field (p.144). In the second place, only a minority is engaged in the transmission of specialist/systematic knowledge on the history, theory and nature of comparative education. Evidence of this is that out of the 417 respondents, only 37 per cent had ever taught an introductory course in comparative education. Rather, society members had multidisciplinary interests, listing 211 areas of primary disciplinary emphasis with a wide information scatter, of which educational planning and policy ranked first (16.9 per cent of responses), while comparative international studies ranked sixth (2.9 per cent of responses). Relating this to the findings of CIECAP on the practice of comparative education teachers to prescribe rarely textbooks in comparative education but instead to give preference to journals also partly explains the lack of substantive cohesion in the transmission of specific knowledge on the field and its history. Textbooks offer a systematic and comprehensive treatment of a subject, whereas journal articles focus on the transmission and creation of new knowledge but in a fragmentary way. Thus Cook et al. (2004, p.148) aptly observed: "Those entrusted to transmit the field do it in widely disparate ways, both in subject matter and method of approach". All of these factors contribute to the absence of consensual references and to fluidity in the boundaries of the field of comparative education.

Although Cook et al.'s (2004) survey is limited to the North American CIES constituency, its conclusions and reflections have a wider applicability to the field world wide. The societies are generally loose groupings of scholars with disparate multidisciplinary backgrounds and foci, united perhaps by a common interest in the 'other'. Thus, as Cook et al. (2004, p.145) conclude, the field's boundaries are "much more flexible and pliant because of the larger epistemic contests facing other social science disciplines" that comprise it. Comparative education is thus not only an intellectual field with multidisciplinary 'tributaries'. It is also a field that is situated within multiple political and economic fields. Agents who occupy the field and are endowed with their *habitus,* react to these varied constraints and opportunities which the structure of the field presents, thereby constructing a variegated landscape of comparative educations.

Implications: Is Comparative Education a Field?

This chapter has explored the empirical substance of the field, focusing mainly on academic comparative education. During its early history, comparative education had gained institutional independence world-wide in the form of specialist programmes, centres, scholarly journals and books, as well as professional societies. This was partly owing to the synchronisation between the development of the intellectual field of comparative education and the political discourses particularly in the post-World War II period especially in such countries as the USA and England, which, due to their position of influence in the geopolitical sphere, also influenced the adoption of comparative education in other parts of the world. This disciplinary knowledge was thus subtly linked with political power. Once the disciplinary institutions of comparative education were established, the intellectual field acquired a life of its own until the power relations sustaining it were substantially withdrawn.

Interdisciplinary fields such as comparative education perhaps exhibit, in this sense, more sensitivity to movements of power than those which the more intellectually established disciplines.

Being a constructed field, comparative education can also be deconstructed when contingent forces of discourses, structure and agency no longer coalesce to maintain or improve the field's position of power vis-à-vis neighbouring fields in the educational sciences. Thus, in recent decades, it seems that the distinctive academic territory of comparative education is being eroded, not only epistemologically, as corroborated by the results of content analyses of course outlines and specialist publications, but also institutionally, with a declining trend in offering specialist programmes in comparative education and a more common practice of offering it as an optional subject in educational studies, or simply using it as a perspective or method in the different branches of educational studies, and a weak sense of substantive identity in its professional societies. The erosion of a unique space and distinctive identity of comparative education is also attested to by the rather unstable histories or changing landscapes of the professional societies, which, except perhaps for a few of the older societies (CIES, CIESC, BAICE) and some of the newer ones that have gained a rather secure foothold because comparative education has become compulsory in their national curriculum (SEEC, CCES), various others are struggling for survival. Most are loose networks of scholars interested in comparative education but with varying disciplinary loyalties and who identify only weakly with the field. Cook et al.'s (2004) survey of the CIES revealed that comparative education exhibits little or no consensual references or orientations in thematic content, historic tradition or boundary continuity. This observation may, to a certain extent, be extended in its applicability to the wider field of comparative education. In this respect, comparative education probably exemplifies Foucault's concept of a discipline (or field) as a historically contingent discursive formation of heterogeneous objects and practices organised into particular knowledge relations with each other, which emerges from power relations and constitutes power relations. This heterogeneity becomes more salient and is seen as a sign of the field's weakness when the links between power and (comparative education) knowledge weaken.

What implications do these findings have on the institutional and intellectual legitimacy of comparative education? It appears that despite its worldwide diffusion and institutionalisation in past decades, the

field's institutional and intellectual legitimacy as an independent academic field remains contested. Folliet warns that "comparative education is
confronted with the danger of losing its identity in two opposing ways:
one, to be reduced to a general theory of comparison, without any
distinctive content of its own, or to be diluted into an ensemble of
educational and social practices that adopt comparative perspectives"
(1999, p.286). Folliet's prognosis has visibly become a reality in the past
decade, as demonstrated in this chapter. Wolhuter et al. (2008b) contend
that the field's revitalisation is plausibly owed to its reconceptualisation
in higher education curricula as an integral perspective rather than as an
independent specialism of educational studies. Comparative educationists who seek to survive will, with their *habitus*, interact with the
available opportunities in the field and in the wider institutional and
political structures in order to redefine the practices and contents of
comparative education, adapting them to the changing times and needs.

A close examination of the nature and internal consistency of the
various *institutional* forms of comparative education – course outlines,
journals, society membership – reveals problems of a dilution of substantive identity. This leads one to question the nature of comparative
education itself. If its institutional legitimacy is in itself geographically
broad but substantively weak, fragmented and fluid, what does this
reflect of the nature of comparative education? Is there something
distinctive about the field of comparative education that legitimises it
intellectually? Can institutional structures legitimate a field intellectually?
What is the relationship between institutional infrastructures and
intellectual superstructures? And if the institutional infrastructures
exhibit fluidity, centrelessness and marginalisation, as the current picture
drawn here suggests, then does that de-legitimise the field on intellectual
grounds? Is there a relationship between institutionalisation and intellectual legitimation of a field? Is it valid to assume that intellectual
solidity is a result of institutional stability or is it not in fact more valid to
assume the reverse: that institutional strength merely *mirrors* intellectual
robustness just as institutional weakness merely *reflects* intellectual
fragility? In other words, can we validly affirm that the institutionally
blurred boundaries of comparative education are a mere effect of the
intellectually diffuse nature of comparative education itself? Obviously,
as Bourdieu highlights, factors of history, politics and institutional power
and personal biographies intervene and interact in a complex manner in
'materialising' the intellectual into institutional form. Cowen (1982a)

partially explored the reciprocal interaction between the intellectual and institutional forms of comparative educations. I would push the argument further by contending that both epistemological and sociological forms of power interact in dialectic fashion in constructing disciplinary fields (see Chapter 2). Drawing on Foucault's view on power-knowledge relations, I posit that in this dynamic interaction of intellectual and institutional legitimacy or power, at least two possible combinations seem to lead to the creation of a field: first, when both intellectual and institutional legitimacy are strong (pole 1); and, second, when institutional legitimacy is strong even if intellectual legitimacy is weak (pole 2). By contrast, when an area of knowledge has intellectual legitimacy but is unable to secure institutional power (pole 3), or when both intellectual and institutional legitimacies are weak or absent (pole 4), no new field comes to the fore. The histories of comparative education and the surveys of its contours seem to suggest that this field has been constructed initially on the basis of strong institutional power albeit weak intellectual legitimacy (pole 2). It is thus not surprising that, when in some parts of the world, institutional power is significantly withdrawn, the weakness of the field's intellectual legitimacy becomes more visible.

I will discuss this issue more extensively at the end of this chapter. Suffice it here to raise questions about the value of institutional legitimacy and its links with the intellectual legitimacy of a field. Meanwhile, I now turn to explore the other major players in the field: the national and international organisations that engage in comparative education studies outside of academia in pursuit of practical, policy-oriented aims.

Other Institutions

Apart from universities and teacher training institutes, which mainly engage in academic comparative education through teaching and research work, comparative education research is also undertaken by national and international government bodies whose work is probably more fittingly denominated as interventionist comparative education (Cowen, 1982a). Only a brief overview is given here for the purpose of illustrating the wide range of actors in comparative education. Related literature on this topic includes Debeauvais (1980), Jones (1992; 2007), Hallak and Göttelmann-Duret (1994), Henry et al. (1999), Mundy (1999; 2007), and Chabbott (2003).

Bray (2007b) distinguishes between policy makers in individual countries and international agencies, and their respective purposes and interests. While national policy makers examine foreign education systems for policy improvement at home, international agencies do large-scale cross-national comparisons of educational patterns in order to improve the policy advice they offer to national governments.

Figure 3.2 Typology of Comparative and International Education Organisations

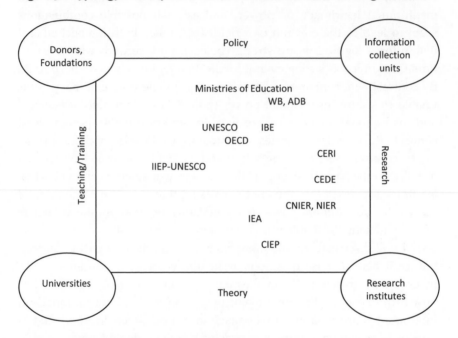

Source: Modified from Loxley (1994), p.936.

Legend:
ADB – Asian Development Bank, The Philippines
CEDE – Centro Europeo dell'Educazione, Italy
CERI – Center for Educational Research and Innovation, France
CIEP – Centre International d'Etudes Pédagogiques, France
CNIER – China National Institute of Educational Research, PRC
IBE – International Bureau of Education, Switzerland
IEA – International Association for the Evaluation of Educational Achievement,
      The Netherlands
IIEP-UNESCO – International Institute for Educational Planning, France & Argentina
NIER – National Institute for Educational Research, Japan
OECD – Organisation for Economic Co-operation and Development, France
OISE – Ontario Institute for Studies in Education, Canada
UNESCO – United Nations Educational, Scientific and Cultural Organization,
      France and global
WB – The World Bank, USA and global

In a typology of comparative and international education organisations, Loxley (1994) differentiates among universities, research institutes, information collection units and education policy-oriented organisations, schematically plotting these entities along the two intersecting continua of teaching/training–research and policy–theory (see Figure 3.2). Despite the limitations of this typology to capture the multiple facets of some organisations such as UNESCO, it is a useful analytical tool. Since universities have been the main focus of the previous sections, I shall limit this discussion to organisations based outside universities.

Research and Information Institutes

These entities serve a practical role by conducting survey research for the use of policymakers such as ministries of education (e.g., CNIER, NIER, CIEP, CEDE) or international bodies (e.g., CERI-OECD). They are established outside universities, either privately or by governments. Both NIER (Japan) and CIEP (France) are attached to their respective ministries of education. The CIEP engages in comparative research on educational systems and hosts meetings on comparative education. It is thus not surprising that the two French comparative education societies, AFEC and AFDECE, have their headquarters at the CIEP (Sutherland, 2007). The NIER collaborates closely with UNESCO in international exchanges of information and personnel. The early history of the Japan Comparative Education Society was intertwined with the NIER, which served as the society's headquarters for 15 years. Similarly, the founding Secretariat of the CCES was located at the CNIER in Beijing. Meanwhile, the CEDE, established as a think-tank of the Italian Ministry of Education, collects and disseminates data on Italian and foreign education through comparative studies, and advises UNESCO, OECD, and other intergovernmental bodies. The Italian comparative education society (SICESE) was formally linked with CEDE, which gave financial and technical support for its conferences and publications (Todeschini, 2004).

The Centre for Educational Research and Innovation (CERI) was established within the OECD (discussed below) to support educational research among OECD member states and to build consensus among government educational research institutes in these industrialised countries.

Education Policy-Oriented Organisations

Major intergovernmental bodies in this category include the World Bank,

UNESCO and OECD, among others. There are also non-governmental organisations such as the IEA. These entities undertake large-scale cross-national comparisons of educational systems to support policy advice given to their respective clientele. They are also significant producers of comparative education documentation in the form of educational statistics, journals, educational yearbooks and other specialised studies. Loxley, however, notes that, in contrast to academic comparative education, "political roles often dominate in this sphere, as these organisations adopt central resource allocation, planning and lobbying functions to influence education" (1994, pp.934-935). They pursue applied/interventionist purposes to promote, for example, best practices in educational governance, educational equality and intercultural understanding. The work of these agencies possibly represents what Foucault would designate as games of truth, since they propose truth claims that are congruent with their institutional aims. The dividing practices (Foucauldian sense) promoted by their authoritative discourses (e.g., publications, policies, statistical data and league tables) serve as a powerful basis for governmental self-evaluation and decision-making.

UNESCO

The United Nations Educational, Scientific and Cultural Organization (UNESCO) was established in 1945 for the purpose of contributing to "peace and security in the world by promoting collaboration among the nations through education, science and culture" (UNESCO, 1945). UNESCO and its specialist institutes and centres in the field of education exercise a strong policy advisory role, particularly for UN member state governments. As Bray (2007b, p.25) highlights, among the strategic objectives of UNESCO for the period 2002-2007 was "promoting experimentation, innovation and the diffusion and sharing of information and best practices as well as policy dialogue in education" all over the world. This necessarily involves the cross-national comparative study of education at a worldwide scale. UNESCO also publishes two specialist journals in the field: the *International Review of Education* and *Prospects: Quarterly Review of Comparative Education*. The IIEP-UNESCO also has a teaching/training focus aside from its policy advisory role.

The International Bureau of Education (IBE) was founded in 1925 in Geneva and has, since 1947, been linked with UNESCO. Among its prominent activities is the International Conference of Education, gathering ministers of education of member countries to deliver national education reports. The IBE has been particularly influential in the field of comparative education, especially in the early years of the WCCES (Masemann & Epstein, 2007), as well as in the 'national' comparative education histories (e.g., Walterová, 2007; Mussin, 2007) and synergies with both IBE and UNESCO continue to the present day (Bray, 2008). Various comparative education society histories (e.g., of Kazakhstan and the Czech Republic) cited the pivotal role these IBE-organised forums played in stimulating the establishment of the field in their countries (Mussin, 2007; Walterová, 2007).

The OECD
The Organisation for Economic Co-operation and Development was formed in 1961, but had its origins in an earlier organisation established in 1947 to help in post-World War II reconstruction of European economies (Bray, 2007b). In 2010, it had 32 member countries (OECD, 2010). Among its multi-sectoral foci is education and its specialist institution, CERI (mentioned above) is particularly active in research publications. The OECD publishes the influential annual *Education at a Glance* (OECD, 2001), and the *OECD Handbook for Internationally Comparative Statistics* (OECD, 2004). The OECD's Programme for International Student Assessment (PISA) has engaged comparative educators and policymakers alike in the comparison of achievement levels of 15-year olds in 41 countries/ states (OECD, 2003).

The World Bank and 'Regional' Banks
Also established in the context of post-World War II reconstruction, the World Bank was founded in 1944 by 44 member nations. It consists of two institutions: the International Development Association (IDA) and the International Bank for Reconstruction and Development (IBRD). Its main mission was to address inter-governmental monetary and financial problems across a wide range of sectors, including education. As a bank, its work is to lend money mainly to governments. Its engagement in comparative education research is for a practical purpose: to serve the bank's worldwide lending programmes. The World Bank publishes cross-national education sector policy reports, educational statistics, and other such comparative education studies with a focus on economics and financing (e.g., World Bank, 1999; Psacharopoulos & Patrinos, 2002).

Entities similar to the World Bank but with a regional focus are the Asian Development Bank (ADB) for the Asia-Pacific region, and the

Banco Interamericano de Desarrollo (BID) in Latin America. They also undertake cross-national comparisons in education to serve their policy advisory and lending activities and publish influential reports (e.g., ADB, 2001).

Other Intergovernmental Organisations

The European Community (EC) has an Education Committee responsible for implementing the community's educational policy. Of particular relevance to comparative education is the information network, EURYDICE, which publishes periodic reports on the educational systems of the EC member states and extensive information databases (García Garrido, 1996).

In Latin America, the Oficina Iberoamericana para la Educación, la Ciencia y la Cultura is becoming an increasingly active and influential body. Previously known as the Oficina de Educación Iberoamericana (OEI), this organisation is based in Madrid. It undertakes research and publication work on the educational systems within the Latin American region.

The IEA

The International Association for the Evaluation of Educational Achievement (IEA) was founded in 1959 in Stockholm and is comprised of ministries of education, universities and educational research institutes which undertake survey research and represent educational systems around the world. Unlike the abovementioned intergovernmental bodies, the IEA is principally engaged in curriculum-based survey research at the primary and secondary school levels. Its work extends to over 60 countries on such themes as mathematics, science, reading literacy, and foreign languages, plausibly the most prominent of which is known as the TIMSS (Third [also Trends in] International Mathematics and Science Study). The IEA's scholarly publications aim to disseminate knowledge and advice on how educational systems work best under diverse conditions (Loxley, 1994, p.942).

Links with Comparative Education

The relationship between comparative education and these national and international organisations has been close ever since their establishment after World War II. As glimpsed above, various comparative education societies have been supported by or have closely collaborated with their national research institutes, and individual comparative scholars have been involved in providing policy advice to their respective educational ministries. In the same vein, various countries have reported the strategic insertion of comparative education in teacher education and/or higher education curricula by national ministries of education during educational reform processes owing to historically contingent factors, such as favourable political and economic structural shifts and the role of human agency. In some cases, institutional links with and support from supranational organisations have likewise served to catalyse or sustain the work of comparative education scholars and, by extension, the professional societies they belong to. Among these, UNESCO and its institutes, most notably the IBE and UIE, as well as the World Bank, OECD, the Council of Europe, the European Union, and the BID and OEI in Latin America are frequently cited in the histories of the development of the field and its professional societies in almost all the world regions (Manzon & Bray, 2007, pp.355-356; Wolhuter et al., 2008b, pp.331-332), but was notably omitted in the country reports on African universities with the exception of Egypt (Wolhuter et al., 2008b, p.332; Megahed & Otaiba, 2008). In microcosm, Cook et al.'s (2004) survey of CIES members revealed that out of 188 governmental and non-governmental organisations listed as the most influential in the field, the World Bank ranked highest with 19.7 per cent of total responses, followed by UNESCO with 15.8 per cent. Despite the contextual limitations of these findings, they are illustrative of the prominent role that national and international bodies play in the field. A good number of comparative education specialists are engaged as experts in these organisations, and some policy specialists have shifted to academic comparative education. This symbiotic relationship is reflected in the membership of the professional societies, which included persons from government bodies, as well as from international agencies and research institutes, especially in those countries where these organisations had a strong presence (Manzon & Bray, 2007, p.356).

Cowen (1982a, pp.108-109) elucidated on the relationship between interventionist (or applied) comparative education and academic comparative education. He posits that in the 1960s and 1970s, the intellectual debates about purpose and method in academic comparative education introduced a new legitimating principle for an 'interventionist comparative education'. British protagonists in these debates were King (1965) and Holmes (1971), who explicitly defined the *practical purpose* of comparative education, and, according to Cowen, intellectually legitimised a close working relationship between academic comparative educationists and government or intergovernmental agencies. (This indicates the power of discourse in constructing the limits of the field and its objects of knowledge, as Foucault suggests.) Meanwhile, the US-based protagonists of the methods debate in the 1960s – Bereday (1964), Noah and Eckstein (1969) – advocated the systematic use of social science methods and quantitative analyses in order to strengthen academic comparative education. Institutionally, these methodological approaches were already rather influential in the work of the international agencies, especially the OECD. Thus, Cowen concludes, academic comparative education and interventionist comparative education were brought closer to each other by both purpose and method.

Moreover, in view of the difficulty and financial outlay involved in large-scale comparative studies based on field work, Cowen describes a natural division of labour in comparative studies, with international and national agencies taking the lead in these global projects, leaving academic comparativists to undertake smaller and more manageable tasks. Nevertheless, as Cowen aptly cautions, the interventionist comparative education work of these policy-making bodies derive from political rather than intellectual principles (1982a, p.112; 2006), which can raise ethical dilemmas.

Nevertheless, a paradoxical relationship between academic and applied comparative education is noteworthy in some countries. Where the academic presence of comparative education has traditionally been weak, the research and consultancy work by international organisations or of national governments in collaboration with comparative education scholars is more salient in countries such as Brazil, Chile, Finland, France, the Netherlands, Switzerland and Uruguay (Wolhuter et al., 2008b, pp.331-332), where the 'comparative education research' undertaken by organisations such as UNESCO, OECD, IEA, and the IBE were given a prominent place in their institutional histories. Whether there is a direct relationship or not between academic comparative education and applied or interventionist comparative education remains to be established. I would posit for now that authors of country reports in publications which aim to describe the position of comparative education in their academic institutions, finding a weak or marginal presence, would intend to balance the description by citing extra-academic activity and thus highlighting the comparative education research done by academics in collaboration with international organisations in their home country. This is probably a discursive move on the part of the authors of those historical narratives to construct the institutional presence of comparative education in their home contexts. In any case, this pattern brings to light that the volume of work produced by international and government educational bodies in the area of comparative education studies and their increasing role in educational policy-making in the world are far too substantial to be ignored (Jones, 2007; Mundy, 2007).

Institutional Construction of the Field

In the foregoing sections, I have presented a fairly global historical narrative of the institutionalisation mainly of academic comparative education, and, secondarily, of interventionist comparative education. This description revealed a very large institutional superstructure and specialist literature. Paradoxically, however, a survey of the field's contours and contents of courses, specialist publications, as well as of society demographics and perceptions suggests that academic comparative education is extremely heterogeneous, extensively inclusive, and without distinctive content, membership or purposes.

This diluted identity of comparative education has led me to raise questions about the relationship between institutional legitimacy and intellectual legitimacy. Cowen (1982a, p.322) posits a reciprocal interacttion between the institutional and intellectual forms of comparative educations, and Epstein (1981, p.269) further contends that the field's tenability depends on whether its professional associations (the institutional component) can capture recognition for their specialisation (intellectual legitimacy). I query, however, the direction of this relationship: can institutional legitimacy justify intellectual legitimacy? Would it not rather be more reasonable to affirm that intellectual legitimacy is the sine qua non for any effort to institutionally legitimise the field to be effective and sustainable in the long-run? Perhaps for some time, sociological inertia and discourse will keep comparative education's institutional infrastructures intact until major upheavals come to unsettle the shaky edifices. But, going beyond the institutional facade, are there not profound intellectual foundations that sustain it? Can we not in fact validly assume that, just as institutional strength *mirrors* intellectual robustness, institutional weakness *reflects* intellectual fragility? In other words, can we validly deduce from the institutionally blurred boundaries of comparative education that the nature of comparative education is itself intellectually diffuse and that this intellectual diffuseness accounts for its institutional weakness? Yet, why is it that comparative education seems to be robust and healthy? Moreover, why does it continue to take root in other parts of the world? Is it the field's alliance with the voluminous interventionist comparative education work of national and international organisations, the discourse of interventionist comparative education, which somewhat gives institutional vitality to the field and at times, overshadows the fragility of academic comparative education? As Cowen (2006, p.568) describes it, the field of study had widened substantially in the post-1945 period, extending to development education, area studies, international education, planning and economics of education, among others. A wide range of activities and literature relating to 'education overseas', he argues, "has claimed or has been given, rather absent-mindedly, the label 'comparative education'".

I argue that comparative education is a constructed field that initially came to be institutionally legitimised as a distinct subfield of educational studies not only out of an inner logic based on cognitive criteria alone, but also as the result of pragmatic and political reasons working through a complex interplay of discourses, social structures and human agency and their respective power relations. The intersections of various discourses – political, economic, intellectual, etc. – as well as power relations in various structural contexts, geopolitics, institutional power and personal biographies, have contributed in diverse ways to the construction of this intellectual field (Bourdieuian sense). Once institutionally legitimised as a field, comparative education had acquired sufficient (ontological) existence that 'materially' demarcated it from other fields, while subjecting it to further workings of political interests among institutions and individuals who naturally attempt to preserve and increase the field's inertial momentum (Mason, 2008c) and their positions within it. As an institutionally independent field, a distinctive discursive formation (Foucauldian sense) developed and took shape in disciplinary-like structures and processes, specific discourses on 'canonical' texts, authors and methods. The discursive formation of a field of 'comparative education' has made possible the stabilisation of otherwise contingent and heterogeneous discourses, which are evidenced by the current state of the field characterised by a wide scope of objects, purposes and social populations. Transposing Wagner and Wittrock's comment on the institutional histories of the social sciences to the context of comparative education: "national profiles [of the social sciences] have their roots in the specific intellectual, institutional, and political constellations under which 'social scientists' have tried to develop discursive understandings of their societies" (1991b, pp.6-7). The previous sections have alluded to this in diverse ways. I now attempt to recapitulate the evidence from the institutional histories to substantiate my argument that comparative education, although apparently a distinct subfield of educational studies, is a heterogeneous field because it has come about as a result not only of pure cognitive criteria but also partly as a result of historically contingent discourses and structural and agency-oriented power struggles. Moreover, the field remains apparently distinct due to the sociological inertia of its institutional infrastructures and discourse as a constitutive shaping force of academic fields. I demonstrate this by examining two main forms of the institutionalisation of comparative education: as a distinct academic programme at universities and as a distinct professional society.

Comparative Education Teaching: Genealogy and Field

In this section, I develop the first part of my argument: that the institutionalisation of comparative education as an academic program distinct from educational studies at universities originated and developed partly due to historically contingent discourses that brought to light the need for this specialised area of study. Applying Foucauldian genealogical lenses, I argue that the formation of new bodies of knowledge presupposes and constitutes power relations, and power relations likewise presuppose and constitute new knowledge. This is particularly salient in some contexts where comparative education has acquired an institutionally distinctive status as an academic specialisation, partly due to its role in maintaining existing power relations at the national government and sometimes at the intergovernmental level, as in the case of the international agencies. Comparative education interacted with discourses of these governmental bodies about the 'education abroad', 'best educational practices' and 'educational reform'.

Complementing this genealogical critique, I further argue that the emergence of comparative education as a distinctly institutionalised field is not simply a direct effect of political or social power. Bourdieuian theory offers the conceptual tools to analyse the complex power struggles that take place in the *intellectual field*. Focusing on the intellectual field at the level of faculties of education at universities, I view comparative education as a subfield in competition with different subject specialisations under educational studies over pertinent forms of capital in order to have the right to define its own subject domain in the field. To some extent, the structure of this intellectual field – educational studies – is homologous to that of the wider field of power. If a certain form of capital, say political capital, is most valued in the field of power in a particular national context, then the possession (actual or potential) of such capital by comparative education vis-à-vis other branches of educational studies, partly accounts for its emergence as an independent body of knowledge. This is not to say that comparative education is entirely about policy advice to governments, but this form of comparative education practice had contributed substantially to the growth of the field. In addition, human agency also plays a part in this endeavour, and Bourdieu's concept of *habitus* – individual and collective – helps explain how agency and structure mutually interact in shaping the intellectual field. To substantiate these claims, I examine three typologies of national cases of substantial institutionalisation / de-institutionalisation discussed in this chapter. A first typology deals with the context of post-war internationalism and interventionism, with the USA as a principal example. A second typology represents a counter-example in the context of socialist and post-war nationalisms. Finally, a third typology examines the close relationship between institutionalisation and national education reforms, taking Spain as an illustrative case. As is the case with typologies, they are limited tools which oversimplify reality, but are nevertheless useful for conceptual understanding. In particular, with the first typology, I do not claim that the field of comparative education came to exist only after World War II. There were already early forms of comparative education teaching as lecture courses and specialist publications. Rather, echoing Foucault (1972) who contends that objects of knowledge emerge only in discourse, I claim that the field became substantially institutionalised only during this post-war period, taking the form of specialist programmes and departments which permitted the drawing of visible, material boundaries distinguishing comparative education from neighbouring educational fields.

Typology 1: USA and Post-war Internationalism (or interventionism)

The formation of specialised academic programmes of comparative education distinct from educational studies took a significant upward turn in the USA after World War II. International cooperation initiatives in the context of the Cold War saw the leadership of the USA in funding the work of comparativists in consonance with its foreign policy aims, especially in those countries viewed to be strategic in countering Communism (Altbach, 1990 cited by Marginson & Mollis, 2002, p.589). Likewise, in line with the spirit of internationalism and global cooperation for world peace, the 1950s and 1960s were particularly expansionary periods in the field's history in Canada, England, West Germany, and Japan (Epstein, 2008a). Formal academic programmes mushroomed and chairs of comparative education' were established in these countries. Alongside these developments came the emergence of a diverse but related field of study: international and/or development education, which focuses on international cooperation with the 'Third World' or 'developing countries'. In Foucauldian terms, this 'discipline' came to be configured as a stable discourse – in the form of academic programmes – as a power-enabled knowledge, which in its turn, was also power-enabling. The 'practices of patronage' from government foreign policy and aid programmes administered by national governments (e.g., in the UK, USA, Canada) and intergovernmental agencies (e.g., World Bank, UNESCO) indirectly empowered the significant institutionalisation of a distinct body of knowledge – 'disciplinary knowledge'. This body of knowledge was perceived to bring social and political benefits to the world in consonance with the social and political aims of a core group of countries – led by the USA – which sought to maintain power balances in the world. Disciplinary institutions such as centres of research and scholarship in the new 'science' of comparative education thus came to be established drawing on economic and social capital from these powerful entities. With disciplinary knowledge and its related institutions and practices, a discursive formation took shape through the building up of discourses (commentaries on works of specific authors, journal articles, textbooks, conference papers, etc.). This is not to say that comparative education courses were, as Marginson and Mollis had put it, "simply 'programmed' in the corridors of power" (2002, p.581). Rather, comparative education enjoys relative intellectual autonomy and has indeed offered reflexive insights to critique the power relations that have partly shaped its disciplinary formation. Nevertheless, Foucault enables us to raise the question: Had there been no Cold War, would comparative education have become institutionalised in the way that it has as a distinct domain from educational studies? Had world history taken a different course, would comparative education have entered significantly into the discourse? After pointing out some of the historical contingencies and power relations involved in the 'disciplinary' institutionalisation of comparative education as a formal academic programme at universities, and the intertwining of comparative education with the discourse on development and international education, I examine more closely the internal dynamics of this *intellectual field* from a Bourdieuian perspective. I argue that comparative education emerged as a distinct subfield of educational studies, initially at American universities, in competition with other subfields for legitimate recognition of its intellectual authority. Bourdieu conceptualised a field as dynamically configured by different forms of capital and the complex interactions between *habitus* and the objective constraints and opportunities of the social world. As demonstrated above, the specialisation of comparative education at American universities took place in consonance with a pro-active interventionist foreign policy in the country. Although macro government policies did not directly interfere with the 'programming' of comparative education, they offered the structural opportunity, the social demand for comparative work and with it, the necessary funding for research and teaching and foreign study visits, and opportunities for international agency work. These social opportunities attracted individuals who had some predisposition (*habitus*) for the field. Such predisposition could take the form of scholarly interest in international education issues, previous international experience (e.g. through the Peace Corps, Canadian University Service Overseas, Voluntary Service Overseas) and possession of pertinent capital (linguistic, social, etc.). Through this encounter between macro-social opportunities and groups of individuals with the pertinent capital and *habitus*, a new intellectual field – comparative education – was taking shape. I follow Bourdieu's view of intellectual fields as a network of competing positions of influence and distinction. I contend that when comparative education was first established as a formal academic programme at American graduate schools, comparative education probably possessed more capital – political, economic, linguistic, and social capital – than other existing subfields of educational studies, but primarily political capital, which at that time was particularly valuable in American interventionist foreign policy aims.

Taking Bourdieu's metaphor of the intellectual field as a field within fields, I contend that the position of certain countries – the United States and to some extent, England – in world affairs and the prestige of their universities partly explains why the academic programmes of comparative education in their institutions served as a model and seedbed for comparative education to take root in other parts of the world. They attracted scholars from those countries on which they had political and/or economic influence. In turn, these scholars who have received 'disciplinary' training in comparative education served as catalysts of the field in their own countries. Countries such as Brazil, Japan, Korea, China, Thailand, to name a few, looked to the USA for models of educational development. Similarly, the dissemination of comparative education in the Commonwealth countries (Australia, Hong Kong, Kenya, etc.) is partly due to the central political position that the UK used to have in colonial history. Had the USA and the UK not occupied a central position in the world system of political power, would they have been as influential in disseminating comparative education throughout the world? The histories of comparative education at universities illustrate Bourdieu's view of the intellectual field as exhibiting homologies with the fields of power. In this case, the leadership of American and British higher education – and within it, comparative education – manifests parallel positions of leadership in the world system of power relations. The 'USA' typology thus highlights the sensitive relationship of comparative education to the directions of foreign policy and international relations among governments.

Typology 2: Socialist Bloc and Post-war Nationalisms

To further highlight that comparative education is a field within fields of power, particularly political power, I also explore the case of the Socialist countries wherein comparative education had been eclipsed, if not 'suppressed', within a radically distinct *episteme* (Foucauldian sense) which viewed comparative education as running counter to the logic of the intellectual field and of the wider field of power. These examples articulate the power-knowledge dialectic and the homology between the intellectual field and the field of power, as shown in the differentiated impact of the same world event – World War II – on different national contexts and their respective comparative educations.

The academic institutionalisation of comparative education was disrupted in the countries of the former Soviet bloc, China, South Africa, Chile and Brazil within a specific historical context where the prevailing political ideology in their respective governments was 'nationalist' or anti-Western/American in orientation. In these places, the teaching of comparative education – which had an American or Western connotation – was either completely removed from universities or underwent severe contraction of institutional support and restriction of the 'objects of knowledge' to those countries that were in consonance with the dominant political ideology. This reinforces my claim above that, as deduced from the case of the USA, comparative education is highly sensitive to the directions of foreign policy and international relations among governments. It illustrates the power-knowledge dialectic from another perspective. In this case, comparative education is a 'power-disabled' knowledge because its knowledge is 'power-disabling', or is at least perceived to pose a threat by those who dominate the field of political power. Also, the 'Socialist/nationalist typology' elucidates Foucault's concept of a discourse, which both constrains and enables what can be said, thought, and written about a specific object or practice – in this case, comparative education – within a specific *episteme*, that of the Socialist regime. In this respect, where both discourse and structure – more specifically, political structure – constrains comparative education activity, even if the field has been institutionally established and has strong individual agency who advocates it, these latter become de-legitimised by the power of the dominant discourse and structure in a particular period.

From a Bourdieuian perspective, we can further imagine the academic field of comparative education as embedded within the field of geopolitical power. The system of positions and oppositions among national governments in the wider field of politics exhibits homologies within the intellectual field of 'national' comparative educations. The East-West German divide in the trajectories of the field, for example, reflects in microcosm a wider geopolitical bi-polarity during the Cold War period. Some countries manifest patterns of insulations and/or spatial attractions (Cowen, 1990) towards certain countries due to their political histories. These patterns are reflected in the differentiated objects and contents of comparative education in each place, creating what Cowen termed as comparative educations (1990, p.335).

Typology 3: Spain and Reformist Policies

Through the first two typologies, I have sought to demonstrate by means of an example and a counter-example the genealogies of comparative education as a field of knowledge that has been highly responsive to geopolitical power relations particularly at some periods of history. I now examine the case of Spain, which also echoes the case of some other countries such as China and Kazakhstan, on a genealogy of comparative education as a compulsory core subject in national educational curricula.

Unlike the 'USA' case which typified a foreign interventionist or 'outward meliorative role' of comparative education, the Spanish narrative exemplifies the 'inward meliorative' value of the field with respect to domestic educational reforms. As in the previous typologies, I tease out how the workings of historical contingencies and power struggles for academic capital, in particular, accounted for comparative education's disciplinary institutionalisation at universities.

Despite its early existence as a subject taught in some Spanish universities since the 1960s, comparative education only became a compulsory core subject for all national universities in the 1990s, enforced by law amidst society-wide educational reforms in a newly-democratised nation. This new development brought about significant specialisation of the field in terms of academic programmes and 'discipline-trained' personnel. From Foucauldian and Bourdieuian lenses, one can identify some contingent factors accounting for such turn of events such as the personal biography of those tasked to intervene in educational policy formulations, the interaction of comparative education with the discourses on educational reform and Spain's opening up to international relations. Ferrer (2006), for example, cited the international background and related work with UNESCO of some key Spanish education ministers who were instrumental in positioning comparative education as a compulsory subject in national educational curricula.

An analysis from a Bourdieuian field perspective offers more insights. Taking comparative education in Spain as a field within fields, I highlight the factors cited by Naya and Ferrer (2004) and Ferrer (2006) related to how the field's specialisation into a distinct area of educational sciences took shape. At the level of regional politics, the discourse on Europeanisation surrounding the formation of the European Union and the linking of the member countries' economic, labour, and educational systems catalysed the 'European' and more outward-looking policies and dispositions in Spain. These transformations were refracted in the intellectual field of educational sciences where, possibly owing to the political capital that comparative education offered, comparative education became a compulsory core subject for all education majors in Spain. At a still lower level, as a field within the intellectual field of educational sciences, university politics and academic capital play a role in determining the 'position' of comparative education in their respective faculties of education. As Naya and Ferrer (2004) comment:

[While] the ministry prescribed a minimum of six credits for teaching comparative education, each university has room to manoeuvre the remaining 150 credits not prescribed by the ministry. Here is where university politics enters: in the power struggles between one area of knowledge and another over institutional space.

This observation echoes Bourdieu's concept of the intellectual field as a power struggle for distinction among agents – in this case, the various subfields of educational studies within a faculty of education. The Spanish case illustrates how comparative education engages in diverse power struggles depending on which social field it is located. Concretely, it highlights that the form of capital at stake or considered more valuable at the institutional level of the university is at variance with that at the national level of an educational ministry. At the level of a faculty of education in a university, comparative education competes with other subjects in educational studies for institutional space. At this level, social capital (with other faculty members and students, university administration) as well as academic capital (power over academic qualifications) might be more important than other forms of capital. By contrast, at the educational ministry level where national educational curricula are formulated and mandated, political and social capital might be more important than academic capital.

This is not to affirm, however, that political capital is what counts most at the national level. The political structure of national governments must be taken account. In the case of Spain and China, significant institutionalisation of comparative education at their universities took place when the respective education ministries, which operated within fairly centralised political structures, made the subject part of the core curriculum for teacher education at universities nationwide. By contrast, I take the case of Germany which, although not properly classified under this typology of 'institutionalisation-for-inward melioration', exemplifies the importance of institutional political power rather than national political capital, given the country's fairly decentralised governance structure. As Waterkamp (2005) highlights, institutional and university politics are more important than national politics in determining the position of the subject (comparative education) at universities:

There is no center which imposes anything because the universities are free to develop their programmes. They have to submit it to their ministries, but the ministry does not intervene. It is the whole community of educationists as such which is important, because it is decided within the schools of education which profile the programmes should have. Therefore it is *important to have a status and to be visible* within the big community of educationists to help this discipline stay and grow in the schools of education. The German Society for Education is a very important institution, and on a lower level, it is the schools of education which have their own mood; rather, *individual professors have their individual weight and influence* and, on this level, it is also possible either to get support for comparative education or not. And this is the most important thing, because (national) politics as such is not very much interested in details in the universities.

Also, the situation or *new tendencies within the education system* have an impact on the interests within the academic field, *which topic comes to the fore*, and which topic loses interest. ... So, the course and trajectories of the field are also interdependent with school politics and educational politics in general.

The two contrasting cases discussed above are instructive for understanding the mechanics of the intellectual field and the variegated intensities of influence that structure, agency and discourse have on the field. Social agents, capitalising on pertinent societal discourses in a particular period, work towards positioning comparative education as a subject at universities depending on the historical structural organisation of power in society and the room for manoeuvre it gives to institutional and individual agents to play their role in the intellectual field. In the case of some centralised societies, political capital – a subject's relevance to national politics – gave a favourable boost to the position of comparative education nationwide. By contrast, in some fairly decentralised societies, institutional and academic capital as well as potential economic capital that a course programme can bring in to the university/department was more pertinent in positioning comparative education at institutions.

A second pair of contrasting cases, those of Italy and Switzerland, serves to counter a possible determinism in the above categorisation. It also highlights further complexities and contingencies in societal responses.

According to Palomba and Paolone (2008), the discourse on the alignment of EU member countries' higher education systems promoted by the Bologna Process served as a catalyst for comparative education, but its impact is variegated in different EU countries. In the case of Italy, the relative autonomy given to universities to re-design their educational offer and establish new courses has led to a wider space given to comparative education, possibly as an offshoot of the "renewed sensibility for the 'international'. This is even more significant considering that, conversely, at the central level, the *Ministry did not prescribe* a place for it" (p.95) [emphasis added]. This example shows that centrally mandated curricula placing comparative education is not the only way to achieve significant institutionalisation. Similar to Germany, the relative autonomy and contribution of institutional and individual agency, aligning itself with opportunities signalled by societal discourses on 'Europeanisation', was more significant to disciplinary institutionalisation.

However, the interplay of discourses and agency are not sufficient to carving a niche for comparative education at universities. The case of Switzerland demonstrates this. Schüssler & Leutwyler (2008) attribute the field's paradoxically weak institutionalisation in Switzerland, despite the penetration of the discourse of the 'international' as well as the organisational presence of international educational organisations (e.g., the IBE), to structural constraints in terms of an educational research framework that neglects macro-approaches, limited economic capital for educational fields, and, what we could call in Bourdieuian terms, a *habitus* of provincialism, partly exacerbated by Switzerland's non-membership of the EU. To this I would add that the discontinuity in/lack of disciplinary institutionalisation of comparative education in Switzerland due to limited human agency who could advocate for its recognition leads to a discontinuity in the 'social gene' of comparativists. Thus, a generally favourable societal discourse on the 'international' in education is insufficient. Both structural opportunities and active advocacy by individual agents are also needed for the sustainable positioning of comparative education in academia. Moreover, the direction and intensity of change is variously shaped not only by what educational traditions had been followed prior to major reforms in curricula (Harbo & Jorde, 2000), but also by the interaction of personal biography, the internal sociology of universities, and the national political work agenda vis-à-vis the geopolitical and domestic contexts in the institutionalisation of comparative education (Cowen, 1982a, p.122).

The above discussion highlights the complexities and discontinuities in patterns in the construction of the field of comparative education. I would claim that in the social construction of a field, one can distinguish a phase by which the institutional boundaries of a field are materially demarcated. A distinct phase ensues with the epistemological construction of a field by agents working in that sociologically delineated intellectual territory. From then on more specialised discourses develop within the specific field. This does not deny the early existence of specialist discourses prior to the material demarcation of a field. It only affirms that such discourses become more distinctive, more peculiar to the field once they are materially embodied in and disseminated through specialist institutions, programmes, societies, publications and conferences. With institutionalisation, the field is perpetuated through discourse. However, through discourse alone, without any institutional structures, it is difficult to distinguish the field.

I now turn to another type of institutionalised comparative education – the professional societies – in order to further substantiate my claim that institutionalisation is not a purely intellectual enterprise but is intricately related to power struggles.

Comparative Education Societies: Distinction

Another form of institutionalisation of comparative education – as a distinct area of educational studies – is as a professional society. I argue that although there is a minimum base of shared intellectual interests that unite members of a comparative education society – some more cohesively than others –, society formation can be understood more dynamically in Bourdieuian thought as a quest for *distinction* in the field. This applies within national boundaries and within a global context. Within a national setting, a comparative education society competes with other educational/social science-related societies in much the same way as it competes for a distinctive institutional space as an academic programme. As Epstein (1981, p.269) claims, "a field's tenability depends on whether the people who run a professional association can capture recognition for their specialisation". Since the power struggles within national boundaries somewhat echo the interactions of discourse, structure and agency already explained earlier, I now focus on the second context: the WCCES and its members.

At a global level, the WCCES, like an intellectual field, is a network of power relations among member societies, who occupy unequal positions in the field based on their unequal possession of pertinent forms of capital. These positions in the WCCES show homologies with the distribution of power in the geopolitical world. However, this correlation does not hold true for all societies, partly because some are not national groupings and partly because other factors intervene in society formation. I argue, however, that in terms of the level of activity in WCCES affairs and forums, those societies – or society representatives – with sufficient economic capital (especially for travel to international meetings), linguistic capital (especially in English and French), in addition to basic academic and scientific capital are most actively and visibly represented. By contrast, those with less of these pertinent forms of capital are hardly able to intervene in World Council meetings. This is evidenced by the attendance patterns, for example, at WCCES Executive Committee meetings.

I argue that the formation of national, language-based, and regional societies, as well as a global body, is a non-discursive move to symbolise academic distinctiveness and belonging to a global network. Societies struggle for distinction within this field of societies – the WCCES – possibly in order to legitimate their existence in the domestic or international scenario. Some comparative education societies (e.g., Spain, Australia, Cuba, Spain, Turkey) explicitly acknowledged that they decided to organise themselves formally as a society in order to be represented on the WCCES as one more entity at par with other entities irrespective of their unequal political, economic and academic power. In some cases, it was merely symbolic representation since what lay behind an organisational façade was nothing but inactivity. In other instances, the formation of new societies represented power struggles over positions and institutional resources in the field, sometimes catalysed by micro-political reasons. Cases include the birth of national societies from regional/international bodies (e.g., NGVO from CESE meetings; SOMEC from CIES meetings), sometimes as the institutional spinning-off of national sections of a regional society into independent national societies (e.g., British Section of CESE to what is now known as BAICE); the formation of a splinter society alongside a national society in the same country (e.g., AFEC and AFDECE; then British CES and LACE); and the birth of new Commissions within a national body of educationists (e.g., the Commission for Education with the Third World from the Commission for Comparative Education within the same German Society for Educationists). The influence of human agency, particularly on the part of leaders of the WCCES and/or more established societies such as the CIES and CESE, and the confluence of scholars at the international/world congresses helped galvanize the decision of groups of scholars to form a distinct society and become eligible members of the WCCES.

Hosting the World Congresses of Comparative Education Societies has also been, in various cases, a struggle for distinction to showcase a particular society's logistical capabilities and social capital, rather than to give evidence of the advanced level of growth of the field in that country. Such were the cases of congresses hosted in Japan, Korea, Southern Africa and Brazil, which managed to attract an international audience, but left little trace in the development of the field in their countries/region.

From a Foucauldian perspective, the historical contingencies underlying society formation and activity within the WCCES are worth noting. In the domain of society organisation, the formation of the CIES was catalysed by a simple event, as Sherman Swing (2007, p.95) recounts: "Although discussion of a formal organisation had antedated this meeting, the impetus for action was the discovery that group rates for study tours required a pre-existing group". Similarly, the birth of the CESHK was a fruit of a 'chance encounter'. According to Wong and Fairbrother (2007, p.245), in 1989 several academics from Hong Kong "bumped into each other" during a CIES conference and the fervour for some form of intellectual exchange in a comparative context led to the society's formation. The protagonist, Bernard Luk, CESHK's founding president, acknowledges the influence of possibly the first comparative educationist in the territory, Cheng Tung Choy, who studied at London Institute of Education.

In summary, in the previous two sections, I have developed the first part of my response to the question: Why is comparative education institutionalised as a distinct area of academic inquiry when its intellectual distinctiveness is or has become contested? I have argued that the academic institutionalisation of comparative education as a distinct subfield of educational studies is partly due to historically contingent discourses, and to the complex interplay of structure and agency. I have demonstrated that the institutionalisation of comparative education was not purely the outcome of intellectual pursuits but also of pragmatic and political reasons. In other words, institutionalisation does not necessarily follow cognitive criteria alone. A complex interplay of forces at the macro- and meso-structural level with micro-political interests of agents in the field, as well as the shaping force of contingent discourses intervene in the field's institutionalisation. I substantiated my claim by examining two main forms of institutionalisation of comparative education – as a distinct academic program at universities and as a distinct professional society – elucidating the underlying power struggles that accounted for their origin and development and illustrating discontinuities and divergences between the institutional and the intellectual. The institutional infrastructures somehow codify the subtle workings of power relations in shaping intellectual fields. Borrowing from Cowen (2000, p.341), the institutional forms of comparative education can be read as educational codings to understand the interaction of history, social structures and pedagogic identities of individuals, of domestic and international forces in the construction of comparative educations.

Conclusion

In this chapter, I have sought to understand the institutional construction of the field of comparative education by examining its institutional histories from the perspectives of Foucauldian and Bourdieuian conceptual frameworks on power-knowledge relations. I have presented a fairly global historical narrative of the field's institutionalisation at universities and in the form of professional societies, specialist books and journals for the period 1900 to 2008. This description revealed a very large institutional superstructure that has been built worldwide and an impressive volume of specialist literature accumulated during this past century.

In more recent decades, however, academic comparative education has become rather marginalised, and its revitalisation has been achieved mainly through its integration as a perspective in education studies. Furthermore, a 'meta-analysis' of the contours and contents of courses, journals, as well as of society demographics and perceptions of comparative education indicated that, despite the impressive institutional machinery, academic comparative education is extremely heterogeneous, extensively inclusive, and not explicitly comparative in content, membership or purposes. This diluted identity of comparative education plausibly reflects the diffuse nature of the field's object, which had widened in more recent decades. At the same time, the field's originally theoretical purpose also became linked and possibly overshadowed by its interventionist aims in conjunction with the development- and policy-oriented work of international and national educational agencies doing comparative education research. This is partly owing to the impact of discourses, including those by comparative education specialists, which serve to construct the field's boundaries and objects, or legitimise its links with sites of political or academic power. The recent advocacy of scholars like Crossley (2008) of a bridging between theoretical and practical purposes and traditions echoes earlier legitimising discourses by Holmes and E. King, as noted by Cowen (1982a).

The above findings have led me to raise questions about the relationship between institutional legitimacy and intellectual legitimacy. Cowen (1982a, p.108) posited a "reciprocal interaction between the intellectual and institutional forms of comparative educations". In the light of the institutional histories reviewed here, I would further affirm that both epistemological and sociological forms of power interact in dialectic fashion in constructing disciplinary fields. Applying Foucault's view on power-knowledge relations to the institutional histories portrayed here, I contend that, in this dynamic interaction of intellectual and institutional legitimacy or power, at least two possible combinations seem to lead to the creation of a field: first, when both intellectual and institutional legitimacy are strong (pole 1); and, second, when institutional legitimacy is strong, even if intellectual legitimacy is weak (pole 2). By contrast, when an area of knowledge has intellectual legitimacy but is unable to secure institutional power (pole 3), or when both intellectual and institutional legitimacies are weak or absent (pole 4), no new field comes to the fore. The histories of comparative education and the surveys of its contours seem to suggest that this field has been constructed initially on the basis of strong institutional power albeit weak intellectual legitimacy (pole 2). When institutional power is significantly withdrawn, the field's intellectual legitimacy becomes challenged and its weakness revealed.

The application of Bourdieu's intellectual field theory and Foucault's genealogical lenses to the analysis of the institutionalisation of comparative education, in the form of academic programmes and professional societies, has revealed some historical contingencies and pragmatic and political (at times, micro-political) interests underlying these formations. A distinct discursive formation had thus developed as a result of complex interactions among historically contingent discourses operating within diverse sociological structures and through the forces of human agency, whose struggles to compete for distinction within the intellectual field provide the very source of dynamism for the field's construction. Through the comparative analysis of historical narratives, I have demonstrated the complexities and discontinuities in the direction of influence and interplay between structure-agency and discourse on the institutional forms of comparative education. Thus, the institutional form of comparative education is not necessarily equivalent to or subservient to purely intellectual criteria. Complex sociological and discursive forces partly account for the divergence between the institutional and intellectual legitimacy of the field. In the next two chapters, I will focus on the intellectual shape and construction of comparative education. I first examine the intellectual histories of the field in the next chapter.

4
Intellectual Histories of Comparative Education

Introduction

Epstein (2008a, p.9) contends that two fundamental characteristics identify comparative education as an academic field. First, it rests on discernible and venerable epistemological platforms that have developed in the 19th century and that have defined its boundaries. Second, since the 20th century, it has had an expanding number of scholars, teachers, and practitioners who identify with and embody a collective consciousness about the venture. He further claims that the epistemological platforms serve as the foundations for identity formation and collective association, to the extent that without a grasp of the accepted ways of knowing educational reality in comparative education, delineating its boundaries through institutional or other means will be superficial. Thus, after having examined the institutional histories and contours of comparative education in Chapter 3, I now explore the intellectual histories of the field. A grasp of the intellectual origins of the field sets the framework for understanding its nature and intellectual shaping (García Garrido, 1996, p.25), a subject discussed in the next chapter.

My purpose in the present chapter is to delineate *an* intellectual history (and possibly histor*ies* rather than *the* history) of the field of comparative education starting from the 19th century to the present. I attempt to integrate an examination of comparative education's epistemological foundations with the take-up of correlative theoretical and disciplinary orientations. The chapter therefore contains a review of the literature on the epistemological roots, theoretical development, and thematic profiles of comparative education. For these sections, my main sources are Epstein (2008b), Paulston (1994) and Cowen (2003a), respectively. In a fourth section, I draw on my own research work, in addition to published literature, to present alternative histories to these earlier interpretations.

Epistemological Boundaries of Comparative Education

Epstein (2008a, p.9) argues that systematic comparative education studies rest on epistemological platforms or currents which define its bound-aries – "the 'visions', the foci, around which scholars could gather sys-tematiccally to study international issues of education and share their ideas and findings with others". He calls them 'epistemological bench-marks' to connote their normative feature in shaping the conceptual frameworks in the field. In a related work (2008b), Epstein contends that comparative education has three epistemological platforms – positivism, relativism and historical functionalism – each of which can be traced to three scholars of the 19th century: Marc-Antoine Jullien of France (1817), K.D. Ushinsky of Russia (1857), and Wilhelm Dilthey of Germany (1888), respectively.

In the first place, Epstein (2008b) positions *Jullien's positivism* as the founding epistemology. Epstein makes a distinction between a 'found-ing' and a 'beginning'. A beginning or antecedent, never precise in any field, refers to its initial seeds. A founding, by contrast, marks a single event, a defining moment by which a field becomes a professional (or systematic) field of study. For many scholars in the field starting with Brickman (1960, 1966), the publication of Marc-Antoine Jullien's *Esquisse et vues préliminaires d'un ouvrage sur l'éducation comparée* [Plan and Preliminary Views for a Work on Comparative Education] in 1817 marks the founding of comparative education as a field of study. The positivist approach that Jullien ushered in is therefore the founding epistemology, according to Epstein, the first epistemological platform of comparative education. Positivism (or scientism) is the philosophy which explains the physical facts by themselves, verifiable through observation. According to Auguste Comte (1830, cited by Epstein, 2008b), positivism views phenomena as subject to invariable laws. Jullien, who was ahead of Comte by more than a decade, proposed a systematic observation of educational phenomena in order to discover law-like principles (a nomothetic approach) to improve public systems of education. As Jullien states in his *Esquisse* (cited in Palmer, 1993, p.171):

> Education, like all other arts and sciences, is composed of facts and observations. It thus seems necessary to produce for this science, as has been done for other branches of knowledge, collections of facts and observations arranged in analytical tables, so that these facts and observations can be compared and certain principles and definite rules deduced from them, so that education may become an almost positive science…

To this end, Jullien designed tables with six main categories of education and a questionnaire in two series: "A" for elementary education (120 questions) and "B" for secondary education (146 questions) (Palmer, 1993, p.171). The questionnaire, however, was never implemented and was soon forgotten. It left hardly a trace in the education literature of the time, until its 're-discovery' in the 1940s by Ferenc Kamény, who donated it in 1935 to the International Bureau of Education in Geneva, where Pedro Roselló brought it to international fame through its publication in 1943 and 1962, respectively.

García Garrido (1996, pp.32-35) contends that Jullien's *Esquisse* was not a theoretical piece on the application of the comparative method to education, nor was it laying the foundation of a systematic new science called 'comparative education'. It was a practical schema, a preliminary report, a working proposal to set up under the protection of sovereign states a Special Commission on Education tasked with collecting data about the institutions and methods of education in different European states and comparing them. National educational data was to be collated and juxtaposed in tables in order to discern trends and rank their performance, as well as determine their underlying causes and identify what best practices might be transferred to other countries. But Jullien's work gave a scientific (in its systematic study of causes) and practical characteristic to comparative education and endowed it with epistemological autonomy: it now had a proper object and method (positivist) of study, and a practical purpose of informing and reforming education. It gave a clear, empirical, *positivist* orientation to the science of education in general and to comparative education in particular. García Garrido, however, disagrees with those who designate Jullien as the 'father' or 'founder' of comparative education (1996, pp.36-37). He claims that the title, 'pioneer', of a scientific field should be reserved for those who have truly initiated such an undertaking with tenacity and with the clear consciousness of their foundational role. This was not the case with Jullien, who neither fought for his cause nor sought out some few disciples. After 1817, Jullien got absorbed with other endeavours, including running for election to the Chamber of Deputies and taking part in founding a journal, *Le Constitutionnel*, a major organ of liberal thinking (Palmer, 1993, pp.173-174). His *Esquisse* was forgotten until its 'rediscovery' a century later. Thus García Garrido tends to consider Jullien a forerunner not so much of comparative education in general (or of modern comparative education, according to Noah and Eckstein [1969, p.15]), but of a particular stream within the field: the positivist stream, as Epstein suggests (1983, p.27). This is of no small merit on the part of Jullien, who was ahead of the times in terms of positivist thought. In any case, Jullien's positivist platform gained dominance in the field in the 1950s and 1960s, particularly in North America (e.g., Anderson, 1961; Noah & Eckstein, 1969), and gained further prominence in the International Evaluation of Educational Achievement (IEA) studies (Husén, 1967).

Epstein's second epistemological platform for the field is *relativism* (2008b). It succeeds positivism, but does not surpass it, and continues on a parallel line in juxtaposition with positivism. This form of relativism, which embodied the concept of 'national character', became dominant around the second half of the 19th century. K.D. Ushinsky of Russia and Michael Sadler of England are both noteworthy authors of this relativist epistemology in comparative education. Ushinsky's essay, entitled *On National Character of Public Education* (1857), and Sadler's conference address (1900), *How far can we learn anything of practical value from the study of foreign systems of education?*, are both regarded as paradigmatic texts. Both authors professed an ideographic approach to the study of education systems, emphasising their 'national character'. Education was inextricably bound to its social and cultural context, and knowledge derived from its study was not transferable to other contexts. Sadler's advance from Ushinsky, Epstein continues, lies in his proposal of 'understanding in a sympathetic spirit' a foreign system of education in order to understand more deeply our own education (2008b). Key representatives of relativist 'national character' approaches in comparative education include Mallinson (1957), E. King (1968), and Masemann (1990).

A third epistemological platform, according to Epstein, is *historical functionalism*, which presents in comparative education a synthesis of positivism and relativism, and is attributable to the late 19th century German historian and philosopher, Wilhelm Dilthey (although he himself denied that he was a historical relativist). Both Friedrich Schneider (1961a; 1961b) and Isaac Kandel (1933; 1955a) ushered in this platform in comparative education, taking inspiration from Dilthey (see Epstein, 2008b). Epstein defines historical functionalism as a fusion of (relativistic) history and (positivistic) macro-sociology. It examines education as "interrelated with other social and political institutions; and it can best be understood if examined in its social context" (Kazamias & Massialas, 1982, p.309). Epstein explains that this inextricable relation between education and other social institutions, viewed from a macro-sociological perspective (e.g., Archer, 1979) exhibits universally general-isable features, or "composition laws" (2008b, p.9). But, historical func-tionalists would argue that such positivist laws governing education can best be understood within their historical (and therefore relativist) context. Epstein thus contends that historical functionalist epistemology in comparative education synthesises positivist cross-national generalis-ation – to show the universality of theories about education –, relativist in-depth understanding of 'national character' and the mutual influence between education and its socio-historical context.

This approach diverges from histories that portray comparative education in evolutionary and incremental development along stages or phases (such as Noah & Eckstein, 1969; Phillips & Schweisfurth, 2006). These other histories, Epstein claims, elide the importance of episte-mological currents underlying the field's intellectual development. Instead he posits that comparative education has "not evolved as a unitary field but as a loose unity of separate though thriving currents" (1983, p.28). More recently, he contends that the field "has developed along parallel lines, not by one stage eclipsing another but by the positioning of conceptual frameworks in juxtaposition and in tension with one another" (2008b). Thus, Jullien's positivist approach endures alongside Ushinsky's relativist methods as well as Dilthey's historical functionalism. These normative epistemological benchmarks all offer a framework for generalisation, but they view reality through different lenses and thus lead to different approaches.

Theoretical and Methodological Currents in Comparative Education

Epstein (2008b) convincingly demonstrates the epistemological roots of comparative education reaching back to the 19th century. To this article, Paulston (2004, p.1) would have reiterated his criticism of earlier works of Epstein (2001; Carroll & Epstein, 2001) as an "attempt to police com-parative education discourse using an exclusive canon of supposedly foundational texts ..., [contending that such] an orthodox canonical perspective advocates the need for a closed linear logic of either-or patriarchal binaries" (also Paulston, 1994, p.927). This contestation between Epstein and Paulston is an example of the dynamic construction of the intellectual field through the discursive interaction between opposing positions within the field, as Bourdieu conceives it. Although I disagree with Paulston's indictment of Epstein's position as a closed linearity, I find that Paulston adequately accounts for the theories and paradigms that have branched out from the three root epistemologies that Epstein identified and their dynamic interrelationships. Epstein recognises this, but he immediately follows with a detailed critique of the epistemological weaknesses of Paulston's phenomenological approach as a form of extreme relativism and of his cartography as a rigid reification and distortion of the intellectual platforms it categorises (Epstein & Carroll, 2005, p.81). With a like mind, I consider Paulston's work here with an explicit expression of disagreement with his ultra-relativist and non-essentialist epistemological position. Concretely, I do not share the subjectivist view of some postmodern thinkers. In this, I echo Epstein and Carroll's critique of 'cartography' proponents and postmodern writers who claim that reality is reducible to "language inventions and mental representations ... [and that] all concepts and the conceptualising process itself [are] fluid and unknowable" (2005, pp.69-70). What I take from Paulston's work are the dominant root paradigms and their branching theories as they become salient in particular historical periods. What Paulston and other scholars (who do not explicitly subscribe to Paulston's mapping assumptions, e.g., Kubow and Fossum, 2003) contribute in a complementary way to Epstein's tri-lineal epistemological benchmarks are the dimensions of structure-agency, macro-micro, and society-individual, and how these relate to stability and change, and to consensus and conflict (functionalism and humanism and their opposite radical/critical forms). They trace the take-up of grand social theories in comparative education, and within these grand theories, of such mid-range theories as modernisation, human capital theory, and so on. I briefly introduce these theories before proceeding to describe their impact on comparative education.

Shifts in Philosophical and Sociological Worldviews

Kubow and Fossum (2003, pp.27-28) distinguish between grand social theories that seek to describe broad human and social phenomena, and middle-range theories which apply these broader theoretical assumptions and propel more context-specific attempts to organise thought and action. Both these theoretical frameworks, originating mainly from sociology and philosophy, have an influence in the intellectual shaping of comparative education. A further major classification is between modernist and postmodernist perspectives. From a modernist perspective, a subsequent grouping encompasses two grand social theories: structural functionalism (or functionalism) and Marxist conflict theory.

Prior to the 1970s, a modernist view of the world and of knowledge of the world prevailed. This perspective views knowledge as inherently progressive and linear in time; it was certain, rational, objective, autonomous, and oriented towards a search for the universal truth (Grenz, 1996). But the publication in 1979 of Jean-François Lyotard's *The Postmodern Condition* marked a new epistemological challenge. The postmodernist turn in the 1970s introduced social constructivist, anti-essentialist and counter-ontological theories. A postmodernist perspective might be said to reject any single universal worldview and instead to celebrate difference and localisation; reason and knowledge are held suspect; knowledge is understood primarily as historically and culturally conditioned; truth and reality are relative; and time is not linear but discontinuous (Grenz, 1996).

In parallel with these epistemological shifts (and perhaps informed by them) were transformations in the dominant worldviews prevalent in the social sciences, which were functionalist theory, Marxian-inspired conflict theories, and interpretivist theories. The debates in these social theories oscillate between structural determinacy and individual agency.

Functionalist theory explains social phenomena in terms of their contribution to the operations of a larger social phenomenon, institution, or society. Educational institutions and their various organisational components thus evolve in response to or as a function of the needs of the larger society. Metaphorically, it typically compares society to a biological organism or system made up of many interdependent and co-operative parts. School is viewed as an 'organ' of society (Feinberg & Soltis, 2004). Functionalism views society optimistically as a unitary system that seeks shared norms and values, and assumes that consensus and equilibrium are preferred states. Functionalist theory rests on the Enlightenment's elevated view of human rationality, as depicted by the modernist outlook described above. Functionalism was at its zenith in the 1960s and 1970s until it was challenged by the conflict and inter-actionist theories at the turn of the 70s (Turner & Mitchell, 1997).

Conflict theory underscores the effects of educational (macro) structures on maintaining social inequality and stratification. It takes at least two principal forms: Neo-Marxist conflict theory and Neo-Weberian conflict theory. They differ as to the degree to which school structures and processes correspond to, reflect, or reproduce the relations of production. While Marxian-inspired conflict theory assumes a relatively tight connection between substructure and superstructure, neo-Weberian theorists view class as a multidimensional phenomenon involving more than relations of production. In the latter, boundaries separating status groups are more permeable and less enduring than Marx's social classes (Turner & Mitchell, 1997).

The *Marxist conflict theories* emphasise the role of structure, primarily economic structure, as the overall explanatory framework for society. This means that educational institutions and knowledge are viewed as sites either for the maintenance of existing power relations or of resistance to them. School is considered as an 'instrument' of class domination (Feinberg & Soltis, 2004). Marxist theory, unlike functionalism, questions the authenticity of assumed consensus and the very possibility of authentic consensus, and asserts that conflict, rather than equilibrium, is the overriding catalyst for social change (Kubow & Fossum, 2003, p.28).

Weberian-inspired *interpretivist theory* offers an alternative explanation to mechanistic and deterministic models found in certain forms of Marxian and functionalist theories. It focuses on the role of human agency, particularly on the observation and theoretical interpretation of the subjective 'states of mind' of human actors. Interpretivist theory sees the social world as made up of purposeful actors who acquire, share, and interpret a set of meanings, rules, and norms that make social interaction possible. The social forces at work are shared meanings and interpreting individuals who interact in particular social contexts (Feinberg & Soltis, 2004).

Theoretical Shifts in Comparative Education

These shifts in philosophical and sociological worldviews had their echo in comparative education, but with some time lag (Paulston, 1994). Paulston posits three major periods in the field's intellectual history: *orthodoxy* of functionalism and positivism in the 1950s and 1960s; *heterodoxy* among functionalism, humanism and their respective radical counterparts during the 1970s and 1980s; and *heterogeneity* since the 1990s, with the acceptance of the complementarity of different paradigms and their eclectic intertwining (p.923). Paulston arrived at this classification of changing representations of knowledge by means of textual analysis and interpretation. His classification may be questionable on the grounds of the representativeness of the literature he surveyed and of the objectivity of his textual interpretation and classification of those works, but his framework will suffice as a working schema subject to verification and elaboration. I reproduce in Table 4.1 two columns (root paradigms and branching 'theories') of his table of a heuristic taxonomy of knowledge perspectives in comparative and international education texts, and insert three domains – epistemology, orientation, foci – taken from his macro-mapping of these paradigms.

Table 4.1 Paulston's Taxonomy of Root Paradigms and Branching Theories in Comparative Education

Epistemology	Orientation	Foci	Root paradigms/ world views	Branching 'theories'
Realist-objectivist	Equilibrium	Structure	Functionalist 1950-60s orthodoxy	Modernisation / human capital
				Neofunctionalist
				Rational choice / micro-macro
				Conflict theory
				Dependency
	Transformation		Radical Functionalist 1970s heterodoxy	Historical materialist
				Neo-Marxist / post-Marxist
				Cultural rationalisation
Idealist-subjectivist	Equilibrium	Agency	Humanist 1970s heterodoxy	Ethnographic / ethnological
				Phenomenographic / ethnomethodological
	Transformation		Radical Humanist 1980s heterodoxy	Critical theory / critical ethnography
				Feminist (1990s-)
				Poststructuralist / postmodernist
				Pragmatic interactionist

Source: Extracted from Tables and Figures in Paulston (1994), pp.924, 928, 931.

Note: Regarding the 'foci' column, Paulston did not use the terms 'structure' and 'agency'. Rather he used 'structure and society' and 'consciousness and culture'.

According to Paulston (1994), the period of the *1950s and 1960s* witnessed the dominance of positivist and *functionalist* paradigms in comparative education, particularly in North America, increasingly influenced by approaches from the social and the natural sciences in pursuit of law-like cross-national generalisations (e.g., Anderson, 1961; Husén, 1967; Noah & Eckstein, 1969). Bereday (1964) diverged in his advocacy of an inductive non-social science comparative methodology, though still within a positivist framework. In the late 1960s educational planning and development aid to newly independent countries gained ascendancy in some countries. In this, both modernisation and human capital theories thrived as mid-range applications of functionalism's assumptions regarding consensus and stability, in their attempt to explain issues of change and development. Modernisation theory assumes strong causal linkages between processes of modernisation and national development (e.g., Fägerlind & Saha, 1989). It prescribes the education of individuals in desired values, attitudes and behaviours of 'modern' persons as a necessary means to achieve societal progress. Human capital theory, from economics, likewise assumes a direct and functional relationship between education and development. It assumes a causal relationship between investment and education within a func-tional and harmonious society, and elaborates econometric methods with formulae and calculations of returns on investment (e.g., Schultz, 1963; Psacharopoulos, 1973).

By the *early 1970s*, functionalism's dominance was receding, when conflict and interactionist theories challenged the adequacy of functional analysis (Turner & Mitchell, 1997). Paulston (1994) groups neo-Weberian conflict theory and dependency theory under functionalism, but classifies Marxist-inspired conflict theory (e.g., neo-Marxist, post-Marxist, historical materialist positions) under *radical functionalism*. I, however, disagree with Paulston's classification of conflict and dependency theories under functionalism, since functionalism views institutions in a harmonious and organic cooperation. By contrast, conflict theories critique these institutions as engaged in a conflict over limited resources and as agents of reproduction of social inequalities. In this respect, I agree with Gottlieb (2000) who diverges from Paulston's taxonomy, and instead classifies such theories – conflict, dependency, and Marxist-inspired – under *radical structuralism*. This position views education as part of the structure of dominance by the state and the economy. According to Gottlieb (2000, p.162), examples of this genre of work in comparative education include Carnoy (1974), Altbach (1977) and Arnove (1980). Paulston (1994) suggests that American neo-Marxists tended to focus on the macro-sociological conflict approach, while their British counterparts (e.g., Bernstein, 1977) focused on microsociological interpretivist studies.

This relates to interactionist theory, another counter-orthodox attack on functionalism, which began between the late 1940s and the 1970s outside of comparative education (e.g., Saussure, 1949; Levi-Strauss, 1953; Young, 1971). Interactionism focuses on meso and micro level analysis of individual behaviour within educational settings. Paulston labels this the *'humanist'* paradigm and highlights the important work of Berger and Luckmann (1966), *The Social Construction of Reality*, as a foundational text introducing a humanist and subjectivist orientation to knowledge. Berger and Luckmann's early form of social constructionism posits that the social world external to individual actors is created through intersubjectively constituted meanings and everyday practical activities, which, as they become habitual, become 'objectivated' as our taken-for-granted reality: they are real because we define them as such and can, through habit and history, become institutionalised. Berger and Luckmann do not deny that there is an objective world, but argue that that reality is *realised* through human activity. Gottlieb maintains that, strictly speaking, no (albeit little) comparative work is done within the interpretive paradigm, since "the interpretivist seeks to understand how the actors of a culture experience and understand their own social world" (2000, p.164), and not to theorise using transcultural categories. However, Paulston (1994, pp.926-927) gives some examples of para-digmatic texts advocating the humanist perspective in comparative education, including Heyman (1979), who argued for ethnographic and ethnomethodological approaches, and Clignet (1981). Paulston also cites the ethnographic research of Avalos (1986) and Gibson and Ogbu (1991). A more recent work is done by Mehta (2003).

By the *early 1980s*, a more humanistic Marxism, or *radical humanism* (Paulston, 1994, p.926), emerging from the intellectual movement of critical theory, began to gain a presence in comparative education. Gottlieb describes radical humanism as the positioning of a state of 'full humanity' as a point of departure for critiquing the present state of education as a state of alienation (2000, p.164). By way of background, critical theory traces its roots in the Frankfurt School (1930s) as a renewal of Marxism. Habermas led a second generation of critical theorists in the 1960s. By 'critical', he meant the unmasking of the illegitimate intrusion of (ideological) science into the realm of social norms (Lakomski, 1997). At that time, traditional theory (which critical theory meant to critique) sought knowledge about social phenomena in the form of law-like explanatory generalisations modelled after the natural sciences. By contrast, critical theory considers the social and historical conditions of knowledge. It critically examines how categories and ideas emerge from and support the social order. Habermas's *Knowledge and Human Interests* (1978) is a form of critical theory that offers a higher order synthesis to critique positivism as reductionist and interpretivism as relativist. Habermas addressed these deficiencies by allocating the empirical-analytical (natural sciences) and the historical-hermeneutic sciences to their own, mutually exclusive, object domains endowed with their respective methodologies. A third order of knowledge, the critical sciences, is guided by the goal of social emancipation (Lakomski, 1997). Gottlieb (2000, p.164) suggests that Freire's *Education for Critical Consciousness* (1973) served as a paradigmatic text of consciousness-raising among comparative educators about the oppressive conditions of education among poor populations. Paulston (1994, p.929) lists a few prominent American comparativists who projected a radical humanist perspective (e.g., Kelly & Nihlen, 1982; Stromquist, 1989). Alternative approaches to critical theory are represented by Pierre Bourdieu and Michel Foucault. Bourdieu elaborated a self-reflexive theory of the reproduction of social inequalities in different social fields (Austin Harrington & Marshall, 2006). With Foucault, interpretivist theories, such as social constructionism, take on a linguistic turn in the 1970s, focusing on *power-discourse* relations, which produce reason, the subject, and well-ordered societies. Poststructuralist forms of social constructionism replace the 'objective world' anterior to discourse with the regular formation of objects that emerge *only* in discourse (Foucault, 1972, p.47). Poststructuralist and postmodernist perspectives started to gain attention in the comparative education literature in the 1990s, as documented by Ninnes and Burnett (2003). Among the early examples of texts of this genre identified by Paulston (1994, p.930) are Cherryholmes (1988) and Rust (1991).

Thus, Paulston characterises the intellectual shape of comparative education by the *late 1980s and in the 1990s* as veering away from heterodoxy to a new stage of heterogeneity, mirroring the pervading air of scepticism of grand theories and paradigms in the social sciences, partly brought about by postmodernism. A parallel shift of interest from macro-structural studies to micro-agency interpretative analyses is noticeable in the literature in the 1990s (Paulston, 1994, p.928). While functionalist theory-based studies remain, Paulston notes that neo-functionalist versions manifest an openness to hermeneutic and interpretivist perspectives (e.g., Adams, 1988), and the adoption of rational choice theory (e.g., Turner, 1987). Radical functionalist (radical structuralist) theories have also shifted towards a less deterministic neo-Marxist or post-Marxist stance, particularly after the collapse of communism in 1989 in Eastern Europe (e.g., Carnoy & Samoff, 1990). With respect to the humanist interpretivist paradigm, Paulston points to the emergence of phenomenographic studies in comparative education in the form of conceptual maps based on textual analysis (e.g., Paulston,

1993; 1996). These aim to "characterise how researchers see, apprehend, and think about knowledge constructs such as 'paradigms and theories' at different times and in different knowledge cultures and subcultures" (Paulston, 1994, p.932). Rather than a mapping of things 'as they are', phenomenographic analyses – like that of Paulston's map – present ways of thinking about the world.

At the *turn of the 21ˢᵗ century*, an increasing intertwining of paradigms, disciplinary approaches, macro and micro levels of analysis, quantitative and qualitative methodologies, theory and praxis, is being advocated by comparativists and is gaining salience in the literature. Rather than viewing positions as dualist, dichotomous and disputatious 'either-or' statements, there is a noticeable shift towards viewing positions as decentred and located along a continuum allowing for varying degrees of interaction between two polarities. Probably one paradigmatic text is Crossley's *Bridging Cultures and Traditions in the Reconceptualisation of Comparative and International Education* (2000).

Dominant Themes of Comparative Education

In the previous sections of this chapter I considered the work of Epstein (2008b), which demonstrated the root epistemological platforms of comparative education, and of Paulston (1994), who elucidated the dynamic interrelationships among the dominant theories and perspectives that have characterised the field. What is missing from these discussions is a typological classification of the 'over-arching' or paradigmatic themes that have attracted comparative educators over time. Noah and Eckstein (1969), Ferrer (2002), Crossley and Watson (2003), Cowen (2003a), and Phillips and Schweisfurth (2006), offer diverse readings of the field's history. Cowen's schematic overview of dominant themes in the field serves as a useful means to pull together the various aspects of the field's intellectual history discussed in this chapter. I consider it in the first place, and afterwards review alternative readings.

Cowen's Paradigmatic Themes

Cowen (2003a, pp.6-7) defines 'paradigmatic issues' as having three features:

- a specific *agenda of attention* which delimits the social (dimension), defines some educative process as more important than others, and details a choice among the many possible relations of the social and the educational which might be analysed;

- a *mega-unit of comparative analysis*; and
- an attraction of major bodies of *substantive comparative description*.

He then posits four paradigmatic themes which have produced a sub-stantive discourse within comparative education. These are Sadler, the Chicago/New York Schools, Development Discourse, and Trends. I summarise the main points in Table 4.2.

The dominant position in the 1960s of what Cowen termed the 'Chicago/New York Schools' to refer to the salience of the empirical social sciences in comparative education eclipsed much of the valuable historical-culturalist and interpretive work in the 1930s to 1950s. To cite Cowen (1996, p.152):

> [A]lternative traditions available in the literature were rejected, bypassed and marginalised. Thus the work of Hans and Schneider, drawing centrally on history, was not refuted: it was merely avoided in the search for a relevant science. Similarly, the culturalist motif in the work of Ulich (1964), Lauwerys (1967), Nash et al. (1965), Halls (1973), Mallinson (1975), and King (1979), became overwhelmed by the search for scientific rigour and precision. The dominant paradigm, for research, became positivist economics and positivist sociology, particularly in the USA.

Phillips and Schweisfurth (2006, p.93) echo this observation by Cowen. Concretely, they critique Gottlieb's (2000, p.155) dismissal of valuable historical approaches in the tradition of Kandel and Hans, describing them as "simplistic, subjective and totalistic".

These critiques of the marginalisation of alternative disciplinary traditions can be extended to the eclipsing of alternative disciplinary histories of comparative education. Cowen himself acknowledges this (1990, 2002), pointing out that these histories are not universal enough and do not offer any sustained analysis of the "theoretical *Gestalt* (unmistakable form) of comparative education" (2002, p.414). Crossley and Watson (2003, p.76) echo this critique about the deficiency, from a cross-cultural perspective, of generic Western phases that claim to represent the global history of the field. These authors also point to the limitations of such historical periodisations in oversimplifying reality. Crossley and Watson (2003, p.21), in their use of Brickman's (1966) four historical phases of comparative education, point out that these types of demarcations mask the fact that these phases are "not necessarily linear

Table 4.2 Paradigmatic Themes in Comparative Education (Cowen, 2003a)

	Sadler	Chicago & New York Schools	Development Discourse	Trends
Paradigmatic text(s)	Sadler (1900)	Convergence strand: Halsey et al. (1965); Anderson & Bowman (1966)	Arnove (1980) Carnoy (1974) Altbach & Kelly (1978)	Jullien (1817) Rosselló (1960)[d]
		Control strand: Noah & Eckstein (1969)		
Agenda of attention	*Impalpable forces*: - historical, culturalist - national character	*Economy, education and society* Convergence: economic world (modernisation and human capital) and selective functions of educational systems	*Education and development*: neo-Marxist dependency theory - social inequalities - subordinated identities in educational processes - feminist and anthropological interpretations -postcolonialism, gender and race	*Educational trends*
		Control and science: quantitative analysis		
Mega-unit of Comparison	Society-nations	Convergence: technological imperative	World-system in neo-Marxist terms	Educational trends (also)
		Control: educational outcomes		
Substantive discourse	Academic, university-based: e.g., Kandel, (1933) & Hans (1950)[a]; Schneider (1964)[b]; Lauwerys (1965)[c]; Mallinson (1957); E. King (1968)	Policy-useful knowledge about educational efficiency:	Emancipatory and positional knowledge: e.g., Burns & Welch (1992)	Policy-useful information for educational amelioration: World Bank and International Bureau of Education (IBE) educational statistics reports. e.g., Cowen, 1982b; World Bank (1995)
		Convergence: Inkeles & Smith (1974)		
		Control: IEA studies		

Notes: Ferrer (2002, pp.33-36) further classifies this historical interpretive paradigm into three branches: [a]interpretive-historical; [b]interpretive-anthropological; and [c]interpretive-philosophical. Ferrer also cited some typical authors whom Cowen did not cite, e.g., Kandel (1933) and Schneider (1964). [d]Cowen mentioned that Rosselló raised this issue in 1920, but did not give the full reference. I thus make reference to Rosselló's 1960 work.

or consistent across time, cultures or individuals". A similar critique could apply to Phillips and Schweisfurth's model of historical emphases in comparative analysis (2006, p.28). Building on Noah and Eckstein's (1969) five developmental stages of comparative education, Phillips and Schweisfurth propose a sequential chain of seven lines of historical emphases in comparative analysis, each of which begins at a defined historical point and continues alongside already existing emphases, interacting with them. While such frameworks are useful for a broad understanding of shifts in intellectual thought, Foucauldian perspectives point out their limitations in projecting a linear, smooth, unidirectional, and apparently universal historical progress. This leads to the importance of exploring 'other' intellectual histories of comparative education.

Alternative Intellectual Histories of Comparative Education

In this section, I attempt to highlight the 'other' histories that challenge the dominant discourses on the intellectual history of comparative education, as discussed above. I limit myself to the discourse constellations starting in the 20th century. To cite Crossley and Watson (2003, p.140), comparative education is perhaps best visualised as a "creative, and multi-disciplinary, constellation of fields", or what Cowen (1990, p.333) termed as comparative education*s*. I draw on Cowen's thesis that: a strongly visible discontinuity in the literature [Kuhn's paradigmatic shift] only results when a *combination* of the internal reading of *episteme* (advocacy of a disciplinary form) and an external reading of *kosmos* (a specific global time-space social world) makes sense to a generation of scholars in a particular place (2003b, p.301). Cowen has probably applied these lenses to a Western reading of comparative education*s* in a Western world (e.g., 1996, 2000, 2002). But, as Schriewer (2003, p.279) contends, significant differences are manifest not only between diverse linguistic discourse communities (e.g., Chinese, Spanish, Russian), but also within each of these discourse constellations, influenced by radical transformations in their political systems and dominant ideologies. These diverse constellations are not only separated from each other by linguistic barriers, but also by structural walls of a political, ideological, disciplinary, and economic nature. This echoes Foucault's concept of a discursive formation which enables and constrains what can be said or thought about within a particular episteme or historical period. Likewise, from a Bourdieuian perspective, it can be said that these discursive constellations were operating within distinct epistemes given the distinct structural constraints within which agents (comparativists) could work in the intellectual field of comparative education. One could thus visualise communities of scholars excluded from the opposing discourses mapped by Paulston (1994) during the period of heterodoxy in the 1970s and 1980s, as if they were 'onlookers to a boxing match' between functionalists and their radical critiques, or even left unaware that such contestations were taking place.

To a certain extent, the work of documenting a global history and inventory of comparative education was accomplished by Halls (1990a). This edited volume features regional reports on Western Europe (Holmes), Socialist countries (Hofmann & Malkova), North America (Lawson), Latin America (Oliveros), Asia and the Pacific (Kobayashi; Burns), Africa (Fafunwa), and the Arab states (Benhamida). But, the socio-political world has dramatically changed since. One major geopolitical change is the collapse of communism and the end of the Cold War in 1989. Thus, a case in point is a chapter in that book on the Socialist countries (Hofmann & Malkova, 1990), which depicts mainly the situation of the field in the Soviet Union as a whole, while the 'individual voices' of Soviet-occupied countries are 'silenced'. Here I attempt to further widen and update the discourse, applying Cowen's 'doubled-reading' lenses to a more national/local reading of comparative educations by national/local voices of comparativists speaking about their own local history. In this I employ both published literature, including work I had directly participated in as a co-editor of two volumes on the histories of the field (Masemann, Bray & Manzon, 2007; Wolhuter, Popov, Manzon & Leutwyler, 2008a) and interviews conducted with comparative education scholars who served as leaders of the professional societies of comparative education around the world.

Mainland China

Bray (2001b) contrasts the representation of the history of the field of comparative education in Noah and Eckstein's (1998) *Doing Comparative Education: Three Decades of Collaboration* and Gu Mingyuan's (2001a) *Education in China and Abroad: Perspectives from a Lifetime in Comparative Education*. Noah and Eckstein's work spanned the period of the 1960s to the 1990s, based mainly within an industrialised North America and, for the most part, within the political context of the Cold War. This is also the main context within which the Western writers cited above, particularly Epstein (2008b), Cowen (2003a) and Paulston (1994), traced the 'global' intellectual history of comparative education. Noah and Eckstein, and other Anglo-American scholars in the 1950s and the 1960s, appeared to be absorbed by methodological debates about a positivist science of comparative education, and to be oriented to the industrialised world (see also Bray, 2007c, p.352; Bray & Gui, 2001), and if they focused on the 'developing' world it was to offer educational prescriptions to achieve national development. As described in Chapter 3, this was partly fuelled by the work of national and international organisations in the industrialised countries, who offered development assistance to poorer countries, influenced by modernisation and human capital theories. By contrast, Gu was beginning his university studies in a communist world that operated in the framework of Marxist-Leninist ideology. The 1949 Communist revolution saw the abolition of comparative education as a field of study in China (as it was in many countries under the Soviet bloc, only to be later resumed during the Open Door Policy since 1979. Moving on to the period of the 1960s to the 1970s, which Paulston characterised as the stage of heterodoxy in his 'global map', functionalism and the consequent dominance of the empirical social sciences were challenged by radical structuralist and interpretivist theories. The development discourse was on the rise, where neo-Marxist theorists critiqued functionalist-oriented theories and capitalist economies for the inequalities in the world system. Anglo-American scholarly literature projected a sense of crisis in the field. By contrast, the 1980s witnessed a renaissance of comparative education in China. In 1986, for example, Gu underscored that the "ultimate aim" of comparative education research in China "is to promote educational development and reform in our own country" (2001b, p.221), and that "we should not conduct research for research's sake". He further elaborated on the research methodology:

> We should adopt a positive attitude towards the application of natural sciences' research methodology in comparative education research. We should seriously consider how to analyse contemporary educational phenomena in a scientific and effective manner.... However, we have to emphasise here that no matter which method we employ, we must not abandon the most basic research methodology – the Marxist-Leninist tenets (pp.224-225).

A later article by Gu explicates the workings of Marxist ideology in Chinese comparative education research: "The educational system of a country cannot be detached from its political economy and cultural traditions ... the deepest level is the ideology.... [I]deology belongs to the domain of the superstructure, and it reflects the economic foundation and political climate. ... If we ignore this aspect (ideology), the research will definitely be superficial" (2001c, p.233). In the same year, he urged Chinese comparativists to break away from Eurocentric research methodologies and to construct a comparative education with Chinese characteristics that rest on the socialist doctrines of Karl Marx and Mao Zedong as its methodological foundations (Gu, 2001d, p.242). A decade later, and in view of the changing political climate in China, allusions to Marxist and Maoist doctrines were less overt in the work of Chinese scholars (see e.g., Gu, 2003).

These rather lengthy citations of Gu Mingyuan, one of the leading figures of comparative education in China, are to make the point that the historical phases of paradigmatic changes in comparative education represented for example by Paulston's 'global map' (1994) do not match the picture of global reality. Comparative education in China is a case in point. Thus, while post-World War II depictions of the field portrayed a 'scientific' comparative education, the field of study was so to speak 'dead' in China. And, when the dominance of the empirical social sciences in comparative education was critiqued and partly eroded in the Anglo-American discourse, it is in that same and succeeding decade advocated in the field in China, but within a Marxist framework. In this respect, there is some convergence between the radical functionalism (or radical structuralism) identified by Paulston in the 1970s and 1980s with the mainstream epistemology in China. For comparative educationists based in a 'capitalist' context, a (neo)Marxist framework was one of several frameworks in an epistemologically pluralistic world, but in China, Marxist epistemology was *the* epistemology. In Foucauldian terms, it was the discursive formation operating within that episteme. A further divergence is that, while theoretical and methodological debates have absorbed the energies of scholars in North America, parts of Europe, Australia and Canada, theoretical pursuits were of lesser importance to Chinese counterparts whose main aim, at that time, was research for educational development and reform in their home country. Zhao (2005), echoing Gu (2003), contends that Anglo-American comparative educa-tion research serves an academic purpose, while Chinese comparative education research is for application. This, however, was not the case in nearby Chinese societies as in Hong Kong and Taiwan, where a theoretical and academic thrust developed alongside applied work (see

Bray & Gui, 2001; Manzon, 2008a, pp.214-215).

Socialist Eastern Europe

Hofmann and Malkova (1990) explained the role and state of comparative education in the Socialist countries forming the then Union of Soviet Socialist Republics (USSR). Almost two decades have passed since the political shifts in 1989 and the break-up of the Soviet Union. My work thus draws on more recent literature (Wolhuter et al., 2008a; Masemann et al., 2007) on the histories of comparative education in some countries formerly comprising the Soviet bloc. In these two recent volumes, various chapters are dedicated to the now independent countries formerly under Soviet occupation (e.g., Bulgaria, Czech Republic, Hungary, Kazakhstan, Poland), aside from Russia and united Germany (then divided between East and West).

The period of the 1940s witnessed the annexation of parts of Eastern Europe by the Soviet regime. This curtailed the existing comparative education activity in the Soviet-occupied countries. As Manzon and Bray (2007, p.346) observe, this disruptive political context muted comparative work in Bulgaria, Czechoslovakia, East Germany, Hungary, Poland, and Russia. The 1930s witnessed the rise of the totalitarian regime in the USSR, and the designation of Leninism as the only epistemological foundation for all sciences (Borevskaya, 2007, p.300). In Bulgaria, Popov commented, the "second half of the 1940s and the 1950s were the darkest years. The slightest interest in education in Western countries was considered a provocation and potentially even a crime" (2007, p.271). For the then Czechoslovakia, similar disruptive process took place in 1968 which witnessed the censure of leading members of its professional comparative education society after their public criticism of the prevailing ideology (Walterová, 2007, p.261).

A commonality among these countries was epistemological monism under a Marxist-Leninist ideology. To cite Walterová:

> The political bipolarity of the world was reflected in 'socialist education' from the 1950s through the 1980s: a strong and uncritical orientation to the East and overestimation of Soviet education, and one-sided criticism of Western education. An epistemological unification under the ideological umbrella of Marxism-Leninism did not permit the development of objective and methodologically transparent comparative research (2007, p.257).

Thus, the world behind the Iron Curtain was spared the active methodological and theoretical debates that besieged their Western counterparts. In this, comparative education in a large part of Europe was more similar to China, than it was to European and North American counterparts.

South America

As discussed in Chapter 3, political events in the form of nationalism intervened in several countries. This meant political isolation of the country in question, and its corollary, the disruption of international contacts, since foreign influence was viewed by the government as a form of cultural imperialism. This situation of political closure impacted on the disruption of then existing comparative education activity. These communities of comparativists were thus excluded from the global discourse, not because of linguistic differences or epistemological monism: comparative work was constrained by the prevailing political ideologies which filtered into universities.

In Brazil, Sisson de Castro (2007) reports that after the deposition of its authoritarian political regime, which governed the country for two decades (1964-1985), in the newly democratised country "everything had to be black or white, leftist or rightist" (p.241). Previously, that is, in the 1930s, comparative education was a compulsory subject in teacher education. However, in 1969, it was excluded from the national curriculum (Sisson de Castro & Gomes, 2008). In the 1980s, the politicisation of academic circles in the newly democratised nation further marginalised comparative education, viewing with suspicion its practice of policy borrowing from other nations. It was seen as an instrument of American imperialism and colonisation (Nogueira, 2004; Verhine, 2004). As Verhine (2004) contends, the 'non-nationalistic' connotation of comparative education was in contrast with the 'nationalistic' current prevailing in Brazil. In that context, policy borrowing was not in vogue. Comparative education was further de-institutionalised from the postgraduate programmes of Brazilian universities in the mid-1990s.

A similar discontinuity owing to nationalism occurred in the history of comparative education in Chile. In 1967, comparative education was taught at universities in the country. However, it was removed from university curricula during the military dictatorship (1973-90), during which the country was closed to foreign ideological influence (Rodríguez, 2008).

European Patterns

An alternative view to Paulston's global map comes from the observation of epistemological differences between British and American comparativists. Although the literature has been dominated by Anglo-American scholars, these two communities also differ in their epistemologies (Cowen, 1980) and, within their own national groupings further divergences occur (Crossley & Watson, 2003).

Cowen draws a distinction between European and American comparativists in the post-World War II period:

> The intellectual definition of European comparative education is sharply different from that of American comparative education. The major founding fathers of European comparative education from the mid-twenties were working on themes which were comprehensible in terms of Durkheim, Weber, and Marx. The search for new methodological approaches in the United States and the confidence that American comparative educationists have had in positivist techniques drawn from other social sciences has meant that a field of study with a common name has diverged sharply (1980, p.108).

In the same vein, Waterkamp (2007) claims that historiographic methods tended to dominate comparative research in Germany, until such hegemony was questioned in the late 1960s by scholars who stressed the importance of sociological, political and economic theories. García Garrido (2004) also contends that Spanish comparative educationists mostly adopt historical-culturalist approaches, and much less positivist sociological positions or radical humanist positions. This is partly evidenced by the results of a content analysis of the *Revista Española de Educación Comparada* (Martínez & Valle, 2005), which reveals that most studies are of a qualitative nature, in the form of document analysis and literature reviews, and minimally, those in the form of ethnographic studies (pp.80-81). Ferrer (2004) underscores that the difference in historical tradition and language barrier are among the reasons why Spanish comparativists did not usually participate in the conferences of BAICE and CIES (also Vilanou and Valls, 2001).

Mitter (2007), however, contends that over time, the differences between European and North American comparativists have become less 'sharp' as when Cowen wrote his article in 1980. To cite Mitter, "empirical methodology has long gained access to comparative education theory and research in European universities and research institutes, while social theories have exerted their impact on comparative education in the USA" (p.126).

The above demonstrates that, on the one hand, Paulston's mapping elides divergences, not only in the dominant theories and paradigms across sub-communities of comparativists, but also in terms of the historical period when they were dominant. Through interaction and dialogue among these divergent communities, their different approaches have tended to *mutually* interpenetrate each other's theoretical boundaries, as Mitter described above.

Africa and Asia

A final argument involves the uneven penetration of postmodern perspectives in the scholarly community of comparativists worldwide. I contend that some countries of Africa and Asia, whether due to their cultural conservatism or to the attention paid to more basic needs of education, have paid less attention to postmodernist critiques and methodological debates in their discourses. I support my argument with an analysis of the aims of and textbooks used in teaching comparative education in some African and Asian countries profiled in Wolhuter et al. (2008b). In Asia, they include China, Japan, Kazakhstan, Korea, Malaysia, Oman and Thailand. In Africa, they comprise Burundi, Egypt, Tanzania and Uganda. My selection of these countries is influenced by Cowen's (1996) critique of the possibility of a universal appeal of postmodernism. He argues that:

> The corpus of writing on the poststructuralist and postmodern has attracted international attention but the contributions to this corpus of knowledge have necessarily local trajectories.... Postmodernism, in its comparative dimensions, is impressively parochial: it does not reflect or read the structural socioeconomic conditions, ideological projects, educational systems or self-society issues of identity in Japan, Taiwan or South Korea and, still less, China. It cannot easily be extended to understand the state projects for the construction of Islamic identity in Algeria, Iran, Malaysia or Pakistan and it would seem to have remarkably little to say about the crisis of state legitimation and educational reform in Central and Eastern Europe. Perhaps this is because much of the writing on post-modernism has tipped too far in the direction of asking about the destruction of the

'enlightenment' self, the autonomous individual ... (pp.165-166).

This analytical comment finds an echo in the empirical data on the current position of comparative education at universities. With respect to the aims of teaching comparative education, a focus in Kazakhstan, where the resumption of comparative activity is fairly recent, is for a predictive purpose: to identify future trends and outcomes of educational reforms in other countries (Kussainov & Mussin, 2008). In China, Malaysia, Oman and Thailand, the informative and reformative purposes of comparative education are of more interest than theoretical pursuits (e.g., Al-Harthi, 2008; Manzon, 2008a; Mohd. Meerah & Halim, 2008; Thongthew, 2008).

In terms of textbooks, as I note in Wolhuter et al. (2008b, p.336), several countries are narrowly limited to using old foreign books and/or journal articles (e.g., Burundi, Malaysia, Tanzania, Thailand, Uganda). Works date back to Kandel (1933), with the most 'recent' being Altbach and Kelly (1986) and Halls (1990a). One reason, and a noteworthy one, is that these are classics. But, a constraining factor, in some cases, is financial resources. Anangisye (2008) and Ocheng Kagoire (2008) note the limited endowment of university libraries in Tanzania and Uganda, respectively, leaving scholars with little choice for research and teaching resources. Weeks (2004) identified a similar constraint to the development of comparative education in Zambia, Zimbabwe and Malawi, particularly due to the collapse of the library system after the countries' independence. As Anangisye further highlights, not only are materials outdated, but they are also written in Northern socio-economic contexts not applicable to local users (2008, p.308). Among the classics used, most operate under a functionalist and positivist framework. Another limiting factor is language. In the case of Korea, foreign books are seldom used because of language limitations (Park & Hyun, 2008). Limited access to newer Western textbooks implies limited access to more recent intellectual discourses, not the least on postmodernism. On the other hand, in Egypt, Megahed and Otaiba (2008, p.283) surprisingly note an opposite trend. Despite Egyptian scholars' access to and engagement with the international discourse on development and world systems theory, the recent textbooks in use at their universities adopt a national, functionalist and evolutionary approach to classifying countries.

The above examples illustrate that postmodernism has indeed been parochial. Although Ninnes and Burnett (2003) have documented its increasing presence in the comparative education literature during the decade of the 1990s, a 2008 survey of teaching aims and textbooks used in some African and Asian countries point to the slow take-up, if at all, of postmodernist perspectives in these regions. There, comparative education aims to address more immediate pragmatic and informative needs of the domestic education system, while academic theorisation and methodological debates are left out of the discourse. In this vein, more traditional approaches and classic textbooks are employed, also in the light of financial and language constraints by some communities. This is one more alternative history to that mapped by Paulston (1994).

Conclusion

In this chapter, I have attempted to map the intellectual histories of comparative education from the 19th century to the present. I have endeavoured to integrate an exploration of the field's epistemological foundations with the take-up of correlative theoretical and disciplinary orientations, and related these to genres of comparative studies. Following Epstein (2008b), I first described three main epistemological roots of the field: positivism (Jullien), relativism (Ushinsky), and historical functionalism (Dilthey). To complement this intellectual history, I referred to Paulston (1994) who mapped the development of theories and paradigms in comparative education that have branched out from these epistemological platforms and from mid-range philosophical and sociological theories from the 1950s onwards. Four main paradigms served to influence the diverse types of comparative education studies: functionalism, radical structuralism, humanism and radical humanism. To further enrich the theoretical history of comparative education, I discussed Cowen's (2003a) typology of dominant thematic foci of comparative studies since Jullien in 1817. He categorised comparative studies into four main 'schools' or paradigmatic themes: Sadler, the Chicago/New York School, Development Discourse, and (Jullien's) Trends. They were distinguished by their specific combination of agenda of attention, mega-unit of comparison, and the substantive comparative discourse that is produced about them. Finally, applying Foucauldian lenses to a critical interpretation of disciplinary histories, I noted that these intellectual histories have presented partial views of the global histories of the field. In order to widen the discourse and raise awareness that disciplinary histories are not linear and evolutionary, but are discontinuous and far from unitary, I expounded in the final section of this chapter on alternative histories and interpretations from other cultures. These 'other' intellectual histories bring to light Bourdieu's insights on the intellectual field as the result of the complex interplay between structural constraints/opportunities and human agency, through which comparative education scholars formulate the pertinent objects and purposes of their work and thus shape the intellectual discourse. These historical perspectives on comparative education's intellectual bases set the stage for a contextualised understanding of the nature of the field, the topic of the next chapter.

5
Mapping the Intellectual Discourse on 'Comparative Education'

Introduction

After having delineated the intellectual foundations and development of comparative education in the previous chapter, this chapter explores the nature of comparative education by analysing the intellectual definitions of the field constructed by comparativists. I denote the constructed nature of these definitions in the title of this chapter by placing the term 'comparative education' in quotes. The purpose of this chapter is two-fold: first, to 'map'[1] the discourse on comparative education as a discipline, a field, a method, or such other designation coined by academics working in comparative education. How do comparativists define 'comparative education' and distinguish it from related fields? Second, to evaluate these different positions critically in the light of the conceptual framework on academic fields and disciplines elaborated in Chapter 2 in order to arrive at a clearer understanding of the epistemological status of comparative education. I draw on realist (e.g., Hirst, 1974c), as well as on constructionist perspectives, particularly from Foucault and Bourdieu.

This work responds to Rosselló (1978, p.18, cited in Martínez, 2003, p.28), who, in view of the lack of a unanimous definition of comparative education, ironically said that "one has to begin, then, with a comparative study of the numerous definitions of comparative education". A decade after Rosselló's work, W.D. Halls's worldwide survey of the state of comparative education (1990a) continues to signal as problematic the lack of a precise definition of the field of comparative education and notes the discrepancy between the name 'comparative education' which connotes comparison, and the actual non-comparative (albeit often implicitly comparative) work published in its journals (p.26).

The chapter therefore contains a thematic categorisation of the multiple definitions of comparative education in the specialist literature

---

[1] The term 'mapping' is not used in Paulston's (1994) sense, but in the ordinary usage connoting a review of the literature, tracing the salient definitions of comparative education.

reflecting on the field. The thematic approach is preferable to the chron-ological approach in achieving the purpose of elucidating the substantive content of the definitions, rather than the main tendencies within a particular historical period. After a brief preamble on definitions, I proceed to categorise the definitions of comparative education according to object, method, and purposes, in order to set the groundwork for the next step of establishing whether comparative education is a discipline, a field or a method. I then distinguish comparative education from related fields and conclude the chapter by proposing a definition of comparative education and an explanation of the process of its intellectual con-struction.

Marginson and Mollis (2002, p.615) note the way in which diverse languages "shape the multiplicity and variety of phenomena accounted for by comparative education" (p.615) and the lack of linguistic diversity in the literature on the field, with Anglo-American voices dominating the discourse. They therefore advocate the use of a multilingual approach in comparative studies. This is my approach here: while surveying mainly the Anglo-American literature for academic definitions of comparative education, I have also attempted to go beyond its boundaries and have explored other perspectives in the Spanish, Chinese, French and German discourses.

Preamble on Definitions
Types of Definitions
Ruscoe and Nelson (1964, p.386) offer a prolegomena to a definition of comparative education. Among general definitions, they cite three broad types distinguished on the basis of the intent of the person defining the terms. First, the *stipulative* definition specifies how a term is to be used; second, the *descriptive* definition summarises prior usages of the term; and third, the *programmatic* definition promotes a programme of action, which connotes a moral and practical dimension. Koehl (1977, pp.177-178) designates the stipulative definition as prescriptive, while he also calls the programmatic definition normative. He further explains that "the programmatic definition makes plain that the method is there for a purpose, usually meliorist and reforming" (p.178).

Definitions and terminologies do not exist in a vacuum. From a Bourdieuian field perspective, definitions, theories and concepts – like art works – can only be fully understood in relation to the position held within the intellectual field by those who produced them (Johnson, 1993).

As Cowen (1990, p.333) cautions, "the academic definitions [of comparative education by comparative educationists] should be noted, but should also be understood as reflecting some of the institutional, social and political contexts of their work. This social contextualisation of comparative education leads to different comparative educations in different parts of the world". Anweiler (1977, p.110) further argues that "theoretical subject definitions are the result of practical developments and the questions of research that emerge from these".

Definitions are therefore *positional*. They are formulated by persons who occupy different locations within the intellectual field, giving them symbolic power to define and delimit the boundaries and objects of study of their field. These intellectuals perceive reality at a given point in time and address themselves to a given audience. This is not to say that all definitions are subjective and relative, or that they have no generalisable value as conceptual abstractions. Caution should, however, be exercised when reading and interpreting them.

Discourse

To recapitulate from Chapter 2, *discourse* from a Foucauldian perspective refers to the entire set of statements about a topic, which establish the conditions of truth within a specific historical period (Ball, 1990). These statements could comprise oral or written words, graphics or symbols, that is, texts (Foucault, 1972). Discursive formations contribute to the construction of academic disciplines by organising ideas and producing 'objects of knowledge'. Transposing these ideas to the field of comparative education, Mehta and Ninnes (2003, pp.240-241) argue that since discourse shapes and constructs the relations of power, it has material effects, such as the construction of 'truth' about the boundaries of the field. The particular discourses by prominent individuals in the field influence the intellectual shaping of the field. Thus, Ninnes's (2004, p.44) reply to the question, 'What is comparative education?': "It is whatever comparative educators and other people who engage with the field say it is. ... Like other disciplines, comparative education is constructed through the process of people talking and writing about its 'nature'".

Discipline and Field

In Chapter 2, I elucidated the nature of disciplines and fields. From a realist stance, a *discipline* is ordinarily identified by these epistemological features: a common object, point of view, truth-criteria, conceptual structure and theoretical integration, methods and skills, and products of knowledge. By contrast, a *field* is unified by a common material object or phenomena of study, or a common practical pursuit. The approaches which a field uses to study its proper object are multiple and are drawn from more than one discipline (Hirst, 1974c). Moreover, Becher and Trowler (2001, p.23) conceive of an academic discipline as the result of a mutually dependent interplay of the structural force of the epistemological character of disciplines that conditions culture, and the capacity of individuals and groups as agents of autonomous action, including interpretive acts. Thus, epistemological features structure the field as do the sociological factors of structure, agency and discourse.

From a critical perspective, however, disciplines and fields are viewed as sites of contestation for power. As alluded to earlier, Foucault (1972) views disciplines as historically contingent discursive formations comprised of heterogeneous elements. Disciplines emerge from power struggles and constitute power relations. Bourdieu (1969) likewise views the intellectual field as embedded in fields of power, defining it as a dynamic system of positions and oppositions among agents, who shape the field through their competition over valued capital in order to obtain distinction for their intellectual work. Bourdieu further claims that the discussion on the canon of a field (e.g., the literary canon) is a "site and stake of contention as different groups have argued for its rearrangement along lines more favourable to their divergent interests and agendas" (Johnson, 1993, p.19). For Bourdieu, herein lies the very dynamics of change in the field, for what is always at stake is the legitimate definition of the field and field practice.

Comparison

Schriewer (2000, pp.9-10) distinguishes between 'simple' and 'complex' comparisons. Simple comparison, "as a *universal mental operation* embedded in everyday social life, ... [is aimed at] establishing relations between observable facts". By contrast, complex comparison is a *social scientific method* aimed at "establishing relations between relationships". This latter operation is concerned with "relationships between varying object areas or system levels and with setting these in relation to one another" (p.9). Comparison, in its usage as a social scientific method, is pertinent to understanding the nature of comparative education.

Comparative Education: A Discipline, a Field, a Method?

Kelly, Altbach and Arnove (1982, pp.509-510) describe the intellectual crisis that comparative education entered in the 1960s as one that boiled down to answering the questions: What is comparative education? Is it really a distinct field of study? This spurred new debates centred on five main issues: (1) Is comparative education defined by method or by content? (2) If by content, then of what should that specific content consist? (3) If the specific content of comparative education is constituted by school/society relationships, then how distinct is it from sister disciplines that study similar content? (4) If the specific focus is only on school phenomena detached from context, then how distinct is it from educational psychology, educational administration, or curriculum and instruction? And (5) What distinct contribution does comparative education make to policy formation and to teacher education? This concern for academic recognition as a social science with a distinct methodology generated a substantial literature (Price, 1992, p.95).

Although nearly five decades have passed since comparative education entered this identity crisis, the debate is far from resolved, and the question 'what is comparative education?' continues to be asked (e.g., Carnoy, 2006; Bray, 2007d; Kubow & Fossum, 2007; Klees, 2008). Wolhuter (2008, p.323) graphically describes the actuality of this condition by recalling that when Erwin H. Epstein, commencing his presentation at the XI World Congress in Korea in 2001, asked 'What is comparative education?', his question was met by a dumb silence from an audience of eminent comparativists.

In this section, I will trace the discourse on this issue in two stages. First, I will examine the discourse on the specific object, purpose and method of comparative education in order to further substantiate the argument as to what its nature might be. As noted above, while a field should have at least either a common material object or a common practical purpose, disciplines require in addition a common method and theoretical base. After having established the specific object, purposes and methods of comparative education, I aim to define more conclusively what it is. Thus, in the second part, I will evaluate the statements of comparativists who have attempted to justify whether comparative education is a discipline, a field, a method, or such other classifications, and evaluate them in the light of the conclusions of the first part.

Several scholars (e.g., Jones, 1971, pp.142-169; Kelly, Altbach & Arnove, 1982, pp.511-515; García Garrido, 1996, pp.92-103) have summarised the debate on the nature of comparative education along these lines. Among the pertinent categories they used to classify the different definitions of comparative education were: by *content* or *object of study*; by *method*; and by *purposes*. These are therefore the three categories that I adopt in the first part of this section.

As in any classificatory work, there is a danger of thinking in rigid and exclusive terms. Definitions of comparative education by a single author do not always fall neatly into any single category, but do at times extend to other categories. Following my predecessors in this work, I have attempted to classify definitions given by comparativists according to the salient feature(s) of each, or what Kirkwood (2001) refers to as 'author emphasis'. Thus, if one defines comparative education by giving more emphasis to its 'comparative method' as a defining feature, even if it enumerates various objects of study, I categorise this definition as 'defined by method'.

Defined by Object

García Garrido (1996, pp.92-96) classifies the debate about the object of comparative education into six main positions:

1. There is *no specific object* and therefore there is no comparative science of education. It is only a methodology - the comparative methodology - applied to education.
2. There is a comparative science of education which is the *comparative method* applied to educational problems.
3. There is a comparative science of education because it has a *specific object though not its proper methodology*.
4. Comparative education is substantially *'geography of education'*.
5. Comparative education is substantially *'comparative history* of contemporary education'.
6. Comparative education is the *comparative study of educational systems* operating in today's world.

In this section, I focus on the third, fourth and sixth positions, which specify the object of comparative education, and leave the other points for discussion in later sections of this chapter.

There are those who claim that comparative education is a science because it *has a specific object,* but *not a specific method*. Their assumption is that for a science, what matters is the object, not the method. Lê Thành Khôi (1981, p.43, cited in García Garrido, 1996, p.94) defines the object of comparative education as the comparison of educational facts/realities and of their relationships with their environment. García Garrido points out, however, the problematic issue of defining as comparative education's object the act of comparison per se.

In this respect, the definition advanced by Olivera (2009, p.32) distinguishes between the material and formal objects of comparative education. He states comparative education is the discipline which investigates, through a comparative approach, global or particular educational phenomena in two or more societies or human groupings with respect to their similarities and differences and their interaction with their respective social environments.

Some other scholars, such as Debesse and Mialaret (1974, cited in García Garrido, 1996, p.94) define comparative education as '*geography of education*', whose object is countries or nations seen from the viewpoint of their educational organisation. The descriptive method is adopted in these studies. Fletcher (1974, p.353) echoes the view that comparative education is distinguished fundamentally by "its geographical orientation, in its concern for ecological analysis and aerial differentiation". Bereday (1964) also uses the term 'educational geography' to emphasise the spatial orientation of comparative education's object of study, but he does not view comparative education as merely a descriptive activity. Cowen (2008) thus makes a distinction between Auslandspädagogik (description of foreign educational practices) and comparative education, which tries to understand education in its social context.

The last position cited by García Garrido (1996, p.95) defines comparative education as the *comparative study of educational systems*. He claims that this is the commonly held definition of comparative education and one which he shares as well. The specific object of comparative education is educational systems. This object is not studied by any other sciences of education, even if some (e.g., sociology of education and general pedagogy) have included them as part of their curricula. But García Garrido recognises that 'educational systems' is a problematic concept. He uses educational systems in the wide sense: as a system, or some of its aspects or parts or problems. He categorises two main usages of the term (1996, p.102): (1) understood as 'national educational systems' (e.g., Hans, 1950), and (2) understood in practice, owing to the work of international organisations, as 'public school systems'. Finally, he points out that the debate about the proper object of comparative education is inconclusive.

Additionally, Martínez (2003, p.32) reviewed the definitions by a variety of authors, some of whom are not usually cited in the Anglo-American literature. They included Schneider (1964), Lauwerys (1974), Vexliard (1970), Quintana (1983) and Raventos (1990). She concluded that the objects defining comparative education are: educational systems, educational policy, educational problems and educational processes.

The specific objects of comparative education that have thus far been identified range from the general – comparison of educational facts – to the specific – national educational systems. Other scholars highlight different aspects of this object, such as the cross-national, or school-society relations. I list them below, categorised according to the salient features of the object of comparative education that they focus on. I also explore alternative positions on the wider object of comparative education and recapitulate the common elements by viewing them through Cowen's (2009b) 'unit ideas'.

The Cross-national or Cross-cultural Camp

Kazamias and Massialas (1965, p.14) describe the subject matter of comparative education as "coterminous with the subject matter of education itself", except that comparative education "goes beyond the confines of education in one nation, society or group, and it uses cross-national or cross-cultural methods and techniques".

Trethewey (1976, p.2) compares the definitions or descriptions of the field of comparative education by Bereday (1964), Kandel (1955b) and Noah and Eckstein (1969), and concludes that their commonality lies in a cross-national or cross-cultural emphasis on the study of education and educational systems. Other authors who adopt this stance are Mallinson (1975) and Parkyn (1977). Parkyn asserts that the object of study is what distinguishes comparative education from other comparative disciplines:

> [I]n the particular sense in which it (comparative) is used in the term comparative education, the usual limitation of meaning is that what are being compared are aspects of education that are evidenced in different societies, cultures, or states .... The problems and topics to be studied, then, are *educational*, not simply sociological, psychological, economic, philosophical, and so on. Moreover, they are to be *studied comparatively* across societies and cultures, for one of the main purposes of such study is to derive generalisations that are valid across education systems (pp.89-90).

Epstein (1994, p.918) uses a more generic term in defining the object of comparative education as "transsocietal study of education", likening it to other fields of academic study that are dedicated to the transsocietal study of other social institutions, such as comparative government, comparative economics, and comparative religion. He also regards both explicit and implicit comparisons as acceptable objects (p.922), where explicit comparison has two or more units of analysis (societies or historical periods), while implicit comparison refers to inquiry in one particular society or historical period, but where the analytic scheme can be extended to problems in other societies and periods (also Epstein, 2004).

Phillips and Schweisfurth (2006, p.24) define comparative education as "the study of any aspects of educational phenomena in two or more different national or regional settings in which attempts are made to draw conclusions from a systematic comparison of the phenomena in question". Their definition explicitly takes a comparative cross-national or cross-regional focus.

The School-Society Relations Camp

Scholars such as Anderson (1961) as well Noah and Eckstein (1969), Kneller (1972), and Khôi (1981), diverge from those who hold the view that the national educational system is the primary unit of analysis in comparative education. Instead, they consider that school-society relations – the relation of school systems to national systems of social stratification – is the essential content of comparative education (Kelly, Altbach & Arnove, 1982; Martínez, 2003). Anderson defines comparative education broadly as the "cross-cultural comparison of the structure, operation, aims, methods, and achievements of various educational systems, and the societal correlates of these educational systems and their elements" (1961, p.4). He further delimits the field's content thus:

> The field could be defined in terms of its content – *school/society relations*, which could be studied using methodologies derived from history and the social sciences, including economics, political science, sociology, and anthropology. *No one method* could encompass the field or define it. In addition, work in comparative education did not necessarily have to be comparative; in-depth studies of educational phenomena *within one country* were useful in identifying school/society relations, which then could be verified through testing in other national contexts (cited in Kelly, Altbach & Arnove, 1982, p.513). [emphases added]

This last point on single-unit studies qualifying as comparative work is echoed by former editors of the journal *Comparative Education Review* (Epstein, 1992; Rust, 2001). This move, in my view, weakens by dilution the identity of comparative education by treating all such studies as 'implicitly comparative'. One has to ask, then, what is not comparative? However, there is no unanimity on this point (as discussed in Chapter 3) and the more common view is perhaps that of explicit comparison between educational systems or problems in two or more (national) contexts (Rust, 2001, p.iii). This is not to say, however, that having two or more units of comparison would suffice to constitute a 'comparative education' study. Cowen (2008) contends that adopting an 'A vs. B' form is not a 'comparative education' study unless it also has a specific episteme: a disciplinary approach or intellectual framing.

Widening the Object in the 1980s

Ferrer (2002, pp.49-50) enumerates four major changes (of which I list three, since the fourth could be combined with the first) that have impacted on widening the object of comparative education from its traditional object, educational systems. In the first place, the consequences of globalisation for education have led many to question the relevance of the nation-state in educational affairs (e.g., Dale, 2000, Arnove & Torres, 1999). Green (2003, p.95) claims that globalisation has created new "educational spaces which belong exclusively to neither nations nor systems". Ferrer refers, in second place, to a greater emphasis on some aspects of educational systems, such as the discourses proper to each educational system (e.g., Schriewer, 2000). A third change observed by Ferrer is the increased importance given to history, in contrast to the predominantly sociological emphasis in comparative education studies, and, in particular, to socio-historical comparisons (e.g., Nóvoa, 2000).

Ferrer (2002, p.50) concludes that all of these new approaches still take the educational system as a point of reference, but enrich it with new approaches and analyses that allow for a better understanding of its complex nature. In addition to common references to the nation-state as author of its (national) education system, Ferrer (2002, p.51) cites various authors who propose different classifications of educational systems: Khôi (1981) categorises them into supranational, international and intra-national levels of comparison; Halls (1990a) classifies them into comparisons among nation-states, world systems, ideological systems, world regions, according to levels of economic prosperity ('Three Worlds',

North-South), and local or intra-national. Bray and Thomas (1995) plotted on a cube the objects of comparison (aspects of education and of society), locational/geographic contexts (from world regions down to intra-national units such as states, districts, schools, classrooms and individuals), and demographic groups (e.g., minority groups, religious groups, entire population). A more recent volume by Bray, Adamson, and Mason (2007a) offers new understandings of the more established units of comparison – places, systems, time – as well as other units such as cultures, values, policies, curricula, educational achievements, educational organisations, ways of learning and pedagogical innovations. They encourage multi-level comparative analyses, and portray different models, including comparison of two locations; of a focal location with other locations as appropriate; and of multiple locations.

While these new foci and approaches are insightful, in hindsight, I concur with Mason (2008a) in arguing that the Bray and Thomas cube countenances and probably contributes to legitimating a dilution of the distinct nature of comparative education, precisely due to its advocacy of a wider object of comparison, shifting from the traditional cross-national units to intra-national units of analysis. To some extent, this may be too widely interpreted to the point of eclipsing the cross-national element. I posit, however, that both object – cross-national/cross-cultural educational systems – and explicit use of comparative methodology have to be present for a study to be distinctively categorised as 'comparative education'. If the cross- or inter-national element is absent, then the distinctive nature of comparative education becomes blurred and comparison may become a 'pedestrian' activity: any other educational researcher can and actually does compare two classrooms within the same school or classroom (in a single city or province or state of one's origin) before and after a pedagogical experiment; any other sociologist of education can and actually does compare minority education policies and practices in two provinces within the same country, and so forth. Comparison is, anyway, an integral part of scientific investigation. But what makes comparative education distinct from branches of educational studies that also use the comparative method? I would argue that it is the 'spatial contexts' in which an 'educational' object of comparison is located – the cross-national – which makes the difference. Both cross-national *contexts* (the 'where' question) and explicit comparative methodology are among the elements *sine qua non* that make comparative education a distinct subfield of education studies. There are other elements, which I will discuss in the next section.

The definitions of comparative education reviewed above have thus far identified the field's object as education, educational issues and problems, and more specifically, educational systems viewed from a trans-national perspective. Explicit comparisons entail that the number of objects of comparison is more than one (beyond one nation, society or group), although some view single-unit studies also as 'comparative' provided they are framed within a comparative perspective (e.g., Epstein, 1994). However, various scholars recognise that 'educational system' is a complex concept, the understanding of which continues to be debated (e.g., García Garrido, 1996, pp.102, 110; Ferrer, 2002, pp.50-51; Bray & Jiang, 2007, pp.125-127). By way of conclusion to this section on the specific object of comparative education, I now turn to Cowen's rather comprehensive analysis of the issue.

Cowen's 'Unit Ideas' of Comparative Education

Cowen (2009b) suggests that a set of core ideas serve to intellectually frame comparative education, giving it some continuity throughout its variegated and apparently discontinuous histories. These 'unit ideas' are: space, time, the state, educational system, educated identity, social context, transfer, and praxis. He contends that academic comparative education typically works within a combination of these core ideas, which acquire different emphases and meanings over time, in response to varied political contexts and disciplinary backgrounds and interests of authors. According to him, a core theme of comparative education is the triadic relations between transfer, translation and transformation, which he defines thus (2006, p.566):

- *Transfer* is the movement of an educational idea or practice in supra-national or trans-national or inter-national space;
- *Translation* is the shape-shifting of educational institutions or the re-interpretation of educational ideas which routinely occurs with the transfer in space;
- *Transformations* are the metamorphoses which the compression of social and economic power into education in the new context imposes on the initial translation: that is, a range of transformations which cover both the indigenisation and extinction of the translated form.

Based on these elements, he proposes a permanent agenda of academic comparative education as that of revealing the compressions of social and economic and cultural power in educational forms especially in their most visible moments of transfer, translation and transformation (Cowen, 2009b). He further defines academic comparative education as "the university-based study of educational patterns as part of international political and economic relations" (2008). By a 'good comparative education', he proposes a university-voiced endeavour to understand the C. Wright Mills' problematic of the intersection of history, social structures and individual biographies (2003a, 2008).

Defined by Method

While most of the scholars cited above define comparative education by its object and what that object consists of, there are those who argue that comparative education should be defined by its method: the *comparative method*. Advocates include Bereday (1964), Tusquets (1969), Brembeck (1975) and Green (2003).

In his classic book, *Comparative Method in Education*, Bereday (1964, p.ix) defines comparative education as "the analytical survey of foreign educational systems". Although defined by its method, Bereday acknowledged that comparative education had to rely on a host of methods from other disciplines.

Tusquets (1969, p.18) affirms that "comparative pedagogy is substantially a method". Vexliard (1970, cited by Martínez, 2003, pp.30-31) further remarks that "comparative pedagogy is a discipline that investtigates and attempts to gain new knowledge, both theoretical and practical, *by means* of juxtaposing two or more educational systems in different countries, regions, or different historical periods" [emphasis added].

Brembeck (1975, p.371) emphasises that the key to delimiting comparative education is the word 'comparative':

> I define the field of comparative and international education broadly: it is the comparative study of educational phenomena, formal and non-formal, domestic and international. To me the key word is 'comparative', rather than 'international'. By 'study', I mean to include both research and self-examined practice, both the scholar and the practitioner. By 'domestic', I mean that we should be as concerned about comparative studies 'here' as we are 'there'. By 'international', I mean to include comparative study both across national boundaries and within foreign boundaries.

Finally, Green (2003, p.95) reminds of the need for comparative education to have a distinctively comparative methodology to identify its academic territory:

> Comparative education needs to compare, and to do this systematically, if it is to avoid the accusation that it too often degenerates into a catalogue of traveller's tales, policy advocacy and opportunistic rationalisation of unscientific policy-borrowing. One way that it can do this is to draw more on the mainstream of comparative history and social science research for its concepts, methodology and evidence.

Some scholars are, however, cautious about defining comparative education by its method alone. Jones (1971) notes the interlocking relationship between method and purpose. Anweiler (1977, p.113), meanwhile, highlights the interdependence between method and subject matter (object of study), and argues that "the method of comparison shows itself to be a scientific procedure, which ... does not adequately account for the special nature of comparative education, ... but is required by the subject. Seen as such, the controversy about the priority of 'Subject' or 'Method' within comparative education becomes meaningless". Meanwhile, Horner (2000) notes that the debate about whether comparative education is defined by its object or by its method, is rooted in the logic of language, particularly the German language. He observes that in French, the term *éducation comparée* names the object of investigation (education), conjoined with a past perfect participle to designate that the object has already been compared (method). Something similar occurs in the Spanish, Italian and Portuguese versions of the term (educación comparada, educazione comparata, and educação comparada). In these languages, therefore, object and method are conjoined and inseparable. But in English and German, and perhaps some other languages, these semantic nuances are less overt, giving rise to such debates.

A contemporary advocate of the view that comparative education is defined by method is Mason (2008a). He contends that comparative education is a methodologically, and not a substantively, distinct subfield of education studies. Using logical argumentation, he demonstrates that comparative education does not have content that is substantively distinct from or that could be more broadly defined than that of the field of education studies, and that "all that distinguishes it from the field of education studies is the explicit use of the comparative method" (p.1). In other words, the substantive content or subject matter of comparative education is co-extensive with that of education studies.

I examine Mason's claims in detail, likewise using logical argumentation, in order to answer the question: Is it possible to isolate comparative education as a distinct field or subfield of education studies, and if so, on what grounds? Is it merely on the grounds of methodological distinction or also of substantive distinction?

According to Mason (2008a, p.3), two conditions need to be met for the definition of comparative education and its delimitation as a distinct field or subfield of education studies. First, it should have a *necessary* or essential feature (that is, all aspects of comparative education exhibit this), and second, a *sufficient* or unique feature (that is, only comparative education contains this). He claims that both the necessary and sufficient aspects of comparative education are: its content/substance deals with education and its method is comparative. Thus, the essential content or substance of comparative education cannot be more broadly defined than that of education studies, but is circumscribed within the boundaries of education studies. The only unique aspect of comparative education, distinguishing it from education studies, is the (explicit use of the) comparative method. He therefore concludes that the field of comparative education is not a substantively distinct field of education studies, but a methodologically distinct subfield of education studies.

I concur with Mason on the premises of his conclusion: that the necessary subject matter of comparative education falls within, not outside, the scope of education studies as a whole, and that its unique treatment of this object is through the application of the comparative method or methods (since there is no one method used in comparative education). However, I disagree with his reductionist view of comparative education as only a methodologically distinct field of education studies. I argue that despite being a useful method/approach, it is not only or merely these, but a distinct field as well.

First, that the content of comparative education is education is undeniable. If it were something else outside education studies, then it would not be comparative *education*. Unlike the disciplines of history, philosophy, sociology, psychology, which lie outside of education studies and whose intersection with the latter produces such subfields as history *of* education, philosophy *of* education, and so forth, there is no such thing as a 'comparative field' that lies outside of education studies (or outside of any discipline for that matter) and only partly intersects with it. Thus, we cannot speak of a 'comparative *of* education' or 'comparative *of* history'. Furthermore, we would not be able to know of something about education that absolutely falls outside the domain of education studies as a whole. If something studied comparatively were to fall outside of education studies, then it would be comparative "x": thus, if its object is legal systems, then it would be comparative law. Comparative education is about education. But, are not education studies and its subfields also about education? Are there not other smaller circles – subfields – within the big circle of education studies? Not all education studies are comparative, just as not all education studies are sociological or historical or philosophical. But are these sub-specialisations not unified by the common denominator of 'education' or the educational phenomenon as their object of study? The question that needs to be asked, perhaps is: What then differentiates education studies from the subfields that constitute it? I posit that the principles of differentiation on the theoretical plane are perhaps reducible to these three: a narrower *subject matter* (subject fragmentation or specialisation), alternative and/or specialised *methodological or disciplinary* approaches, and *teleological* reasons (purpose).

On subject fragmentation, Special Education is a specialised sub-field, as is Early Childhood Education. On teleological grounds, Theory of Education would differ from Didactics. Finally, on disciplinary differentiation, there are the subfields of Psychology of Education or History of Education, for example, which are the result of the intersection between psychology or history with education studies. Subject speciali-sation allows for deepening or widening understanding of educational realities and mastery of skills in pedagogy and educational organisation and policy. I contend that comparative education deserves a rightful place as a distinct subfield of education studies on these three grounds: subject specialisation, methodological and (inter)disciplinary approaches, and teleology.

In terms of subject specialisation, comparative education can lay claim to a *narrower* subject matter than that of education studies as a whole. Thus, in contrast to Mason (2008a), who contends that the content of comparative education is as broad as education studies itself, and that the two domains are only distinguished methodologically, García Garrido (1996, pp.100-102) expresses wariness about defining compara-tive education by its method alone, of claiming that it consists funda-mentally in the application of the comparative method to education. In his view, this position could lead to two aporias: first, it could lead to a very wide interpretation of the scope of comparative education, that all comparative studies in education (e.g., in psychology of education, sociology of education, history of education, etc.) are reducible to comparative education. On the other hand, it could also lead to a narrowing down of the scope of comparative education, or a blurring of its distinctive nature, thereby depriving it of legitimate autonomy from other subfields of education studies. He therefore proposes that method and object should go together in defining the field:

> Comparative education needs to have, aside from a specific methodology, a specific object of study. Its object cannot be education in general, or all that is related to education. Most comparativists agree that this specific object is educational systems. But the problem lies in understanding what 'educational system' means.

Following Cowen (1982a), I posit that the substantive content of comparative education is educational phenomena *elsewhere*, usually in *two or more nations*, and more specifically, it examines *educational systems* and their *relations with intra- and extra-educational phenomena*. The specific object of comparative education thus involves an *Other*ly dimension (commonly cross-cultural, cross-national, cross-regional, cross-/transsocietal) of the educational system, which dimension education studies encompasses implicitly, but does not address as explicitly and as extensively as does comparative education. Theoretically speaking, education studies or educology (Olivera, 1988) examines educational reality in its entirety, abstracted from spatial, cultural and temporal dimensions and eliding their important differences, interrelationships, and consequent implications. The substantively distinct subfield of comparative education teases out the impact of spatial and cultural contexts on educational processes and institutions, just as the subfield of history of education deals with the temporal factor. Thus, comparative education is necessarily about education, but only comparative education deals systematically with 'other educations' or 'other educational systems', in particular, and the interactions among them and their environments. The knowledge that it contributes is different from that of education studies in general, or from psychology of education, education policy studies, history of education, but there are overlaps, since comparative educations draws on several disciplines. Yet, would we be able to know about the nature of education policy transfers from the USA to Germany and Meiji Japan (Shibata, 2005) through education studies, history of education, or rather through comparative education? This leads to a few remarks on the second principle of differentiation, which I posit lies in comparative education's methodology.

Comparative education, though a methodologically distinct sub-field of education studies, does not have a unique set of methods. In addition to comparative methods (in plural), it makes use of concepts, theories and methodological approaches in the social sciences and the humanities (history, linguistics, etc.) as well as educology. Moreover, comparative education differs from education studies in terms of the number of units of educational phenomena or 'educations' analysed. For explicit comparisons, two or more educational systems are required. Mason (2008a, p.4) claims that what would locate a study, say of 'factors that enhance learning at school' within the comparative education is if it were a *'comparative* study of factors that enhance learning'. Thus, he concludes that the methodological criterion, rather than the substantive criterion, is what distinguishes comparative education from education studies. I would, however, counter-argue that (systematic) comparison is part of all scientific inquiry. How can it then be made the unique factor for delimiting the boundary of one scientific field from another? What would then differentiate comparative literature from comparative law, if both use the comparative method? Even within the larger circle of education studies, there are smaller circles circumscribing subfields such as psychology of education, sociology of education, history of education, etc., wherein the comparative method is used systematically. How are they then distinguished from each other and from comparative education? Do they become 'comparative education' when they *compare* their respective objects of study or does a comparative education study become labelled as 'psychology of education' when it compares two contexts from a psychological perspective? If, as Mason claims, "all substantively defined topics in the field of education studies are able to be researched comparatively", then not only is "there no field of comparative education substantively distinct from the field of education studies" (2008a, p.5), but the obverse proposition also holds: there is no field of education studies that is not potentially the field of comparative education. As mentioned above, García Garrido (1996, p.101) aptly identified the aporia that defining comparative education merely or only as a *methodologically distinct* subfield with no distinct and necessary content could lead to.

In order to address this problem, I posit that there must be a *co-principle* to the comparative method that distinguishes one scientific field from another, one comparative field from another, and two or more subfields (of a parent field) that both use the comparative method from each other. I contend that a specific *object* of comparison must serve as the *co-principle* of the comparative method, both principles being essential co-constitutive elements for defining the distinct substance of any field. Thus, responding to Mason's claim that comparative education is only a methodologically distinct subfield of education studies, I would counter that comparative education is both a methodologically *and* a substantively distinct subfield of education studies. But, in what does the distinct substantive content of comparative education consist of?

Extracting diverse elements from the definitions given by several scholars (Cowen, 1982a; García Garrido, 1996; Epstein, 1994), I would provisionally define comparative education as

> *the subfield of education studies that systematically examines educational systems and their relations with intra- and extra-educational phenomena within and among two or more nations. Its specific object is 'educational systems' and the interactions among them, examined from a cross-cultural (or cross-national, cross-regional, cross-societal) perspective through the systematic use of the comparative method.*

A sceptical reader might concede to the above, but only in part, recognising that in the 'world of ideas' (Platonic sense), these arguments make sense, but not so in the 'world of reality'. He or she might counter-claim that in the real world, comparative education exhibits both a substantive and methodological centrelessness (as discussed in Chapter 3), and as countenanced and legitimated by the all-inclusive Bray and Thomas (1995) framework of comparative education analyses. I agree that this claim is true, but would point out that an appeal to empirical arguments is an indefensible leap in logical argumentation. I reiterate my stance that it is logically comprehensible and desirable that a subfield be delineated not only on methodological grounds, but also on and inseparably from substantive grounds.

I propose a third principle of differentiation within education studies (and within any discipline or field, for that matter): teleology. Jantsch, in stating the unique feature of interdisciplinarity (1972, pp.106-107), claims that it introduces a teleological dimension, a sense of purpose that unites several disciplines at a higher level. I would therefore argue that comparative education is a substantively and methodologically distinct subfield of education studies, which, because of its interdisciplinarity, provides a platform for dialogue and interaction among other subfields of education studies, and these with other extra-educational disciplines. As defined by Epstein (1994, p.918), comparative education is concerned with "international problems of education", with the "transsocietal study" of education, applying interdisciplinary theories and methods. I claim that comparative education not only exhibits the abovementioned features of interdisciplinarity, in that it draws its theoretical frameworks from established disciplines, but also in the sense of giving a distinct and higher purpose to comparative education studies. Hirst (1974c) argues that a field is not only defined by its object; it could also be defined by a common higher pursuit. This higher pursuit could be synoptic or instrumental (Lynton, 1985, cited in Klein, 1990, p.41). A synoptic purpose of interdisciplinarity, as discussed in Chapter 2, seeks unity and synthesis in knowledge, while an instrumental justification attempts to solve problems usually practical in origin. These two purposes have bound (and continue to bind) the (sub-)field of comparative education together, one perhaps more saliently than the other at different points in time and space, and perhaps overshadowing at times the common object of study and/or methodology in the field. I visualise comparative education as an interdisciplinary subfield of education studies, substantively and methodologically distinct from it and intersecting with other educational sciences. As Olivera (1988) posits, comparative education works at a higher level of analysis, drawing on previously elaborated comparative analyses as well as theoretical inputs from the fields of education studies, the social sciences and other disciplines.

Defined by Purpose

Teleology is the doctrine that the existence of phenomena may be explained with reference to the purposes they serve. This is the approach taken in this section to explain or define comparative education. In the first place, I survey three principal purposes of comparative education as prescribed or described by comparativists: the theoretical, pragmatic and critical.

Several authors have attempted to synthesise the main purposes of comparative education (e.g., Jones, 1971; Arnove, 2007). Arnove proposes three principal thrusts of comparative and international education: scientific, pragmatic, and international/global understanding, viewing these dimensions as closely related and converging. The *scientific* dimension refers to the goal of comparative education to contribute to theory building: to the formulation of generalisable propositions about the workings of school systems and their interactions with their surrounding economies, polities, cultures, and social orders. The *pragmatic* dimension aims to discover what can be learned from other societies' education systems that will contribute to improved policy and practice at home. And the third thrust is to contribute to *international*/global understanding and peace, a goal that is perhaps more pertinent to international education than to comparative education. Martínez (2003) adds the *critical* dimension or aim of comparative education, important for the interpretation of educational phenomena and comparative studies. These three dimensions – theoretical, pragmatic and critical/emancipatory – echo the three cognitive interests of Habermas (1971), who is also cited by Kubow and Fossum (2007) in their discussion of the field's purposes.

I therefore review the salient points of the authors who define comparative education by its purposes, which I group into three: theoretical, pragmatic and critical. Despite these classifications, these purposes overlap in reality, and will likely continue to do so, further to such calls for the purposeful 'bridging' of the theoretical and the practical purposes, traditions and cultures of comparative education research (Crossley, 2008; Klees, 2008).

Theoretical Purpose

Several authors defend the theoretical aim of comparative education as inseparable from the practical. I highlight a few of their statements below.

Kandel (1933, p.xix) describes the scientific function of comparative education thus:

> The chief value of a comparative approach to such problems lies in an analysis of the causes which have produced them, in a comparison of the differences between the various systems and the reasons underlying them, and, finally, in a study of the solutions attempted.

A few years later, he reiterated that "[t]he purpose of comparative education, as of comparative law, comparative literature or comparative anatomy, is to discover the differences in the forces and causes that produce differences in educational systems" (Kandel, 1936, p.406). In my view, Kandel prescribes in these two statements the theoretical purpose of comparative education at the service of the practical. The aim of discovering general principles (scientific/theoretical) is in order to understand better the solutions (pragmatic) attempted to address diverse educational problems.

A more explicit advocate of the theoretical purpose of comparative education is Bereday (1964, p.5). He suggests that the foremost justification for comparative education is intellectual: knowledge for its own sake. Immediately following this description, however, he cites the two practical goals that comparative education serves:

> first, to deduce from the achievements and mistakes of school systems other than their own, lessons for their own schools ....; and second, to appraise educational issues from a global rather than an ethnocentric perspective, or in other words, to be aware always of other nations' points of view.

These two practical goals could be interpreted as policy amelioration and international understanding.

Holmes (1971, pp.x-xi) echoes similar two-pronged objectives: "One aim of comparative education is theoretical. It is to improve our understanding of education as such; and in particular of our own national problems in education. Comparative education has a practical purpose too. It should help administrators to reform their schools more effectively and efficiently".

Parkyn (1977, p.88-89) defines the specific purpose of comparative education as increasing our understanding of the relationship between education and society through the comparative analysis of trans-societal factors. Martínez (2003, p.58) also cites various authors who argue that the comparative method should produce generalisable knowledge (e.g., Anderson, 1961; Farrell, 1979).

Pragmatic Purpose

Arnove (2007) emphasises that the pragmatic dimension of comparative education lies in discovering what can be learned from studying other societies' education systems in order to contribute to the amelioration of policy and practice at home. Two 'ancestors' of comparative education, namely Marc-Antoine Jullien (1817) and Michael Sadler (1900, reprinted 1964) claim that the international transfer of educational policies and practices is at the heart of the field of comparative education. E. King (1965, p.148) suggests that the implicit purpose of comparative education is "to be useful in the improvement of school systems", and reiterates this policy-oriented stance of comparative education in later works (King, 1977; 1997). This meliorist purpose of comparative education is echoed by Pedró (1993).

Although Jones (1971) does not claim to define comparative education by its purpose, he lists the following practical aims (pp.22-26): humanitarian, communication and understanding among peoples, and educational planning. García Garrido (1996, p.111), however, argues that the purpose of comparative education is "not to offer models to be imitated or rejected, but to understand others and learn from their educational and cultural experiences".

Rosselló (1972, 1978), cited by Martínez (2003, p.60), defines the role of comparative education in terms of determining and interpreting educational trends, as well as being able to predict future directions.

The pragmatic purpose is also salient in the definition of the aims of comparative education by Chinese comparativists. In the first textbook on comparative education published after 1949, Wang, Zhu and Gu (1982, cited in Gu, 2001d, p.238), the authors define the aim of comparative education as: to discover the common educational principles and trends in educational development in other countries, and to draw lessons from other countries' experiences.

Critical Purpose

A third purpose of comparative education, according to Martínez (2003), is to offer a critical interpretation of educational issues, as advocated by various scholars (e.g., Altbach, 1991; Ferrer, 2006; Nóvoa, 2000). Phillips and Schweisfurth (2006, p.19) describe the critical purpose of comparative education, particularly in the area of educational policy transfers, as two-fold: to produce "checks and balances and to provide critical commentary – often commentary which warns against proposed courses of action based on models superficially observed elsewhere". This aspect of the field echoes Bourdieu's (1969) idea of the relative autonomy of the intellectual field – its capacity of refracting external social power – by being able to transform its objects of knowledge into objects of critique. McClellan defines this 'critical' contribution of comparative education in the following terms (1957, p.9):

> Comparative education ... proves nothing, but what it disproves is of utmost importance. It is something like a gigantic magnifying mirror; it reveals to us our own faces pitilessly.... [T]he study of comparative education protects us from resting content with super-

ficial assurances while fundamental uncertainties still remain.

From another perspective defending a critical approach in a Habermasian sense, Mason (2007, p.196) goes further in saying that "comparative education is best conceptualised as a critical social science, incorporating an emancipatory interest focused on the distribution of power and its associated attributes: economic wealth, political influence, cultural capital, social prestige and privilege, and the like … to the end of educational equity". This is probably more within the interests of international education development than comparative education per se.

By way of summary, García Garrido (1996, p.98) lists six uses of comparative education:

1. Comparative education helps in knowing and understanding educational activity in different communities, countries, nations, regions, etc.
2. Knowledge of others' systems enables us to have a more sufficient knowledge and better understanding of our own system.
3. Thus knowledge about others and our own educational systems can lead to an understanding of the principal trends of world education and the choice of better educational futures.
4. Comparative education is an indispensable instrument for the design and implementation of educational reforms and innovations.
5. Comparative education can decisively contribute to international understanding, peace in the world and a gradual elimination of ethnocentric attitudes.
6. It can also be a powerful instrument of educational technical assistance in less developed countries.

Conclusion: Defining Features of Comparative Education

Based on the prescriptive definitions of comparative education surveyed above, certain constitutive elements emerge. Comparative education is a substantively and methodologically distinct subfield of education studies, delimited by its specific subject matter, method and purposes. Educational systems and their relations with intra- and extra-educational phenomena within two or more nations (or regions, cultures, societies) constitute its *object* of study. The comparative *method*, which draws on different disciplinary approaches and theories from the social sciences and humanities, is employed for synoptic and instrumental *purposes*. The synoptic purpose seeks to achieve unity and synthesis in educational knowledge, while its instrumental purpose attempts to throw light on relevant educational problems worldwide.

Now that the distinctive features of comparative education have been established, I proceed to analyse the debates on whether comparative education is a discipline, a field or a method.

Considered as a Discipline

Heath (1958-59) raised the question as to whether comparative education is a discipline. Defining a discipline as a "calling requiring a specialised body of knowledge which is applied with skill for a humanitarian purpose" (p.31), Heath outlines ten criteria which define a discipline, and poses them as a mirror to examine the nature of comparative education (pp.31-32). A summary is given below:

1. A discipline defines its body of specialised knowledge.
2. A discipline is intellectual in character and presupposes a liberal education as a foundation.
3. A discipline requires its practitioners to have specialised training.
4. A discipline requires an in-service learning period for those wishing to enter the field.
5. A discipline is a career field – not a stepping-stone to another career.
6. A discipline performs a function which no other field of endeavour performs.
7. A discipline defines and establishes the paths of entry – formal education, in-service training, and practical experience required, and a system of recognition for those who qualify – and then gains recognition for its standards by others.
8. A discipline establishes a code of procedure to which its practitioners agree to adhere.
9. A discipline exists for the benefit of humanity.
10. A discipline binds its practitioners together in formal association. Through such formal association, members set and maintain their standards, assure ethical practice, encourage likely candidates to qualify for entry into the field, and exchange information and experience for the sake of helping each other to improve their service to mankind.

Most of the criteria for a discipline listed by Heath above converge with the earlier definitions except for three. First, that a discipline presupposes a liberal education background is a dubitable contention. Second, that a discipline is for a practical humanitarian purpose is not a necessary feature for all disciplines, as discussed in Chapter 2. Lastly, I also contest her last criteria citing the existence of a professional society as a justification that comparative education is a discipline. As I have demonstrated in Chapter 3, comparative education societies, including the CIES, are loose groupings of scholars with a relatively flexible professional identity, and who share little or not consensual references on the core content of the field.

Among the early authors who designate comparative education as a discipline are: Vexliard (1970), referring to 'Comparative Pedagogy'; Koehl (1977); and Olivera (1988). More recent authors include Higginson (1999), Gu (2001d), Martínez (2003), and Sutherland (2007).

Others refer to comparative education as a scientific discipline or a science: Kandel (1933), Schneider (1964) and Tusquets (1969), who both use the name 'comparative pedagogy' to designate the field, Noah and Eckstein (1969) and Martínez (2003). García Garrido (1996, p.210) contends that comparative education *is* a discipline, a science, because it has its proper object (educational systems) and method (the comparative method).

Other authors have, however, dismissed the designation of comparative education as a discipline as a misnomer. Anderson (1961) viewed comparative education as multidisciplinary because it could not lay claim to a single method. Bereday (1964, p.x) also echoes this stance proposing that comparative education's

> specific task is to bring several of the concerns of the humanities and the social sciences together in application to a geographical perspective of education.... Comparative education is not any of these disciplines (history of education, anthropology or sociology or economics of education) alone. Rather, it is partly all of them together.

Related positions on the multi- or interdisciplinary nature of comparative education are discussed in the following section. Meanwhile Bray (2007d, p.35) considers that the few who have described comparative education as a discipline have perhaps used the term loosely (e.g., Sutherland [1997, p.42]; Chabbott [2003, p.116]). It could be surmised that aside from the loose usage of the term 'discipline' to designate comparative education, language translation issues also have a role to play in adding to the confusion. In Spanish, for example, 'discipline' is also used to designate a university subject, a course taught at the university level.

The debate about whether comparative education is or is not a discipline continues. Phillips and Schweisfurth (2006, pp.9-10) raise some questions below:

> Does comparative education fulfil the essential requirement for a *discipline* to be 'a branch of learning or scholarly instruction' with its own discrete rules and methods? Or should comparative education rather be seen, as Epstein and Halls indicate, as a contributing field within the cross-disciplinary activity that constitutes 'education' as a subject, in much the same way that educational philosophy or psychology or history provide necessary support within that multi-faceted area of academic activity?

Phillips and Schweisfurth conclude that it is not a discipline in the strict sense of the word, but that it has "sufficient discipline-like qualities to be described as a 'quasi-discipline'" (pp.12-13), playing an important role in educational as well as in cross-disciplinary areas such as assessment, special needs, early childhood learning, home-school relations, accountability, and the like.

Considered as a Field

As mentioned earlier, Bereday (1964) and Anderson (1961) are of the view that comparative education is a multidisciplinary field. Similarly, Parkyn (1977, p.90) alludes to the interdisciplinary nature of the field, wherein several disciplines are brought together to achieve a higher purpose.

Kubow and Fossum (2007) take the view that comparative education is a field and not a discipline, citing both Broadfoot (1977) and Parkyn (1977), who have defended this position. Kubow and Fossum claim that comparative education is not a discipline but a field because

> the word *discipline* itself connotes dedication to a specified set of rules and standards. Any discipline's adherents dedicate themselves to techniques and procedures belonging to that discipline while implicitly or explicitly rejecting methods and techniques of other paths. ... Comparative education, however, assumes no such hierarchy; rather as a *field*, it draws on a variety of disciplines to better understand the complexity of particular educational phenomena (p.7).

Taking a logical (rather than a chronological) approach to the usages of the term 'field' to designate comparative education, I list the following significant statements from leading comparativists. Among the clearest and fundamental statements was that of Lawson (1975, p.346) who uses the term 'field' following the definition by Hirst (1966) as "a collection of knowledge from various forms which has unity solely because the knowledge all relates to some object or interest".

Altbach (1991, p.491) argues that comparative education is a *multidisciplinary* field that examines education in a cross-cultural context He explains that the reason why comparative education is not a discipline is its lack of a standard methodology. This stance echoes the previous definition of a field by Lawson (and Hirst) as one unified by object, not by method.

A rather subtle advance is made by Epstein (1994) in his designation of comparative education as an *inter*disciplinary field, rather than a *multi*disciplinary one. The term 'interdisciplinary', as defined in Chapter 2, introduces a sense of purpose – teleology – that unites several disciplines at a higher level, whereas multidisciplinarity refers to the simultaneous but disjointed application of various disciplines/ disciplinary approaches (Jantsch, 1972, pp.106-107). Thus Epstein defines comparative education as

> a field of study that applies historical, philosophical, and social science theories and methods to international problems in education. Its equivalents in other fields of academic study are those dedicated to the transsocietal study of other social institutions, such as comparative government, comparative economics, and comparative religion. Comparative education is primarily an academic and interdisciplinary pursuit (p.918).

A narrower definition of comparative education as a field comes from Noah and Eckstein (1969), who circumscribe the field's interface with social sciences, but not with liberal arts, as was the case with Bereday (1964) and Altbach (1991). Noah and Eckstein (1969, p.121) declare that

> Comparative education is potentially more than a congeries of data and perspectives from the social sciences applied to education in different countries. Neither the topic of education nor the cross-national dimension is central to any of the social sciences; nor are social science concerns and the cross-national dimension central to the work of educators. The field of comparative education is best

defined as an *intersection of the social sciences, education, and cross-national study.* [emphasis added].

While the term 'field' is perhaps the more common designation of comparative education currently, Laska (1973) notes that comparative education is not an independent academic field, but one primarily dependent upon the area of foundations of education or educational studies (p.296), and not on a variety of non-education fields (e.g., economics, government, sociology, anthropology, and history) (p.297). However, what does this 'dependent' relationship mean? In what way is comparative education dependent upon education studies? Some scholars contend that it is not even a distinctive field within education studies, but only a distinctive method or a context.

Considered as a Method or a Perspective

In the previous sections, I reviewed the statements of comparativists who defended the position that comparative education is a discipline, or a science, or a field that is distinguished primarily by the cross-national study of education and its use of the comparative method. By contrast, in this section, I examine the contentions of some scholars who deny that comparative education is even a distinct field, but view it only as a distinctive method, or a context or perspective within the field of education.

Among the earlier scholars who claimed that comparative education is not a discipline but a *context* was Broadfoot (1977, p.133). She contends thus:

> The comparative study of education is not a discipline: it is a context. It allows for the interaction of perspectives arising out of a number of social science disciplines and from a wide range of national backgrounds. It allows for a greater understanding of the interrelationship of educational variables through the analysis of similar and different educational outcomes of national case studies. In a highly practical sense, comparative studies can provide a context for decision-making on matters of planning and policy.

Broadfoot argues that the distinct contribution of comparative education is to offer a context or platform for interdisciplinary and cross-national analysis of education. A decade later, Broadfoot elaborates on her earlier statement, explaining that comparative education "needs to be seen as the expression of a more generally conceived social science perspective" (1999, p.29). She further claims that comparative education is "not so much a context, more a way of life", in the sense of being the "means of highlighting the multiple levels of cultural perspective and ideological and institutional constraints that constitute the territory for social science" (p.28). In this sense, comparative education is not reified as an independent academic field, but as a distinct perspective or context for critical cultural analysis. E. King's response to Broadfoot's paper (cited by Betts & Wilde, 1999) echoes this position and adds that comparative education, rather than an arena, is an area of complementary investigation.

In the same vein, Kubow and Fossum (2007, p.7) assert that comparative education "serves as *a* device to mediate the relationships among the foundations of education (e.g., history, philosophy, and sociology) and to challenge students to consider the interplay of philosophical, historical, and sociological factors as they analyse the educational approaches of foreign cultures". The authors, echoing Trethewey's (1976, p.ix) description of comparative education as "a sprawling and ill-defined field of study", refrain from defining it and instead take a practical approach, recognising the advantage of including comparative education in teacher education as a means to foster critical thinking among educators and helping them to realise that education does not exist in a vacuum (Kubow & Fossum, 2007, p.18).

There are, however, those who claim that comparative education is *only a method* used in education studies, that it has no specific and unique object of study or content distinct from education studies, and that therefore there is no comparative 'science' of education, only a comparative methodology applied to education. Tusquets and Rosselló, influential Spanish comparativists in the 1960s, concurred in affirming that "comparative pedagogy rather than a science, is a method" (Vilanou & Valls, 2001, p.282; also Tusquets, 1969). Vilanou and Valls further explain that for Tusquets, "comparative pedagogy is not an autonomous science, but a method applicable to all the aspects of the different branches of pedagogy/education, which takes three forms: 1) pedagogical comparison; 2) educational comparison (didactic and psycho-pedagogical aspects); and 3) historical comparison" (2001, p.282). García Garrido (1996, p.93) notes that a few other Latin American comparativists (e.g., Villalpando, 1961; García Hoz, 1968) who supported this view argued that the comparative method should be used within each specific part of education studies, e.g., within Didactics, Psychology of Education, History of Education, etc., but that it was not necessary to have an autonomous educational science claiming an exclusive use of the comparative method. The justifications they offer resemble those set out by Mason (2008a) and discussed extensively in the previous section.

Conclusion: Comparative Education is a Field

I have examined the debates in the literature on whether comparative education is a discipline, a (sub)field, or simply a method or perspective in education studies. The above discussion has demonstrated that comparative education is widely viewed as an interdisciplinary subfield of education studies that draws on various disciplines of the social sciences for its theoretical and methodological resources in order to adequately study cross-societal issues or systems of education. After this examination of the 'anatomy' of comparative education, I now turn to examine its distinct nature from an external viewpoint by comparing it with fields of study with which it shares similarities, either in the use of the comparative method or in its focus on education and/or its international dimensions.

Distinguishing Comparative Education from Related Fields

In this section, I first discuss the disciplines/fields in the social sciences and the humanities that make use of the comparative method, in view of the close links that the educational sciences has with these academic domains. Secondly, I examine the educational sciences and the place of comparative education within this body of knowledge. Finally, I clarify the meaning and relationships between comparative education and related fields which also study international issues in education. This narrowing down of focus then leads to the final section of this chapter, which recapitulates my main findings on the specific nature of comparative education: its object, method, purpose and status within education studies.

Comparative Social Sciences and Humanities

I undertake an examination of comparative fields in the social sciences and humanities in what is essential to them as a comparative field of a broader discipline. This would help put the debate on the position of comparative education within the framework of the educational sciences in a wider perspective.

First, I examine the definitions of some comparative fields. Second-ly, I abstract the elements that define them as a field apart from their parent discipline, in order to capture the necessary and sufficient elements that distinguish them as comparative fields. Are they distinguished only by the use of the comparative method? What do they understand by the term 'comparison'?

Before descending into particular comparative branches of the social science, it would be useful to begin with a 'definition' of comparative social science by Ragin (1987, p.5): "What distinguishes comparative social science is its use of attributes of macrosocial units in explanatory statements". The two elements – macrosocial and explanatory – deserve to be highlighted here. Goedegebuure and van Vught (1996) clarify the term 'macrosocial units' to include "all kinds of social entities beyond the behaviour and the opinions of individuals" (p.378). As to the explanatory value of comparative studies, the comparative method acquires a significant role in offering causal explanations to phenomena.

Comparative Politics

I examine the field of comparative politics and two of its subfields: comparative public administration and comparative policy studies. The discourses about their nature are useful in enlightening the issue of the nature of comparative education.

Roberts (1972, p.63) defines comparative politics as "the study of the relationship of theories and concepts to the universe of political systems, past and present, and necessarily employing comparison as a means of explanation". Roberts highlights the specific subject matter as 'systems', not states; the theoretical purpose of the field; and the comparative approach as a necessary element. He argues that although comparative analysis is inextricably part of political analysis, "there is none the less a legitimate, fairly logical and pedagogically valid area of the discipline which deserves the label 'comparative politics'" (p.9). This discursive move echoes similar discourses about comparative education's distinct academic territory.

Lane and Ersson (1994, p.6) expand on the discourse about the 'crisis' in comparative politics. In the first place, they contend that comparative politics is distinct from and not reducible to the comparative method. While comparative politics is "the study of politics at the macrolevel, referring to units denoted by words such as 'political system', 'state', or 'nation-state' and 'government' (Scarrow, 1969), [t]he comparative method ... is a methodology for the study of any kind of social unit, for example, political parties or societies, diachronically or synchronically" (also Roberts, 1972; Øyen, 1990). These definitions delimit the object of study of comparative politics to the *macroscopic level*. Lane and Ersson further point out, however, that there is no unanimity among political comparativists as to what constitutes the 'discipline's' substance. Three historical emphases could however be identified in the study of comparative politics. First, the 'traditional' approach of configurative description of single country studies (non-comparative) dominant until the 1950s. Then, there was an emphasis on 'craft' or the use of the research outcomes of comparative politics as a tool for guiding policy-making in newly-independent states of the world during the decades of the 1960s and 1970s (what is known as development studies). A third historical emphasis that started in the mid-1950s was the concern with (scientific) interpretation and explanation, taking comparative politics as a "nomothetical enterprise that, as an art, should have a strict structure comprising well-defined concepts and a hierarchical net of hypotheses to be corroborated by cumulative research" (Lane & Ersson, 1994, p.5). These competing (as well as complementary) purposes and thematic emphases mirror the variegated intellectual histories of comparative education as described in Chapter 4.

The political 'system' is taken as the basic unit of analysis. More specifically, Peters (1998, p.22) remarks that 'system' is used to refer to the nation-state or country as well as to sub-national units within a single nation-state. He classifies studies within the field of comparative politics into five types: (1) single-country studies; (2) process and institution studies comparing a few countries; (3) typology formation studies of countries or sub-national units; (4) regional statistical studies from a subset of the world's countries; and (5) global statistical studies (p.10). Single-country case studies or area studies are typically descriptive and only implicitly comparative (where the case is other than that of the author and the intended audience) and basically explicate politics 'elsewhere'. This was – and continues to be – a dominant form of comparative political studies (see e.g., Peters, 1998, p.11; Munck & Snyder, 2007, p.25), although there is an increasing consciousness of the need for explicitly comparative studies in contemporary research (Goedegebuure & van Vught, 1996, p.376). On the other extreme is the global statistical study, whose purpose is to test relationships among political variables for the entire population of countries, abandoning the details of thick descriptions of individual countries. The diversity in the types of studies under the label 'comparative politics', while viewed by some as a weakness (e.g., Wiarda, 1986, cited in Peters, 1998, p.9), is seen by others as a sign of the field's vitality (e.g., Verba, 1986, cited in Peters, 1998, p.10). This discourse echoes similar contestations about the field of comparative education. It can be said that while the foci of comparative politics are political institutions and processes viewed comparatively, the foci of comparative education are educational institutions and processes analysed comparatively. As regards purposes, the comparative analyst is concerned with both practical and theoretical aims in conducting comparative studies. With respect to the theoretical purpose, Peters (1998) claims that, as in any social science, "[t]o be effective in developing theory, and ... to make statements about structures larger than an individual or the small group, the social sciences must be comparative" (p.25). To this end, a specific task incumbent upon the comparativist is methodological elaboration in order to make meaningful statements of practical or theoretical value.

Kesselman, Krieger and Joseph (2007, p.8) define 'comparative politics' as a "subfield within the academic discipline of political science as well as a method or approach to the study of politics. The subject matter of comparative politics is the domestic politics of countries or peoples", usually taking as its unit of analysis the political institutions and processes across *two or more* nation-states or through time in one or more countries.

In summary, the essential object of comparative politics is the macro-social unit of the political system, or more widely, the domestic political institutions, processes, attitudes and issues in two or more countries, or in one or more countries through time. The explicit use of comparison is a clear distinguishing mark, although the historical trajectory of comparative politics has exhibited a widening of subject matter and surface forms of 'A vs. B' studies. Both theoretical and practical aims underlie its study.

Comparative Law

Bogdan (1994, p.17) describes that in the discipline of law, the systematic ordering of legal subjects and fields of research usually mirrors the common way of dividing the legal system. For example, penal law is concerned with the rules prescribing the punishment of criminal acts. Yet, some fields of legal science deal with problems of a general nature which affect the entire, or almost the entire, legal system. To this category belong theoretical subjects such as legal history, sociology of law, and comparative law. He defines comparative law as the subject that encompasses (p.18):

> the *comparing* of different *legal systems* with the purpose of ascertaining their similarities and differences; working with the similarities and differences ascertained, for instance explaining their origin, evaluating the solutions utilised in the different legal systems, grouping of legal systems into families of law, or searching for the common core of the legal systems (*theoretical purposes*); and the treatment of the *methodological problems* which arise in connection with these tasks, including methodological problems connected to the study of foreign law. [emphasis added]

As highlighted in the above citation, the essential elements that constitute comparative law are: comparison (method), legal systems (object), theoretical understanding (purpose), and concern for methodological issues governing comparison. It tends towards generalist, theoretical and scientific pursuits, rather than pragmatic ends. Although comparative legal studies may also have a practical value, including greater understanding of the comparativist's own law, Bogdan's view is that this field is mainly concerned with theoretical and scientific questions He claims that comparative law is an independent science to the extent that it concerns questions which lie on a higher level of abstraction (a comment that resembles Olivera's (1988) view of comparative education), for example "when one searches for the common core of the legal systems, or when one attempts to group the legal systems into families of law" (p.24). Also, research in comparative law normally involves collaboration with other fields of legal research, in which case, Bogdan claims that comparative law is *distinguished by its use of the comparative method*. Bogdan recognises that the boundaries dividing the established legal disciplines are blurred and porous, normally determined by practical reasons (pedagogic, in particular), than by theoretical or scientific grounds (p.25), an important observation that is resonant with the discourse on the boundaries of comparative education.

Comparative Sociology

Sociology is essentially a comparative discipline. Thus, Émile Durkheim posits that "comparative sociology is not a particular branch of sociology; it is sociology itself, in so far as it ceases to be purely descriptive and aspires to account for facts" (1895 [trans.1982], p.157). Higgins echoes this by saying that comparative sociology is better understood as "a method, not a field" (1981, p.3, cited by Crow, 1997, p.24), echoing the insecure position of comparative studies in the social sciences.

Debates are rife on what comparative sociologists compare (Crow, 1997, pp.13-30). The conventional unit of comparison – 'societies' – is problematised by sociologists who claim that there is no unitary concept-tion of society, but that its spatial and temporal boundaries are fluid and tenuous (e.g., Mann, 1986; Runciman, 1989, cited in Crow, 1997). Also, new units of comparison at different levels – other than the dominantly used macro-social unit of the nation-state – are coming into use.

According to Crow, comparative sociology has three main purposes: to 'deprovincialise' sociological thought by revealing the immense diversity of social configurations; to discover systematic patterns of variations observed from social arrangements to extract "that which was, if not universal, at least generally true of a large number of cases" (Inkeles & Sasaki, 1996, p.xi, cited in Crow, 1997, p.2); and to system-atically analyse and explain why social phenomena differ. Crow further claims that comparative sociology takes historical sociology (temporal foci) and area studies (geographic foci) as its points of departure (p.10). It can thus be extrapolated from this that comparative sociology analyses social phenomena at a higher epistemological level and at a higher level of abstraction.

Comparative Literature

Aldridge (1969, p.1) defines comparative literature as "the study of any literary phenomenon from the perspective of more than one national literature or in conjunction with another intellectual discipline or even several". He distinguishes comparative literature from general literature by highlighting that this comparative field focuses on "the relations between one particular literature and others", where such relations may take the form of "affinity, tradition, or influence" (p.3). 'Affinity' refers to similarities in style, structure, idea or mood between two works which are otherwise unrelated, while 'tradition' studies examine resemblances between works which are part of a large group of similar works sharing a common historical, chronological, or formal bond. A third type of comparative literary studies investigates the relationships of 'influence' or inspiration between one work and its precedents.

Remak (1971, p.1) offers a more elaborate and inclusive definition of comparative literature as the study of literature *beyond the confines of one particular country,* and the study of the relationships *between literature* on the one hand *and other areas of knowledge* and belief, such as the arts, philosophy, history, the social sciences, the sciences, religion, etc., on the other. In brief, it is the comparison of one literature with another or others, and the comparison of literature with other spheres of human expression.

Remak, however, qualifies that comparisons between literature and extra-literary fields, if they are to be considered 'comparative literature', must be systematic and be between literature and a "separable, coherent discipline outside of literature" (1971, p.7). In other words, in Remak's view, comparison of literatures may either be *cross-national* or *cross-disciplinary.* These features resemble those of comparative education.

As to the position and role of comparative literature within literary studies, Remak (1971, p.8) conceives of it not as an independent discipline, but as an auxiliary discipline whose purpose is to bridge organically related but physically separated areas of human creativeness, giving a more comprehensive understanding of literature as a whole by extending the investigation of literature both geographically and generically. While recognising overlaps among comparative literature, national literature and world literature, Remak distinguishes from each other in these terms. First, comparative literature transcends national literature in its study of the "contact or collision *between different cultures,* ... and the problems connected with translation" (1971, p.8). Secondly, comparative literature is distinct from world literature in five domains: *spatially,* comparative literature has a more restricted geographic scope than world literature which has a universal scope. In terms of *time* and *quality,* comparative literature has a wider scope than 'world literature', which is limited to literature of world renown whose quality has withstood the test of time, or recent works that have received intense applause abroad. Lastly and more importantly, comparative literature prescribes a specific method – the *comparative approach* – while world literature does not and usually studies individual masterpieces as stand-alone works. Thus, the distinctive element of comparative literature consists in its cross-cultural study of national literatures.

Further contestations have ensued about Remak's fairly inclusive definition of comparative literature (e.g., Bassnett, 1993; Tötösy de Zepetnek, 1998) attempting to redefine the 'discipline' of comparative literature and reflecting the mood of intellectual insecurity that pervades it this comparative field. These debates are similar to those about comparative education and exemplify Bourdieu's concept of the intellectual field as a system of positions and oppositions among agents competing to define the dominant area of their intellectual topography.

Conclusion: Essence of Comparative Fields of Study

The above discussion has demonstrated that the discourse about the position, boundaries and specific contribution of various comparative fields in the social sciences and humanities are rehearsed in the comparative education literature. The continuous problematisation of what is the proper object of study of a particular comparative field and the delimitation of its academic territory from perhaps more established cognate fields or disciplines, is a common feature of the comparative fields surveyed above. These fields converge on the following elements: a concern with *theoretical*, generalist issues; the *'system'* (political, legal, educational) as the specific object of study; the *spatial* dimension (taking the object from *two or more national contexts*); and the use of the *comparative method*. Comparative literature introduces another type of element, similar to that of comparative education: its *cross-disciplinarity*. These fields share a common tool for research – the comparative method – yet are not only methodologically, but also substantively distinct subfields of their respective parent disciplines, whose contribution lies in serving as a bridge to link the national with the trans-national domain, a single discipline with multiple disciplines. This is the essence of comparative interdisciplinary fields: to overcome disciplinary fragmentation and to 'de-provincialise' knowledge from ethnocentric lenses. Together with these shared epistemological criteria, the embodiment of these fields into academic institutions also commonly exhibit high sensitivity to variegated practical and socio-historical reasons that intervene in their establishment and development.

Perhaps due to the breadth of its object and its generalist focus, the identity of comparative fields is usually contested by neighbouring fields, a feature common among intellectual fields, as Bourdieu (1969) observes. Thus, a common derogatory view of comparativists, particularly in their 'pre-scientific' stage, recurs in the above narratives on different fields of comparative study. Non-sympathisers regarded "comparative law as being a play-house for escapist theoreticians having rather peculiar interests" and comparative jurists as "jurists who in their own country pretended to be experts on foreign law, while abroad representing themselves as experts on the law of their home country" (Bogdan, 1994, p.25). Similarly, comparative public administration has been regarded as "a series of excursions into the exotica of world political systems with the intention of describing different administrative systems and, with any luck, developing a repertoire of amusing anecdotes based on field work" (Peters, 1988, p.8 cited in Goedegebuure & van Vught, 1996, p.391). The above has shown that interdisciplinary fields like comparative studies are always faced with the challenging question: what is the necessary and sufficient subject matter of your field? All of the above cited fields are grappling with this question, so is comparative education.

Comparative Education within the Educational Sciences

In this section, I seek to elucidate the different subfields of education studies and the specific role of comparative education in this disciplinary map. Among the works that have discussed the place of comparative education within the educational sciences are Cowen (1982a), Mitter (1982), García Garrido (1996), Olivera (1988, 1990), Ferrer (2002), and Martínez (2003).

Cowen (1982a, p.119) briefly describes the transformation of education studies in the 20th century, from a discipline that was unified by a moral/philosophical view of education and nourished by principles of great educational thinkers in the past, to its fragmentation by the introduction of the social sciences into its ranks. Thus, particular sciences of education took shape, and the moral core of education studies became differentiated into philosophy of education, history of education and comparative education.

With this historical background in mind, the taxonomy proposed by García Garrido (1996, p.209) offers a clear and useful framework for the purposes of this discussion, of which a simplified version is presented in Figure 5.1). He explains that the object of the educational sciences is the educational process. This object can be understood from three different basic elements: the *subjects* or *actors* of the educational process, the *ends/aims* of education, and the *means* to achieve those ends. For the first grouping, he denominates the sciences concerned with the study of the subjects or actors of education as the *anthropological* sciences of education, since they deal with human realities. These include psychology, sociology and anthropology of education. The second grouping, which is concerned with the means or methods to achieve those ends, he calls *methodological* sciences of education. These encompass didactics, school organisation, politics of education, economics of education, and educational planning. Finally, the third grouping, which is concerned with the aims of education, he denominates *teleological* sciences of education, under which he classifies philosophy and theology of education. All of these three groupings tend to focus on a part of the educational process, thus they could also be called *analytical sciences* of education. By contrast, there are those that deal with the entire process of education, which he designates as the *synthetic* sciences of education (e.g., general pedagogy). And lastly, in between these two are the *analytical-synthetic* sciences of education, which initially analyse parts of the educational process (historical or comparative analysis) before culminating in a synthetic study. They can take as an object of study the entire educational process or some aspects of it (e.g., the ends, means or the actors). Under this grouping, García Garrido classifies history of education and comparative education. Mitter (1982) highlights the unique contribution of these two subjects to education sciences as that of providing a historical and geographic perspective, respectively. The analytical-synthetic sciences, in particular, make it possible to transcend disciplinary (or subfield) boundaries within education studies, by using the time and space dimensions. This is what the historical and comparative sciences achieve. Thus, Sutherland (2007, p.197) notes that "comparative education has the difficult task of recognising and synthesising the contribution of many different aspects of systems of education", which individual branches of education studies tackle separately. Such synthesis is necessary for a holistic understanding of the educational process.

Figure 5.1 A Classification of the Educational Sciences

Analytical Sciences of Education

Anthropological Sciences	*Methodological Sciences*	*Teleological Sciences*
• Psychology of Education	• Didactics	• Philosophy of Education
• Sociology of Education	• School Organisation	• Theology of Education
• Anthropology of Education	• Politics of Education	
	• Economics of Education	
	• Educational Planning	

Analytical-Synthetic Sciences
- History of Education
- Comparative Education

Synthetic Sciences
- General Pedagogy
- Special Pedagogy

In positioning comparative education within this framework of educational sciences, García Garrido differentiates between the proper object of comparative education – in his view, educational systems – and the proper object of the specific science(s) of education (psychology, sociology, philosophy, etc.). He acknowledges the complexity of delimiting the different educational sciences, and I will not replicate here the long discussions on the topic. My purpose here is to illuminate the distinctive nature of comparative education from these other constituencies of educational sciences and to argue that it therefore deserves a place in the map of educational sciences, despite obvious overlaps in themes and sharing of comparative methodologies.

In the following paragraphs, I will discuss some of the branches of educational sciences listed above and their relationship with comparative education. Unless otherwise indicated, the ideas are taken from García Garrido (1996). I start with the anthropological sciences, followed by the methodological, then the teleological sciences. After discussing these analytical sciences, I then explore the analytical-synthetic science of history of education.

Psychology of Education

This branch of psychology is concerned with the educational process and specifically the actors of education, their interactions, and the relationships between the individual and culture. Particularly pertinent to comparative education are the subfields of social psychology and the psychology of learning.

Sociology of Education

In broad terms, the object of sociology of education includes "social phenomena", and the "social institutions and relationships with reference to education and society" (Martínez, 2003, p.45). This evidently overlaps with the object of comparative education – educational systems – which are essentially social institutions. A specific contribution of sociology of education to comparative education is its analysis of the behaviour of specific social groups in different contexts (educational, social, political, and economic).

Anthropology of Education

This field of educational sciences is an interface between education and cultural anthropology. It studies the development of education in living cultures (as opposed to prehistoric cultures, which is the object studied by archaeology). The anthropologist can contribute to education an inter-cultural understanding of human behaviour as well as the knowledge of culture itself (Nicholson, 1969, pp.8-9, cited by García Garrido, 1996, p.224). This has particular resonance in comparative education.

After a discussion of the sciences that deal with the actors in the educational process, I now explore the sciences that deal with the means and methods of education.

School Organisation (also Educational Administration)

School Organisation studies the means and methods that guarantee the efficiency of schools, individually considered. Specialists in school organisation/administration have recourse to foreign educational experi-ences and comparative methodology. Conversely, comparativists need a sound knowledge of school organisational issues.

Politics of Education

García Garrido (1996) defines this branch of study as the science that investigates the right use of political power with a view to achieving the highest possible level of education for its citizens. It concerns the methods or the means of achieving educational ends. It needs compara-tive education to offer a critical view of educational policy at home and abroad. At the same time, comparativists need to have some knowledge of political science and educational politics since educational systems are in themselves political systems, influenced by political objectives and established through political means.

At the service of educational policy are Economics of Education and Educational Planning. The first deals with the financing of education, and the second with the application of systematic and rational analysis to education in order to enable it to meet most effectively the needs and aims of students and society (Coombs, 1970, p.14, cited by García Garrido, 1996, p.235).

Philosophy of Education

García Garrido (1996) defines it as the study of the aims/ends of education. In its study of educational systems, comparative education ought to be concerned with the aims and objectives of educational systems, and needs to be familiar with philosophical concepts. Lauwerys, for example, was a comparativist who adopted a philosophical approach, identifying world education systems by the underlying philosophical traditions in each country (Martínez, 2003, p.46).

History of Education

History of education studies both the history of educational thought and of educational reality. García Garrido (1996) classifies both history of education and comparative education as analytical-synthetic sciences. The relationship between the two fields has been long-standing and strong, particularly in Europe (Ferrer, 2002, p.189). Ferrer identifies two schools of thought with respect to the relationship between history of education and comparative education: first, the fusion of these two branches of knowledge by the socio-historical camp (e.g., Archer, 1979; Pereyra, 1989; Ringer, 1992; Schriewer, 2000); and second, the auxiliary role of history of education to comparative education espoused by García Garrido (1996). Ferrer resolves this apparent dichotomy by distinguishing between diachronic and synchronic comparative studies (2002, pp.193-194). When the diachronic approach is used, then a study more clearly belongs to history of education. However, when a synchronic approach is employed, then history of education becomes at the service of comparative education, because what dominates is not the evolution of an educational system, but the study of several systems at one point in time.

Conclusion: Positioning Comparative Education within Education Studies

By employing the analytical framework offered by García Garrido (1996), which classified the educational sciences by their proper object of study, the discussion above has clarified the distinct position of comparative education within educational studies. While the analytical subfields of the educational sciences study a specific aspect of the educational process – the actors, the means, or the ends –, and the synthetic subfields (e.g., general pedagogy) study the entire educational process, comparative education as well as history of education study *both analytical and synthetic* aspects from the perspective of space and time. The hybrid nature of comparative education, with its specific object (educational systems), has the challenging task of synthesising the contribution of many different aspects of systems of education.

Comparative Education and Related Fields

Various typologies have been offered to distinguish the different fields closely allied to comparative education. Halls (1990b, pp.23-24) offered a preliminary model reproduced in Figure 5.2. Ferrer (2002, p.196) cited the work of Van daele (1993), who distinguished among the following related terms: comparative education, international education (as a subfield of comparative education), education for development, and multicultural (and intercultural) education. It will be noted that Halls locates comparative education as the overarching field which encompasses subfields such as international education, intercultural education and development education, among others.

Figure 5.2 Halls's Typology of Comparative Education

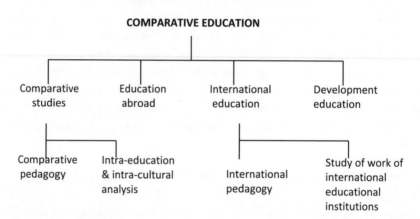

Source: Halls, 1990b (p.23)

In this respect, Phillips and Schweisfurth (2006) disagree with Halls' positioning of international education as a sub-set of comparative education. They propose instead that 'comparative education' and 'international education' be viewed as "consanguineous fields" (2006, p.154; also Wilson, 1994a), as equal and essentially related starting points for 'mapping' the field (see Figure 5.3). Phillips and Schweisfurth contend that both terms – comparative and international – are needed to describe the field adequately, since "[c]omparative education without the 'international' qualifier might be comparing anything ... [while] international education without comparison denies its intellectual foundations" (2006, pp.152-153). However, Manzon (2008b) disagrees with their claim that comparative education and international education are consanguineous fields because they actually have different ancestors (Epstein, 1994) and rather incommunicable bodies of literature: international educationists talk less of comparative education than the reverse. Moreover, the intertwining of the comparative and international education fields was peculiar to some countries, as demonstrated in the professional society histories (Manzon & Bray, 2007), and as Cowen (2009b, p.3) points out, was politically positioned in terms of US and British foreign policy. These different typologies can thus be viewed as varied discursive moves to legitimate one or another definition of the field by locating visually its position with related fields. Halls (1990b) maps comparative education as an umbrella field encompassing a whole range of cross-national educational activities, including international education. By contrast, Phillips and Schweisfurth (2006) place comparative education and international education on equal footing with each other, treating them as inseparable and symbiotic fields.

Figure 5.3 Schema for the Field of Comparative and International Education

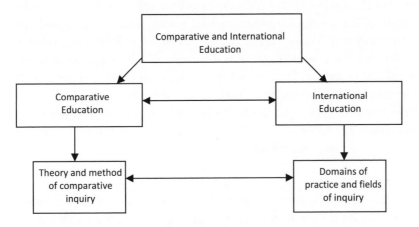

Source: Phillips and Schweisfurth, 2006 (p.10).

For discussion purposes, I employ Halls's typology. After giving a brief definition of these major headings, I proceed to elucidate the terms which have been debated in the recent literature, namely Foreign Education, International Education, Development Education Global Education, and Intercultural Education. I partly follow Cheng (2003) in this approach, who elucidated the linkages between comparative education and these other fields of inquiry, though he excluded Intercultural Education.

Halls sub-divides the first category, Comparative Studies, into two:

Comparative Pedagogy refers to the study of teaching and the classroom process in different countries. Intra-educational and intra-cultural analysis involves the investigation of

> education by its various levels, and also systematically researches the historical, social, cultural, political, religious, economic and philosophical forces that partly determine and are partly determined by the character of education systems, and compares the resultant outcomes in two or more systems, areas or even globally (1990, p.24).

A second category is Education Abroad (Auslandspädagogik) or foreign education which studies the aspects of an educational system or systems other than one's own. A third grouping is International Education which is sub-divided into: International pedagogy "which is the study of teaching multinational, multicultural and multiracial groups, or the education of linguistic or ethnic minorities; it is also the study of such subjects as education for international understanding, peace education, and international population and ecological studies" (1990, p.24). Meanwhile, the Study of the Work of International Educational Institutions overlaps with International Pedagogy, but deals with policy matters (e.g., promotion of educational exchanges, establishment of international acceptability of qualifications). The last grouping proposed by Halls (1990b, p.24) is Development Education, which deals with the "production of information and plans to assist policymakers, the development of appropriate educational methods and techniques, and the training of personnel to implement programmes".

Foreign Education

A term that has been often associated and confused with comparative education in its earlier history is 'foreign education'. Rust (2001, p.iii) cites Friedrich Schneider's notion of foreign education as including those works which mainly *describe and explain* educational phenomena in a *single country*. This is similar to what Bereday (1964) identified as area studies, which are normally concerned with one country or region, in contrast to comparative studies which juxtaposed data from different countries and compared simultaneously their units of analysis. Rust, however, argues that not all single-country studies are descriptive and therefore classifiable as 'foreign education'. They could also be comparative if they "allow readers outside that educational system to understand how its problems might illuminate problems elsewhere" or if "they rely or test more general theories" (2001, p.iv). These criteria concur with those laid down by Rust's predecessor as editor of *Comparative Education Review*: Erwin H. Epstein (see Epstein, 1994, p.922) as well as by Anderson (1961).

Foreign education is less utilised in the contemporary literature and in institutional names. Its use in the 1950s can partly be explained by the then prevailing ideologies (Manzon and Bray, 2007, p.353). Institutions in East Germany (German Democratic Republic) used the term 'foreign education' or 'education abroad' to denote the work that was descriptive or consisted of translations of foreign-authored articles. They avoided the term 'comparative education' because any comparisons were viewed as ideologically risky, until the reunification of East and West Germany in 1989.

International Education

Bray (2007d, pp.51-53) traced the debates that tried to define international education and distinguish it from comparative education. He cited four different meanings of international education. First, Scanlon and Shields (1968, p.x) define international education as "the various types of educational and cultural relations among nations". Distinguishing comparative education from this definition, Epstein claims that international education "tends to be less scientific than comparative education", and that it was less concerned with analysis and study, but more with practice and implementation of policy (1968, pp.376-377). He later defines comparative education as "a field of study that applies historical, philosophical, and social science theories and methods to international problems in education", and contrasts it with international education which "fosters an international orientation in knowledge and attitudes, and among other initiatives, brings together students, teachers, and scholars from different nations to learn about and from each other" (1994, p.918). He claims that comparativists are primarily scholars interested in explanation and analysis of why educational systems and processes vary and how they relate to their wider societal contexts, while international educators are more focused on descriptive information about nations and societies' educational systems and engaged in *policy-making* in the area of *international exchange and understanding*. This second definition of international education seems to differ only slightly from Scanlon and Shield's, particularly in its delimitation of scope to formal education.

Wilson (1994a, p.452) contests Epstein's dichotomous conceptual-isation of comparative versus international education. Instead, he claims that the two fields – comparative education and international education – are *twin fields* and that international educators were concerned with the improvement of national educational systems through the borrowing or transfer of educational models, practices, innovations from other national educational systems. Wilson thus 'appropriates' the *melioristic purpose* as a differentiating factor of international education. In this typology, he includes the work of "personnel in bilateral, multilateral, and non-governmental organisations engaged in national studies, usually related to a development project" (p.455). Several others echo this explicitly *applied and action-oriented* feature of international education, also under-stood as international development aid (e.g., Crossley, 1999; Watson, 1999).

Another definition cited by Bray (2007d) is from Postlethwaite (1988b, p.xvii) who classifies under the heading of 'international educa-tion' those studies that "do not compare, but rather describe, analyse or make proposals for a particular aspect of education in *one* country other than the author's own country." Comparative education, Postlethwaite specifies, is strictly concerned with 'comparing', with examining two or more entities (between or within education systems) by juxtaposing them and looking for similarities and differences between or among them. Postlethwaite thus reserves for comparative education the explicit use of the comparative method, and leaves for international education the wide ranging area of *non-comparative, descriptive and/or pragmatic foreign edu-cation* studies.

Comparing the different definitions of international education cited above, the following elements tend to distinguish it from comparative education: international education is not explicitly comparative, it works on one foreign country/culture, it has a pragmatic/applied purpose, it concerns with fostering international exchanges and understanding, and with the work of international educational organisations.

Nevertheless, the definitions of international education by interna-tional education scholars (who may not explicitly consider themselves as comparativists) offer different perspectives from those presented above. Cambridge and Thompson (2004) identify the use of the term 'interna-tional education' with the work of international schools (e.g., Lowe, 1998). Associated with this usage, they introduced two current interpretations of international education. One follows an 'internationalist' ideological slant, which "identifies international education with the development of international attitudes, international awareness, international-mindedness and international understanding" (also Gellar, 2002). Another is in line with the pragmatic 'globalist' trend concerned with "serv[ing] a market that requires the global certification of educational qualifications" (p.173).

Furthermore, the purposes of international education have been widened by some authors (e.g., Sylvester, 2007, p.11; Vestal, 1994) to include education for international understanding and education for world citizenship, linking it with activities and subject disciplines under the name of international affairs, global education, multicultural education, peace education, exchange programmes, globalisation and intercultural studies. Further confusion is introduced by Marshall's (2007) broad usage of 'global education' (see below).

Despite these distinctions, comparativists recognise that comparative education and international education complement each other. Thus Crossley (1999; also Crossley & Watson, 2003) proposes a fundamental 'reconceptualisation and rapprochement' of the two fields. Epstein (1994, p.922) elucidates this symbiotic relationship between the two:

> International education, by setting the framework for observations of education in other countries, is the starting point for comparative education. Comparison gives meaning to the observations made possible by international education, by expanding the possibilities of analysis. To understand why and how something functions requires inquiry into the relationship among its parts.... Countless statistics can be amassed on education in a particular country, but unless they are incorporated within a comparative framework, the analysis will be limited.

Development Education

Expanding further the brief definition offered by Halls (1990b) above, I cite a few other authors in this section. Parkyn (1977, pp.88-89) clearly defines this area of study thus:

> Basically the distinction between 'development education' and 'comparative education' is one of purpose. Development education is specifically concerned with the immediate need of the developing countries to achieve economic, political, and social modernisation.

He contrasts this with the purpose of comparative education, which is "to increase our understanding of the relationship between education and development" through a comparative study of transsocietal factors (p.89). Kazamias and Massialas (1982, p.314) echo this understanding of development education, and alternatively designate it as 'education-for-development'. Comparative education is thus more academic and traditionally focused on 'developed' countries, while development education is more policy-oriented and focused on 'less-developed' countries. In its applied aims, development education is more akin to international education than to comparative education.

Adams (1977) points out two nuances in the use of the term 'development education'. First, it has been used to refer to "that kind of education peculiarly designed both to reflect the poverty of the environment and to promote community or societal change". Second, it has also referred to "studies and policies of relationships between education and the general process of development" (p.296).

Ishii (2001) traces the emergence of development education as a subject in schools back to the 1960s. After the birth of newly independent countries, the industrialised nations realised their moral and ethical responsibilities towards them and among the means they applied was the introduction of development education in schools (e.g., Sweden, Norway, Canada, France and UK, and later the Netherlands). Its purpose was to enable students in developed countries to be more aware of the existence of economic inequality and unequal life chances in developing countries, and the importance of a just international society (p.330). Ishii further points out that the term used in the USA for this type of studies was 'global education'.

Global Education

Marshall (2007, p.38) uses the term 'global education' to encompass "development education or world studies (relating to the work of organisations and individuals advocating the inclusion of a global dimension in mainstream school teaching and curriculum) *and* the tradition of international education (often defined in relation to the international schools and curricula models such as the International Baccalaureate, IB)". He traced the emergence of the field to 19th century peace movements in the USA, Britain and continental Europe, and the emergence of the terms 'global education', 'education for world citizenship' and 'education for international understanding' in the 1950s, particularly in the UK (pp.39-40). The 1960s and 1970s fuelled the growth of global education, with the rise of NGOs and globally-oriented policies in this area (e.g., UNESCO's 1974 *Recommendation on Education for*

International Understanding). Fujikane (2003) adds to the list of predecessors of global education the following: development education, multicultural education and peace education. Kirkwood (2001, p.12) compared major definitions of global education by global scholars and concluded that they converged on four major themes: *multiple* perspectives, *comprehension* and appreciation of cultures, knowledge of *global issues*, and the *world as interrelated* systems.

In terms of distinguishing global education from international education, (Cheng, 2003, p.20) elucidates that, although both fields promote peace and understanding, "international education conceptualises human beings as political and cultural individuals with a national identity and an international mind, [while] global education tends more to conceptualise that we are inhabitants of the global earth". As Fujikane (2003) describes, after the 1990s the focus of global education has changed: "we are now embracing the idea of new 'world citizens', who acknowledge interdependency, act independently of their nation states, and are constructing universal morality in order to create a more just global society" (p.145).

Marshall (2007) cites two traditions that have tried to articulate the boundaries of global education: the human rights tradition and the International Schools/IB tradition. Human rights education gives an identifiable substance and focus to global studies, while the IB tradition delimits the scope of global education to the role of international schools in the education on international values. The purpose of global studies in this light is to foster a sense of 'international-mindedness'. Marshall, however, qualifies his understanding of global education to the UK context, as does Fujikane (2003) who limits his notion to the contexts of the USA, UK and Japan. This qualification is important since the same term lends itself to contrasting meanings depending on who defines it. My interview with a Chinese scholar, for example, gives another perspective. Zhao (2004) explains that the renaming of the journal *Foreign Education: Information and Reference Materials* to *Global Education* in 2001 sought to widen the scope of research to include Greater China and comparisons within China. Previously, foreign education was limited to foreign countries. Names and definitions thus have a history to them.

Intercultural Education

Dasen (2000, p.11, cited in Ferrer, 2002, p.199) describes Intercultural Education as encompassing three types of studies: the study of a phenomenon within one culture; the comparative study of a phenomenon in various cultures; and the study of the processes involved in the gathering together of several persons from different cultures of origin. Ferrer (pp.199-200) opines that it is in the last type of studies where intercultural education intersects with comparative education. He points out their common focus on 'the other' and similar interest in culture, although while culture is at the core of intercultural education, for comparative education, it is an interpretative medium for understanding educational systems (Pérez, Groux, & Ferrer, 2000). This is obviously only one view of culture in relation to comparative education. Culture itself is a complex term to define, as Mason (2007) demonstrates.

A related and sometimes interchangeably used term is multicultural education. Fujikane (2003, p.137) analyses variations in meanings and in the importance of this area from country to country. In the UK and parts of Continental Europe, USA and Japan, it was associated with the growing problems of immigration within the host society and fostered a sympathetic understanding of the different cultures and races that make up its society. Banks and McGee Banks (2004, p.7) remark that multicultural education is used to describe a wide range of educational programmes and practices related to ethnic groups, language minorities, low-income groups and people with disabilities.

Conclusion: Distinguishing Comparative Education from Cognate Fields

The above taxonomy has illuminated the elements distinguishing comparative education from related fields that likewise explore 'foreign' or 'other' educational realities and attitudes, for diverse purposes. The contrast with related fields brings into perspective the distinctive, albeit not always exclusive, territory of comparative education. *Comparative education, strictly speaking, refers to the academic subfield of education studies, which analyses in comparative perspective educational systems and processes in two or more national or cultural contexts, and their interaction with their social environments. Its purpose is academic, that is for theoretical understanding and theory building. In these three domains – object of study, method and purpose – comparative education is distinguishable from neighbouring fields closely associated with it.* Thus foreign education is usually concerned with a single 'foreign' country or region, and is mainly descriptive or informative. International education is a broad term that, depending on a particular historical period and country, may encompass global education, intercultural education, and development education. International education is also concerned with foreign education systems and practices, but it is not explicitly comparative and its purposes are usually pragmatic – that of improving educational policy and practice – usually carried out in collaboration with international educational organisations. In this respect, it is associated with development education. International education is also closely associated with fostering international exchanges and attitudes of international understanding, and, in this vein, overlaps with global and intercultural education. Global education differs from international education in its interest in fostering an attitude of being responsible citizens of the global world, unlike the latter which is narrower in scope by focusing on several nations (inter-national). Intercultural education and multicultural education are concerned with education of immigrant communities. And development education is generally taken to mean educational assistance to 'less-developed' or 'developing' countries provided by developed or industrialised nations.

Given their different emphases, albeit the absence of a consensus on their exact boundaries, institutional infrastructures (university programs and courses, research centres, specialist publications, professional societies, university chairs) have been named with one or several of these terms combined. The most common (though not universal) combination is between comparative and international education. Among the 37 professional societies of comparative education, six combine comparative and international education on their names, and one of them includes intercultural education as well. Among the society journals, the Greek society is named *Comparative and International Education Review* and the Australian and New Zealand society's is called *The International Education Journal: Comparative Perspectives*. As for postgraduate programmes in Canada, for example, names include: M.A. in Comparative, International and Development Education, M.A. in Comparative and Intercultural Education, M.A. in International Development Studies, M.A. in Globalisation and International Development (Larsen, Majhanovich, & Masemann, 2008).

In view of this diversity in foci and purposes, Cheng (2003, p.26) proposes an alternative to Halls' (1990b) framework. Rather than viewing comparative education as an umbrella field that embraces the related fields of foreign education, international education and development education, it may be considered instead as an independent but overlapping field with its 'sister' fields. I concur with Cheng and would only add that perhaps comparative education could be viewed as a *primus inter pares*, since it provides the theoretical backbone or foundation for the other fields.

Defining Comparative Education

As mentioned in the prolegomena to this chapter, definitions and terminologies do not exist in a vacuum. They are formulated by persons who perceive reality at a given point in time and who address themselves to a given audience. Take for example the definition of comparative education offered by Gu (2001d) in China. The salient emphasis on 'education development' contrasts with more common definitions by Anglo-American scholars of the same period. Another example is with the use of terminologies. At an institutional level, the change in the names of some of the professional societies of comparative education was catalysed by contextual factors (Manzon & Bray, 2007, pp.347-353). This is not to say that all definitions and terminologies are subjective and of relative value. These are only a few examples that serve to make the point that definitions and terminologies have a genesis and ought to be critically viewed *in context*, that is, in relation to its position within an intellectual field.

Comparing Definitions of Comparative Education

In this section, I seek to pull together the main points demonstrated in this chapter. I consider it important not only to compare definitions of comparative education as suggested by Rosselló (1978) but also to do so across linguistic communities (Marginson & Mollis, 2002). This is what I undertook in Manzon (2007, pp.11-13). I selected and juxtaposed the definitions of comparative education by comparativists from the Spanish (Continental Europe), American, Chinese, and South American settings, respectively. First, Martínez (2003), who compared definitions of comparative education by Anglo-Saxon, European and Spanish scholars. Second, Epstein (1994) from the USA, third Gu (2001d) from China, and lastly, Olivera (2009) from Costa Rica, who also compared definitions of comparative education by scholars from different traditions. Table 5.1 shows a juxtaposition of these various definitions.

Perhaps more than linguistic diversity, these definitions might be considered as typologies of contextualised definitions. I recognise the limits and dangers of reifying these definitions into specific types, but this comparison of comparisons is useful for abstracting at a higher level the nature of comparative education. While Epstein's definition may perhaps reflect the North American, industrialised country context, Gu's emerges from a 'developing' country perspective, one that is a new entrant and becoming a major player in the world system. Martínez, having been based on a comparison of many definitions of comparative education somewhat represents the 'mainstream' view, while Olivera could be considered an 'idealistic' view of comparative education (see García Garrido, 1996). I classify the definitions according to three principal domains: object, method and purposes.

Mapping the multilingual/multi-contextual definitions of comparative education confirms that comparative education is an interdisciplinary field, with a proper object, method and purpose. From Table 5.1, we can abstract certain common or shared elements that can constitute an internationally and cross-contextually consistent definition of comparative education. First, the distinct *object* of comparative education

Table 5.1 A Comparison of Typological Definitions of Comparative Education

	Mainstream Martínez (2003, Spain)	Industrialised Epstein (1994, USA)	Developing Gu (2001d, PRC)	Idealistic Olivera (2009, Costa Rica)
Object	Educational systems, problems, processes	International issues of education	Education in foreign countries or regions in a particular country	Educational phenomena in two or more societies
Method	Comparative	Historical, philosophical, social scientific theories and methods	Comparative; from social sciences	Comparative
Purposes	Basic: To understand educational phenomena's interaction with context Applied: to solve current educational problems	To explain how and why education relates to social factors and forces that form its context.	To identify principles and trends of education development as a reference for local educational reform	To understand the similarities and differences between educational phenomena and their forms of interaction with their social environment, and to enlighten decision-making for educational improvement

consists of educational systems, issues and patterns in two or more national/cultural contexts. Second, the *method* employed is essentially comparative, with theoretical frameworks drawn from the social sciences, history and philosophy. Third, the principal *purpose* of comparative education is for theoretical understanding of the relationships between inter-nation educational patterns and their respective societal contexts.

On epistemological criteria, we can conclude that comparative education is not a discipline, but an interdisciplinary subfield of education studies. It is a substantively distinct subfield from education studies, since the proper object of comparative education, *in strictu sensu*, consists of two or more educational systems, or previously elaborated sets of relationships between two or more educational systems. This object is essentially different from the proper objects of the other subfields of education studies. Neither is comparative education simply a method or only a methodologically distinct subfield. Diluting it to a distinctive method in education studies ignores that it has a distinctive object and purpose, and that it does not have a single distinctive method, but draws its methods and theories from multidisciplinary sources.

However, as demonstrated in Chapter 2 (also Manzon, 2007, pp.14-15), disciplines and fields are not only constructed around an epistemological non-arbitrary core, but also around sociologically arbitrary elements. Both sociological power and epistemological power constitute knowledge. The epistemological structure of a field exhibits necessary, permanent and universal features while its sociological forms display contingent, changing and particular characteristics. Both interact with external social structures and the substantive and discursive work of agents who, motivated by intellectual as well as micro-political interests, seek to develop their field and their positions within it. Thus, while comparative education is defensibly a distinct subfield of education studies from a theoretical standpoint (as demonstrated above), it is less clearly so in its empirical substance (as discussed in Chapter 3 and alluded to above on the struggles commonly shared by comparative fields to defend their respective territories). This tension is due partly to the breadth of the object and disciplinary approaches (epistemological factors) used in fields and comparative fields, in particular, and partly to the sociological and discursive forces which intervene in the construction of fields. Drawing on Foucauldian and Bourdieuian perspectives, I now attempt to tease out the way in which sociological and discursive forces construct comparative education as an intellectual field, interacting with its epistemological structure.

Intellectual Construction of Comparative Education

Both Bourdieu and Foucault highlight the socially constructed nature of disciplines and fields, and the historical contingencies surrounding their formation. First, Foucault illuminates the concept of the discursive construction of knowledge fields. As noted in the introduction to this chapter, Foucault views disciplines (and fields) as historically contingent discursive formations of heterogeneous elements, which emerge from power struggles and constitute power relations. Second, and (in my view) complementing Foucault, Bourdieu conceptualises intellectual fields as a dynamic network of hierarchical positions of power held by occupants who compete to define the field, which in turn is a mediating context between forces in the external fields of power and individual and collective *habitus*. The intellectual field's inner logic refracts external forces thereby giving the field intellectual autonomy. In this sense, the intellectual field is constituted both by a cultural or sociological arbitrary and an epistemological non-arbitrary.

Applying Foucauldian lenses to the field of comparative education, Ninnes (2008a) contends that academic fields are *discursively constituted* and reconstituted through the debates of what people within the field and other related parties say it is. He demonstrated this through a historical discourse analysis of the discourses on fear and desire in the comparative education literature. To this view, I further posit that comparative education as a field consists of heterogeneous elements – objects, methods, theories, participants – which, due to historically contingent conditions, have come together to form a more or less stable discursive formation or field known as 'comparative education', institutionalised sociologically in research centres, academic programmes, professional societies, and specialist journals and books. The heterogeneous and contingent features of the field are shown clearly and consistently by surveys of the field's contours (e.g., course outlines, journal content analyses, demographic and citation analyses), as discussed in Chapter 3. Yet, partly through the discursive work of commentaries on specific authoritative works in the field, disciplinary histories, field reviews, and the very contested discourses about comparative education (such as those presented in the previous sections) serve to organise knowledge, institutions, and practices by classifying them and assigning them meanings and values, as well as 'power' hierarchies. A discursive formation of comparative education is thus formed and reformed. A powerful discursive tool is epitomised by the typologies and taxonomies of comparative education formulated by scholars (e.g., Halls, 1990b; Phillips & Schweisfurth, 2006). As noted earlier, Phillips and Schweisfurth diverge from Halls's view of comparative education as the overarching umbrella field that subsumes, among others, international education. They instead argue that international education ought to be positioned at par with comparative education, both subfields thus forming interdependent starting points of an enlarged field. These discursive moves partly shape the hierarchies of power in conceptualising the field. A review of the definitions of comparative education also exhibit what Foucault (1977) denominates as 'dividing practices', by which comparativists distinguish their work from non-scientific comparisons and from uncritical international transfers of educational practices. These dividing practices are salient in the contestation between Epstein (1968) and Wilson (1994a) on the nature of comparative education vis-à-vis international education. While Epstein characterised international education as being descriptive, policy-oriented and "less scientific than comparative education" (1968, pp.376-377), Wilson dissented with this view and argued for positioning international education on equal footing with comparative education as its twin field.

I would, however, caution against a simplistic interpretation of the struggle to define the field misconstruing it as a purely discursive construction that eclipses or decentres the subject (the agent of discourse). In this sense, I use the term *'quasi-discursive' construction* of comparative education to highlight that discourses have a human subject as their author. It is also to focus on the role of structure and agency, which, in Bourdieuian theory, are viewed to likewise intervene conjoined with cognitive interests, in constructing the field. Bourdieuian thought offers insights into the dynamic *sociological construction* of intellectual fields through the interaction of social structure and agency. For Bourdieu, the contestation among occupants in the field who compete for positions of authority to define their field is the very source of the field's dynamism, for "what is always at stake is the legitimate definition of the field and field practice" (Johnson, 1993, p.19). Transposing Bourdieu's insights into the literary/cultural field to the field of comparative education, I view the struggle among comparativists to define a 'comparative education canon' as representing a site and stake of contention where different scholars argue for a canonical redefinition along lines more favourable to or in consonance with their different interests and agenda. This is evidenced in the contrasting definitions between Carnoy (2006) and Epstein (2006), on one hand, and Klees (2008) and Cowen (2006) on the other. Carnoy adopts a positivist view of comparative (and international) education knowledge, in contrast to Epstein, who views positivism as only one of the three epistemological platforms, the other two being relativism and historical functionalism (see Chapter 4). Another position, proposed by Klees (2008, p.303), sets "relevance to the central dilemma of our time (*what to do* about poverty, inequality and development)" as one of the criteria that gives coherence to the comparative and international education agenda. Cowen (2006), however, takes an opposite stance to Klees's advocacy of educational action, by expressing his wariness towards comparative educationists who 'act comparatively upon the educational world', and instead puts forth a distinction between 'academic comparative education' and 'applied comparative education'. This resonates with Bourdieu's ideas on the field of cultural production as structured by an opposition between two subfields: the field of restricted production, as in high art, and the field of large-scale production, as represented by popular art (Johnson, 1993, p.15).

A Bourdieuian field perspective further contributes the notion that definitions of a field are 'positional'. In other words, theoretical definitions of a field can be understood comprehensively if they are examined in the light of the positions and interests held by those who produce them within the intellectual field, which is where *habitus* and the external field of power – academic-institutional, national, and international – intersect and interact. Proponents of diverse definitions of comparative education compete with each other for the legitimacy to define the field. These human authors – agents – occupy different positions of power inside the intellectual field, and interact with intellectual traditions and with external opportunities and demands in the academic-institutional and social/political fields of power. Agents within the intellectual field compete for valuable capital within the field in order to define the direction of their field, and they define it substantively through scholarly discourse. Discourse is thus the (textual) medium by which power relations between agency-structure and epistemology are translated into definitions of the field, thus the *quasi-discursive construction* of the field. These considerations imply that academic definitions are not a priori conceptual abstractions by scholars based on cognitive criteria alone. Rather they are a posteriori definitions based not only on certain epistemological structures, but also on cumulative work done in the field (which is partly determined by practical developments outside the intellectual field and areas of teaching/research that arise from them), and on the position of power and breadth of vision of the academic defining the field in relation to other positions in the field. The intellectual definitions of the field of comparative education are thus constructed partly by epistemology and partly by the interplay of objective social structures and subjective dispositions of agents and their divergent (micro-) political interests. I would go further in saying that, academic definitions of the field represent the *quasi-discursive intellectual construction* of comparative education by individual academics who, through scholarly discourse, codify the relations of power between the external social structures within which they work (from international, national down to the local university), the various forms of capital they hold and the intellectual traditions and criteria that govern their intellectual field.

These insights into the 'positional properties' of definitions of comparative education have already been noted by comparativists (e.g., Anweiler, 1977; Kelly et al., 1982; Cowen, 1990; Marginson & Mollis, 2002). A socially positioned understanding of academic definitions is particularly pertinent to a critical reading of the historical contingencies which led to the emergence of fields related to but distinct from comparative education: international education, global education, development education. Thus, Kelly et al. (1982, p.515) noted that the methodological debates and identity crises in comparative education did not occur in a vacuum. They were intimately linked with the empirical work carried out by comparativists – studies that were largely generated to address the pertinent interests or concerns of national governments, international organisations, and private funding agencies. They also took place against the backdrop of intellectual upheavals in the social sciences and philosophy (e.g., postmodernism, etc). The dialectical interaction of these forces has brought about growth and diversity in the social community populating comparative education, introducing further challenges to its intellectual foundations and definitions. I take the theme of the intellectual construction of comparative education and international education to illuminate the question on how the forces of epistemology, structure and agency, and discourse construct the intellectual field of comparative education.

Extending the insights of the abovementioned scholars to the present work, I argue that the definitions of '(academic) comparative education' vis-à-vis the definitions of 'comparative and international education' can be better understood by teasing out the positional properties of the agents who advocated them and the varied social structural forces with which agents interact. As discussed in Chapter 3, the typology of the USA and post-war internationalism elucidates the intertwining between the discourses on comparative education and international and development education. Favourable American foreign policy, in view of geopolitical concerns to balance world power, offered structural opportunities to extend foreign aid to other countries, partly through the work of international organisations and philanthropic foundations. Within this conducive structure, individual scholars who possessed pertinent forms of capital (linguistic, cultural, political, social) and *habitus* later formed the foundations of a new intellectual field: the field of comparative *and* international (and/or development) education. Due to varied contingent reasons, the growing community of international and/or development-oriented practitioners became associated with comparative education scholars. In some cases, pragmatic and institutional reasons prevailed over epistemological considerations, thereby leading to coalitions between these different subfields. Nevertheless, the comparative *and* international education strand is not a universal and necessary phenomenon. One indicator is the names (and underlying histories) of the professional societies. Of the 37 member societies of the WCCES, only six have the 'comparative *and* international education' in their names. They are the societies of the USA, UK, Germany, Canada, Australia and New Zealand, and the Nordic countries. These societies exhibit a common feature: the existence of a community of scholars working in the field of international and/or development education, a feature less salient albeit absent in other societies (Manzon & Bray, 2006; 2007). Thus, comparative and international education epitomises a sociologically constructed subfield formed within contingent historical circumstances and due to specific power relations, particularly in those countries active in international development assistance or international agency work.

Macro-social factors such as foreign policy are not, however, the only shapers of comparative and international education. Academic-institutional politics at the meso-level as well as individual *habitus* and micro-political interests also play a role. As Bourdieu (1969) contends, macro-political forces do not shape the intellectual field directly, but impacts on it in subtle ways. One way is through institutional policies governing universities, particularly, through resource allocation (e.g., budget cuts/subsidies, research grants policies) and through structural policies which impact on the position of power of one academic field over another (e.g., the contraction or expansion of teacher education, or its structural location within a university department or in a teachers' college). Individual *habitus* and political interests also intervene in the sociological construction of the field. Thus, even within the same national and institutional boundaries, an individual scholar may identify more with comparative education, while another scholar next door may more likely work in the area of international education. Thus, as Marginson and Mollis (2002, p.582) appositely observed: the "match between power and knowledge reflects the economic/intellectual weight of the leading world powers, the geographical and political location of agencies such as the World Bank, and the biographies of academic faculty and agency personnel".

Viewing academic definitions of comparative education as positioned within an intellectual field thus illuminates their constructed nature. Nevertheless, this is not to say that academic fields and their definitions are purely subjective and have limited generalisable value. As earlier indicated, both epistemological forces and sociological-discursive forces interact in the structuring of academic fields. While epistemological structure exhibits universal and necessary features, structural, agency-oriented and discursive forces draw out the particular and contingent aspects of the intellectual field. This echoes Cowen's (2009b) claim that, while the field of comparative education is highly sensitive to the intersection of local and international politics and epistemic transformations, as reflected in its changing agendas of attention, certain core ideas remain that unite the field.

Conclusion

This chapter has mapped the discourse on 'comparative education' in order to clarify the necessary, epistemological structure of the field in response to the question: what is comparative education? I have examined the definitions of this area of study formulated by comparativists coming from multiple linguistic and historical contexts. Concretely, the period covered is from 1933, with the work of Isaac L. Kandel, up to 2009. Efforts were made to go beyond the Anglo-American literature so as to include Spanish, Chinese, French and German discourses.

Applying the conceptual framework on the nature of academic fields and disciplines elucidated in Chapter 2, I categorised the definitions according to object, method, and purpose. I compared four typological definitions of comparative education, thus conducting some form of 'meta-analysis', in order to discern the necessary and permanent epistemological features of comparative education. The analysis revealed that there is consensus that the distinct *object* of comparative education consists of educational systems, patterns and issues in two or more national contexts. Its *method* is essentially comparative, with theoretical and methodological approaches drawn from multidisciplinary sources, mainly from the historical and social sciences. The principal *purpose* of (academic) comparative education is for theoretical understanding of the relationship between education and societal contexts.

Having established the specific object, method and purposes of comparative education, I argued that comparative education is not merely a distinct method in education studies. While it does perform a useful methodological function for other branches of education studies, reducing it to a methodologically distinct subfield within education studies leads to a serious aporia. Since all the topics of education studies are researchable comparatively, then not only is there no distinct field of comparative education, but there is also no distinct field of education studies that is not potentially the field of comparative education. Rather, comparative education is not only a methodologically, but also a substantively distinct subfield of education studies. These epistemological features distinguish comparative education from related fields which study international or global issues in education.

Summarising the results of the above analysis, I therefore define academic comparative education strictly speaking as

> an interdisciplinary subfield of education studies that systematically examines the similarities and differences between educational systems in two or more national or cultural contexts, and their interactions with intra- and extra-educational environments. Its specific object is educational systems examined from a cross-cultural (or cross-national, cross-regional) perspective through the systematic use of the comparative method, for the advancement of theoretical understanding and theory building.

Complementing this epistemological analysis, in the penultimate section of this chapter, I pulled together the considerations made in previous chapters on the contingent features of the field resulting from its sociological and discursive construction. I went further in proposing that the forces of structure, agency, discourse and epistemology interact in a quasi-discursive intellectual construction of the field of comparative education. I view academic definitions of the field as 'positional', that is, as statements formulated by human authors who occupy different positions of power within the intellectual field. These human authors, in interaction with intellectual traditions and criteria, institutional demands and opportunities and wider societal structural forces, compete to define their field, and do so substantively through scholarly discourse. Discourse is thus the (textual) medium by which power relations between agency-structure and epistemology are translated into definitions of the field, thus the *quasi-discursive construction* of the field to highlight the positioned nature and human authorship of discursive definitions of a field. In this chapter, I have thus demonstrated that comparative education is not only constructed by epistemological traditions and criteria, which endow it with relative intellectual autonomy, but also by the discourses among scholars who compete to define their field which, in its turn, is socially located within wider fields of power. I thus construe definitions of the field as codifications of both sociological and epistemological forms of power, that is, as co-constituted by structured and positioned social power and by structuring and non-arbitrary epistemological criteria.

6
Reconstructing Comparative Education

This book has investigated the problem of what comparative education is and how it came to be constructed as a field. Adopting a philosophical and sociological approach, the study sought to understand the institutional and intellectual shaping of academic comparative education by epistemological, as well as structural, agency-oriented and discursive forces. This section recapitulates the essential arguments and proposes a theorisation of the relationship between the institutional and intellectual re-shaping of comparative education in terms of a 'quasi-discursive' construction of the field.

A Paradoxical Relationship

In the previous chapter, I have clarified the question on the intellectual legitimacy of comparative education by identifying the discernible epistemological boundaries which define it as a field with a proper object of study, method and purpose. However, disciplines and fields are constructed not only around an epistemological non-arbitrary core, but also around sociologically and discursively arbitrary elements. While the epistemological structure of a field exhibits necessary, permanent and universal characteristics, its sociological and discursive morphologies display contingent, changing and particular features.

The fairly global historical narrative of the institutionalisation of academic and interventionist comparative education, presented in Chapter 3, reveals a very large institutional superstructure (academic programmes, professional societies) and specialist literature (journals, books) worldwide. Paradoxically, however, recent surveys of the field's contours and contents as embodied in academic programmes, specialist publications, as well as society demographics and perceptions reveal that academic comparative education is extremely heterogeneous, inclusive, lacking a distinctive content, membership and purposes, and rather marginalised at faculties of education globally. Thus, while comparative education is demonstrably a distinct subfield of education studies from a theoretical standpoint, it becomes less clearly so in its empirical substance.

But, why does comparative education continue to be institutionalised as a distinct field in new places despite a dilution in its intellectual identity and institutional status? What accounts for the divergent trajectories between the field's intellectual vis-à-vis institutional legitimacy? I have contended that the dialectic between sociological and epistemological forms of power partly explain the divergent institutional and intellectual constructions of the field. I recapitulate my arguments in the following two sections.

Institutional Construction of Comparative Education*s*

I have demonstrated in Chapter 3 that the institutionalisation of comparative education was not purely the outcome of intellectual pursuits but also of pragmatic and political factors. Institutionalisation did not necessarily follow cognitive criteria alone. A complex interplay of sociological forces at the macro- and meso-structural level and micro-political interests of agents in the field, as well as the shaping force of contingent societal discourses intervened in the field's institutionalisation. I substantiated my claim by examining two main forms of institutionalisation of comparative education as a distinct academic programme at universities and as a distinct professional society, elucidating the underlying power struggles that accounted for their origin and development, and illustrating discontinuities and divergences between institutional and intellectual principles.

In the case of academic institutionalisation as university courses and programmes, the 'USA' typology exemplifies intertwining of discourses on comparative education with those on international and development education, within a favourable structure of American foreign policy and global leadership after World War II. Academics who had the *habitus* and pertinent capital (linguistic, social, political) received the impetus and structural support, particularly from philanthropic foundations, to institutionalise the intellectual field of comparative education in a substantial way at American universities. From this followed the substantial formation of the corpus of the field: academic programmes, professional societies and the publication of specialist journals and books in the USA and outside, partly owing to the influence of American scholarship. This case highlights the sensitive relationship of comparative education to the directions of geopolitical power, particularly in the area of international relations among governments. Moreover, the central position then enjoyed by the USA and England in world affairs, and the corresponding prestige of their universities, partly explains why the academic programmes of comparative education in their institutions served as a model and seedbed for comparative education to take root in other parts of the world. These power-knowledge relations in the intellectual field thus reflect homologies with the external field of world power.

By way of contrast, a similar power-knowledge dialectic is evident in the typology of the then 'Soviet Socialist Bloc', where academic comparative education had been eclipsed, if not 'suppressed', within a radically distinct *episteme* (Foucauldian sense) which viewed comparative education as running counter to the logic of the intellectual field and of the wider field of power. This pair of typologies articulates the power-knowledge relations that have divergently shaped comparative education at universities, ensuing from the same world event – World War II – but differently shaping national contexts and their respective comparative educations.

The formation of national, language-based, and regional societies of comparative education – another form of institutionalisation – I have argued, also illustrates the sociological construction of the field owing more to pragmatic and (micro) political reasons than to purely intellectual criteria. As explicated in Chapter 3, society formation can be understood more dynamically as a quest for *distinction* in the field. Professional societies struggle for distinction within this global field of societies – the WCCES – partly in order to legitimate their existence in the domestic or international scenario as one more entity at par with other entities irrespective of their unequal political, economic and academic power. Evidence of this lies among the responses of some comparative education society leaders (e.g., Australia, Cuba, Spain, Turkey) who explicitly acknowledged that their decision to form a society was motivated by the desire to be represented on the WCCES. In some cases, it was merely symbolic representation since what lay behind an organisational facade was inactivity. In other instances, the formation of new societies represented power struggles over positions and institutional resources, sometimes catalysed by micro-politics. The dynamism of the intellectual field, owing to the competition for 'distinction' among its participants, has contributed to the 'proliferation' of these societies. However, a close examination of the nature and internal consistency of these scholarly infrastructures has revealed problems of a dilution of substantive identity among some societies. Thus, it is not sufficient to argue that comparative education is a well-established field on the grounds that it has a global network of almost 40 comparative education societies worldwide. The varied and less-intellectual motivations and criteria that have led to society formation and that maintain some of them further demonstrate that the institutional construction of the field follows sociological forces and not purely epistemological criteria.

Intellectual Construction of Comparative Education*s*

In the previous section, I have offered the first part of my response to the question: why do the intellectual and institutional trajectories of comparative education diverge? I have thus examined the sociological factors accounting for the institutional construction of the field. I now recapitulate my apologia from the perspective of the intellectual construction of the field, or what I would denominate its *quasi-discursive* intellectual construction.

In Chapter 5, I have elucidated, through a 'meta-analysis' of the definitions of the field made by comparativists, that comparative education is a distinct interdisciplinary subfield of education studies, displaying a minimum base of necessary and sufficient epistemological elements and intellectual foundations (discussed in Chapter 4) that constitute it as a distinct academic domain. However, fields incorporate both an epistemological non-arbitrary core and a sociological arbitrary component. While the epistemological principle exhibits necessary, permanent and universal characteristics, the sociological principle exhibits contingent, changing and particular features. How does the interface of these two co-principles in the discursive activity by academics of defining their field account for the divergence between the intellectual and the institutional aspects of comparative education and, possibly, for the field's metamorphosis over its century-long history?

I have argued in the previous chapter that academic definitions of the field are not static, isolated and based on purely intellectual criteria. Rather they are dynamic, relational and power-laden 'positional' definitions. The variegated and at times contested definitions of comparative education reflect that comparative education is like an intellectual field, within which comparativists occupy different positions and compete for the legitimacy to define the field. The hierarchical positions of power that comparativists occupy in the field are a result of the interactions between agents' *habitus* and micro-political interests, on one hand, and the pertinent forms of capital (political, economic, linguistic, cultural, and partly through cultural capital, also intellectual traditions and criteria) valued in the academic-institutional and, more widely, in the national and international fields of social and political power, on the other. From these unequal positions of power, comparativists substantively define their field through scholarly discourse. Discourse is thus the (textual) medium by which power relations between agency-structure and epistemology are codified into definitions of the field, thus the *quasi-discursive construction* of the field. This implies that although there are epistemological elements by which comparative education can be defined theoretically as a distinct (sub-)field, the sociological dynamism of the intellectual field within which comparativists work, and their interest to preserve and increase their position in the field by adapting to new structural demands and opportunities objectively laid down by the institutions in which they work and the wider field of political-economic power, introduce contingency, diversity and discontinuities in the field's intellectual contours. Major shifts in intellectual thought likewise impact on the field's definitions, as discussed in Chapter 4. These sociological and epistemological principles inject dynamism into the intellectual construction of the field. Thus, the interplay between sociological and epistemological forces, each with varying intensities and 'chemistry', underlie the tension between the intellectual and institutional trajectories.

Comparative Education as a Constructed Field of Power

Integrating the results discussed above, I draw three conclusions: first, comparative education is a constructed field; second, the mutual interaction of sociological and epistemological forms of power are codified by comparativists into the quasi-discursive intellectual and institutional construction of the field; and third, two particular combinations of intellectual and institutional legitimacy seem to lead to the construction of the field or its continued development.

First, I conclude that comparative education is a constructed field. It is constructed both institutionally and intellectually. Both sociological and epistemological forms of power interact dialectically in shaping the field's contours. Thus, academic comparative education initially came to be institutionally legitimised as a distinct subfield of educational studies not only out of an inner logic based on cognitive criteria alone, but also as the result of pragmatic and political reasons working through a complex interplay of power relations among discourses, social structures and human agency. The intersections of various discourses – political, economic, intellectual, etc. – power relations in various structural contexts (geopolitical, academic-institutional) and personal biographies, have contributed in diverse ways to the institutional construction of this intellectual field. These diverse discourse constellations and power relations have intersected within the intellectual field and, ultimately, through the work of individual agents (comparativists), have led to the institutionalisation of the field of comparative education. Once institutionally legitimised as a field and endowed with disciplinary-like structures (e.g., research centres, academic programmes, professional societies), comparative education acquired sufficient ontological existence that 'materially' demarcated it from other fields and enabled it to be perpetuated epistemologically over time. As an institutionally independent field, a distinctive discursive formation, embodied in specialist journals, books, courses and conferences, further developed in the form of specialised discourses on definitions of the field, 'canonical' texts, authors and methods, disciplinary histories, field reviews, which served to organise knowledge, institutions, and practices by classifying them and assigning them meanings and values as in a power hierarchy. Through scholarly discourse, comparativists have thus competed (and continue to compete) to define and redefine their field. Thus, through the quasi-discursive intellectual formation and institutionalisation of a field of 'comparative education', the stabilisation of otherwise contingent and

Figure 6.1 Intellectual and Institutional Construction of Comparative Educations

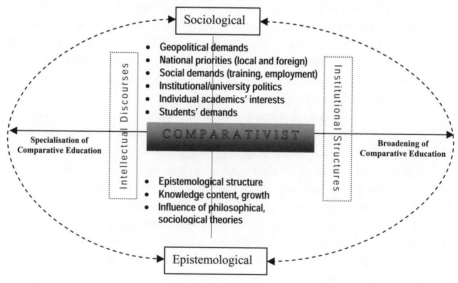

heterogeneous discourses is made possible. However, this stability is not perpetual. Both sociological and epistemological worlds change, and so do fields of knowledge embedded within them.

A second conclusion thus deals with how the interplay between epistemological and sociological domains can be understood in relation to the intellectual and institutional shaping of comparative education. I propose an analytical framework (see Figure 6.1), which pulls together the results of this study. The framework modifies an earlier version offered in Chapter 2 (Figure 2.1) as a 'preliminary mapping of disciplinary change'. As in the original framework, I plot the epistemological forces at one end of the y-axis, and the multi-level sociological forces (geopolitical, national, labour market, academic-institutional, individual academic and students) at the other end. Since both epistemological and sociological factors mutually influence each other, they are connected with two-sided arrows. The present framework, however, incorporates new elements. On the x-axis, I plot on a continuum the two directions of disciplinary change in comparative education: its specialisation into an independent (sub-)field, on one end, or its broadening as a perspective/method integrated into education studies, on the other. These two disciplinary directions may be interpreted either in institutional form (embodied in courses or journals) or in intellectual form (e.g., academic definitions). Thus we can plot the comparative educations resulting from the dialectic of varied combinations of sociological and epistemological forces in different places and at different periods as occupying different positions of the diagram. This analytical framework thus avoids a unilinear, mono-directional interpretation of the intellectual and institutional trajectories of comparative education, and instead allows for discontinuities and differential combinations and gradations in intensity on the way sociological and epistemological forces shape the intellectual field.

I further highlight the role of structure, agency and discourse in this new framework. First, I position the 'comparativist' at the centre of the diagram, precisely at the intersection of the two axes: the field of comparative education and the sociological-epistemological fields, respectively. Second, I also make more explicit the place of discourse in both sociological and epistemological domains. Third, by structure I refer to both sociological and epistemological fields (plotted on the y-axis) as 'structured structures', in the Bourdieuian sense of objective social and/or epistemological conditions. I thus view the 'comparativist' (individually or collectively as a group or institution) as playing a central role in defining the direction of the field along the lines of either integration or specialisation, partly through scholarly discourse, and partly through institutional forms. Comparativists, as 'structuring structures' (transposing Bourdieu's use of the term to describe *habitus*), generate and organise practices and representations in their field in response to the structured structures prevalent in each historical period, while at the same time refracting those external forces by taking societal discourses as the object of study and critique. In these processes, discourses serve as the textual medium by which multi-level power relations between structure-agency and epistemology are codified. Discourse is also the medium by which these power relations are compressed into intellectual definitions of the field, thus its quasi-discursive intellectual construction. Meanwhile, institutional structures serve to 'materialise' those discourses into sociological reality with its respective existential principles of dynamism.

A third conclusion responds to the question: what is the relationship between the institutional and intellectual legitimacy of the field? If, as the current state of comparative education drawn here suggests, the institutional infrastructures exhibit fluidity and marginalisation, then will it lead to an intellectual de-legitimisation of the field? Or is the case the reverse: that intellectual fragility is at the root of the field's institutional weakness? The answer is not straightforward. Obviously, factors of history, politics and institutional power, and personal biographies intervene and interact in a complex manner in 'materialising' the intellectual into institutional form, and, possibly, the reverse as well: in 'discursively' constituting the institutional into intellectual form. Building on and going beyond Cowen's (1982a) investigation of the reciprocal interaction between the intellectual and institutional forms of comparative educations, I conclude that while the institutional and intellectual forms of comparative education mutually interact and often legitimise each other, at least two scenarios seem to lead to the field's establishment or continued development. Based on the variegated intellectual and institutional scenarios reviewed in this book, the dynamic interaction of intellectual and institutional power can lead to the 'creation' or propagation of a field in two ways: first, when both intellectual and institutional legitimacy are strong (pole 1); and, second, when institutional legitimacy is strong even if intellectual legitimacy is weak (pole 2). By contrast, when an area of knowledge either has intellectual legitimacy but is unable to secure institutional power (pole 3), or when both intellectual and institutional legitimacies are weak or absent (pole 4), no new field comes to the fore or the existing field eventually becomes eclipsed, if not extinct. The histories of comparative education and the surveys of its contours seem to suggest that this field has been constructed initially on the basis of strong institutional power but weak intellectual legitimacy (pole 2). As some cases reviewed here have shown, when institutional power is significantly withdrawn, the weakness of the field's intellectual legitimacy becomes more visible. Yet, owing to the field's inertial momentum (Mason, 2008b) and partly to the dynamism arising from the relational-positional nature of the intellectual field, wherein agents – individuals and institutions – interact and compete to make their field develop and their positions within it flourish, the field continues to exist.

Acknowledging Positionalities in the Field

This research raises two main implications for the field of comparative education. First, academic comparative education will benefit from the recognition of the power-knowledge relations that shape it institutionally and intellectually, thereby avoiding its instrumentalisation. Second, academic comparative education needs to be more universal in outlook, adopting not only a multilingual but also a 'multidiscursive' approach that is able to acknowledge one's position as related to other positions and to engage in dialogue with them.

On its first main implication for the field, this research has shown that comparative education is partly a socially-constructed field that is largely determined by the purposes which it serves in its host society. Comparative education initially became institutionalised as having a distinct discursive space partly because of the discourse on its 'usefulness' to governments whether during the era of post-war reconstruction and national modernisation, or after an era of politico-ideological isolationism. Institutional boundaries or intellectual classifications of knowledge, therefore, do not necessarily and absolutely follow purely rational criteria. There are knowledge-constitutive interests at work. Academic comparative education is thus highly sensitive to international and national societal discourses on education, which are then filtered through academic-institutional politics and market forces, and comparativists' cognitive and micro-political interests in the field. But, can an intellectual field's existence be determined solely, if not largely, on the grounds of its usefulness? Can a field claim to be useful because it exists?

Can it exist without necessarily being useful? A lack of discernment as to who defines the field and for what purpose it is so defined runs the risk of the field's potential instrumentalisation. By elucidating the subtle power-knowledge relations that are codified in the institutional and intellectual forms of the field, this research raises awareness among comparativists and educational practitioners to this danger and brings into focus the importance of clarifying what epistemological and axiological lenses influence in their work (McClellan, 1957).

This book has illustrated how the interplay of structure-agency and epistemology has discursively and institutionally shaped comparative educations. In this view, the second main implication of this research suggests that comparative education practitioners need to exercise a greater sensitivity by explicitly acknowledging the positional nature of their institutional and intellectual configurations of the field, and to recognise and dialogue with *other* positions in order to give a balanced and comprehensive view of it. It also raises the ante for the need for those transmitting the field to the next generations to incorporate and acknowledge the diverse epistemological foundations – the epistemologically necessary core – in their definitions of the field, as well as the variegated histories of comparative education – the sociologically contingent manifestations – thereby adopting a universal outlook and avoiding ethnocentric and reductionist perspectives in their work.

The epistemological and axiological lenses are important in any educational research endeavour. In this light, human agency needs to regain its rightful place in (self-) determining the rightful use of comparative education. I join the voices that call for an increased awareness among the field's practitioners of the potential instrumentalisation (and risk of extinction) of comparative education if it does not pay attention to the values that orient its work. In this sense, philosophical reflection plays an important role in comparative education (McLaughlin, 2004).

Towards a Reflexive Comparative Education?

The contribution of this research to the scholarly literature on the nature of the field of comparative education, and of academic fields in general, can be summarised in two main points. First, it represents a globally extensive and systematically comparative philosophical and sociological analysis of the institutional histories and intellectual definitions of the field of comparative education. Second, it refines the explanatory framework on the intellectual and institutional construction of academic fields, by employing both realist and constructionist perspectives, and reconciling the roles of epistemology, structure-agency and discourse in this process, as it addresses some limits in Foucauldian and Bourdieuian frameworks and in contemporary studies analysing the development of comparative education mainly through historical discourse analysis.

This book is perhaps the first systematic, globally comprehensive and explicitly comparative analysis of the nature of comparative education and of its institutional histories. It draws from a wealth of data that the researcher has gathered in the course of her four year study and direct participation in global research projects on the institutional histories of comparative education and in WCCES forums. This work takes a multilingual, multi-contextual approach to substantiate and enrich the philosophical and sociological arguments presented. Through the diversity of cases explored, I hope to have raised the awareness and questioned some of the long-held assumptions regarding comparative education.

Second, this research refines the explanatory framework on the intellectual and institutional construction of the field of comparative education in particular, and of academic fields in general. By synthesising Foucault and Bourdieu, and recognising the role of epistemological power, the framework herein proposed reconciles the dichotomy between structure-agency oriented theories and discourse-oriented frameworks. It shows that neither is comparative education an absolutely autonomous body of knowledge governed purely by its own cognitive logic, nor is it merely a reflection of social power in the external world or a result of language games. The relation between power in the social world and knowledge in this intellectual field is neither direct nor unidirectional. Comparative education is a field constructed by both epistemological and sociological power, which interact in complex ways through the discourses of comparative education scholars and their work on the institutionalisation of the field. This research re-positions academics in a central place as they, in interaction with objective sociological and epistemological structures, codify power-knowledge relations into their discursive intellectual definitions of the field and in the edification of its institutional structures. It thus recovers the crucial role of the individual comparativist (the human agent) in determining the direction of the field, within the objective social conditions posed by external fields of power and by the intrinsic epistemological structure of knowledge. In this aspect, it diverges from some Foucauldian interpretations of discourse as all-encompassing and eclipsing a human author, and their consequent reductionist interpretations of knowledge construction as purely 'text-driven'. Instead, discourse is viewed here only as a textual medium through which scholars construct the field. However, this quasi-discursive intellectual construction is only fully empowered when it becomes incarnated in institutional structures, or, as the case may be, when it aligns itself with and intellectually legitimises existing institutional forms, a point that seems to be weakly addressed by historical discourse analyses of the field. Thus, in my view, discourse is constituted or positioned within the boundaries of objective epistemological and sociological structures, and is defined by human authors.

The analytical framework proposed in this book views the interrelation between the socio-political world, within which comparative education is embedded, and the field of academic comparative education, not as a one-to-one reflection. Rather, it highlights the agency of the scholars involved, mediated through the intellectual traditions (epistemological domain) which they have acquired, and the academic institutions in which their discourses were to be positioned. The present research therefore extends the explanatory framework of Bourdieu by incorporating the explicit role of discourse, as a medium used by scholars to intellectually define the contours of their field. It also applies realist philosophical insights to elucidate the nature of academic disciplines and fields, thereby illuminating their intrinsic epistemological structure as the necessary, non-arbitrary core of knowledge. The multi-dimensional framework used in this book thus gives due recognition to the crucial role of discourse, while avoiding the reduction of the field's reality and construction to discourse by recognising the centrality of human authors who freely and responsibly interact with objective sociological and epistemological structures in shaping the intellectual field.

The field of comparative education is a field in construction. The cross-contextual comparisons presented here have illustrated that the institutional history of an intellectual field is not linear, unidirectional and necessary. Rather they are non-linear, multidirectional and contingent. This study may contribute to helping comparativists, and other scholars working in other interdisciplinary fields, to reflect on the purposes and processes by which their fields have come to be, and on the consequences of their action on it. It may thus contribute to re-conceptualising our understanding of the nature and development not only of comparative education, but also of other fields. Its detailed analysis of the complex interactions among structure, agency and discourse in shaping a variety of 'intellectual fields' within comparative education raises awareness on the need for a critical attitude towards meta-narratives on disciplinary histories. My interpretation of the field is only one view, and it stands to benefit from the ensuing contestation and debate to which this work aspires to contribute.

Appendix 1
List of Key Informants Interviewed
(October 2004 to January 2007)

		Name	Date Interviewed	No.
WCCES Presidents	1980-83	Erwin H. Epstein	Oct '04	3
	1983-87	Michel Debeauvais	Oct '04	2
	1987-91	Vandra Masemann	Oct '04	11
	2001-04	Anne Hickling-Hudson	Oct '04	1
WCCES Standing Committees	Research	Juergen Schriewer	Aug '05	30
	Congress; Secretary General	Christine Fox	Aug '05	25
REGIONAL	SACHES	Sheldon Weeks	Oct '04	14
	ANZCIES	Anthony Welch	Jan '05	21
	CESA	Kengo Mochida	May '05	23
NATIONAL	SEEC	José Luis García Garrido	Oct '04	5
		Ferran Ferrer	Oct '04	8
			Jan '06	31
		Luís María Naya Garmendia	Oct '04	9
	SIIVEDGE	Dietmar Waterkamp	Oct '04	7
			May '05	24
	BAICE	Michael Crossley	Oct '04	10
			Apr '05	22
	SBEC	Robert Verhine	Oct '04	6
		Sonia Nogueira	Oct '04	13
	AFDECE	Dominique Groux	Oct '04	17
	CCES	Gu Mingyuan	Nov '04	18
			Aug '05	28
		Wang Yingjie	Nov '04	19
		Zhao Zhongjian	Nov '04	20
			Aug '05	26
		Zhong Qiquan	Aug '05	29
		Gao Yimin	Aug '05	27
	CESI	Nina Dey-Gupta	Oct '04	15
	TÜKED	Fatma Gök	Jan '07	32
	CCEK	Kulamergen Mussin	Jan '07	33
LANGUAGE-BASED	AFEC	Alain Carry	Oct '04	16
		Pierre-Louis Gauthier	Oct '04	12
	NGVO	Sylvia van de Bunt-Kokhuis	Oct '04	4

Total: 33 interviews (including 5 with 2nd interviews)

A Chronology of the Institutionalisation of Comparative Education World Wide

Appendices 2 to 6

Notes: Entries in the chart list the commencement of comparative education as institutionalised in the form of a university course, specialised publication and as a professional society. It is not comprehensive, but I have attempted to include as far as possible all the available data from the sources cited.

(1) *University courses* could either be as a lecture course or as an academic programme. The teaching of comparative education usually commences in the form of a lecture course, oftentimes, an optional course, and only later develops into a formal academic programme. Course names vary from comparative education, comparative pedagogy, educational systems abroad, and similar terms.

(2) *Publications* are listed in two categories: (a) specialist textbooks/encyclopedias, and (b) journals/yearbooks. Textbooks are listed by author(s) name; complete book titles are listed in the References section. The textbooks listed are probably the first original works published under the title 'comparative education' or 'comparative pedagogy' by indigenous authors in the local language of the country of publication.

(3) Professional societies are listed by year of establishment. Complete society names are listed in Table 3.12. For those societies that have changed names over time, the names used here are their current names, not the original name when they were established.

(4) Countries/universities are also listed using their current denomination.

Sources: Dey Gupta (2004); Epstein (2008); Frenay et al. (1999); Gök (2007); Groux & Paul (1999); Halls (1990a); Makatiani & Chege (2008); Masemann et al. (2007); Soudien (2007); Wolhuter (2006); Wolhuter et al. (2008a).

A Chronology of the Institutionalisation of Comparative Education World Wide

Appendix 2   North America

	1900 - 1945	1945 - 1970	1970 - 2000	2000 - 2008
UNIVERSITY COURSES	1900: J. Russell, Columbia University, USA 1913: P. Sandiford, University of Toronto, Canada (Anglophone) 1924: Institut pedagogique de Westmount, Canada (Francophone)			
PUBLICATIONS **Textbooks and Encyclopedias**	Sandiford (1918, Canada) Kandel (1933, USA)		Encyclopedia: Kurian (1988); Wickremasinghe (1992)	
Journals and Yearbooks	*The Educational Yearbook* (1924-44)	*Comparative Education Review* (1957, USA)	*Canadian and International Education* (1972, Canada); *Current Issues in Comparative Education* (1997, USA)	
PROFESSIONAL SOCIETIES		1956 CIES (USA) 1967 CIESC (Canada)		

A Chronology of the Institutionalisation of Comparative Education World Wide

Appendix 3   Europe

1900 - 1945	1945 - 1970	1970 – 2000	2000 - 2008
UNIVERSITY COURSES			
1905: I. Kandel, Manchester University, England 1920s: S. Hessen, Prague (now Czech Republic) & Warsaw (Poland) 1925: C. Negentzov, Bulgaria 1930s: University of Oslo, Norway	1950: University of Hamburg, Germany (1st chair) 1951: R.L. Plancke, Ghent, Flanders 1956: P. Idenburg, Amsterdam, The Netherlands; Hungary 1957: Academy of Pedagogical Sciences, Moscow, Russia 1958: M. Debesse, Sorbonne, France 1960: University of Zagreb, Croatia 1961: T. Husén, University of Stockholm, Sweden 1962: Université de Liège, Belgium 1963: H-G. Hofmann, East Berlin, Germany 1964: J. Tusquets, Barcelona, Spain 1965: K. Grue-Sørensen, Copenhagen, Denmark late 1960s: Ankara, Turkey; Helsinki, Finland *Hiatus*: Socialist countries (1945-1989)	1973: P. Furter, University of Geneva, Switzerland 1979: A. Kazamias, M. Eliou, Greece 1990s: resumption in former countries of the Soviet Union (Czech, Poland, new Russia, etc.)	2002: T. Winther-Jensen, Danish University of Education (1st Danish professorship in comparative education; despite early introduction in1965).

Appendix 3 Europe (cont'd)

	1900 - 1945	1945 - 1970	1970 – 2000	2000 - 2008
PUBLICATIONS				
Textbooks and Encyclopedias	Czech Encyclopedia of Education (1891-1909)	Schneider (1947, Germany); Hans (1949, UK); Sjösted & Sjöstrand (1952, Sweden); E. King (1958, England); Idenburg (1959, the Netherlands); Chakarov (1969, Bulgaria); Vexliard (1967, France); Tusquets (1969).	Franković (1972, Croatia); Glenstrup (1973, Denmark); Orizio (1977, Italy); Sokolova et al. (1978, USSR); Mitrović (1981, Bosnia & Herzegovina); Raivola (1984, Finland); García Garrido (1986 [1996], Spain); Bishkov & Popov (1994, Bulgaria); Pachocinski (1995, Poland); Malkova & Wulfson (1996, new Russia); Vánova (1998, Czech Republic) Encyclopedias: Postlethwaite (1988a, UK); Husén & Postlethwaite (1994, UK)	Bouzakis (2002, 2003, 2005, Greece)
	1900 - 1945	**1945 - 1970**	**1970 – 2000**	**2000 – 2008**
Journals and Yearbooks	*International Education Review [IER]* (1930, Germany); *Year Book of Education* (1932, University of London Institute of Education); *International Yearbook of Education* (1933, IBE)	*IER* became *International Review of Education* (1955, UNESCO, Germany); *Perspectivas Pedagogicas* (1958-84, Spain); *Comparative Education* (1964, UK); *Compare* (1970, UK); *Prospects* (1970, UNESCO)	*International Journal of Educational Development* (1979, UK); *Revista Española de Educación Comparada* (1995, Spain); *Oxford Studies in Comparative Education* (1990, UK); *Bildung und Erziehung* (Germany)	*Politiques de éducation et de formation* (2001-2004/05, France) ; *Comparative and International Education Review* (2002, Greece); *Research in Comparative and International Education* (2006, UK)

Appendix 3   Europe (cont'd)

1900 - 1945	1945 - 1970	1970 – 2000	2000 - 2008
PROFESSIONAL SOCIETIES			
	1961 CESE (European)	1973 AFEC (Francophone), NGVO (Dutch)	2004 MESCE (Mediterranean)
	1964-70 CSPS-CES (Czech)	1974 SEEC (Spain)	2006 TÜKED (Turkey)
	1966 BAICE (British Section of CESE), SIIVEDGE (German Section of CESE)	1986 SICESE (Italian Section of CESE)	2010 UCES (Ukraine-new)
	1970 HPS-CES (Hungary)	1990 CPS-CES (new Czech)	
		1991 BCES (Bulgaria), GCES (Greece), PCES (Poland)	
		1992 NOCIES (Nordic)	
		1995 RCCP (new Russia)	
		1998 AFDECE (France)	
		1990s: Portugal and Ukraine CE society (defunct in 2000s)	

A Chronology of the Institutionalisation of Comparative Education World Wide

Appendix 4   Africa

	1900 - 1945	1945 – 1970	1970 - 2000	2000 - 2008
UNIVERSITY COURSES	1925: Makerere University, Uganda 1945: National University of Lesotho	1957: University of Zimbabwe 1957: Ain Shams University, Egypt mid-1960s: South African universities 1966: National Institute of Education, Rwanda 1970: Kenyatta University, Kenya; University of Dar es Salaam, Tanzania	1977: University of Burundi 1990s University of Namibia 1998: Université de la Réunion	2005: University of Swaziland
PUBLICATIONS				
Textbooks and Encyclopedias		Samaan (1958, Egypt)	Potgieter (1972, South Africa) Rwantabagu (1990, Kenya)	
Journals and Yearbooks			*Southern African Review of Education with Education with Production* (1995, South Africa)	
PROFESSIONAL SOCIETIES			1980s An Egyptian and a Nigerian society were admitted to the WCCES, but became defunct in the 1990s. 1991 SACHES (Southern Africa) 1991 ECEEAS (Egypt- new society)	

A Chronology of the Institutionalisation of Comparative Education World Wide

Appendix 5   Asia and Australasia

	1900 - 1945	1945 - 1970	1970 - 2000	2000 - 2008
UNIVERSITY COURSES	1938: Tokyo University, Japan 1930s: Beijing Normal University, Zhongshan University, People's Republic of China [PRC]; (hiatus 1937-1970s) 1939: The University of Hong Kong 1945: University of Sydney, Australia	1953: Yonsei University, South Korea 1960: Chulalongkorn University, Thailand 1965: University of New Delhi, India 1970: University of Malaya, Malaysia	1986 Sultan Qaboos University, Oman 1991 Kazakhstan	
PUBLICATIONS				
Textbooks and Encyclopedias	Higuchi (1928, Japan) Chang (1930, PRC)	Mukherjee (1959, India) Rim (1961, Korea) Lei (1967, Taiwan, Republic of China [ROC]) P.E. Jones (1971, Australia)	Wong (1973, Malaysia) Wang, Zhu & Gu (1982, PRC) Belkanov (1994, Kazakhstan)	Issan (2006, Oman) Bray et al. (2007, Hong Kong) Encyclopedia: Taneja (2000, India)
Journals and Yearbooks		*Comparative Education Review* [Beijing] (1965, PRC)	*Global Education* (1972, PRC) *Korean Journal of Education* (1971, Korea) *Comparative Education Studies* (1975, Japan) *Journal of Comparative Education* (1997, Taiwan) *Comparative Education Bulletin* (1998, Hong Kong)	*Compare* [CESA Journal] (2006, Malaysia) *The International Education Journal* (2007, Australia)

Appendix 5 Asia and Australasia (cont'd)

1900 – 1945	1945 - 1970	1970 - 2000	2000 – 2008
PROFESSIONAL SOCIETIES			
	1965 JCES (Japan)	1973 ANZCIES (Australia & New Zealand)	2001 CESP (Philippines)
	1968 KCES (Korea)	1974 CCES-T (Taipei, Taiwan)	2005 CCEK (Kazakhstan)
		1979 CCES (PRC); CESI (India)	
		1988 ICES (Israel)	
		1989 CESHK (Hong Kong)	
		1995 CESA (Asian)	

A Chronology of the Institutionalisation of Comparative Education World Wide

Appendix 6   Latin America and the Caribbean

	1900 – 1945	1945 – 1970	1970 - 2000	2000 - 2008
UNIVERSITY COURSES				
	1939: University of Brazil 1944: University of Havana, Cuba	1955: Universidad Nacional Autónoma de México 1967: University of Chile (discontinued in 1973)	1976: Universidad de Buenos Aires, Argentina	2005: Universidad de la Empresa, Uruguay
PUBLICATIONS				
Textbooks and Encyclopedias	Pérez (1945, Cuba)	Filho (1961, Brazil) Villalpando (1961, Mexico)	Marquez (1972, Argentina) Fuentealba (1985, Chile)	Olivera (2009, Costa Rica)
PROFESSIONAL SOCIETIES			1980s An Argentinean and a Colombian society were admitted to the WCCES, but became defunct in the 1990s 1980s SVEC (Venezuela) 1983 SBEC (Brazil) 1994 APC-SEC (Cuba)	2001 SAECE (Argentina- new) 2003 SOMEC (Mexico)

Appendix 7
Number of Universities where
Comparative Education is Taught
(June 2008)

Country	Source	Bache-lor's	Mas-ter's	Specialist Programme
EUROPE TOTAL		**161**	**27**	
Bulgaria	Wolhuter et al., 2008b	6	n.a.	n.a.
Croatia	Vrcelj, 2008	3	---	---
Czech Republic	Walterova, 2008 (1)	10	n.a.	---
Denmark	Winther-Jensen, 2008 (1)	n.a.	1	---
Finland	Raivola, 2008	n.a.	n.a.	---
France	Poizat, 2008	n.a.	n.a.	---
Germany	Waterkamp, 2008 (3)	20	n.a.	---
Greece	Karras, 2008	9	n.a.	---
Hungary	Holik, 2008 (1)	4	n.a.	---
Ireland	O'Sullivan, 2008	3	n.a.	---
Italy	Palomba & Paolone, 2008	25	n.a.	---
Norway	Brock-Utne & Skinningsrud, 2008	2	2	M. in CIE (Oslo)
Poland	Potulicka, 2007 (1)	5	5	
Portugal	Senent, 2005 (1)	4	n.a.	---
Russia	Golz, 2008	6	n.a.	
Spain	Naya et al., 2008	39	n.a.	n.a.
Switzerland	Schussler & Leutwyler, 2008	2		M. in Inter-cultural & CE (Fribourg)
The Netherlands & Flanders	Boerma et al., 2008	3	1	---
UK	Wilson, 2005	20	18	M. in CE (London, Oxford, Bristol) (1)
NORTH AM TOTAL		**21**	**46**	
Canada	Larsen et al., 2008	n.a.	25	MA/MEd CIDE (Toronto)
USA	CIECAP, 2008 (1),(4)	21	21	M.CIE/ICE, etc. (Stanford, Columbia, etc.)
LAT AM TOTAL		**52**	**15**	
Argentina	Marquina & Lavia, 2007	19	n.a.	---
Brazil	Sisson de Castro & Gomes, 2008	3	n.a.	---
Chile	Rodriguez, 2008	---	---	---
Cuba	Masson & Torres, 2008	n.a.	3	---
Mexico	Navarro-Leal, 2008	30	11	---
Uruguay	Martinez, 2008	---	1	---

Appendix 7
(Cont'd)

Country	Source	Bache-lor's	Mas-ter's	Specialist Programme
ASIA TOTAL		**153**	**185**	
China	Gu, 2005 (1)	100	100	MEd CE (10 universities)
Hong Kong	Manzon, 2008a	---	1	MEd CIED (HK)
Japan	Takekuma, 2008 (1) (3)	5	12	M. in CE
Kazakhstan	Kussainov & Mussin, 2008	n.a.	n.a.	---
Korea	Park & Hyun, 2008	42	61	---
Macao	Manzon, 2008a	---	1	---
Malaysia	Mohd. Meerah & Halim, 2008	1	2	---
Oman	Al-Harthi, 2008	1	---	---
Taiwan	Manzon, 2008a (1)	4	4	M. ICE (Chi Nan)
Thailand	Thongthew, 2008	---	4	---
AFRICA TOTAL		**56**	**25**	
Botswana	Bulawa & Tsayang, 2006	1	---	---
Burundi	Rwantabagu, 2008	1	---	---
Egypt	Megahed & Otaiba, 2008	8	3	---
Kenya	Makatiani & Chege, 2008	6	6	M. in CE (in 6 universities, e.g. Kenyatta U)
La Reunion	Lucas et al., 2006	1	---	---
Lesotho	Seotsanyana & Ntabeni, 2006	1	1	---
Namibia	Likando et al., 2006	1	1	---
Rwanda	Nzabalirwa, 2008	---	---	---
South Afr	Maarman & Wolhuter, 2006 (1)	6	9	M. in CE
Swaziland	Mazibuko, 2006	1	1	---
Tanzania	Anangisye, 2008; Muganda & Alphonce, 2006	1	1	M. in CE
Uganda	Ocheng Kagoire, 2008 (1)	27	1	M. in CE (Makerere)
Zimbabwe	Machingura & Mutemeri, 2006	2	2	---
GRAND TOTAL		**443**	**298**	

Notes:

(1) The numbers are not precise. Some country reports indicate a few sample institutions, but do not give the total number.; (2) N.A. - not available; (3) Based on academic chairs at universities

Legend: CE - Comparative Education; CIE - Comparative & International Education; ICE - International Comparative Education; CIED/CIDE – Comparative and International Education and Development.

Appendix 8   Key Data on WCCES Member Societies

	Society	Location	Region/ Other	Type	Year Estab.	Year joined WCCES	World Congress	Members 2004/05	Source
1	CIES	USA	N AMER	N	1956	founder		1345	Cook et al. 2004
2	JCES	JAPAN	ASIA	N	1965	founder	1980	850	JCES 2007
3	CCES	CHINA	ASIA	N	1979	1984		500	CCES 2007
4	KCES	KOREA	ASIA	N	1968	founder	2001	400	KCES 2007
5	BAICE	UK	EU	N	1966	1980		101-300	Turner 2008
6	CCES-T	TAIWAN, ROC	ASIA	N	1974	1990		101-300	Turner 2008
7	CPS-CES	CZECH REPUBLIC	EU	N	1964	1990	1992	272	CPS 2005
8	CESE	EUROPE	EU	R	1961	founder	1977	271	Luzon 2005
9	CESA	ASIA	ASIA	R	1995	1997		262	CESA 2007
10	SEEC	SPAIN	EU	N	1974	1974		143	SEEC 2005
11	SBEC	BRAZIL	S AMER	N	1983	1984	1987	121	SBEC 2007
12	SIIVEDGE	GERMANY	EU	N	1966	1980		<100	Turner 2008
13	ANZCIES	AUSTRALIA & NZ	ANZ	R	1973	1974	1996	<100	Turner 2008
14	SACHES	SOUTHERN AFRICA	AFR	R	1991	1992	1998	<100	Turner 2008
15	MESCE	MEDITERRANEAN	EU	R	2004	2004	2007	<100	Turner 2008
16	SICESE	ITALY	EU	N	1986	1987		<100	Turner 2008
17	NOCIES	NORDIC	EU	R	1992	1997		<100	Turner 2008
18	SAECE	ARGENTINA	S AMER	N	2001	2005		<100	Turner 2008
19	NGVO	NETHERLANDS	EU	L	1973	1974		<100	Turner 2008

Appendix 8   (cont'd)

	Society	Location	Region/Other	Type	Year Estab.	Year joined WCCES	World Congress	Members 2004/05	Source
20	CIESC	CANADA	N AMER	N	1967	founder	1970,1989	100	CIESC 2006
21	ECEEAS	EGYPT	AFR	N	1991	2006		100	ECEEAS 2006
22	AFEC	FRANCOPHONE	EU, AFR	L	1973	1973	1984	99	AFEC 2007
23	GCES	GREECE	EU	N	1991	1994		93	GCES 2005
24	APC-SEC	CUBA	CARIBB	N	1994	2002	2004	90	APC 2007
25	CESHK	HONG KONG	ASIA	N	1989	1992		80	CESHK 2007
26	CESI	INDIA	ASIA	N	1979	1980		60	CESI 2007
27	AFDECE	FRANCE	EU	N	1998	2004		60	AFDECE 2007
28	PCES	POLAND	EU	N	1991	1992		60	PCES 2007
29	HPS-CES	HUNGARY	EU	N	1970	1994		50	HPS 2007
30	TüKED	TURKEY	ASIA	N	2006	2006	2010	50	TüKED 2007
31	CCEK	KAZAKHSTAN	ASIA	N	2005	2006		41	CCEK 2007
32	SOMEC	MEXICO	N AMER	N	2003	2004	2013	40	SOMEC 2007
33	RCCE	RUSSIA	EU	N	1995	1996		28	RCCE 2007
34	ICES	ISRAEL	ASIA	N	1988	1989		20	ICES 2007
35	BCES	BULGARIA	EU	N	1991	1992		15	BCES 2004
36	CESP	PHILIPPINES	ASIA	N	2001	2002		5	CESP 2007
37	UCES	UKRAINE	EU	N	2010	2010		<50	UCES 2010

Source: WCCES Minutes; Chapters in Masemann et al. (2007); society information sheets; Turner (2008); Except for UCES, which was added in 2010, the rest of the data were collected in 2008.

Appendix 8 (cont'd)

Note: The societies have been grouped by size of membership based on the following fee structure:

Tier 1: Over 600 members - US$400   2 societies
Tier 2: 301-600 members - US$300   2 societies
Tier 3: 101-300 members - US$200   7 societies
Tier 4: < 100 members - US$100   26 societies

No. of members	
Exact #s	5155
101-300*	400
<100*	245
Total	**5800**

*For those societies where precise data on membership size was not available, I assumed (a) average of 200 members for 2 societies in Tier 3; and (b) average of 25 members for 8 societies in Tier 4.

By type of society	No.	%
National	29	78%
Regional	6	16%
Language-based	2	6%
Total	**37**	**100%**

By Region	No.	%
Europe	17	46%
Asia	11	30%
N Amer	3	8%
S Amer & Carib	3	8%
Africa	2	5%
Australasia	1	3%
Total	**37**	**100%**

Appendix 9   Citation and Content Analysis Comparative Education Journals

Source Article	Scope of Analysis	Purpose	Methodology	Results	Limitations
1. Koehl (1977)	CER (Chicago) 1957-76 CE (UK) 1964-75 IRE 1954-75	To discern trends in prescription and practice of comparative education	Content analysis of articles, book reviews, etc.		Only internal analysis: not correlated content with authors' or readers' demographics
2. Halls (1990b)	IRE 1975-85 Total 60 papers	To discern trends	Content analysis	40% are one-country studies 30% are 2-6 country studies 13% on 7 or more countries 17% not classifiable	
3. Lawson (1990)	CER (Chicago) 1975-86	To discern trends	Content analysis	Top themes were: theory and methodology, financing, cultural reproduction, higher education, labor market and professional training, women's studies	
4. Rust et al. (1999)	CER (Chicago) 1957-95 CE (UK) 1964-95 IJED 1981-95	To discern methodological trends	Content analysis	Less than 1/3 do direct comparison. More area studies/foreign education. A large number of publications are area studies/foreign education examining educational phenomena in single countries	
5. Little (2000)	CE (UK) 1977-98 Total 472 articles	To determine the nature of 'comparison'	Analysis of article titles	53% are one-country studies Has a comparative 'dimension' in the sense of locating the study in more general literature of the field. 62% on developed countries 18% about education reform	Internal analysis. Title analysis is superficial. It would have been more appropriate to undertake a content analysis.

Appendix 9   (cont'd)

Source Article	Scope of Analysis	Purpose	Methodology	Results	Limitations
6. Ferrer (2002, expanded version of Palaudàrias, 2000)	CER (Chicago) 1979-2000 Total 286 articles ERIC 1979-2000 (English) FRANCIS 1979-2000 (Francophone)	To determine priority themes	Content analysis of CER Citation analysis in ERIC and FRANCIS	Top priority theme out of a total of 14 categories: Politics and education, levels of education. Comparative education theory and methodology also ranked among top three themes in ERIC and FRANCIS, but not in CER.	
7. Wolhuter (2008)	CER (Chicago) 1957-06 Total 1157 articles	To discern trends in contents, methods, units of analysis, etc.	Content analysis of CER	Nation-state as main unit; Mostly single-unit studies;	
8. Martínez and Valle (2005)	REEC 1995-04 (Spanish) Total 98 articles	To discern trends on themes, units of comparison	Content analysis	Extreme heterogeneity in themes, types of study and units of comparison: Top 22% on education reform; only 6% on comparative education theory Top 23% on one unit (while 34% not specific) – Limited explicit comparison	
9. Yung (1998)	CER (Chicago) 1987-97 CER (Beijing) 1987-97 (Chinese)	To discern trends on themes, units	Content analysis	CER (Beijing) 89% single-unit study; CER (Chicago) 81% single unit Top 3 themes out of 24 themes: For CER (Beijing) they were higher education (19%), educational theory (12%), and curriculum and pedagogy (10%). For CER (Chicago), the themes were evenly distributed, the highest being on politics and education (10%).	

Appendix 9   (cont'd)

Source Article	Scope of Analysis	Purpose	Methodology	Results	Limitations
10. Cheng (2003)	CER (Beijing) 1996-2002 Total 683 articles GE/JFES (Shanghai) 1996-2002. Total 820 articles. Both in Chinese	To discern trends	Content analysis	CER Top theme is higher education (30%). GE top theme is Pedagogy (75%). One-unit studies dominated (75%).	
11. Manzon (2005)	Journal of CE (Taipei) 1995-2004. Total 97 articles. In Chinese	To discern trends	Content analysis	75% area studies; 21% on comparative education theory. 75% in one location. 57% of area studies focus on developed countries (Germany, USA, UK, Japan).	
12. Shang & Chen (2008)	CER (Beijing) 1979-2006 Total 252 articles In Chinese		Citation analysis / "CNKI"	Top themes are research paradigms (32%) and disciplinary construction (28%).	
13. Kitamura (2005) cited by Ninomiya (2007)	CE (Japanese) 1975-2004 Total 454 articles			From 1975-85: Top two countries studied were Japan and USA (35%), but in 1990s they only accounted for 19%, with the distribution of geographic foci becoming more even across regions.	
14. Otsuka (2005) cited by Ninomiya (2007)	CE (Japanese) 1975-2003			From 1975-1990 focused on area studies; 1990s more explicit comparisons.	

Note: The articles are listed following two criteria: 1st , the language medium of the journals analysed; and 2nd , the date of publication of the review article.

Legend:
CE – *Comparative Education*   GE – *Global Education*   IJED – *International Journal of Education Development*
CER – *Comparative Education Review*   JFES – *Journal of Foreign Education Studies*   IRE – *International Review of Education*
REEC – *Revista Española de Educación Comparada*

Appendix 10 Attitudinal & Demographic Surveys of the Field of Comparative Education

Source Article	Scope of Analysis	Purpose	Methodology	Results	Limitations
1. Epstein (1981)	WCCES General Assembly (1980)	To determine the background characteristics and attitudes of Congress participants	Questionnaire survey	Congress was highly inclusive: low percentage of participants were specialists in the field.	Too small sample (only 13% of total participants)
2. Ross et al. (1992)	CIES national meeting attendants (1979, 1988) Attitudinal survey	To determine the objectives, methods and trends in comparative education	Questionnaire survey	Top objective for research: (1) study other's systems to better understand own system; (2) appraise educational issues from a global rather than ethnocentric perspective Top objective for the field: (1) find facts about educational systems; (2) discern direction of change Methodological eclecticism	Reliability: too small sample
3. Cook et al. (2004)	CIES membership (419 respondents or 49% of accessible members) Demographic survey and bibliometric/ citation analysis	To discern how perceptions converge on the content of comparative education (important themes, works, figures, centres and international organizations), and correlate these with respondents' demographics (gender, academic degree, disciplinary orientation, formal induction through an introductory course of comparative education)	Questionnaire survey Citation analysis (CER, CE, IJED)	Among a predominantly North American membership, the field remains distinctively heterogeneous in its disciplinary composition, its research interests, and its thematic content.	Focused only on CIES, North American constituency.

References

Adams, D. (1977). Development Education. *Comparative Education Review, 21*(2-3), 296-310.

Adams, D. (1988). Extending the Educational Planning Discourse: Conceptual and Paradigmatic Explorations. *Comparative Education Review, 32*(4), 400-415.

Aldridge, A.O. (Ed.) (1969). *Comparative Literature: Matter and Method.* Urbana, Chicago & London: University of Illinois Press.

Alexander, R., Broadfoot, P. & Phillips, D. (Eds.) (1999). *Learning from Comparing: New Directions in Comparative Educational Research* (Vol.1). Oxford: Symposium Books.

Al-Harthi, H.K. (2008). Comparative Education in Universities in the Sultanate of Oman. In C. Wolhuter, N. Popov, M. Manzon & B. Leutwyler (Eds.), *Comparative Education at Universities World Wide* (pp.259-265). Sofia: Bureau for Educational Services.

Allemann-Ghionda, C. (2004). *Einführung in die Vergleichende Erziehungswissenschaft.* Weinheim/Basel: Beltz.

Altbach, P. (1977). Servitude of the Mind? Education, Dependency and Neo-Colonialism. *Teachers College Record, 79*(2), 187-204.

Altbach, P. (1991). Trends in Comparative Education. *Comparative Education Review, 35*(3), 491-507.

Altbach, P. (1994). International Knowledge Networks. In T. Husén & T.N. Postlethwaite (Eds.), *The International Encyclopedia of Education* (2nd ed.) (pp.2993-2998). Oxford: Pergamon Press.

Altbach, P. (2007). The Imperial Tongue: English as the Dominating Academic Language. *International Higher Education, 49*, 2-4.

Altbach, P. & Kelly, G. (Eds.) (1978). *Education and Colonialism.* London: Longman.

Altbach, P. & Kelly, G. (Eds.) (1986). *New Approaches to Comparative Education.* Chicago: The University of Chicago Press.

Altbach, P. & Tan, E.T.J. (1995). *Programs and Centers in Comparative and International Education: An International Inventory.* Buffalo, NY: SUNY-Buffalo Graduate School of Education.

Anangisye, W. (2008). Reflecting on Comparative Education Teaching in Tanzania: The Case of the University of Dar Es Salaam. In C. Wolhuter, N. Popov, M. Manzon & B. Leutwyler (Eds.), *Comparative Education at Universities World Wide* (pp.303-310). Sofia: Bureau for Educational Services.

Anderson, C.A. (1961). Methodology of Comparative Education. *International Review of Education, 7*(1), 1-23.

Anderson, C.A. & Bowman, M.J. (Eds.) (1966). *Education and Economic Development.* London: Frank Cass.

Anweiler, O. (1977). Comparative Education and the Internationalization of Education. *Comparative Education, 13*(2), 109-114.

Aquinas, T. (1952). *De Veritate*, Vol.1. (Trans. R. Mulligan, J. McGlynn & R. Schmidt). Chicago: Henry Regnery Co. www.diafrica.org/kenny/CDtexts/QDde Ver. Downloaded 29/3/09.

Archer, M. (1979). *Social Origins of Educational Systems*. London: Sage.

Aristotle (1993). *Metaphysics. Book 4-6*. (2nd ed.). (Trans. C. Kirwan). Oxford: Clarendon Press.

Arnove, R.F. (1980). Comparative Education and World Systems Analysis. *Comparative Education Review*, 24(1), 48-62.

Arnove, R.F. (2007). Introduction: Reframing Comparative Education. In R.F. Arnove & C.A. Torres (Eds.), *Comparative Education: The Dialectic of the Global and the Local* (pp.1-20). Lanham, MD: Rowman & Littlefield Publishers, Inc.

Arnove, R.F. & Torres, C.A. (Eds.) (1999). *Comparative Education: The Dialectic of the Global and the Local* (1st ed.). Lanham, MD: Rowman & Littlefield Publishers.

Arnove, R.F. & Torres, C.A. (Eds.) (2007). *Comparative Education: The Dialectic of the Global and the Local* (3rd ed.). Lanham, MD: Rowman & Littlefield.

Asian Development Bank (ADB) (2001). *Education and National Development in Asia: Trends, Issues, Policies, and Strategies*. Manila: ADB.

Austin Harrington, B. & Marshall, H.M. (Eds.) (2006). *Encyclopedia of Social Theory*. London & New York: Routledge.

Avalos, B. (1986). *Enseñando a los Hijos de los Pobres: Un Estudio Etnográfico en América Latina*. Ottawa: International Development Research Center.

Baeck, L. (1999). Text and Content in the Thematization on Development. *Prospects, XXIX*(4), 459-477.

Ball, S. (1990). Introducing Monsieur Foucault. In S. Ball (Ed.), *Foucault and Education: Disciplines and Knowledge*. London/New York: Routledge.

Banks, J. & McGee Banks, C. (Eds.) (2004). *Multicultural Education: Issues and Perspectives* (5th ed.). Hoboken, NJ: John Wiley & Sons, Inc.

Bassnett, S. (1993). *Comparative Literature: A Critical Introduction*. Oxford, UK: Blackwell.

Becher, T. & Trowler, P. (2001). *Academic Tribes and Territories: Intellectual Enquiry and the Culture of Disciplines* (2nd ed.). Buckingham; Philadelphia, PA: Society for Research into Higher Education & Open University Press.

Belkanov, N. (1994). *Introduction to Comparative Education*. Алматы: РИК. [in Russian]

Benedek, A., Illés, M., Tóth, P. (2007). The Last 40 Years of the Comparative Education Section in the Hungarian Pedagogical Society. Unpublished manuscript. Hungarian Pedagogical Society-Comparative Education Section, Hungary.

Benson, R. (1998). Field Theory in Comparative Context: A New Paradigm for Media Studies. *Theory & Society, 28*, 463-498.

Bereday, G.Z.F. (1963). James Russell's Syllabus of the First Academic Course in Comparative Education. *Comparative Education Review*, Vol.7, No.2, pp.189-196.

Bereday, G.Z.F. (1964). *Comparative Method in Education*. New York: Holt, Rinehart & Winston, Inc.

Berger, P.L. & Luckmann, T. (1966). *The Social Construction of Reality: A Treatise in the Sociology of Knowledge* (1st Ed.). Garden City, N.Y.: Doubleday.

Bergh, A-M. (comp.) in collaboration with Claassen, C., Horn, I., Mda, T. & van Niekerk, P. (1999). *Teaching Comparative and International Education*. Report on a Workshop held at the 10th World Congress of Comparative Education Societies in Cape Town, South Africa (14-15 July 1998). Pretoria: Comparative and International Education Interest Group, Faculty of Education, University of South Africa.

Bergh, A-M. & Soudien, C. (2006). The Institutionalization of Comparative Education Discourses in South Africa in the 20th century. *Southern African Review of Education* with *Education with Production, 12*(2), 35-60.

Bernstein, B. (1977). Class, Codes and Control, Vol.3: *Towards a Theory of Educational Transmission* (2nd ed.). London: Routledge & Kegan Paul.

Betts, J. & Wilde, S. (1999). Postscript. In R. Alexander, P. Broadfoot & D. Phillips (Eds.), *Learning from Comparing: New Directions in Comparative Educational Research* (Vol. 1, pp. 102-106). Oxford: Symposium Books.

Bhaskar, R. (1986). *Scientific Realism and Human Emancipation*. London: Verso.

Biraimah, K. (2006). Knowing Others and Knowing Self: Patterns of Differentiated Publishing in Education Journals from the North and South. *Southern African Review of Education* with *Education with Production*, Vol.12, No.2, pp. 81-92.

Bishkov, G. & Popov, N. (1994). *Comparative Education*. (1st Ed.) Sofia: St. Kliment Ohridski University Press. [in Bulgarian]

Bochaca, J.G. (2001). *Curso de Filosofía*. Madrid: Ediciones Rialp, S.A..

Boerma, E., Bunt-Kokhuis, S. van de, Karsten, S., Louwyck, A. & Standaert, R. (2008). Comparative Education in the Netherlands and Flanders In C. Wolhuter, N. Popov, M. Manzon & B. Leutwyler (Eds.), *Comparative Education at Universities World Wide* (pp.96-104). Sofia: Bureau for Educational Services.

Bogdan, M. (1994). *Comparative Law*. Deventer & Cambridge, MA: Kluwer.

Borevskaya, N. (2007). The Russian Council of Comparative Education. In V. Masemann, M. Bray & M. Manzon (Eds.), *Common Interests, Uncommon Goals: Histories of the World Council of Comparative Education Societies and its Members* (pp.299-308). Dordrecht & Hong Kong: Springer & Comparative Education Research Centre, The University of Hong Kong.

Bourdieu, P. (1969 [Fr.1966]). Intellectual Field and Creative Project (Trans. S. France). *Social Science Information 8*(2), 89-119.

Bourdieu, P. (1975). The Specificity of the Scientific Field and the Social Conditions of the Progress of Reason. *Social Science Information 14*, 19-47.

Bourdieu, P. (1977 [Fr.1972]). *Outline of a Theory of Practice* (Trans. R. Nice). Cambridge: Cambridge University Press.

Bourdieu, P. (1990 [Fr.1980]). *The Logic of Practice* (Trans. R. Nice). Oxford: Polity.

Bourdieu, P. (1991 [Fr.1981]). *Language and Symbolic Power*. Cambridge, Mass.: Harvard University Press.

Bourdieu, P. (2000 [Fr.1997]). *Pascalian Meditations* (Trans. R. Nice). Oxford: Polity Press.

Bourdieu, P. & Wacquant, L. (1992). *An Invitation to Reflexive Sociology*. Chicago:

The University of Chicago Press.

Bouzakis, S. (2002). *Comparative Education I: Theoretical, Methodological Problems and the Modern Trends in International Education.* Athens: Gutenberg [in Greek].

Bouzakis, S. (2003). *Comparative Education II: Theoretical Approaches and the Educational Systems Abroad.* Athens: Gutenberg [in Greek].

Bouzakis, S. (2005). *Comparative Education III.* Athens: Gutenberg [in Greek].

Bray, M. (2001a). Comparative Education as a Field of Study: Overview and Historical Development. M.Ed. Course handout. Unpublished manuscript. The University of Hong Kong, Hong Kong.

Bray, M. (2001b). Foreword. In M. Gu, *Education in China and Abroad: Perspectives from a Lifetime in Comparative Education* (pp.1-4). Hong Kong: Comparative Education Research Centre, The University of Hong Kong.

Bray, M. (2002). Comparative Education in East Asia: Growth, Development and Contributions to the Global Field. *Current Issues in Comparative Education, 4*(2), 70-80.

Bray, M. (Ed.) (2003). *Comparative Education: Continuing Traditions, New Challenges, and New Paradigms.* Special double issue of *International Review of Education, 49*(1-2). Republished 2003 as book with same title, Dordrecht: Kluwer Academic Publishers.

Bray, M. (2004). *Comparative Education: Traditions, Applications, and the Role of HKU.* Hong Kong: Faculty of Education, The University of Hong Kong.

Bray, M. (2007a). Expanding the Coverage and Hearing More Voices: 2004-2007. In V. Masemann, M. Bray & M. Manzon (Eds.), *Common Interests, Uncommon Goals: Histories of the World Council of Comparative Education Societies and its Members* (pp.83-93). Hong Kong: Comparative Education Research Centre, The University of Hong Kong, and Dordrecht: Springer.

Bray, M. (2007b). Actors and Purposes in Comparative Education. In M. Bray, B. Adamson & M. Mason (Eds.), *Comparative Education Research: Approaches and Methods* (pp.15-38). Hong Kong: Comparative Education Research Centre, The University of Hong Kong, and Dordrecht: Springer.

Bray, M. (2007c). Scholarly Enquiry and the Field of Comparative Education. In M. Bray, B. Adamson & M. Mason (Eds.), *Comparative Education Research: Approaches and Methods* (pp.341-361). Hong Kong: Comparative Education Research Centre, The University of Hong Kong, and Dordrecht: Springer.

Bray, M. (2007d). International and Comparative Education: Boundaries, Ambiguities and Synergies. In M. Hayden, J. Levy & J. Thompson (Eds.), *The SAGE Handbook of Research in International Education* (pp.51-56). London: Sage Publications Ltd.

Bray, M. (2008). The WCCES and Intercultural Dialogue: Historical Perspectives and Continuing Challenges. *International Review of Education, 54*(3-4), 299-317.

Bray, M., Adamson, B. & Mason, M. (Eds.) (2007a). *Comparative Education Research: Approaches and Methods.* Hong Kong: Comparative Education Research Centre, The University of Hong Kong, and Dordrecht: Springer.

Bray, M., Adamson, B. & Mason, M. (2007b). Different Models, Different Emphases, Different Insights. In M. Bray, B. Adamson & M. Mason (Eds.), *Comparative Education Research: Approaches and Methods* (pp.363-379). Hong Kong: Comparative Education Research Centre, The University of Hong Kong, and Dordrecht: Springer.

Bray, M. & Gui, Q. (2001). Comparative Education in Greater China: Contexts, Characteristics, Contrasts and Contributions. *Comparative Education, 37*(4), 451-473.

Bray, M., & Jiang, K. (2007). Comparing Systems. In M. Bray, B. Adamson & M. Mason (Eds.), *Comparative Education Research: Approaches and Methods*. Hong Kong: Comparative Education Research Centre, The University of Hong Kong, and Dordrecht: Springer.

Bray, M. & Manzon, M. (2005). El *World Council of Comparative Education Societies* (WCCES): Equilibrios, Misiones y Prospectivos. *Revista Española de Educación Comparada, 11*, 189-213.

Bray, M., Manzon, M. & Masemann, V. (2007). Introduction. In V. Masemann, M. Bray & M. Manzon (Eds.), *Common Interests, Uncommon Goals: Histories of the World Council of Comparative Education Societies and its Members* (pp.1-12). Dordrecht & Hong Kong: Springer & Comparative Education Research Centre, The University of Hong Kong.

Bray, M. & Thomas, R.M. (1995). Levels of Comparison in Educational Studies: Different Insights from Different Literatures and the Value of Multilevel Analyses. *Harvard Educational Review, 65*(3), 472-490.

Brembeck, C.S. (1975). The Future of Comparative and International Education. *Comparative Education Review, 19*(3), 369-374.

Brickman, W.W. (1960). A Historical Introduction to Comparative Education. *Comparative Education Review, 3*(3), 6-13.

Brickman, W.W. (1966). Prehistory of Comparative Education to the End of the Eighteenth Century. *Comparative Education Review, 10*(1), 30-47.

Brickman, W.W. (1988). History of Comparative Education. In T.N. Postlethwaite (Ed.), *The Encyclopedia of Comparative Education and National Systems of Education* (pp.3-10). Oxford: Pergamon Press.

Broadfoot, P. (1977). The Comparative Contribution-Research Perspective. *Comparative Education, 13*(2), 133-137.

Broadfoot, P. (1999). Not So Much a Context, More a Way of Life? Comparative Education in the 1990s. In R. Alexander, P. Broadfoot & D. Phillips (Eds.), *Learning from Comparing: New Directions in Comparative Educational Research* (Vol.1, pp.21-31). Oxford: Symposium Books.

Brock-Utne, B. & Bøyesen, L. (Eds.) (2006). *Coping with the Educational System in the North and the South. An Introduction to Multicultural and Comparative Education, Education and Development*. Bergen: Fagbokforlaget. [in Norwegian]

Brock-Utne, B. & Skinningsrud, T. (2008). Comparative Education in Norway. In C. Wolhuter, N. Popov, M. Manzon & B. Leutwyler (Eds.), *Comparative Edu-*

cation at Universities World Wide (pp.105-112). Sofia: Bureau for Educational Services.

Bulawa, P. & Tsayang, G. (2006). The Present and the Future of Comparative Education and History of Education in Botswana. In C. Wolhuter (Ed.). *Aurora Australis: Comparative Education and History of Education at Universities in Southern Africa/Education comparée et histoire de l'éducation dans les universités d'Afrique Australe* (pp.1-14). Potchefstroom: C.C.Wolhuter.

Bunt-Kokhuis, S. van de & Van daele, H. (2007). The Dutch-speaking Society for Comparative Education (NGVO). In V. Masemann, M. Bray & M. Manzon (Eds.), *Common Interests, Uncommon Goals: Histories of the World Council of Comparative Education Societies and its Members* (pp.210-213). Dordrecht & Hong Kong: Springer & Comparative Education Research Centre, The University of Hong Kong.

Burns, R. (1990). Australia, New Zealand and the Pacific. In W.D. Halls (Ed.), *Comparative Education: Contemporary Issues and Trends* (pp.226-256). Paris: UNESCO and London: Jessica Kingsley.

Burns, R.J. & Welch, A. (Eds.) (1992). *Contemporary Perspectives in Comparative Education.* New York: Garland Publishers.

Cambridge, J., & Thompson, J. (2004). Internationalism and Globalization as Contexts for International Education. *Compare: A Journal of Comparative Education, 34*(2), 161-175.

Carnoy, M. (1974). *Education as Cultural Imperialism.* New York: Longman.

Carnoy, M. (2006). Rethinking the Comparative–and the International. *Comparative Education Review, 50*(4), 551-570.

Carnoy, M. & Samoff, J. (1990). *Education and Social Transition in the Third World.* Princeton, NJ: Princeton University Press.

Carroll, K. & Epstein, E.H. (2001). Understanding Ancestors: Foundations of Comparative Thought. Paper presented at the 45th Annual Meeting of the Comparative and International Education Society, Washington, D.C..

Carry, A. (2004). Interview by Maria Manzon, 30 October. Havana, Cuba. [in Spanish]

Carry, A., Frenay, M., Perez, S., & Gorga, A. (2005). L'éducation comparée dans l'espace francophone: tendances et perspectives. *Revista Española de Educación Comparada, 11,* 135-159.

Cavicchi-Broquet, I. & Furter, P. (Eds.) (1982). *Les sciences de l'éducation: perspectives et bilans européens. Actes de la Xe Conférence de l'Association d'éducation comparée pour l'Europe.* Genève: Section des sciences de l'éducation, Faculté de psychologie et de sciences de l'éducation, Université de Genève.

Chabbott, C. (2003). *Constructing Education for Development: International Organisations and Education for All.* New York: RoutledgeFalmer.

Chakarov, N. (1969). *Problems of Comparative Pedagogy.* Sofia: Narodna Prosveta. [in Bulgarian]

Chang, D. (1930). *Comparative Education.* Shanghai: China Book Co. [in Chinese]

Chen, S.C. (1992). Comparative Education Studies in the People's Republic of

China. PhD dissertation. State University of New York at Buffalo.

Cheng, M.W. (2003). *Comparative Education in Mainland China: Globalization and Localization.* Unpublished M.Ed. thesis. The University of Hong Kong, Hong Kong.

Cherryholmes, C. (1988). *Power and Criticism: Post-structural Investigations in Education.* New York: Teachers College Press.

Chinese Comparative Education Society-Taipei (CCES-T) (2000). *Comparative Education Theory and Practice.* Taipei: Taiwan Bookstore Press. [in Chinese]

Chu, S.H. (2005). *Introduction to Comparative Education.* Seoul: Korean Studies Information. [in Korean]

CIECAP (2008). Comparative and International Education Course Archive Project. www.luc.edu/cce/ciecap.shtml. Downloaded on 3/24/08.

CIECAP (2010). Comparative and International Education Course Archive Project. www.luc.edu/cce/ciecap/courseoutlines_ciecap.shtml. Downloaded 1/8/10.

Clark, B.R. (1987). *The Academic Life: Small Worlds, Different Worlds.* Princeton: The Carnegie Foundation for the Advancement of Teaching.

Clignet, R. (1981). The Double Natural History of Educational Interactions: Implications for Educational Reforms. *Comparative Education Review, 25*(3), 330-352.

Comte, A. (1830). *Introduction to Positive Philosophy.* Indianapolis, IN: Bobbs-Merrill. Republished 1970.

Cook, B.J., Hite, S.J. & Epstein, E.H. (2004). Discerning Trends, Contours, and Boundaries in Comparative Education: A Survey of Comparativists and Their Literature. *Comparative Education Review, 48* (2), 123-149.

Coombs, P.H. (1970). *What is Educational Planning?* Paris: UNESCO-IIEP.

Coser, L. (1965). *Men of Ideas.* New York: Free Press of Glencoe.

Cowen, R. (1980). Comparative Education in Europe: A Note. *Comparative Education Review, 24*(1), 98-108.

Cowen, R. (1982a). The Place of Comparative Education in the Educational Sciences. In I. Cavicchi-Broquet & P. Furter (Eds.), *Les Sciences de l'éducation: Perspectives et Bilans Européens. Actes de la Xe Conférence de l'Association d'éducation Comparée Pour l'Europe* (pp.107-126). Genève: Section des Sciences de l'éducation, Faculté de Psychologie et de Sciences de l'éducation, Université de Genève.

Cowen, R. (1982b). *International Yearbook of Education,* Vol. XXXIV. Paris: UNESCO.

Cowen, R. (1990). The National and International Impact of Comparative Education Infrastructures. In W.D. Halls (Ed.), *Comparative Education: Contemporary Issues and Trends* (pp.321-352). Paris: UNESCO and London: Jessica Kingsley.

Cowen, R. (1996). Last Past the Post: Comparative Education, Modernity and Perhaps Post-modernity. *Comparative Education, 32*(2), 151-170.

Cowen, R. (2000). Comparing Futures or Comparing Pasts? *Comparative Education, 36* (3), 333-342.

Cowen, R. (2002). Moments of Time: A Comparative Note. *History of Education, 31*(5), 413-424.

Cowen, R. (2003a). Paradigms, Politics and Trivial Pursuits: A Note on Comparative Education. Unpublished manuscript. Institute of Education, University of London.

Cowen, R. (2003b). Agendas of Attention: A Response to Ninnes and Burnett. *Comparative Education, 39*(3), 299-302.

Cowen, R. (2006). Acting Comparatively upon the Educational World: Puzzles and Possibilities. *Oxford Review of Education, 32* (5), 561-573.

Cowen, R. (2008). A Paradigm Shift in Comparative Education. Seminar Given at the Hong Kong Institute of Education, 9 October.

Cowen, R. (2009a). On History and on the Creation of Comparative Education. In R. Cowen & A.M. Kazamias (Eds.), *International Handbook of Comparative Education* (pp.7-10). Dordrecht: Springer.

Cowen, R. (2009b). Then and Now: Unit Ideas and Comparative Education. In R. Cowen & A.M. Kazamias (Eds.), *International Handbook of Comparative Education* (pp.1277-1294). Dordrecht: Springer.

Cowen, R. & Kazamias, A.M. (2009). *International Handbook of Comparative Education*. Dordrecht: Springer.

Crane, D. (1972). *Invisible Colleges: Diffusion of Knowledge in Scientific Communities*. Chicago: University of Chicago Press.

Crossley, M. (1999). Reconceptualising Comparative and International Education. *Compare: A Journal of Comparative Education, 29*(3), 249-267.

Crossley, M. (2000). Bridging Cultures and Traditions in the Reconceptualisation of Comparative and International Education. *Comparative Education, 36* (3), 319-332.

Crossley, M. (2008). Bridging Cultures and Traditions for Educational and International Development: Comparative Research, Dialogue and Difference. *International Review of Education, 54,* 319-336.

Crossley, M., Broadfoot, P. & Schweisfurth, M. (Eds.) (2007). *Changing Educational Contexts, Issues and Identities: 40 Years of Comparative Education*. London: Routledge.

Crossley, M. & Jarvis, P. (2000). Comparative Education for the Twenty-first Century. Special Number of *Comparative Education, 36*(3).

Crossley, M. & Watson, K. (2003). *Comparative and International Research in Education. Globalisation, Context and Difference*. London: Routledge Falmer.

Crow, G. (1997). *Comparative Sociology and Social Theory: Beyond the Three Worlds*. New York: St. Martin's Press.

Dale, R. (2000). Globalization: A New World for Comparative Education? In J. Schriewer (Ed.), *Discourse Formation in Comparative Education* (pp.87-109). Frankfurt: Peter Lang.

Danaher, G., Schirato, T. & Webb, J.J. (2000). *Understanding Foucault*. London: SAGE Publications.

Dasen, P. (2000). Approches interculturelles: acquis et controverses. *Raisons educatives, 1-2,* 7-28.

Debeauvais, M. (1980). The Role of International Organisations in the Evolution of Applied Comparative Education. In B. Holmes (Ed.), *Diversity and Unity in Education: A Comparative Analysis* (pp.18-30). London: George Allen & Unwin.

Debesse, M. & Mialaret, G. (Eds.) (1974). *Pedagogía Comparada*, 2 Vols. Barcelona: Oikostau.

Delanty, G. (2001). *Challenging Knowledge: The University in the Knowledge Society.* Buckingham; Philadelphia, PA: The Society for Research into Higher Education & Open University Press.

Dey-Gupta, N. (2004). Interview by Maria Manzon, 30 October. Havana, Cuba.

Dilthey, W. (1888). *Über die Möglichkeit einer Allgemeingültigen Pädagogischen Wissenschaft.* Reprinted 1961. In H. Nohl (Ed.), *Gesammelte Schriften*, Vol. V. Weinheim: Beltz.

Durkheim, E. (1982). *The Rules of Sociological Method.* London & Basingstoke: Macmillan.

Epstein, E.H. (1968). Letter to the Editor. *Comparative Education Review, 12*(3), 376-378.

Epstein, E.H. (1981). Toward the Internationalization of Comparative Education: A Report on the World Council of Comparative Education Societies. *Comparative Education Review, 25*(2), 261-271.

Epstein, E.H. (1983). Currents Left and Right: Ideology in Comparative Education. *Comparative Education Review, 27*(1), 3-28.

Epstein, E.H. (1992). Editorial. *Comparative Education Review, 36*(4), 409-416.

Epstein, E.H. (1994). Comparative and International Education: Overview and Historical Development. In T. Husén & T.N. Postlethwaite (Eds.), *The International Encyclopedia of Education* (pp.918-923). Oxford: Pergamon Press.

Epstein E.H. (2001). An Examination of Content Boundaries and Standards in the Teaching of Comparative Education. Paper presented at the 45th Annual Meeting of the Comparative and International Education Society, Washington, D.C..

Epstein, E.H. (2004). Interview by Maria Manzon, 25 October. Havana, Cuba.

Epstein, E.H. (2006). Commentary on Carnoy. *Comparative Education Review, 50*(4), 578-580.

Epstein, E.H. (2008a). Crucial Benchmarks in the Professionalization of Comparative Education. In C. Wolhuter, N. Popov, M. Manzon & B. Leutwyler (Eds.), *Comparative Education at Universities World Wide* (pp.9-24). Sofia: Bureau for Educational Services.

Epstein, E.H. (2008b). Setting the Normative Boundaries: Crucial Epistemological Benchmarks in Comparative Education. *Comparative Education, 44*(4), 373-386.

Epstein, E.H. & Carroll, K. (2005). Abusing Ancestors: Historical Functionalism and the Postmodern Deviation in Comparative Education. *Comparative Education Review, 49*(1), 62-88.

Fägerlind, I. & Saha, L.J. (1989). *Education and National Development: A Comparative Perspective* (2nd ed.). Oxford: Pergamon Press.

Farrell, J.P. (1979). The Necessity of Comparisons in the Study of Education: The Salience of Science and the Problem of Comparability. *Comparative Education Review, 23*(1), 3-16.

Feinberg, W. & Soltis, J. (2004). *School and Society*. New York: Teachers College Press.

Fernández Lamarra, N. (2007). Personal communication.

Fernández Lamarra, N., Mollis, M. & Dono Rubio, S. (2005). La Educación Comparada en América Latina: Situación y Desafíos para su Consolidación Académica. *Revista Española de Educación Comparada, 11*, 161-187.

Ferrer, F. (2002). *La Educación Comparada Actual*. Barcelona: Ariel.

Ferrer, F. (2004). Interview by Maria Manzon, 27 October. Havana, Cuba. [in Spanish]

Ferrer, F. (2006). Interview by Maria Manzon, 26 January. Hong Kong, China. [in Spanish]

Filho, L. (1961). Comparative Education. São Paulo: Melhoramentos. [in Portuguese]

Fletcher, L. (1974). Comparative Education: A Question of Identity. *Comparative Education Review, 18*(3), 348-353.

Folliet, H. (1999). En guise de conclusion: mondialisation ou spécificités de l'espace francophone? In Leclercq, J-M. (Ed.), *L'éducation comparée: mondialisation et spécificités francophones* (pp.285-286). Sèvres: Association francophone d'éducation comparée; Paris: Centre national de documentation pédagogique.

Foucault, M. (1972[Fr.1969]). *The Archaeology of Knowledge*. London: Tavistock Publications.

Foucault, M. (1977[Fr.1975]). *Discipline and Punish: The Birth of the Prison*. London: Allen Lane.

Foucault, M. (1980). *Power/Knowledge: Selected Interviews and Other Writings 1972-1977*. London: Harvester Press.

Fox, C. (2005). Interview by Maria Manzon, 19 August. Hong Kong, China.

Fox, C. (2007). The Australian and New Zealand Comparative and International Education Society (ANZCIES). In V. Masemann, M. Bray & M. Manzon (Eds.), *Common Interests, Uncommon Goals: Histories of the World Council of Comparative Education Societies and its Members* (pp.200-209). Dordrecht & Hong Kong: Springer & Comparative Education Research Centre, The University of Hong Kong.

Franković, D. (1972). *Komparativna pedagogija*. Beograd: Institut za pedagoška istraživanja.

Freire, P. (1970). *Pedagogy of the Oppressed*. New York: Continuum.

Freire, P. (1973). *Education for Critical Consciousness*. New York: Seabury.

Frenay, M., Mc Andrew, M., Perez, S. & Lessard, C. (1999). La situation de l'éducation comparée en belgique, au canada francophone et en suisse. In Leclercq, J-M. (Ed.), *L' éducation comparée: mondialisation et spécificités francophones* (pp.125-148). Sèvres: Association francophone d'éducation comparée; Paris: Centre national de documentation pédagogique.

Fuentealba, L. (1985). *Educación comparada y otros ensayos*. Santiago: Editorial Universitaria.

Fujikane, H. (2003). Approaches to Global Education in the United States, the United Kingdom and Japan. *International Review of Education, 49*(1-2), 133-152.

Fuller, S. (1993). Disciplinary Boundaries and the Rhetoric of the Social Sciences.

In E. Messer-Davidson, D.R. Sumway & D.J. Sylvan (Eds.), *Knowledges: Historical and Critical Studies of Disciplinarity* (pp.125-149) Charlottesville: University of Virginia.

Gallo, L. (2006). *Problemi e Prospettive dell'Educazione Comparata*. Bari: Laterza.

Gao, Y. (2005). Interview by Maria Manzon, 23 August. Beijing, China. [in Chinese]

García Garrido, J.L. (1996). *Fundamentos de Educación Comparada*. Madrid: Editorial Dykinson S.L.

García Garrido, J.L. (2004). Interview by Maria Manzon, 26 October. Havana, Cuba. [in Spanish]

García Garrido, J.L. (2005a). Diez Años de Educación Comparada en España. *Revista Española de Educación Comparada, 11,* 15-36.

García Garrido, J.L. (2005b). Personal communication. 13 March.

García Hoz, V. (1968). *Principios de Pedagogía Sistemática*. Madrid: Rialp.

García-Villegas, M. (2006). Comparative Sociology of Law: Legal Fields, Legal Scholarships, and Social Sciences in Europe and the United States. *Law & Social Inquiry, 31*(2), 343-382.

Gellar, C.A. (2002). International Education: A Commitment to Universal Values. In M. Hayden, Thompson, J. & Walker, G (Eds.), *International Education in Practice: Dimensions for National and International Schools* (pp.30-35). London: Kogan.

Gibson, M.A. & Ogbu, J.U. (1991). *Minority Status and Schooling: A Comparative Study of Emigrant and Involuntary Minorities*. London: Garland.

Glenstrup, C. (1973). *Comparative Education*. Copenhagen: Gjellerup. [in Danish]

Goedegebuure, L. & van Vught, F. (1996). Comparative Higher Education Studies: The Perspective from the Policy Sciences. *Higher Education, 32*(4), 371-394.

Gök, F. (2007). Interview by Maria Manzon, 10 January. Hong Kong, China.

Golz, R. (2008). Comparative Pedagogy in Russia: Historic and Current Discourses. In C. Wolhuter, N. Popov, M. Manzon & B. Leutwyler (Eds.), *Comparative Education at Universities World Wide* (pp.113-120). Sofia: Bureau for Educational Services. (pp.113-120)

Gomis, S. (2008). L'éducation comparée en Afrique de l'Ouest: le cas du Sénégal. Unpublished manuscript. Université Cheikh Anta Diop, Senegal.

Gonzales, P. (2007). Personal communication.

Gottlieb, E.E. (2000). Are We Post-Modern Yet? Historical and Theoretical Explorations in Comparative Education. In B. Moon, Ben-Peretz & S. Brown (Eds.), *Routledge International Companion to Education* (pp. 153-176). London & New York: Routledge.

Graham, L., Lepenies, W. & Weingart, P. (Eds.) (1983). *Functions and Uses of Disciplinary Histories*. Dordrecht/Boston/Lancaster: D. Reidel Publishing Company.

Green, A. (2003). Education, Globalisation and the Role of Comparative Research. *London Review of Education, 1*(2), 83-97.

Grenfell, M.J. (2007). *Pierre Bourdieu: Education and Training*. London & New York: Continuum.

Grenz, S. (1996). *Primer on Postmodernism.* Grand Rapids, Mich.: William B. Eerdmans Pub. Co.

Groux, D. & Paul, J-J. (1999). L'éducation comparée en France: état des lieux. In Leclercq, J-M. (Ed.), *L'éducation comparée: mondialisation et spécificités franco-phones* (pp.107-123). Sèvres: Association francophone d'éducation comparée; Paris: Centre national de documentation pédagogique.

Groux, D. & Tutiaux-Guillon, N. (Eds.) (2000). *Les échanges internationaux et la comparaison en éducation.* Coll. éducation comparée. Paris: L'Harmattan.

Gu, M.Y. (2001a). *Education in China and Abroad: Perspectives from a Lifetime in Comparative Education.* Hong Kong: Comparative Education Research Centre, The University of Hong Kong.

Gu, M.Y. (2001b). Issues in the Development of Comparative Education in China. *Education in China and Abroad: Perspectives from a Lifetime in Comparative Education* (pp.219-226). Hong Kong: Comparative Education Research Centre, The University of Hong Kong. Original published in Chinese in *Foreign Education, 6* (1986).

Gu, M.Y. (2001c). Comparative Education: Retrospect and Prospect. *Education in China and Abroad: Perspectives from a Lifetime in Comparative Education* (pp.227-235). Hong Kong: Comparative Education Research Centre, The University of Hong Kong. Original published in Chinese in *Foreign Education Conditions, 67*(1), 5-8 (1991).

Gu, M.Y. (2001d). Comparative Education in China: Name and Reality. *Education in China and Abroad: Perspectives from a Lifetime in Comparative Education* (pp.236-242). Hong Kong: Comparative Education Research Centre, The University of Hong Kong. Original published in Chinese in *Journal of Foreign Education Studies, 1* (1991).

Gu, M.Y. (2003). The Mission of Comparative Education in the Era of the Knowledge Economy. *Policy Futures in Education, 1*(2), 225-233.

Gu, M.Y. (2005). Comparative Education and Me. *Comparative Education Review* (Beijing), Vol.26, No.1, pp.1-4. [in Chinese]

Gu, M.Y. & Gui, Q. (2007). The Chinese Comparative Education Society (CCES). In V. Masemann, V., M. Bray & M. Manzon (Eds.), *Common Interests, Uncommon Goals: Histories of the World Council of Comparative Education Societies and its Members* (pp.225-239). Hong Kong: Comparative Education Research Centre, The University of Hong Kong, and Dordrecht: Springer.

Habermas, J. (1971). *Knowledge and Human Interests* (J.J. Shapiro, Trans.). Boston: Beacon Press.

Habermas, J. (1978). *Knowledge and Human Interests* (2nd ed.). London: Heinemann.

Hallak, J. & Göttelmann-Duret, G. (1994). United Nations Organisations: Research and Service in Comparative and International Education. In T. Husén & T.N. Postlethwaite (Eds.), *The International Encyclopedia of Education* (2nd ed.) (pp.6523-6530). Oxford: Pergamon Press.

Halls, W.D. (1973). Culture and Education: The Culturalist Approach to Comparative Education. In R. Edwards, B. Holmes & J. Van de Graff (Eds.), *Relevant Methods in Comparative Education* (pp.119-135). Hamburg: UNESCO Institute for Education.

Halls, W.D. (Ed.). (1990a). *Comparative Education: Contemporary Issues and Trends*. Paris: UNESCO and London: Jessica Kingsley.

Halls, W.D. (1990b). Trends and Issues in Comparative Education. In W.D. Halls (Ed.), *Comparative Education: Contemporary Issues and Trends* (pp.21-65). Paris: UNESCO and London: Jessica Kingsley.

Halsey, A.H., Floud, J. & Anderson, C.A. (Eds.) (1965). *Education, Economy and Society: A Reader in the Sociology of Education*. London: Collier-Macmillan Ltd.

Hans, N.A. (1949). *Comparative Education: A Study of Educational Factors and Traditions*. London: Routledge.

Hans, N.A. (1950). *Comparative Education: A Study of Educational Factors and Traditions* (2nd ed.). London: Routledge & Kegan Paul.

Harbo, T. & Jorde, D. (2000). Comparative Education in Current Educational Studies: Four Nordic Universities in Context. *Comparative Education, 36*(2), 143-155.

Harbo, T. & Winther-Jensen, T. (Eds.) (1993). *Vi og de Andre. Komparative, Internationale og Flerkulturelle Studier i Norden*. Oslo: Ad Notam Gyldendal.

Harrison, R., Jones, A. & Lambert, P. (2004). The Institutionalization and Organization of History. In P. Lambert & P. Schofield (Eds.), *Making History: An Introduction to the History and Practice of a Discipline* (pp.9-25) Oxon/New York: Routledge.

Haskell, T.L. (2000). *The Emergence of Professional Social Science*. Baltimore and London: Johns Hopkins University Press

Heath, K.G. (1958-59). Is Comparative Education a Discipline? *Comparative Education Review, 2*(2), 31-32.

Heckhausen, H. (1972). Discipline and Interdisciplinarity. In CERI, *Interdisciplinarity: Problems of Teaching and Research in Universities* (pp.83-89) Paris: CERI, Organisation for Economic Co-operation & Development.

Henry, M., Lingard, B., Rizvi, F. & Taylor, S. (1999). *The OECD, Globalization and Education Policy*. Oxford: Pergamon Press.

Heyman, R. (1979). Comparative Education from an Ethnomethodological Perspective. *Comparative Education, 15*(3), 241-249.

Hickling-Hudson, A. (2004). Interview by Maria Manzon, 6 October. Hong Kong, China.

Hickling-Hudson, A. (2007). Improving Transnational Networking for Social Justice: 2001-2004. In V. Masemann, M. Bray & M. Manzon (Eds.), *Common Interests, Uncommon Goals: Histories of the World Council of Comparative Education Societies and its Members* (pp.69-82). Dordrecht & Hong Kong: Springer & Comparative Education Research Centre, The University of Hong Kong.

Higgins, J. (1981). *States of Welfare: Comparative Analysis in Social Policy*. Oxford: Basil Blackwell.

Higginson, J. H. (1999). The Development of a Discipline: Some Reflections on the Development of Comparative Education as seen through the Pages of *Compare*. *Compare: A Journal of Comparative Education, 29*(3), 341.

Higginson, J.H. (2001). The Development of a Discipline: Some Reflections on the Development of Comparative Education as seen through the Pages of the Journal *Compare*. In K. Watson (Ed.), *Doing Comparative Education Research: Issues and Problems* (pp.373-388). Oxford: Symposium Books.

Higuchi, C. (1928). *Comparative Education*. Tokyo: Hobun-do. [in Japanese]

Hirst, P. (1966). Educational Theory. In J.W. Tibble (Ed.), *The Study of Education* (pp.44-48). London: Routledge and Kegan Paul.

Hirst, P. (1974a). *Knowledge and the Curriculum: A Collection of Philosophical Papers*. London: Routledge & Kegan Paul.

Hirst, P. (1974b). The Forms of Knowledge Re-visited. In P. Hirst, *Knowledge and the Curriculum: A Collection of Philosophical Papers* (pp.84-100) London & Boston: Routledge & Kegan Paul.

Hirst, P. (1974c). Liberal Education and the Nature of Knowledge. In P. Hirst, *Knowledge and the Curriculum: A Collection of Philosophical Papers* (pp.30-53) London & Boston: Routledge & Kegan Paul.

Hofmann, H.G. & Malkova, Z. (1990). The Socialist Countries. In W.D. Halls (Ed.), *Comparative Education: Contemporary Issues and Trends* (pp.109-144). Paris: UNESCO and London: Jessica Kingsley.

Holik, I. (2008). The Role of Comparative Education in Hungary. In C. Wolhuter, N. Popov, M. Manzon & B. Leutwyler (Eds.), *Comparative Education at Universities World Wide* (pp.81-87). Sofia: Bureau for Educational Services.

Holmes, B. (1965). *Problems in Education: A Comparative Approach*. London: Routledge & Paul.

Holmes, B. (1971). Foreword. In *Comparative Education: Purpose and Method* (pp.ix-xi). St. Lucia, Queensland: University of Queensland Press.

Holmes, B. (1990). Western Europe. In W.D. Halls (Ed.), *Comparative Education: Contemporary Issues and Trends* (pp.69-108). Paris: UNESCO and London: Jessica Kingsley.

Horner, W. (2000). 'Europe' as a Challenge for Comparative Education: Reflections on the Political Function of a Pedagogical Discipline. *European Education, 32*(2), 22-35.

Husén, T. (Ed.) (1967). *International Study of Achievement in Mathematics: A Comparison of Twelve Countries*. Stockholm: Almqvist & Wiksell.

Husén, T. & Postlethwaite, T.N. (Eds.) (1994). *The International Encyclopedia of Education* (2nd ed.). Oxford: Pergamon.

Idenburg, Ph.J. (1959). *Introduction to Comparative Education*. Groningen: Wolters. [in Dutch]

Inkeles, A. & Sasaki, M. (1996). Preface. In A. Inkeles & M. Sasaki (Eds.), *Comparing Nations and Cultures: Readings in a Cross-Disciplinary Perspective* (pp.xi-xv). Englewood Cliffs, NJ: Prentice Hall.

Inkeles, A. & Smith, D.H. (1974). *Becoming Modern: Individual Change in Developing Societies.* London: Heinemann.

Ishii, Y. (2001). Teaching about International Responsibilities: A Comparative Analysis of the Political Construction of Development Education in Schools. *Comparative Education, 37*(3), 329-344.

Issan, S. (2006). *Education in the Arab Gulf States and the Sultanate of Oman.* Muscat: Sultan Qaboos University Press.

Jantsch, E. (1972). Towards Interdisciplinarity and Transdisciplinarity in Education and Innovation. In CERI, *Interdisciplinarity: Problems of Teaching and Research in Universities* (pp.97-121) Paris: CERI, Organisation for Economic Co-operation & Development.

Jenkins, R. (1992). *Pierre Bourdieu.* London: Routledge.

Johnson, R. (Ed.) (1993). *The Field of Cultural Production: Essays on Art and Literature.* Cambridge: Polity Press.

Jones, P.E. (1971). *Comparative Education: Purpose and Method.* St. Lucia: University of Queensland Press.

Jones, P.W. (1992). *World Bank Financing of Education: Lending, Learning and Development.* New York: Routledge.

Jones, P.W. (2007). Education and World Order. *Comparative Education, 43*(3), 325-337.

Jullien, M.-A. (1817). *Esquisse et Vues Préliminaires d'un Ouvrage sur l'Éducation Comparée.* Paris: Société Établie à Paris pour l'Amélioration de l'Enseignement Elémentaire. Reprinted 1962. Genève: Bureau International d'Éducation.

Kandel, I.L. (1933). *Comparative Education.* New York: Houghton-Mifflin.

Kandel, I.L. (1936). Comparative Education. *Review of Educational Research, 6*(4), 400-416.

Kandel, I.L. (1955a). The Study of Comparative Education. *Educational Forum, 20* (November), 5-15.

Kandel, I.L. (1955b). *The New Era in Education: A Comparative Study.* Boston: Houghton Mifflin.

Karras, K. (2008). Comparative Education: The Case of Greece. In C. Wolhuter, N. Popov, M. Manzon & B. Leutwyler (Eds.), *Comparative Education at Universities World Wide* (pp.73-80). Sofia: Bureau for Educational Services.

Kazamias, A. & Massialas, B.G. (1965). *Tradition and Change in Education: A Comparative Study.* Englewood Cliffs, N. J.: Prentice-Hall.

Kazamias, A. & Massialas, B.G. (1982). Comparative Education. In H.E. Mitzel (Ed.), *Encyclopedia of Educational Research*, Vol.1 (5th ed.) (pp.309-317). New York: Free Press.

Kazamias, A. & Schwartz, K. (1977). Editorial: The State of the Art. *Comparative Education Review, 21* (2-3), 151-152.

Kazamias, A. with Spillane, M.G. (Eds.) (1998). *Education and the Structuring of the European Space.* Athens: Seirios Editions.

Kelly, G.P. & Altbach, P.G. (1981). Comparative Education: A Field in Transition. In P.G. Altbach, G.P. Kelly & D.H. Kelly (Eds.), *International Bibliography of*

Comparative Education (pp.1-27). New York: Praeger.

Kelly, G.P., Altbach, P. & Arnove, R. (1982). Trends in Comparative Education: A Critical Analysis. In P. Altbach, R. Arnove & G. Kelly (Eds.), *Comparative Education* (pp.505-533). New York & London: Collier Macmillan.

Kelly, G.P. & Nihlen, A.S. (1982). Schooling and the Reproduction of Patriarchy. In M. Apple (Ed.), *Cultural and Economic Reproduction in Education* (pp.79-126). London: Routledge & Kegan Paul.

Kesselman, M., Krieger, J. & Joseph, W.A. (Eds.) (2007). *Introduction to Comparative Politics: Political Challenges and Changing Agendas* (4th ed.). Boston & New York: Houghton Mifflin Company.

Khôi, L.T. (1981). *L'éducation comparée*. Paris: Armand, Colin.

King, E.J. (1958). *Other Schools and Ours*. New York: Holt, Rinehart & Winston.

King, E.J. (1965). The Purpose of Comparative Education. *Comparative Education, 1*(3), 147-159.

King, E.J. (1968). *Comparative Studies in Educational Decision Making*. London: Methuen.

King, E.J. (1977). Comparative Studies: An Evolving Commitment, a Fresh Realism. *Comparative Education, 13*(2), 101-108.

King, E.J. (1979). *Other Schools and Ours: Comparative Studies for Today* (4th ed.). London: Holt, Rinehart and Winston.

King, E.J. (1997). A Turning-Point in Comparative Education: Retrospect and Prospect. In C. Kodron, B. von Kopp, U. Lauterbach, U. Schäfer & G. Schmidt (Eds.), *Vergleichende Erziehungswissenschaft: Heraus-forderung, Vermittlung, Praxis : Festschrift fur Wolfgang Mitter zum 70. Geburtstag* (pp.81-90). Frankfurt am Main: Bohlau Verlag.

Kirkwood, T.F. (2001). Our Global Age Requires Global Education: Clarifying Definitional Ambiguities. *The Social Studies, 92*(1), 10-15.

Kitamura, Y. (2005). Comparative Education and its Relation with Development Studies. *Comparative Education* [Japan], *31*, 241-252. [in Japanese]

Klees, S. (2008). Reflections on Theory, Method, and Practice in Comparative and International Education. Presidential Address. *Comparative Education Review, 52*(3), 301-328.

Klein, J.T. (1990). *Interdisciplinarity: History, Theory, and Practice*. Detroit: Wayne State University Press.

Klein, J.T. (1993). Blurring, Cracking, and Crossing: Permeation and the Fracturing of Discipline. In E. Messer-Davidson, D.R. Sumway & D.J. Sylvan (Eds.), *Knowledges: Historical and Critical Studies of Disciplinarity* (pp.185-211). Charlottesville: University of Virginia.

Kneller, G.F. (1972). Las Perspectivas de la Educación Comparada. In A.D. Marquez (Ed.), *Educación Comparada. Teoría y Metodología* (pp.81-89). Buenos Aires: Ateneo.

Koehl, R. (1977). The Comparative Study of Education: Prescription and Practice. *Comparative Education Review, 21*(2/3), 177-194.

Kozma, T. (2006). *Basic Concepts in Comparative Education*. Budapest: ÚMK. [in Hungarian]

Kubow, P. & Fossum, P. (2003). *Comparative Education: Exploring Issues in International Context*. Upper Saddle River, NJ: Merrill/Prentice Hall.

Kubow, P. & Fossum, P. (2007). *Comparative Education: Exploring Issues in International Context* (2nd ed.). Upper Saddle River, NJ: Pearson Education/Merrill Prentice Hall.

Kubow, P. & Fossum, P. (2008). Comparative Education in the USA. In C. Wolhuter, N. Popov, M. Manzon & B. Leutwyler (Eds.), *Comparative Education at Universities World Wide* (pp.157-166). Sofia: Bureau for Educational Services.

Kurian, G. T. (Ed.) (1988). *World Education Encyclopedia* (3 volumes). New York: Facts on File Publications.

Kussainov, A. & Mussin, K. (2008). Comparative Education at Universities in the Republic of Kazakhstan. In C. Wolhuter, N. Popov, M. Manzon & B. Leutwyler (Eds.), *Comparative Education at Universities World Wide* (pp.237-241). Sofia: Bureau for Educational Services.

Lakomski, G. (1997). Critical Theory and Education. In L.J. Saha (Ed.), *International Encyclopedia of the Sociology of Education* (pp.57-62). Oxford: Pergamon.

Lambert, P. (2003). The Professionalization and Institutionalization of History. In S. Berger, H. Feldner & K. Passmore (Eds.), *Writing History: Theory and Practice* (pp.42-60) London: Arnold.

Lane, J-E. & Ersson, S. (1994). *Comparative Politics: An Introduction and New Approach*. Cambridge, UK: Polity Press.

Larsen, M., Majhanovich, S. & Masemann, V. (2008). Comparative Education in Canadian Universities. In C. Wolhuter, N. Popov, M. Manzon & B. Leutwyler (Eds.), *Comparative Education at Universities World Wide* (pp.145-156). Sofia: Bureau for Educational Services.

Laska, J. A. (1973). The Future of Comparative Education: Three Basic Questions. *Comparative Education Review, 17*(3), 295-298.

Lauwerys, J. (1959). Comparative Education at the University of London. *Comparative Education Review, 3*(2), 3-4.

Lauwerys, J. (1965). General Education in a Changing World. *International Review of Education, 11*(4), 385-401.

Lauwerys, J. (1967). Opening Address in *General Education in a Changing World: Proceedings of the Comparative Education Society in Europe*. Berlin: CESE.

Lauwerys, J. (1974). La Pedagogía Comparada: Su Desarrollo, Sus Problemas. In M. Debesse & G. Mialaret (Eds.), *Pedagogía Comparada* (Vol.1, pp.19-47). Barcelona: Oikos-Tau.

Lawson, R. (1975). Free-Form Comparative Education. *Comparative Education Review, 19*(3), 345-353.

Lawson, R. (1990). North America. In W.D. Halls (Ed.), *Comparative Education: Contemporary Issues and Trends* (pp.145-174). Paris: UNESCO and London: Jessica Kingsley.

Leclerq, J-M. (1999). *L'éducation comparée: mondialisation et spécificités francophones*. Actes du congrès international sur «L'histoire et l'avenir de l'éducation comparée en langue française». Paris: Association francophone d'éducation comparée.

Lee, B.J. & Kwon, D.T. (2007). The Korean Comparative Education Society (KCES). In V. Masemann, M. Bray & M. Manzon (Eds.), *Common Interests, Uncommon Goals: Histories of the World Council of Comparative Education Societies and its Members* (pp.183-188). Dordrecht & Hong Kong: Springer & Comparative Education Research Centre, The University of Hong Kong.

Lei, G. (Ed.) (1967). *Comparative Education Systems*. Taipei: Taiwan Bookstore. [in Chinese]

Lenoir, T. (1993). The Discipline of Nature and the Nature of Disciplines. In E. Messer-Davidow, D. Shumway & D. Sylvan (Eds.), *Knowledges: Historical and Critical Studies in Disciplinarity* (pp.70-102). Charlottesville & London: University Press of Virginia.

Levi-Strauss, C. (1953). Social Structure. In A. Kraeber (Ed.), *Anthropology Today*. Chicago, Ill.: The University of Chicago Press.

Likando, G. N., Katzao, J.J. & Lijambo, T.C. (2006). The State of History of Education and Comparative Education in Namibia: An Overview. In C. Wolhuter (Ed.), *Aurora Australis: Comparative Education and History of Education at Universities in Southern Africa / Education Comparée et Histoire de l'éducation dans les universités d'Afrique Australe* (pp.67-88). Potchefstroom: C.C.Wolhuter.

Little, A. (2000). Development Studies and Comparative Education: Context, Content, Comparison and Contributors. *Comparative Education, 36*(3), 279-296.

Llano, A. (2001). *Gnoseology*. Manila: Sinag-tala Publishers, Inc. [Spanish 1983]

Lowe, J. (1998). International and Comparative Education. *International Schools Journal, XVII*(2), 18-21.

Loxley, W. (1994). Comparative Education and International Education: Organisations and Institutions. In T. Husén & T.N. Postlethwaite (Eds.), *The International Encyclopedia of Education* (2nd ed.) (pp.933-942). Oxford: Pergamon Press.

Lucas, R., Alaoui, D., Si Moussa, A. & Tupin, F. (2006). Histoire de l'éducation, éducation comparée à La Réunion: Situation, défis. In C. Wolhuter (Ed.), *Aurora Australis: Comparative Education and History of Education at Universities in Southern Africa/Education Comparée et Histoire de l'éducation dans les universités d'Afrique Australe* (pp.101-118). Potchefstroom: C.C.Wolhuter.

Luk, B. (2005). Address at the History of CESHK Panel. Annual Conference of the Comparative Education Society of Hong Kong, January 29.

Luzón, A. (2005). La Sociedad Europea de Educación Comparada (CESE) en una época de cambios. *Revista Española de Educación Comparada, 11*, 215-240.

Lynton, E. (1985). Interdisciplinarity: Rationales and Criteria of Assessment. In L. Levin & I. Lind (Eds.), *Inter-Disciplinarity Revisited: Re-assessing the Concept in Light of Institutional Experience* (pp.137-152). Stockholm: OECD, SNBUC, Linköping University.

Lyotard, J-F. (1979). *The Postmodern Condition: A Report on Knowledge*. Manchester: University of Manchester Press.

Maarman, R.F. & Wolhuter, C.C. (2006). Thematic and Infrastructural Overview of Comparative Education and History of Education at South African Universities. In C. Wolhuter (Ed.), *Aurora Australis: Comparative Education and History of Education at Universities in Southern Africa / Education Comparée et Histoire de l'éducation dans les universités d'Afrique Australe* (pp.41-50). Potchefstroom: C.C.Wolhuter.

Machingura, V. & Mutemeri, J. (2006). The State of Comparative and History of Education in Zimbabwe. In C. Wolhuter (Ed.), *Aurora Australis: Comparative Education and History of Education at Universities in Southern Africa / Education Comparée et Histoire de l'éducation dans les universités d'Afrique Australe* (pp.89-100). Potchefstroom: C.C.Wolhuter.

Makatiani, M. & Chege, F. (2008). Comparative Education and Its Development in Kenya. Unpublished manuscript. Kenyatta University, Kenya.

Malkova, Z. & Wulfson, B. (1996). *Comparative Pedagogy*. Moscow: Voronezh [in Russian]

Mallinson, V. (1957). *An Introduction to the Study of Comparative Education*. London: Heinemann.

Mallinson, V. (1975). *An Introduction to the Study of Comparative Education* (4th ed.). London: Heinemann.

Manicas, P. (1991). The Social Science Disciplines: The American Model. In P. Wagner, B. Wittrock, & R. Whitley (Eds.), *Discourses on Society: The Shaping of the Social Science Disciplines* (pp.45-71) Dordrecht: Kluwer Academic Publishers.

Mann, M. (1986). *The Sources of Social Power, Vol. I: A History of Power from the Beginning to A.D. 1760*. Cambridge: Cambridge University Press.

Manzon, M. (2005). Analysis of Contents of Comparative Education Journals. Unpublished manuscript. Hong Kong: Comparative Education Research Centre, The University of Hong Kong.

Manzon, M. (2006). The Necessary and the Contingent: On the Nature of Academic Fields and of Comparative Education. *Comparative Education Bulletin, 9,* 5-22.

Manzon, M. (2007). Comparative Education as a Field? In N. Popov, C. Wolhuter, B. Leutwyler, M. Kysilka & M. Černetič (Eds.), *Comparative Education, Teacher Training and New Education Agenda*, Volume 5 (pp.9-16). Sofia: Bureau for Educational Services & Bulgarian Comparative Education Society.

Manzon, M. (2008a). Teaching Comparative Education in Greater China: Contexts, Characteristics and Challenges. In C. Wolhuter, N. Popov, M. Manzon & B. Leutwyler (Eds.), *Comparative Education at Universities World Wide* (pp.211-228). Sofia: Bureau for Educational Services.

Manzon, M. (2008b). Review of 'Comparative and International Education. An Introduction to Theory, Method and Practice. D. Phillips & M. Schweisfurth, 2006'. *International Journal of Educational Development, 28,* 768-771.

Manzon, M. & Bray, M. (2006). The Comparative and International Education Society (CIES) and the World Council of Comparative Education Societies

(WCCES): Leadership, ambiguities and synergies. *Current Issues in Comparative Education, 8*(2), 69-83.

Manzon, M. & Bray, M. (2007). Comparing the Comparers: Patterns, Themes and Interpretations. In V. Masemann, M. Bray & M. Manzon (Eds.), *Common Interests, Uncommon Goals: Histories of the World Council of Comparative Education Societies and its Members* (pp.336-363). Dordrecht & Hong Kong: Springer & Comparative Education Research Centre, The University of Hong Kong.

Marginson, S., & Mollis, M. (2002). The Door Opens and the Tiger Leaps: Theories and Reflexivities of Comparative Education for a Global Millennium. *Comparative Education Review, 45* (4), 581-615.

Marquez, A.D. (Ed.) (1972). *Educación Comparada: Teoría y Metodología.* Buenos Aires: El Ateneo.

Marquina, M. & Lavia, P. (2007). La Formación en Educación Comparada en las Universidades Argentinas: Hacia la Consolidación de un Espacio de Reflexión e Intervención. Paper presented at the Second National Congress of the Argentinean Comparative Education Society, Buenos Aires.

Marshall, H. (2007). The Global Education Terminology Debate: Exploring Some of the Issues. In M. Hayden, J. Levy & J. Thompson (Eds.), *The SAGE Handbook of Research in International Education* (pp.38-50). London, Thousand Oaks, New Delhi: SAGE Publications.

Martínez, E. (2008). Educación Comparada en Universidades Sudamericanas: El Caso de Uruguay. In C. Wolhuter, N. Popov, M. Manzon & B. Leutwyler (Eds.), *Comparative Education at Universities World Wide* (pp.201-210). Sofia: Bureau for Educational Services.

Martínez, M.J. (2003). *Educación Comparada: nuevos retos, renovados desafíos.* Madrid: Editorial La Muralla, S.A.

Martínez, M.J., & Valle, J.M. (2005). 10 años de la REEC. Una mirada en perspectiva. *Revista Española de Educación Comparada, 11*, 37-93.

Masemann, V. (1990). Ways of Knowing: Implications for Comparative Education. *Comparative Education Review, 34*(4), 465-473.

Masemann, V. (1997). Recent Directions in Comparative Education. In C. Kodron, B. von Kopp, U. Lauterbach, U. Schäfer & G. Schmidt (Eds.), *Vergleichende Erziehungswissenschaft: Herausforderung, Vermittlung, Praxis. Festchrift für Wolfgang Mitter zum 70 Geburtstag* (pp. 81-90). Koln: Bohlau.

Masemann, V. (2004). Interview by Maria Manzon, 29 October. Havana, Cuba.

Masemann, V. (2006). Afterword. *Current Issues in Comparative Education, 8*(2), 104-111.

Masemann, V., Bray, M. & Manzon, M. (Eds.) (2007). *Common Interests, Uncommon Goals: Histories of the World Council of Comparative Education Societies and Its Members.* Hong Kong: Comparative Education Research Centre, The University of Hong Kong, and Dordrecht: Springer.

Masemann, V. & Epstein, E.H. (2007). The World Council from 1970 to 1979. In V. Masemann, M. Bray & M. Manzon (Eds.), *Common Interests, Uncommon Goals:*

Histories of the World Council of Comparative Education Societies and its Members (pp.13-19). Dordrecht & Hong Kong: Springer & Comparative Education Research Centre, The University of Hong Kong.

Mason, M. (2000). *The Ethics of Integrity: A Defense of Core Ethical Principles for Education in Late Modernity*. Ed.D. Dissertation. Teachers College, Columbia University.

Mason, M. (2007). Comparing Cultures. In M. Bray, B. Adamson & M. Mason (Eds.), *Comparative Education Research: Approaches and Methods* (pp.165-196). Hong Kong: Comparative Education Research Centre, The University of Hong Kong, and Dordrecht: Springer.

Mason, M. (2008a). What Is Comparative Education, and What Values Might Best Inform Its Research? Presidential Address Given at the Annual Conference of the Comparative Education Society of Hong Kong.

Mason, M. (2008b). What Is Complexity Theory and What are Its Implications for Educational Change? *Educational Philosophy and Theory*, 40(1), 35-49.

Mason, M. (2008c). Personal communication, 2 June. Hong Kong, China.

Massón, R.M. (Ed.) (2006). *Educación Comparada. Teoría y Práctica*. La Habana: Editorial Pueblo y Educación.

Massón, R.M. & Torres, A. (2008). La Educación Comparada como Disciplina Universitaria en Cuba. In C. Wolhuter, N. Popov, M. Manzon & B. Leutwyler (Eds.), *Comparative Education at Universities World Wide* (pp.185-191). Sofia: Bureau for Educational Services.

Maton, K. (2000). Language of Legitimation: The Structuring Significance for Intellectual Fields of Strategic Knowledge Claims. *British Journal of Sociology of Education*, 21(2), 147-167.

Mazibuko, E.Z. (2006). The State of History of Education and Comparative Education in Swaziland. In C. Wolhuter (Ed.), *Aurora Australis: Comparative Education and History of Education at Universities in Southern Africa / Education Comparée et Histoire de l'éducation dans les universités d'Afrique Australe* (pp.15-26). Potchefstroom: C.C.Wolhuter.

McClellan, J.E. (1957). An Educational Philosopher Looks at Comparative Education. *Comparative Education Review*, 1(1), 8-9.

McDade, D. (1982). The Things that Interest Mankind: A Commentary on Thirty Years of Comparative Education. *British Journal of Educational Studies*, 30(1), 72-84.

McGovern, S. (1999). *Education, Modern Development, and Indigenous Knowledge: An Analysis of Academic Knowledge Production*. New York: Garland Publishing Inc.

McIntosh, C. (2002). International Review of Education: A Journal of Many Incarnations. *International Review of Education*, 48(1/2), 1-20.

McLaughlin, T.H. (2004). Education, Philosophy and the Comparative Perspective. *Comparative Education*, 40 (4), 471-483.

Megahed, N. & Otaiba, A. (2008). Comparative Education at Universities in Egypt. In C. Wolhuter, N. Popov, M. Manzon & B. Leutwyler (Eds.), *Comparative Education at Universities World Wide* (pp.280-286). Sofia: Bureau for Educational Services.

Mehta, S. (2003). *Mapping Excluded Knowledge in Comparative Education Discourse: Opening pedagogy*. Ph.D. Dissertation. State University of New York at Buffalo.

Mehta, S. & Ninnes, P. (2003). Postmodernism Debates and Comparative Education: A Critical Discourse Analysis. *Comparative Education Review, 47*(2), 238-255.

Messer-Davidow, E., Shumway, D. & Sylvan, D. (1993). Introduction: Disciplinary Ways of Knowing. In E. Messer-Davidow, D. Shumway & D. Sylvan (Eds.), *Knowledges: Historical and Critical Studies in Disciplinarity* (pp.1-21). Charlottesville & London: University Press of Virginia.

Millán-Puelles, A. (2002). *Léxico Filosófico* (2nd ed.). Madrid: Ediciones Rialp, S.A..

Mitrović, D. (1981). *Moderni tokovi komparativne pedagogije*. Sarajevo: Svijetlost.

Mitter, W. (1982). Educational Sciences or Educational Science? Some Considerations on a Basic Issue. In I. Cavicchi-Broquet & P. Furter (Eds.), *Les Sciences de l'éducation: Perspectives et Bilans Européens. Actes de la Xe Conférence de l'Association d'éducation Comparée Pour l'Europe* (pp.83-95). Genève: Section des Sciences de l'éducation, Faculté de Psychologie et de Sciences de l'éducation, Université de Genève.

Mitter, W. (2007). The Comparative Education Society in Europe (CESE). In V. Masemann, M. Bray & M. Manzon (Eds.), *Common Interests, Uncommon Goals: Histories of the World Council of Comparative Education Societies and its Members* (pp.116-127). Hong Kong: Comparative Education Research Centre, The University of Hong Kong, and Dordrecht: Springer.

Mitter, W. & Swift, J. (Eds.) (1983). *Education and the Diversity of Cultures / L'Éducation et la diversité des cultures / Erziehung und die Vielfalt der Kulturen. Bericht der 11. Konferenz der Comparative Education Society in Europe (Würzburg)*. Köln, Wien: Böhlau. I. und II. Teilband: XXI, 719 S. = *Bildung und Erziehung*, Beiheft 2/I und 2/II.

Mochida, K. (2005). Interview by Maria Manzon, 31 May. Bangi, Malaysia.

Mohd. Meerah, T.S. & Halim, L. (2008). The Status of Comparative Education in Malaysia. In C. Wolhuter, N. Popov, M. Manzon & B. Leutwyler (Eds.), *Comparative Education at Universities World Wide* (pp.252-258). Sofia: Bureau for Educational Services.

Moore, R. (2004). Cultural Capital: Objective Probability and Cultural Arbitrary. *British Journal of Sociology of Education, 25*(4), 445-455.

Mucklow, N.H. (1980). Grounds for Grouping the Disciplines. *Journal of Philosophy of Education, 14* (2), 225-237.

Muganda, C.K. & Alphonce, N.R. (2006). The State of Comparative Education and History of Education in Tanzania. In C. Wolhuter (Ed.), *Aurora Australis: Comparative Education and History of Education at Universities in Southern Africa / Education Comparée et Histoire de l'éducation dans les universités d'Afrique Australe* (pp.27-40). Potchefstroom: C.C.Wolhuter.

Mukherjee, L. (1959). *Comparative Education*. Allahabad, India: Kitab Mahal.

Munck, G.L. & Snyder, R. (2007). Debating the Direction of Comparative Politics:

An Analysis of Leading Journals. *Comparative Political Studies, 40*(1), 5-31.

Mundy, K. (1999). Educational Multilateralism in a Changing World Order: UNESCO and the Limits of the Possible. *International Journal of Educational Development, 19*(1), 27-52.

Mundy, K. (2007). Global Governance, Educational Change. *Comparative Education, 43*(3), 339-357.

Mussin, K. (2007). Interview by Maria Manzon, 11 January. Macao, China.

Nakajima, H. (1916). *Comparative Study of National Education in Germany, France, Britain and the USA*. Tokyo: Kyouiku-shincho Kenkyukai. [in Japanese]

Nash, P., Kazamias, A.M. & Perkinson, H. (1965). *The Educated Man: Studies in the History of Educational Thought*. New York: John Wiley and Sons.

Navarro-Leal, M. (2008). Un Panorama de la Educación Comparada en México. In C. Wolhuter, N. Popov, M. Manzon & B. Leutwyler (Eds.), *Comparative Education at Universities World Wide* (pp.192-200). Sofia: Bureau for Educational Services.

Naya, L.M. (2004). Interview by Maria Manzon, 27 October. Havana, Cuba [in Spanish]

Naya, L.M. (2005). La Educación Comparada en los Nuevos Espacios Virtuales (1995-2004). *Revista Española de Educación Comparada, 11*, 241-271.

Naya, L.M. & Ferrer, F. (2007). The Spanish Comparative Education Society (SEEC). In V. Masemann, M. Bray & M. Manzon (Eds.), *Common Interests, Uncommon Goals: Histories of the World Council of Comparative Education Societies and its Members* (pp.214-224). Dordrecht & Hong Kong: Springer & Comparative Education Research Centre, The University of Hong Kong.

Naya, L.M., Ferrer, F. & Martínez, M.J. (2008). The Teaching of Comparative Education in Spain. In C. Wolhuter, N. Popov, M. Manzon & B. Leutwyler (Eds.), *Comparative Education at Universities World Wide* (pp.121-127). Sofia: Bureau for Educational Services.

Nicholson, C.K. (1969). *Antropología y educación*. Buenos Aires: Paidós. Original English version: 1968. *Anthropology and Education*. Columbus, Ohio: Merrill Books.

Ninnes, P. (2004). Discourse Analysis and Comparative Education. In P. Ninnes & S. Mehta (Eds.), *Re-imagining Comparative Education: Postfoundational Ideas and Applications for Critical Times* (pp.43-62). New York: Routledge.

Ninnes, P. (2008a). Fear and Desire in Twentieth Century Comparative Education. *Comparative Education Review, 44*(3), 345-358.

Ninnes, P. (2008b). Ancestors, Founders and Heroes in Comparative Education: An Historical Discourse Analysis. In V. Rust & J. Zajda (Eds.), *Globalisation and Comparative Education Research: The History of Comparative Education*. Dordrecht: Springer.

Ninnes, P. & Burnett, G. (2003). Comparative Education Research: Poststructuralist Possibilities. *Comparative Education, 39*(3), 279-297.

Ninomiya, A. (2007). The Japan Comparative Education Society. In Masemann, V.,

Bray, M. y Manzon, M. (Eds.), *Common Interests, Uncommon Goals: Histories of the World Council of Comparative Education Societies and its Members*. Dordrecht & Hong Kong: Springer & Comparative Education Research Centre, The University of Hong Kong, pp.128-138.

Noah, H.J. & Eckstein, M.A. (1969). *Toward a Science of Comparative Education*. New York: Macmillan.

Noah, H.J. & Eckstein, M.A. (1998). *Doing Comparative Education: Three Decades of Collaboration*. Hong Kong: Comparative Education Research Centre, The University of Hong Kong.

Nogueira, S. (2004). Interview by Maria Manzon, 29 October. Havana, Cuba.

Nóvoa, A. (2000). Estat de la qüestió de l'educació comparada: paradigmas, avanços i impassos. *Temps d'Educació 24*, 101-123.

Nzabalirwa, W. (2008). L'éducation comparée au Rwanda: situation, problèmes et perspectives. In C. Wolhuter, N. Popov, M. Manzon & B. Leutwyler (Eds.), *Comparative Education at Universities World Wide* (pp.287-294). Sofia: Bureau for Educational Services.

O'Sullivan, M. (2008). Comparative Education in Teacher Education in the UK and Ireland In C. Wolhuter, N. Popov, M. Manzon & B. Leutwyler (Eds.), *Comparative Education at Universities World Wide* (pp.105-112). Sofia: Bureau for Educational Services.

Ocheng Kagoire, M. (2008). Comparative Education in Universities in Uganda. In C. Wolhuter, N. Popov, M. Manzon & B. Leutwyler (Eds.), *Comparative Education at Universities World Wide* (pp.311-318). Sofia: Bureau for Educational Services.

OECD (2001). *Education at a Glance: OECD Indicators*. Paris: OECD.

OECD (2003). *The PISA 2003 Assessment Framework: Mathematics, Reading, Science and Problem Solving Knowledge and Skills*. Paris: OECD.

OECD (2004). *OECD Handbook for Internationally Comparative Education Statistics: Concepts, Standards, Definitions and Classifications*. Paris: OECD.

OECD (2010). The OECD: What is it? www.oecd.org/document/18/0,2340, 3n_2649_201185_2068050_ 1_1_1_1,00.html. Downloaded on 6/8/10.

Olivera, C.E. (1988). Comparative Education: Towards a Basic Theory. *Prospects, 18*(2), 167-185.

Olivera, C.E. (1990). Comparative Education: What Kind of Knowledge? In J. Schriewer & B. Holmes (Eds.), *Theories and Methods in Comparative Education* (2nd ed., pp.197-223). Frankfurt am Main: Peter Lang.

Olivera, C.E. (2009). *Introducción a la Educación Comparada* (2nd ed.). San José, Costa Rica: Editorial Universidad Estatal a Distancia (EUNED).

Orizio, B. (1977). *Pedagogia Comparativa*. Brescia: La Scuola.

Otsuka, Y. (2005). Fields as Methods. *Comparative Education* [Japan], *31*, 253-263. [in Japanese]

Øyen, E. (Ed.) (1990). *Comparative Methodology: Theory and Practice in International Social Research*. London: SAGE.

Pachociński, R. (1995). *Comparative Pedagogy*. Białystok: Trans Humana. [in Polish]

Palaudàrias, J.M. (2000). *Proyecto Docente*. Universitat de Girona. Documento policopiado.

Palmer, R. (Ed. & Transl.) (1993). *From Jacobin to Liberal. Marc-Antoine Jullien, 1775-1848*. Ewing, NJ: Princeton University Press.

Palomba, D. & Paolone, A. (2008). Comparative Education in Italian Universities: A Renewed Vitality. In C. Wolhuter, N. Popov, M. Manzon & B. Leutwyler (Eds.), *Comparative Education at Universities World Wide* (pp.88-95). Sofia: Bureau for Educational Services.

Park, E.L. & Hyun, K.S. (2008). Comparative Education in Teacher Education in Korea. In C. Wolhuter, N. Popov, M. Manzon & B. Leutwyler (Eds.), *Comparative Education at Universities World Wide* (pp.237-241). Sofia: Bureau for Educational Services.

Parkyn, G.W. (1977). Comparative Education Research and Development Education. *Comparative Education, 13*(2), 87-93.

Paulston, R. (1993). Ways of Seeing Education and Social Change in Latin America: A Phenomenographic Perspective. *Latin American Research Review, 28*(1), 177-202.

Paulston, R. (1994). Comparative and International Education: Paradigms and Theories. In T. Husén, T.N. Postlethwaite (Eds.), *The International Encyclopedia of Education* (pp.923-933). Oxford: Pergamon Press.

Paulston, R. (Ed.) (1996). *Social Cartography: Mapping Ways of Seeing Social and Educational Change*. New York: Garland.

Paulston, R. (2004). Opening up the Canon? How Freedom to Map the Multiple in Knowledge Debates Enhances Comparison for a Disputatious Time. Paper presented at the 48th Annual Meeting of the Comparative and International Education Society, Salt Lake City, 9-13 March.

Pedró, F. (1993). Conceptos alternativos y debates teórico-metodológicos en Educación Comparada: una panorámica introductoria. In J. Schriewer & F. Pedró (Eds.), *Manual de Educación Comparada* (pp.163-188). Barcelona: PPU.

Pereyra, M. (1989). La comparación, una empresa razonada de análisis. Por otros usos de la comparación. *Revista de Educación* (N.° extraordinario sobre Los usos de la comparación en Ciencias Sociales y en Educación), 25-76.

Pérez, E. (1945). *Educación Comparada*. La Habana: Universidad de la Habana.

Pérez, S., Groux, D., & Ferrer, F. (2000). Éducation comparée et éducation interculturelle: éléments de comparaison. *Raisons educatives, 1-2*, 49-65.

Peters, B.G. (1988). *Comparing Public Bureaucracies, Problems of Theory and Method*. Tuscaloosa, AB: University of Alabama Press

Peters, B.G. (1998). *Comparative Politics: Theory and Methods*. New York: New York University Press.

Phillips, D. (1994). Periodisation in Historical Approaches. *British Journal of Educational Studies, 42*(3), 261-272.

Phillips, D. (2002). Comparative Historical Studies in Education: Problems of

Periodisation Reconsidered. *British Journal of Educational Studies, 50*(3), 363-377.

Phillips, D. & Schweisfurth, M. (2006). *Comparative and International Education. An Introduction to Theory, Method and Practice.* London: Continuum International Publishing Group.

Philp, M. (1990). Michel Foucault. In Q. Skinner (Ed.), *The Return of Grand Theory in the Human Sciences.* Cambridge [England] and New York: Cambridge University Press.

Poizat, D. (2008). Considérations sur l'éducation comparée en France. In C. Wolhuter, N. Popov, M. Manzon & B. Leutwyler (Eds.), *Comparative Education at Universities World Wide* (pp.60-65). Sofia: Bureau for Educational Services.

Popov, N. (2007). The Bulgarian Comparative Education Society (BCES). In V. Masemann, M. Bray & M. Manzon (Eds.), *Common Interests, Uncommon Goals: Histories of the World Council of Comparative Education Societies and its Members* (pp.268-277). Hong Kong: Comparative Education Research Centre, The University of Hong Kong, and Dordrecht: Springer.

Popov, N. (2008). Comparative Education in Bulgaria. In C. Wolhuter, N. Popov, M. Manzon & B. Leutwyler (Eds.), *Comparative Education at Universities World Wide* (pp.27-34). Sofia: Bureau for Educational Services.

Postlethwaite, T.N. (Ed.) (1988a). *The Encyclopedia of Comparative Education and National Systems of Education.* Oxford: Pergamon Press.

Postlethwaite, T.N. (1988b). Preface. In T.N. Postlethwaite (Ed.), *The Encyclopedia of Comparative Education and National Systems of Education* (pp.xvii-xxvii). Oxford: Pergamon Press.

Potgieter, F.J. (1972). *Inleiding tot die Vergelykende Pedagogiek.* Johannesburg: Perskor.

Potulicka, E. (2007). Poland. Unpublished manuscript. Adam Mickiewicz University, Poland.

Price, R.F. (1992). Comparative Education Redefined? In R.J. Burns & A.R. Welch (Eds.), *Contemporary Perspectives in Comparative Education* (pp.69-87). New York: Garland Publications.

Psacharopoulos, G. (1973). *Returns to Education: An International Comparison.* San Francisco: Jossey-Bass.

Psacharopoulos, G. & Patrinos, H.A. (2002). *Returns to Investment in Education: A Further Update.* Policy Research Working Paper 2881. Washington DC: The World Bank.

Quintana, J. M. (1983). Epistemología de la pedagogía comparada. *Educar, 3,* 25-26.

Rabinow, P. (Ed.) (1997). *Ethics: Essential Works of Foucault 1954-1984,* Vol.1. London: Penguin.

Ragin, C. (1987). *The Comparative Method: Moving beyond Qualitative and Quantitative Strategies.* Berkeley: University of California Press.

Raivola, R. (1984). *Comparative Education.* Tampereen yliopiston kasvatustieteen laitos, julkaisusarja A:30. [in Finnish]

Raivola, R. (2008). Comparative Education in Finland. In C. Wolhuter, N. Popov, M. Manzon & B. Leutwyler (Eds.), *Comparative Education at Universities World*

Wide (pp.53-59). Sofia: Bureau for Educational Services.

Raventos, F. (1990). *Metodología Comparativa y Pedagogía Comparada*. Barcelona: Boixareu Universitaria.

Remak, H. (1971). Comparative Literature: Its Definition and Function. In N.P. Stallknecht & H. Frenz (Eds.), *Comparative Literature: Method & Perspective* (rev. ed.) (pp.1-53). Carbondale & Edwardsville: Southern Illinois University Press.

Rim, H.Y. (1961). *Comparative Education*. Seoul, Korea: Modern Education Collection, Publication. [in Korean]

Ringer, F. (1992). *Fields of Knowledge: French Academic Culture in Comparative Perspective, 1890-1920*. Cambridge: Cambridge University Press.

Ringer, F. (2000). *Toward A Social History of Knowledge: Collected Essays*. New York: Berghahn Books.

Roberts, G.K. (1972). *What is Comparative Politics?* London and Basingstoke: MacMillan.

Rodríguez, E. (2008). Escenarios y Mediaciones de la Educación Comparada en el Ámbito Universitario de Chile. In C. Wolhuter, N. Popov, M. Manzon & B. Leutwyler (Eds.), *Comparative Education at Universities World Wide* (pp.177-184). Sofia: Bureau for Educational Services.

Ross, H., To, C.Y., Cave, W. & Bair, D.E. (1992). On Shifting Ground: The Post-paradigm Identity of U.S. Comparative Education, 1979-88. *Compare, 22*(2), 113-131.

Rosselló, P. (1943). *Marc-Antoine, Jullien de Paris, Père de l'Education Comparée et Précurseur du Bureau International de l'Education*. Geneva: International Bureau of Education.

Rosselló, P. (1960). *La Teoría de las Corrientes Educativas: Cursillo de Educación Comparada Dinámica*. La Habana: Centro Regional de la UNESCO.

Rosselló, P. (1972). La Estructura de la Educación Comparada. In A.D. Marquez (Ed.), *Educación Comparada: Teoría y metodología* (pp.53-60). Buenos Aires: Ateneo.

Rosselló, P. (1978). *Teoría de las corrientes educativas* (2nd ed.). Barcelona: Promocion Cultural.

Runciman, W.G. (1989). *A Treatise on Social Theory, Vol. II: Substantive Social Theory*. Cambridge: Cambridge University Press.

Ruscoe, G.C., & Nelson, T.W. (1964). Prolegomena to a Definition of Comparative Education. *International Review of Education / Internationale Zeitschrift fur Erziehungswissenschaft / Revue Internationale de l'Education, 10*(4), 385-392.

Rust, V. (1991). Postmodernism and its Comparative Education Implications. *Comparative Education Review, 35*(4), 610-626.

Rust, V. D. (2001). Editorial. *Comparative Education Review, 45*(3), iii-iv.

Rust, V.D., Soumare, A., Pescador, O., & Shibuya, M. (1999). Research Strategies in Comparative Education. *Comparative Education Review, 43*(1), 86-109.

Rwantabagu, H. (1990). *Comparative Education: Global Perspectives*. Nairobi: Kenyatta University.

Rwantabagu, H. (2006). Personal communication. 23 May. Hong Kong, China.

Rwantabagu, H. (2008). Comparative Education in Burundi. In C. Wolhuter, N.

Popov, M. Manzon & B. Leutwyler (Eds.), *Comparative Education at Universities World Wide* (pp.273-279). Sofia: Bureau for Educational Services.

Sadler, M. (1900 [reprinted 1964]). How Far Can We Learn Anything of Practical Value from the Study of Foreign Systems of Education? *Comparative Education Review, 7*(3), 307-314.

Samaan, W. (1958). *Studies in Comparative Education.* Cairo, Egypt: Maktabat ElAnglo ElMisria [in Arabic].

Sandiford, P. (Ed.) (1918). *Comparative Education: Studies of the Educational Systems of Six Modern Nations.* London, Toronto: J.M. Dent & Sons Ltd.

Sapiro, G.L. (2004). Forms of Politicization in the French Literary Field. In D.L. Swartz & V.L. Zolberg (Eds.), *After Bourdieu: Influence, Critique, Elaboration* (pp.145-164). Dordrecht: Kluwer Academic Publishers.

Saussure, F. (1949). *Course on General Linguistics.* Paris: Payot.

Scanlon, D.G. & Shields, J.J. (1968). Introduction: Scope and Purposes of International Education. In D.G. Scanlon & J.J. Shields (Eds.), *Problems and Prospects in International Education* (pp.ix-xxii). New York: Teachers College Press, Columbia University.

Scarrow, H.A. (1969). *Comparative Political Analysis: An Introduction.* New York: Harper & Row.

Schneider, F. (1947). *Triebkräfte der Pädagogik der Völker.* Salzburg: Otto Müller Verlag.

Schneider, F. (1961a). *Vergleichende Erziehungswissenschaft: Geschichte, Forschung, Lehre.* Heidelberg: Quelle and Meyer.

Schneider, F. (1961b). The Immanent Evolution of Education: A Neglected Aspect of Comparative Education. *Comparative Education Review, 4*(1), 136-139.

Schneider, F. (1964). *Pedagogía de los Pueblos: Introducción a la Pedagogía Comparada.* Barcelona: Herder.

Schriewer, J. (2000). Comparative Education Methodology in Transition: Towards a Science of Complexity? In J. Schriewer (Ed.), *Discourse Formation in Comparative Education* (pp.3-52). Frankfurt am Main: P. Lang.

Schriewer, J. (2003). Globalisation in Education: Process and Discourse. *Policy Futures in Education, 1*(2), 271-283.

Schriewer, J. (2005). Interview by Maria Manzon, 23 August. Beijing, China.

Schultz, T.W. (1963). *The Economic Value of Education.* New York: Columbia University Press.

Schüssler, L. & Leutwyler, B. (2008). The Ambiguous Future of a Discipline: Comparative Education in Switzerland. In C. Wolhuter, N. Popov, M. Manzon & B. Leutwyler (Eds.), *Comparative Education at Universities World Wide* (pp.128-135). Sofia: Bureau for Educational Services.

Schweisfurth, M. (1999). Resilience, Resistance and Responsiveness: Comparative and International Education at United Kingdom Universities. In R. Alexander, P. Broadfoot & D. Phillips (Eds.), *Learning from Comparing. New Directions in Comparative Educational Research. Volume 1: Contexts, Classrooms and Outcomes* (Vol. 1, pp. 89-101). Wallingford, Oxford: Symposium Books.

Senent, J.M. (2005). Los Estudios de Pedagogía en Europa en el Contexto de la Implantación del Proceso de Bolonia y la Situación de la Educación Comparada. *Revista Española de Educación Comparada, 11*, 95-133.

Seotsanyana, M. & Ntabeni, M. (2006). The State Of History of Education and Comparative Education at the National University of Lesotho. In C. Wolhuter (Ed.), *Aurora Australis: Comparative Education and History of Education at Universities in Southern Africa / Education Comparée et Histoire de l'éducation dans les universités d'Afrique Australe* (pp.51-66). Potchefstroom: C.C.Wolhuter.

Shang, X. & Chen, S. (2008). Content Analysis of the Disciplinary System of Comparative Education in Mainland China. *Comparative Education Review (Beijing)*, 2, 40-44. [in Chinese]

Sherman Swing, E. (2007). The Comparative and International Education Society. In V. Masemann, M. Bray & M. Manzon (Eds.), *Common Interests, Uncommon Goals: Histories of the World Council of Comparative Education Societies and its Members* (pp.94-115). Dordrecht & Hong Kong: Springer & Comparative Education Research Centre, The University of Hong Kong.

Shibata, M. (2005). *Japan and Germany under the U.S. Occupation: A Comparative Analysis of Post-War Education Reform.* Lanham, MD & Oxford: Lexington Books.

Sisson de Castro, M. (2007). The Brazilian Comparative Education Society. In V. Masemann, M. Bray & M. Manzon (Eds.), *Common Interests, Uncommon Goals: Histories of the World Council of Comparative Education Societies and its Members* (pp.240-244). Dordrecht & Hong Kong: Springer & Comparative Education Research Centre, The University of Hong Kong.

Sisson de Castro, M. & Gomes, C. (2008). Small is Beautiful: Comparative Education in Brazilian Universities. In C. Wolhuter, N. Popov, M. Manzon & B. Leutwyler (Eds.), *Comparative Education at Universities World Wide* (pp.169-176). Sofia: Bureau for Educational Services.

Sjösted, C.E. & Sjöstrand, W. (1952). Schools and Education in Sweden and other Countries. A Comparative Survey. Stockholm: Natur och kultur. [in Swedish]

Sokolova, M.A., Kuzmina, E.N. & Rodionov, M.L. (1978). *Comparative Pedagogy.* Moscow: Prosvescenie. [in Russian]

Soudien, C. (2007). The Southern African Comparative and History of Education Society. In V. Masemann, M. Bray & M. Manzon (Eds.), *Common Interests, Uncommon Goals: Histories of the World Council of Comparative Education Societies and its Members* (pp.284-292). Dordrecht & Hong Kong: Springer & Comparative Education Research Centre, The University of Hong Kong.

Stone, K.M. (2005). Research Note: Comparative and International Course Archive Project (CIECAP). *International Review of Education, 51*(5/6), 517-524.

Stromquist, N. (1989). Determinants of Educational Achievement of Women in the Third World: A Review of the Evidence and a Theoretical Critique. *Review of Educational Research, 59*(2), 143-183.

Sutherland, M. (2007). The Francophone Association for Comparative Education.

In V. Masemann, M. Bray & M. Manzon (Eds.), *Common Interests, Uncommon Goals: Histories of the World Council of Comparative Education Societies and its Members* (pp.189-199). Dordrecht & Hong Kong: Springer & Comparative Education Research Centre, The University of Hong Kong.

Sutherland, M., Crossley, M. & Watson, K. (2007). The British Association for International and Comparative Education. In V. Masemann, M. Bray & M. Manzon (Eds.), *Common Interests, Uncommon Goals: Histories of the World Council of Comparative Education Societies and its Members* (pp.155-169). Dordrecht & Hong Kong: Springer & Comparative Education Research Centre, The University of Hong Kong.

Sweeting, A. (2007). Comparing Times. In M. Bray, B. Adamson & M. Mason (Eds.), *Comparative Education Research: Approaches and Methods* (pp.145-163). Hong Kong: Comparative Education Research Centre, The University of Hong Kong, and Dordrecht: Springer.

Sylvester, R. (2007). Historical Resources for Research in International Education (1851-1950). In M. Hayden, J. Levy & J. Thompson (Eds.), *The SAGE Handbook of Research in International Education* (pp.11-24). London: Sage Publications Ltd.

Takekuma, H. (2008). Comparative Education at Universities in Japan. In C. Wolhuter, N. Popov, M. Manzon & B. Leutwyler (Eds.), *Comparative Education at Universities World Wide* (pp.229-236). Sofia: Bureau for Educational Services.

Taneja, R.P. (Ed.) (2000). *Encyclopaedia of Comparative Education* (1st ed.). New Delhi: Anmol Publications.

Thongthew, S. (2007). Personal communication.

Thongthew, S. (2008). Comparative Education in Thailand. In C. Wolhuter, N. Popov, M. Manzon & B. Leutwyler (Eds.), *Comparative Education at Universities World Wide* (pp.266-270). Sofia: Bureau for Educational Services.

Tikly, L. & Crossley, M. (2001). Teaching Comparative and International Education: A Framework for Analysis. *Comparative Education Review, 45*(4), 561-580.

Todeschini, M. (2004). The Comparative Approach to Education in Italy. Unpublished manuscript.

Tötösy de Zepetnek, S. (1998). *Comparative Literature: Theory, Method, Application.* Amsterdam & Atlanta, Ga: Rodopi.

Toulmin, S. (1972). *Human Understanding* (Vol.1). Oxford: Clarendon Press.

Trethewey, A.R. (1976). *Introducing comparative education.* Rushcutters Bay, Australia: Pergamon Press.

Turner, D.A. (1987). Problem-solving in Comparative Education. *Compare, 17*(1), 39-45.

Turner, D. (2008). Personal communication, 27 May.

Turner, J.H. & Mitchell, D.E. (1997). Contemporary Sociological Theories of Education. In L.J. Saha (Ed.), *International Encyclopedia of the Sociology of Education* (pp.21-31). Oxford: Pergamon.

Tusquets, J. (1969). *Teoría y Práctica de la Pedagogía Comparada.* Madrid: Magisterio.

Tusquets, J. (1979). La Aportación Española al Comparativismo Pedagógico. *Revista de Educación, 260,* 115-131.

Ulich, R. (Ed.) (1964). *Education and the Idea of Mankind.* Chicago: The University of Chicago Press.

UNESCO (1945). *Constitution of the United Nations Educational, Scientific and Cultural Organization.* Paris: UNESCO.

Ushinsky, K.D. (1857). *On National Character of Public Education.* Reprinted 1975, in A.J. Piskunov (Ed.), *K.D. Ushinsky: Selective Works.* Moscow: Progress Publishers.

Van daele, H. (1993). *L'Éducation Comparée.* Paris: Presses Universitaires de France.

Veikshan, V.A. (1959). The Moscow Center in Comparative Education. *Comparative Education Review, 3*(1), 4-5.

Verba, S. (1986). Comparative Politics: Where Have We Been, Where Are We Going? In H. Wiarda (Ed.), *New Directions in Comparative Politics.* Boulder, Co.: Westview Press.

Verhine, R. (2004). Interview by Maria Manzon, 27 October. Havana, Cuba.

Vestal, T. (1994). *International Education: Its History and Promise for Today.* Westport, CT & London: Praeger.

Vexliard, A. (1967). *La Pédagogie Comparée.* Paris: Presses Universitaires de France.

Vexliard, A. (1970). *Pedagogía comparada: métodos y problemas.* Buenos Aires: Kapelusz.

Vilanou, C.Y. & Valls, M. (2001). En el Centenario del Nacimiento de Juan Tusquets (1901-1998), Propulsor de los Estudios de Pedagogía Comparada en España. *Revista Española de Educación Comparada, 7,* 263-294.

Villalobos, E. M. (2002). *Educación Comparada.* México: Publicaciones Cruz.

Villalpando, J.M. (1961). *Líneas Generales de Pedagogía Comparada. Teoría y Técnica.* México: Universidad Nacional Autónoma de México.

Vrcelj, S. (2005). *In Search for Identity - Comparative Pedagogy Perspective.* Hrvatsko futurološko društvo. Rijeka: Graftrade. [in Croatian]

Vrcelj, S. (2008). History of Comparative Education in Croatia. In C. Wolhuter, N. Popov, M. Manzon & B. Leutwyler (Eds.), *Comparative Education at Universities World Wide* (pp.35-41). Sofia: Bureau for Educational Services.

Wagner, P. & Wittrock, B. (1991a). States, Institutions, and Discourses: A Comparative Perspective on the Structuration of the Social Sciences. In P. Wagner, B. Wittrock & R. Whitley (Eds.), *Discourses on Society: The Shaping of the Social Science Disciplines* (pp.331-357). Dordrecht: Kluwer Academic Publishers.

Wagner, P. & Wittrock, B. (1991b). Analyzing Social Science: On the Possibility of a Sociology of the Social Sciences. In P. Wagner, B. Wittrock & R. Whitley (Eds.), *Discourses on Society: The Shaping of the Social Science Disciplines* (pp.3-22). Dordrecht: Kluwer Academic Publishers.

Walterová, E. (2006). *Comparative Education: Development and Changes in a Global Context.* Praha: Ministerstva školtsví. [in Czech]

Walterová, E. (2007). The Comparative Education Section of the Czech Pedagogical Society. In V. Masemann, M. Bray & M. Manzon (Eds.), *Common Inter-*

ests, Uncommon Goals: Histories of the World Council of Comparative Education Societies and its Members (pp.256-267). Dordrecht & Hong Kong: Springer & Comparative Education Research Centre, The University of Hong Kong.

Walterová, E. (2008). Comparative Education for Teachers in the Czech Republic: Aims, Models, Problems. In C. Wolhuter, N. Popov, M. Manzon & B. Leutwyler (Eds.), *Comparative Education at Universities World Wide* (pp.42-46). Sofia: Bureau for Educational Services.

Wang, C. (1999). *History of Comparative Education.* People's Education Press. [in Chinese]

Wang, C., Zhu, B. & Gu, M. (Eds.) (1982). *Comparative Education.* Beijing: People's Education Press. [in Chinese]

Waterkamp, D. (2005). Interview by Maria Manzon, 31 May. Bangi, Malaysia.

Waterkamp, D. (2007). Section for International and Intercultural Comparative Education. In V. Masemann, M. Bray & M. Manzon (Eds.), *Common Interests, Uncommon Goals: Histories of the World Council of Comparative Education Societies and its Members* (pp.139-154). Dordrecht & Hong Kong: Springer & Comparative Education Research Centre, The University of Hong Kong.

Waterkamp, D. (2008). Comparative Education as a Field of Teaching in German Universities. In C. Wolhuter, N. Popov, M. Manzon & B. Leutwyler (Eds.), *Comparative Education at Universities World Wide* (pp.66-72). Sofia: Bureau for Educational Services

Watson, K. (1982). Comparative Education in British Teacher Education. In R. Goodings, M. Byram & M. McPartland (Eds.), *Changing Priorities in Teacher Education* (pp.193-225). London: Croom Helm.

Watson, K. (1999). Comparative Educational Research: The Need for Reconceptualisation and Fresh Insights. *Compare: A Journal of Comparative Education, 29*(3), 233-248.

WCCE [World Council for Comparative Education] (1970). *Proceedings of the First World Congress of Comparative Education Societies,* Vol. 1. Ottawa: Secretariat, World Council for Comparative Education.

WCCES (1996). *Statutes.* World Council of Comparative Education Societies.

WCCES (2005). *By-laws to the Statutes and Rules of Procedures.* World Council of Comparative Education Societies.

WCCES (2010). Member Societies. www.wcces.net. Downloaded 06/08/10.

Weeks, S. (2004). Interview by Maria Manzon, 30 October. Havana, Cuba.

Weeks, S., Herman, H., Maarman, R. & Wolhuter, C. (2006). SACHES and Comparative, International and Development Education in Southern Africa: The Challenges and Future Prospects. *Southern African Review of Education* with *Education with Production, 12*(2), 5-20.

Welch, A. (1997). Things Fall Apart: Dis-integration, Universities, and the Decline of Discipline(s). Problematising Comparative Education in an Uncertain Age. In C. Kodron, B. von Kopp, U. Lauterbach, U. Schäfer & G. Schmidt (Eds.), *Vergleichende Erziehungswissenschaft: Herausforderung, Vermittlung, Praxis:*

Festschrift fur Wolfgang Mitter zum 70. Geburtstag (pp. 182-191). Frankfurt am Main: Bohlau Verlag.

Welch, A. (2005). Interview by Maria Manzon, 14 January. Hong Kong, China.

Wiarda, H.J. (Ed.) (1986). *New Directions in Comparative Politics*. Boulder, Co.: Westview Press.

Wickremasinghe, W. (Ed.) (1992). *Handbook of World Education*. Houston: American Collegiate Service.

Wilson, D. (1994a). Comparative and International Education: Fraternal or Siamese Twins? A Preliminary Genealogy of Our Twin Fields. *Comparative Education Review, 38*(4), 449-486.

Wilson, D. (1994b). On Teaching the Methodology of Comparative Education: Why Are There So Few Courses in Canada? *Canadian and International Education, 23*(1), 13-24.

Wilson, D. (2003). The Future of Comparative and International Education in a Globalised World. In M. Bray (Ed.), *Comparative Education: Continuing Traditions, New Challenges, and New Paradigms* (pp.15-33). Special double issue of *International Review of Education, 49*(1-2). Republished as book with same title, Dordrecht: Kluwer Academic Publishers.

Wilson, M. (2005). *Regression, Repositioning and Regeneration: Comparative and International Education in UK Higher Education Institutions*. Paper presented at the 8th UKFIET International Conference on Education and Development.

Winther-Jensen, T. (2004). *Comparative Education, Scientific Tradition and Global Challenge*. Copenhagen: Akademisk forlag. [in Danish]

Winther-Jensen, T. (2008). Comparative Education in Denmark. In C. Wolhuter, N. Popov, M. Manzon & B. Leutwyler (Eds.), *Comparative Education at Universities World Wide* (pp.47-52). Sofia: Bureau for Educational Services.

Wolhuter, C. (Ed.) (2006). *Aurora Australis: Comparative Education and History of Education at Universities in Southern Africa / Education Comparée et Histoire de l'éducation dans les universités d'Afrique Australe*. Potchefstroom: C.C.Wolhuter.

Wolhuter, C. (2008). Review of the Review: Constructing the Identity of Comparative Education. *Research in Comparative and International Education, 3*(4), 323-344.

Wolhuter, C. & Popov, N. (Eds.) (2007). *Comparative Education as Discipline at Universities World Wide* (1ˢᵗ ed.). Sofia: Bureau for Educational Services.

Wolhuter, C., Popov, N., Manzon, M. & Leutwyler, B. (Eds.) (2008a). *Comparative Education at Universities World Wide*. Sofia: Bureau for Educational Services.

Wolhuter, C., Popov, N., Manzon, M. & Leutwyler, B. (2008b). Mosaic of Comparative Education at Universities: Conceptual Nuances, Global Trends and Critical Reflections. In C. Wolhuter, N. Popov, M. Manzon & B. Leutwyler (Eds.), *Comparative Education at Universities World Wide* (pp.319-343). Sofia: Bureau for Educational Services.

Wolhuter, C. et al. (2008c). Comparative Education at Universities in the Southern African Region: From Decolonization Context to the Challenges of the 21ˢᵗ

Century. In C. Wolhuter, N. Popov, M. Manzon & B. Leutwyler (Eds.), *Comparative Education at Universities World Wide* (pp.295-302). Sofia: Bureau for Educational Services.

Wong, F. (1973). *Comparative Studies in Southeast Asian Education*. Kuala Lumpur: Heinemann Educational Books.

Wong, S.Y. & Fairbrother, G. (2007). The Comparative Education Society of Hong Kong (CESHK). In V. Masemann, M. Bray & M. Manzon (Eds.), *Common Interests, Uncommon Goals: Histories of the World Council of Comparative Education Societies and its Members* (pp.245-255). Hong Kong: Comparative Education Research Centre, The University of Hong Kong, and Dordrecht: Springer.

World Bank (1995). *Priorities and Strategies for Education: A World Bank Review*. Washington, D.C.: World Bank.

World Bank (1999). *Education Sector Strategy*. Washington, DC: The World Bank.

Wulfson, B.L. (2003). *Comparative Pedagogy: History and Modern Problems*. Moscow: University under Russian Academy of Education. [in Russian]

Young, M.F.D. (1971). *Knowledge and Control: New Directions for the Sociology of Education*. London: Collier-Macmillan.

Yu, J. (1917). *Comparative Study of National Education in Germany, France, Britain and the USA*. Shanghai: China Book Co. [in Chinese]

Yung, S-S.C. (1998). *A Comparison of Comparisons in the Field of Comparative Education: A Content Analysis of English-medium and Chinese-medium Journals*. Unpublished M.Ed. thesis. The University of Hong Kong, Hong Kong.

Zajda, J., Majhanovich, S. & Rust, V. with Martín Sabina, E. (Eds.) (2006). *Education and Social Justice*. Special double issue of *International Review of Education*, 52(1-2). Republished 2006 as book with same title, Dordrecht: Springer.

Zhao, Z.J. (2004). Interview by Maria Manzon, November 20, Zhuhai, China.

Zhao, Z.J. (2005). Interview by Maria Manzon, 23 August. Beijing, China.

Notes on the Author

Maria MANZON is a Research Associate of the Comparative Education Research Centre (CERC) at the University of Hong Kong. She has been editor of *CIEclopedia* (www.cieclopedia.org) and was Assistant Secretary General of the World Council of Comparative Education Societies (WCCES) in 2005. Her research interests focus on the history, theory and methodology of comparative education. *Correspondence*: Comparative Education Research Centre, The University of Hong Kong, Pokfulam Road, Hong Kong. E-mail: mimanzon@graduate.hku.hk.

Index

A

academic comparative education
1, 4, 35, 37, 40-1, 50, 56, 58, 83, 98,
107-10, 124, 164-5, 217, 225
academic definitions of comparative education   154, 214
academic disciplines   5-7, 13-7,
20, 25-6, 28, 36, 156, 186
construction of   27, 155
nature of   6, 11, 13-4, 16, 20, 228
academic fields   2, 7, 12, 16, 18-9,
23, 28, 33, 36, 53, 64, 66, 82, 214-5,
226-7
academic programmes   65, 113,
117, 121, 125, 209, 217-8, 222, 232
formal   38, 46, 66, 113-4, 232
Africa   42, 50, 63, 77-8, 143, 149,
237, 242, 245
agency   3, 7, 9, 14, 22, 35-6, 53-4,
99, 104, 112, 119-21, 123, 135, 210,
228-9
human agency   3-4, 7, 32, 48,
50, 52, 80, 87, 110, 112, 122, 125,
152, 221, 226
agents   4, 8, 24, 28-31, 33-6, 52-3,
55, 64, 71-2, 77, 79, 82, 98, 118,
210-1
habitus of   30-1, 34
individual   119-20, 222
subjective dispositions of   5, 7,
212
America see US/USA
Anderson, C.A.   130, 135, 161,
174, 178-9, 199
area studies   92-3, 110, 185, 188,
198, 248
Argentina   43, 56, 59, 61-2, 67,
77-8, 85, 240

Asia   42, 50, 66-8, 75, 77, 82, 90,
143, 149, 238-9, 242, 245
Asian Development Bank (ADB)
102, 105-6
Association Francophone
d'Éducation Comparée (AFEC)
73, 75, 83, 103, 122, 231, 236, 244
Australasia   238-9, 245
Australia   42, 44-5, 50, 59-60, 67,
77, 79, 86, 115, 122, 145, 219, 238
Australian and New Zealand
Comparative and International
Education Society (ANZCIES)
73, 75, 80, 84-5, 239

B

Beijing   71, 103, 238, 247-8
Bereday, George   38, 41, 44, 65-7,
69-70, 88, 93, 108, 135, 159-60,
165, 174, 178-80, 198
boundaries   20, 38, 64-5, 87, 92-3,
98, 127, 134, 154-5, 167, 170, 187,
190, 192, 203
Bourdieu/Bourdieuian   3, 6-9, 11,
13-4, 22-4, 28-33, 45, 48, 53, 63, 72,
114-5, 121, 156, 210, 227-8
Bray, Mark   16, 37, 41, 43, 68-9,
73, 75-8, 80, 83, 92, 94, 104-5, 143-
4, 163, 199-200
Brazil   45, 49, 52, 60-1, 63, 67, 78,
82, 86, 108, 115, 123, 147, 240
British Association for International and Comparative Education (BAICE)   71, 75, 83-4, 99,
122, 148, 231, 236, 243
Bulgaria   44, 48, 67, 78, 146, 234-6

Bulgarian Comparative Education
   Society (BCES)   73, 75, 95, 236,
   244

C

Canada   41, 43-4, 46, 50, 52, 60-3,
   76-8, 83, 86, 90, 113, 145, 202, 205,
   233
capital   8, 23, 28-9, 32, 34-5, 56,
   59, 84, 112, 114, 118, 211-3
   academic   52, 59, 87, 117-9
   social   35, 59, 79, 84-5, 87, 113-
   4, 118, 123
centres   2, 39-41, 45, 52, 65, 74, 76,
   88, 98, 104, 223, 249
China   43-5, 48-9, 52-3, 60, 66, 77,
   82, 84, 115-6, 118, 143-5, 147, 149-
   50, 203, 206-7, 238-9
Chinese Comparative Education
   Society (CCES)   75, 85, 95, 99,
   103, 231, 239, 243
Chinese Comparative Education
   Society-Taipei (CCES-T)   73, 75
Chile   48-9, 60, 67, 108, 115, 147,
   240
Comparative Education Review
   (CER)   71, 91, 96, 233, 238, 246-
   9
Comparative Education Research
   Centre (CERC)   10-11, 72, 91,
   250
Comparative Education Society of
   Asia (CESA)   73, 75, 81, 94, 239,
   243
Comparative Education Society in
   Europe (CESE)   47, 71, 73, 75-7,
   122, 236, 243
Comparative Education Society of
   Hong Kong (CESHK)   72, 75,
   123, 239, 244

Comparative Education Society of
   India (CESI)   75, 83, 239, 244
Comparative Education Society of
   the Philippines (CESP)   75, 239,
   244
Comparative and International
   Education Course Archive Project (CIECAP)   43-4, 69, 88, 91,
   97
Comparative and International
   Education Society (CIES)   71,
   75-6, 84, 94-6, 99, 122-3, 148, 178,
   233, 249
Comparative and International
   Education Society of Canada
   (CIESC)   75, 99, 233, 244
comparative education
   academic field of   33, 56, 116
   academic institutionalisation of
      115, 123
   academic programmes of comparative education   114, 218
   construction of   8, 11, 126, 210
   courses   41, 50, 90, 113
   defining/definition of   66, 86,
      93, 153-4, 158, 160, 164, 170,
      180, 206-7, 210, 212
   dissemination of   45, 115
   distinct object of   207, 215
   distinctive nature of   163, 193
   histories of   101, 115, 125, 225
   intellectual history of   142, 144
   intellectual shaping of   3, 127-
      52
   journals   41, 92
   nature of   1, 6, 13, 19, 36, 87,
      97, 100, 109, 153, 156, 158, 177,
      183-4, 206
   object of   158-62, 164, 169, 193
   positioning of comparative edu-

cation   54, 58, 195

research   47, 68, 88, 101, 105, 108, 144-5, 173

scholars   10-11, 36, 38-9, 107-8, 143, 152, 213, 227

societies   10, 73, 75-9, 82, 84, 86, 88-9, 94, 96, 121-3, 178

society journals   72

studies   101, 105, 109, 151, 162, 170, 172, 175, 238

teaching   10, 37, 42-4, 63, 78, 82, 96, 111-2, 115, 232

theory   149, 247-8

Comparative Education Society of India (CESI)   75, 83, 239, 244

Comparative Education Society of the Philippines (CESP)   75, 239, 244

comparative

   fields   2-3, 167, 171, 183-4, 188, 190, 208

   literature   170, 173, 188-90

   method   129, 158, 163, 165-8, 170-1, 174, 176, 178, 181-4, 187, 190, 200

   pedagogy   47, 165, 178, 182, 198, 232

   politics   184-6

   studies   41, 56, 89, 93, 95, 103, 108, 151, 154, 165, 169-70, 181, 184-6, 190-1, 197-8

comparison   100, 105, 141, 151, 156, 159-60, 162-3, 166, 170, 184, 186-9, 199, 201, 203, 206-7

   implicit   94, 161

   object(s) of   163-4, 171

   units of   162, 247

Council on Comparative Education of Kazakhstan (CCEK)   75, 239, 244

Cowen, Robert   1, 3, 6, 13, 69, 100-1, 107-10, 116, 124-5, 139-42, 148-9, 159-60, 164-5, 191, 211-2

Crossley, Michael   3, 40, 42, 69, 71, 124, 139-40, 142, 173, 200-1

Cuba   45, 61-2, 67-8, 75, 78-80, 85, 122, 219, 240

Current Issues in Comparative Education   72, 233

Czech Republic   39, 58, 67-8, 105, 146, 234-5

Czechoslovakia   44, 47-8, 85-6, 146

D

Deconstructing Comparative Education   1, 3, 5, 7, 9, 11

Denmark   47, 60-2, 67-8, 234-5

developed countries   202, 246, 248

development education   39, 95, 110, 113, 196, 198, 201-5, 213, 218

disciplinary change   11, 14, 20-22, 223

   dynamics of   13, 22

   nature of   20, 36

   socio-historical explanations of   6, 13

disciplinary histories   7, 38, 140, 151-2, 209, 222, 229

disciplinary institutionalisation   16, 25, 59, 113, 120

disciplinary knowledge   7, 14, 17-8, 20, 33, 36, 74, 98, 113

disciplines   1, 5-9, 13-28, 40, 46, 50, 64, 153-7, 165, 167, 171-2, 177-81, 183-6, 190-1, 208-9

   comparative   160, 187

disciplines and fields, nature of   20, 155

disciplines and fields in academic
    discourse   13, 15, 17, 19, 21, 23,
    25, 27, 29, 31, 33, 35
discourses   3-7, 9, 20, 22-8, 35-6,
    53-4, 56, 108-14, 116-17, 119-21,
    124-5, 151-7, 209-14, 223-5, 227-9
    scholarly   211-2, 216, 221-2,
    224
discursive construction   9, 33, 65,
    73, 209-10, 216
discursive formations   7-8, 11,
    23-5, 27-8, 33, 46, 54, 64-5, 74, 110,
    113, 145, 155, 210
distinction   7-8, 26, 28, 30, 32, 34,
    51, 71, 74, 77, 79, 114, 118, 121-3,
    219

E
Egyptian Comparative Education
    and Educational Administration
    Society (ECEEAS)   75, 78, 237,
    244
Eckstein, Max   67, 108, 129, 139,
    142-4, 160-1, 178, 180
    comparative science of   158
    economics of   110, 192
    higher   13, 17-8, 51, 57, 70, 96,
    246-8
    history of   167, 169-70, 178,
    191-3, 195
    international   60, 73, 95, 199-
    200, 212, 235
    sociology of   7, 96, 159, 170,
    193
education(al) studies   3, 5, 9, 34,
    40-1, 43, 45, 57, 59, 64, 88-9, 99-
    100, 118, 121, 123-4, 160, 166-72,
    181-3, 191-2, 195, 204, 208, 215,
    220, 223

branches of   99, 112, 163
    distinct subfield of   2, 4, 8, 32,
    34, 88, 110-1, 114, 163, 166-8, 171-
    2, 176, 208, 215, 217, 221
    interdisciplinary subfield of
    172, 183, 208, 215
education systems   48, 119, 130,
    160, 162, 173-4, 183, 192, 195, 198,
    200
    foreign   102, 205
    higher   58, 60, 119
educational systems   28, 53, 57,
    66, 90, 103-4, 106, 159-62, 164-5,
    169-71, 193-5, 198-9, 204, 208, 215
    comparative study of   158-9
    national   34, 66, 159-61, 200
Egypt   50, 60-1, 67, 77, 107, 149-
    50, 237
England   44, 46, 70, 98, 113-4,
    130, 218, 234-5
epistemological structures   5, 21,
    208-9, 212, 214, 217, 222, 227-8
    intrinsic   227-8
epistemology   3, 5, 9, 135, 145,
    148, 211-2, 216, 221, 224, 226-7
Epstein, Erwin H.   37-8, 40-1, 43-
    6, 50-1, 64-7, 69-70, 74, 85-8, 93-4,
    127-8, 130-2, 161-2, 171-2, 179-80,
    210-1
Europe   42-3, 45, 54, 67-8, 73, 76-
    7, 82, 88, 145, 147, 195, 234-6, 241,
    245
European Union   53-4, 56, 107,
    117

F
Ferrer, Ferran   53-5, 58, 68, 117,
    139, 141, 148, 162, 164, 175, 191,
    195-6, 203-4, 247
Finland   44, 47, 60-2, 67, 108, 235

forces   6-7, 14, 16, 22, 24, 30, 123, 125, 173, 207, 209, 212
    epistemological   22, 214, 221, 223
foreign education   103, 197-9, 203-5
Foucauldian/Foucault   3, 6-9, 11, 14, 23-8, 32-3, 36, 46, 85, 101, 104, 112-3, 123-4, 138, 155-6, 209-10, 227
France   43, 47, 56, 60-2, 67, 70, 78, 102-3, 108, 202, 234-6

G

García Garrido, José Luís   1, 22, 32, 37, 55, 67, 80, 83, 106, 127, 129, 148, 157-9, 164, 170-1, 175-6, 182, 191-5
Greek Comparative Education Society (GCES)   75, 95, 236, 244
Germany   46, 50-2, 60-2, 68, 70, 72, 118, 120, 148, 213, 234-5, 248
global education   72, 201-3, 205, 212, 238, 248
globalisation   57, 59, 90, 162, 201
Greece   52-3, 55, 61-2, 68, 78, 234-6
Greek Comparative Education Society (GCES)   75, 95, 236, 244
Gu, Mingyuan   95, 144-5, 175, 178, 206-7

H

habitus   8, 29-31, 35-6, 52, 59, 98, 100, 112, 114, 120, 211, 213, 218, 220, 224
    individual   30, 213-4

Halls, W.D.   3, 37-8, 42, 45, 65, 89, 92, 140, 143, 150, 153, 162, 179, 196-8, 210
Hirst, P.   6, 13-5, 17-8, 153, 156, 172, 180
histories   10, 27, 37-8, 42-3, 64, 76-7, 96-8, 100-1, 115-6, 124-5, 127, 130-1, 140, 143, 151-2
Hong Kong   10-11, 43-5, 60, 62-3, 68, 72, 77, 83, 90, 115, 123, 238-9, 250
human capital theories   132, 135-6, 144
humanities   170, 176-8, 183, 190
Hungary   47-8, 60-62, 68, 79, 90, 146, 234, 236

I

India   44-5, 50, 55, 67, 77, 238-9
International Bureau of Education (IBE)   102, 104-5, 107-8, 120, 141, 235
Israel Comparative Education Society (ICES)   75, 239, 244
IEA   102, 104, 106, 108, 130
International Journal of Educational Development (IJED)   72, 92-3, 96, 235, 246, 248-9
institutional construction of comparative education   4, 37, 87, 109, 124, 218, 220-2, 226-7
institutional histories of comparative education   4-5, 9-11, 38, 52, 108, 110-11, 124-5, 127, 226-8
institutional legitimacy   2, 50, 88, 100-1, 109, 125, 221, 224-5
institutional power   23, 59, 89, 100-1, 110, 125, 224-5

institutionalisation   9, 16-8, 33, 38, 40-1, 43, 52, 55, 59, 99-100, 112, 121, 123, 217-9, 222

intellectual construction of comparative education   209, 212, 218, 220-1

intellectual field   5, 7-9, 23-4, 28-34, 36, 45, 47-9, 63-4, 77-80, 110-12, 114-9, 154-6, 208-14, 219-23, 227-9

of comparative education   48-9, 52, 59, 71, 89, 98, 143, 218

intellectual histories of comparative education   9, 127, 129, 131, 133, 135, 137, 139, 141-3, 145, 147, 149, 151

intellectual legitimacy of comparative education   4, 55, 99, 217

interdisciplinarity/interdisciplinary fields   19, 21-2, 51, 74, 99, 171-2, 180, 191, 228

international agencies   4, 56, 101-2, 107-8, 111

international education   5, 10, 39-40, 68, 72, 88, 91, 93, 110, 114, 172-3, 196-205, 210, 212-4

International Education Journal   73, 205, 238

International Education Review (IER)   70, 73, 205, 235

International Education Organisations   102-3

international organisations   37, 39, 56, 69, 95, 101, 106, 108, 110, 144, 159, 212-3

International Review of Education (IRE)   70, 73, 92, 104, 235, 246

Israel Comparative Education Society (ICES)   75, 239, 244

Italy   60-3, 68, 90, 119-20, 235

J

Japan   44, 46-7, 60-2, 66, 76-8, 82, 103, 113, 115, 123, 149, 203-4, 238-9, 248

Japan Comparative Education Society (JCES)   75, 103, 239, 243

Journal of Comparative Education   71-2, 238

Jullien, M.A.   128-30, 141, 151

K

Kandel, Isaac   45, 66, 140-1, 150, 160, 173, 178, 233-4

Kazakhstan   52-3, 61-2, 67, 78, 105, 116, 146, 149-50, 238-9

Korean Comparative Education Society (KCES)   75, 239, 243

Kenya   43, 45, 50, 52, 59, 62, 67, 115, 237

Korea   52, 55, 60-2, 67-8, 76-8, 82, 85, 90, 115, 123, 149-50, 238-9

L

Latin America   42-3, 67-8, 77, 106, 143, 240

M

Malaysia   52, 60-2, 149-50, 238

Manzon, Maria   10, 13, 16, 40, 42-4, 53, 65, 68, 76, 80, 83, 90, 92, 94, 146, 150, 250

Masemann, Vandra   38, 46, 65, 76, 78, 81, 83-4, 86, 94, 130, 143, 146, 205, 232, 244

Mason, Mark   1, 4, 27, 69, 110, 163, 166-8, 170, 176, 183, 204, 225

Mediterranean Society of Comparative Education (MESCE)   75, 236

Mexico   60-2, 67-8, 78, 240

N

Namibia   52, 61-3, 237
Naya, Luis M.   47, 52-5, 58, 72, 80, 117
Noah, Harold   67, 108, 129, 139, 142-4, 160-1, 178, 180
Nordic Comparative and International Education Society (NOCIES)   75, 236, 243
North America   42, 79, 130, 135, 143, 145, 233

O

OECD   56, 102-5, 107-8
Olivera, Carlos   1, 68, 159, 169, 172, 178, 187, 191, 206-7, 240

P

Paulston, Rolland   127, 131-2, 134-9, 143-5, 148, 151, 153
Polish Comparative Education Society (PCES)   75, 236, 244
People's Republic of China see China
Phillips, D.   1, 37-8, 66, 68-9, 93, 131, 139-40, 142, 161, 175, 179, 196-7, 210
philosophy   66, 70, 128, 132, 167, 182, 189, 192-3, 208, 212
Poland   43-4, 48, 59, 67, 78, 146, 234-6
Polish Comparative Education Society (PCES)   75, 236, 244
political capital of comparative education   50, 53
political power   34, 52, 82, 98, 115-6, 194, 221
politics, educational   119, 194

Popov, Nikolay   10, 38, 42-3, 48, 143, 146
positivism   128, 130, 134, 151, 211
postmodernism   138, 149-51, 212
power   4-5, 7-8, 22-6, 28, 30-2, 34-5, 48, 65, 99, 112-13, 115-6, 118-9, 155-6, 209-12, 219-21
   academic   31, 58, 122, 124, 219
   epistemological forms of   216, 218, 221
   external fields of   32, 209, 227
   intellectual   31
   position(s) of   82, 211-2, 214, 216
   scientific   31, 56, 71, 79
power relations   3-4, 8, 25-8, 33, 37, 54, 86, 98-9, 110-11, 113, 115, 121, 155-6, 211-3, 221-2

R

Revista Española de Educación Comparada (REEC)   72, 148, 235, 247-8
Russia   48, 52-3, 61-2, 67-8, 78, 146, 234
Russian Council of Comparative Education (RCCE)   75, 94, 244
Rust, Val   92, 138, 162, 198, 246

S

Sadler, Michael   41, 130, 140-1, 151
Schweisfurth, M.   1, 37-8, 66, 68-9, 93, 131, 139-40, 142, 161, 175, 179, 196-7, 210
Sociedad Argentina de Estudios Comparados en Educación (SAECE)   75, 78, 240

Sociedade Brasileira de Educação
    Comparada (SBEC)   75, 83,
    231, 240, 243
Sociedad Española de Educación
    Comparada (SEEC)   75, 80, 83,
    95, 99, 231, 236, 243
social constructionism   137-8
social sciences   24, 55, 110, 133,
    138, 148, 157, 161, 170, 172, 176,
    180-4, 186, 188-91, 207-8
socialist countries   42, 48, 115,
    143, 146, 234
society formation   78, 87, 121-3,
    219-20
sociology   13, 49, 132, 161, 167,
    178, 181-2, 187, 191
Sociedad Mexicana de Educación
    Comparada (SOMEC)   75, 81,
    122, 240, 244
South Africa   48-50, 60-2, 67, 79,
    85, 89, 115, 237
Southern African Review of Edu-
    cation   72, 237
Spain   42, 47, 52-4, 58, 61-2, 67-8,
    77, 82-3, 112, 116-8, 122, 207, 219,
    234-6
specialist journals   2, 18, 69-71,
    92, 104, 209, 218, 222
Sweden   47, 60, 67, 202, 234-5
Switzerland   43, 52, 55-6, 60, 108,
    119-20, 234

T

Taiwan   43, 60-2, 67, 77, 149, 238-
    9, 243
Tanzania   50, 61-2, 149-50, 237
teacher education   49, 51-3, 55-6,
    59, 88, 107, 118, 147, 157, 182, 214
Thailand   45, 47, 60-2, 78, 115,
    149-50, 238

theories   6-7, 14-5, 21-2, 28, 30, 52,
    91-2, 97, 100, 102, 131-2, 135-6,
    138-9, 151, 208-9
    critical   135, 137-8
    functionalist   133-4
    interpretivist   133-4, 138, 144
Tusquets, Juan   47, 67, 80, 165,
    178, 182, 234-5

U

Uganda   44, 61-2, 149-50, 237
UK   43, 45, 50, 60-3, 68, 71-3, 79,
    82, 90, 113, 115, 202-4, 213, 235,
    246
Ukrainian Comparative Education
    Society (UCES)   75, 236, 244
United Nations Educational Scien-
    tific and Cultural Organization
    (UNESCO)   56, 71, 87, 102-5,
    107-8, 113, 117, 202, 235
universities   1-2, 37-8, 40-5, 47-9,
    51-3, 56-60, 62-3, 90-1, 101-3, 111,
    114-5, 117-20, 218-9, 232-4, 241-2
University of Hong Kong   10-11,
    44, 72, 90, 238, 250
US/USA   89, 240, 46, 50, 56, 245,
    38, 43-6, 50, 60-3, 70-1, 76-8, 82-3,
    112-3, 115-7, 202-4, 206-7, 213,
    218, 233, 248

W

Walterová, Eliška   39, 47-8, 58,
    66, 68, 76, 79, 84, 105, 146
Waterkamp, Dietmar   46-8, 51-2,
    118, 148
Watson, Keith   42-3, 51, 69, 139-
    40, 142, 200
Wilson, David N.   3, 37, 43, 51,
    60, 66, 196, 200, 210

Wolhuter, Charl   10, 37-8, 42-4,
    50-2, 59-63, 65, 68, 90-2, 100, 107-
    8, 143, 146, 149-50, 232, 247
World Bank, The   102-3, 105, 107,
    113, 141, 214
World Congress(es) of Compara-
    tive Education Societies   2, 73,
    77, 80-2, 84-6, 89, 94, 123
World Council of Comparative
    Education Societies (WCCES)
    10-11, 41, 74-86, 94, 105, 121-3,
    213, 219, 231, 237, 240, 243-5, 250
World War II   45-6, 106, 112, 115,
    218-9

CERC Studies in Comparative Education (ctd)

12. Robert A. LeVine (2003, reprinted 2010): *Childhood Socialization: Comparative Studies of Parenting, Learning and Educational Change.* ISBN 978-962-8093-61-8. 299pp.

11. Ruth Hayhoe & Julia Pan (eds.) (2001): *Knowledge Across Cultures: A Contribution to Dialogue Among Civilizations.* ISBN 978-962-8093-73-1. 391pp. [Out of print]

10. William K. Cummings, Maria Teresa Tatto & John Hawkins (eds.) (2001): *Values Education for Dynamic Societies: Individualism or Collectivism.* ISBN 978-962-8093-71-7. 312pp. HK$200/US$32.

9. Gu Mingyuan (2001): *Education in China and Abroad: Perspectives from a Lifetime in Comparative Education.* ISBN 978-962-8093-70-0. 252pp. HK$200/US$32.

8. Thomas Clayton (2000): *Education and the Politics of Language: Hegemony and Pragmatism in Cambodia, 1979-1989.* ISBN 978-962-8093-83-0. 243pp. HK$200/US$32.

7. Mark Bray & Ramsey Koo (eds.) (2004): *Education and Society in Hong Kong and Macao: Comparative Perspectives on Continuity and Change.* Second edition. ISBN 978-962-8093-34-2. 323pp. HK$200/US$32.

6. T. Neville Postlethwaite (1999): *International Studies of Educational Achievement: Methodological Issues.* ISBN 978-962-8093-86-1. 86pp. HK$100/US$20.

5. Harold Noah & Max A. Eckstein (1998): *Doing Comparative Education: Three Decades of Collaboration.* ISBN 978-962-8093-87-8. 356pp. HK$250/US$38.

4. Zhang Weiyuan (1998): *Young People and Careers: A Comparative Study of Careers Guidance in Hong Kong, Shanghai and Edinburgh.* ISBN 978-962-8093-89-2. 160pp. HK$180/US$30.

3. Philip G. Altbach (1998): *Comparative Higher Education: Knowledge, the University, and Development.* ISBN 978-962-8093-88-5. 312pp. HK$180/US$30.

2. Mark Bray & W.O. Lee (eds.) (1997): *Education and Political Transition: Implications of Hong Kong's Change of Sovereignty.* ISBN 978-962-8093-90-8. 169pp. [Out of print]

1. Mark Bray & W.O. Lee (eds.) (2001): *Education and Political Transition: Themes and Experiences in East Asia.* Second edition. ISBN 978-962-8093-84-7. 228pp. HK$200/US$32.

Order through bookstores or from:

Comparative Education Research Centre
Faculty of Education, The University of Hong Kong, Pokfulam Road, Hong Kong, China.
Fax: (852) 2517 4737 ; E-mail: cerc@hku.hk; Website: www.hku.hk/cerc

The list prices above are applicable for order from CERC, and include sea mail postage. For air mail postage costs, please contact CERC.

No. 7 in the series and Nos. 13-15 are co-published with Kluwer Academic Publishers and the Comparative Education Research Centre of the University of Hong Kong. Books from No. 16 onwards are co-published with Springer. Springer publishes hardback and electronic versions.

Other CERC Publications

Series: CERC Monographs Series in Comparative and International Education and Development

1. Yoko Yamato (2003): *Education in the Market Place: Hong Kong's International Schools and their Mode of Operation*. ISBN 978-962-8093-57-1. 117pp. HK$100/US$16.

2. Mark Bray, Ding Xiaohao & Huang Ping (2004): *Reducing the Burden on the Poor: Household Costs of Basic Education in Gansu, China*. ISBN 978-962-8093-32-8. 67pp. HK$50/US$10. [Also available in Chinese]

3. Maria Manzon (2004): *Building Alliances: Schools, Parents and Communities in Hong Kong and Singapore*. ISBN 978-962-8093-36-6. 117pp. HK$100/US$16.

4. Mark Bray & Seng Bunly (2005): *Balancing the Books: Household Financing of Basic Education in Cambodia*. ISBN 978-962-8093-39-7. 113pp. HK$100/US$16.

5. Linda Chisholm, Graeme Bloch & Brahm Fleisch (eds.) (2008): *Education, Growth, Aid and Development: Towards Education for All*. ISBN 978-962-8093-99-1. 116pp. HK$100/US$16

6. Eduardo Andere (2008): *The Lending Power of PISA: League Tables and Best Practice in International Education*. ISBN 978-988-17852-1-3. 138pp. HK$100/US$16.

7. Nina Ye. Borevskaya, V.P. Borisenkov & Xiaoman Zhu (eds.) (2010): *Educational Reforms in Russia and China at the Turn of the 21st Century: A Comparative Analysis*. ISBN 978-988-17852-4-4. 115pp. HK$100/US$16.

8. Nirmala Rao & Jin Sun (2010): *Early Childhood Care and Education in the Asia Pacific Region: Moving Towards Goal 1*. ISBN 978-988-17852-5-1. 97pp. HK$100/US$16.

Series: Education in Developing Asia

The five titles in the Series are HK$100/US$12 each or HK$400/US$50 for set of five.

1. Don Adams (2004): *Education and National Development: Priorities, Policies, and Planning*. ISBN 978-971-561-529-7. 81pp.

2. David Chapman (2004): *Management and Efficiency in Education: Goals and Strategies*. ISBN 978-971-561-530-3. 85pp.

3. Mark Bray (2004): *The Costs and Financing of Education: Trends and Policy Implications*. ISBN 978-971-561-531-0. 78pp.

4. W.O. Lee (2004): *Equity and Access to Education: Themes, Tensions, and Policies*. ISBN 978-971-561-532-7. 101pp.

5. David Chapman & Don Adams (2004): *The Quality of Education: Dimensions and Strategies*. ISBN 978-971-561-533-4. 72pp.

CERC Monographs Series No.3

Building Alliances

Schools, Parents and
Communities in
Hong Kong and Singapore

Maria Manzon

Publisher: Comparative Education
Research Centre (CERC)
ISBN 978-962-8093-36-6
September 2004; 117 pages
Price: HK$100/US$16

Governments worldwide are increasingly advocating parental and community partnerships in education. This monograph explores the evolution of parental and community partnerships in Hong Kong and Singapore, and the local and global forces that have shaped those partnerships. It focuses on the work of two government advisory bodies established to spearhead partnership advocacy: the Committee on Home-School Co-operation (CHSC) in Hong Kong, and Community and Parents in Support of Schools (COMPASS) in Singapore. Key policy actors and local academics in the two states were interviewed to gain insiders' perspectives on the 'micro-politics' of educational partnership.

Comparative educators, ministries of education, and educational policy makers will gain from this book a penetrating insight into parent-school-community partnership in a pair of Asian contexts, and may find some good practices and lessons.

Maria Manzon initially studied in the Philippines and in Italy, and then graduated from the MEd programme in Comparative Education at the University of Hong Kong. She has had almost 10 years of working experience in Hong Kong and Southeast Asia, in the fields of finance and education.

More details: www.hku.hk/cerc/Publications/publications.htm

CERC Studies in Comparative Education 21

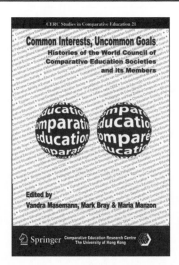

Common Interests, Uncommon Goals
Histories of the World Council of Comparative Education Societies and its Members

Edited by
**Vandra Masemann, Mark Bray
and Maria Manzon**

Publishers: Comparative Education
Research Centre and Springer
ISBN 978-962-8093-10-6
September 2007; 384 pages
Price: HK$250 / US$38

The World Council of Comparative Education Societies (WCCES) was established in 1970 as an umbrella body which brought together five national and regional comparative education societies. Over the decades it greatly expanded, and now embraces three dozen societies.

This book presents histories of the WCCES and its member societies. It shows ways in which the field has changed over the decades, and the forces which have shaped it in different parts of the world. The book demonstrates that while comparative education can be seen as a single global field, it has different characteristics in different countries and cultures. In this sense, the book presents a comparison of comparisons.

Vandra Masemann is a past WCCES President and Secretary General. She has also been President of the US-Based Comparative and International Education Society (CIES), and of the Comparative and International Education Society of Canada (CIESC). *Mark Bray* is also a past WCCES President and Secretary General. He has also been President of the Comparative Education Society of Hong Kong (CESHK). *Maria Manzon* is a member of the CESHK and has been an Assistant Secretary General of the WCCES. Her research on the field has been undertaken at the Comparative Education Research Centre of the University of Hong Kong.

More details: www.hku.hk/cerc/Publications/publications.htm

CERC Studies in Comparative Education 19

Comparative Education Research
Approaches and Methods

Edited by
Mark Bray
Bob Adamson
Mark Mason

Publishers: Comparative Education Research Centre and Springer
ISBN: 978-962-8093-53-3
Date: 2007; 444 pages
Price: HK$250 / US$38

Approaches and methods in comparative education research are of obvious importance, but do not always receive adequate attention. This book contributes new insights within the longstanding traditions of the field.

A particular feature is the focus on different units of analysis. Individual chapters compare places, systems, times, cultures, values, policies, curricula and other units. These chapters are contextualised within broader analytical frameworks which identify the purposes and strengths of the field. The book includes a focus on intra-national as well as cross-national comparisons, and highlights the value of approaching themes from different angles. The book will be of great value not only to producers of comparative education research but also to consumers who wish to understand more thoroughly the parameters and value of the field.

The editors: *Mark Bray* is Director of the UNESCO International Institute for Educational Planning, in Paris; *Bob Adamson* is Associate Professor in the Hong Kong Institute of Education; and *Mark Mason* is Associate Professor in the Faculty of Education at the University of Hong Kong. They have all been Presidents of the Comparative Education Society of Hong Kong (CESHK), and Directors of the Comparative Education Research Centre (CERC) at the University of Hong Kong. They have also written extensively in the field of comparative education with reference to multiple domains and cultures.

More details: www.hku.hk/cerc/Publications/publications.htm

Doing Comparative Education: Three Decades of Collaboration

Harold J. Noah & Max A. Eckstein

with a foreword by
Philip Foster

Publisher: Comparative Education
Research Centre
ISBN 978-962-8093-87-8
1998; 356 pages
Price: HK$250/US$38

The writings of Harold J. Noah and Max A. Eckstein are well known in the field of comparative education. For over three decades, they have worked and published collaboratively. Both separately and together, they have made major contributions to the field.

This book brings together selections from their work, showing how their thinking, and that in the field as a whole, has evolved over the decades. The book makes available extracts from seminal works which had gone out of print, and places them between the covers of a single volume. The book commences with a foreword by Philip Foster, who is another distinguished figure in the field and who analyzes the work of Noah and Eckstein in its historical context. Foster notes that Noah and Eckstein write with "clarity, felicity, and economy". From the earliest stages of their careers they have also written with penetrating insight. The Comparative Education Research Centre at the University of Hong Kong is proud to publish this collection, which will become a major reference work for new generations of scholars in the field of comparative education.

More details: www.hku.hk/cerc/Publications/publications.htm

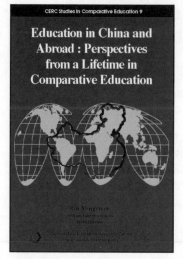

Education in China and Abroad: Perspectives from a Lifetime in Comparative Education

Gu Mingyuan

with an Introduction by
Ruth Hayhoe

Publisher: Comparative Education
Research Centre
ISBN 978-962-8093-70-0
2001; 260 pages
Price: HK$200/US$32

Gu Mingyuan is one of China's most distinguished specialists in the field of comparative education. He is a long-serving of the China Comparative Education Society, and in 2000 he was elected President of the Chinese Education Society. Yet because most of his works have been published only in Chinese, they have been little-known internationally.

The book commences with an Introduction to Professor Gu's life and work by Ruth Hayhoe. She is a Past-President of the Comparative & International Education Society, and has made seminal contributions to the study of education in China from a comparative perspective. Since 1997 she has been Director of the Hong Kong Institute of Education.

The book commences with an Introduction to Professor Gu's life and work by Ruth Hayhoe. She is a Past-President of the Comparative & International Education Society, and has made seminal contributions to the study of education in China from a comparative perspectives. Since 1997 she has been Director of the Hong Kong Institute of Education.

More details: www.hku.hk/cerc/Publications/publications.htm

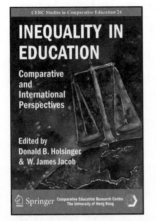

INEQUALITY IN EDUCATION

Comparative and International Perspectives

Edited by Donald B. Holsinger & W. James Jacob

Publishers: Comparative Education Research Centre and Springer
ISBN 978-962-8093-14-4
December 2008; 584 pages
Price: HK$300/US$45

Inequality in Education: Comparative and International Perspectives is a compilation of conceptual chapters and national case studies that includes a series of methods for measuring education inequalities. The book provides up-to-date scholarly research on global trends in the distribution of formal schooling in national populations. It also offers a strategic comparative and international education policy statement on recent shifts in education inequality, and new approaches to explore, develop and improve comparative education and policy research globally. Contributing authors examine how education as a process interacts with government finance policy to form patterns of access to education services. In addition to case perspectives from 18 countries across six geographic regions, the volume includes six conceptual chapters on topics that influence education inequality, such as gender, disability, language and economics, and a summary chapter that presents new evidence on the pernicious consequences of inequality in the distribution of education. The book offers (1) a better and more holistic understanding of ways to measure education inequalities; and (2) strategies for facing the challenge of inequality in education in the processes of policy formation, planning and implementation at the local, regional, national and global levels.

Donald B. Holsinger is Professor Emeritus in Education and Development Studies at Brigham Young University, and has held academic appointments at the University of Chicago, the University of Arizona, and the State University of New York (Albany). He is a former President of the Comparative and International Education Society and Senior Education Specialist at the World Bank.

W. James Jacob is Director of the Institute for International Studies in Education at the University of Pittsburgh's School of Education, and is the former Assistant Director of the Center for International and Development Education at the University of California (Los Angeles).

More details: www.hku.hk/cerc/Publications/publications.htm

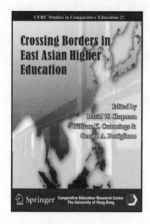

Crossing Borders in East Asian Higher Education

Edited by
David W. Chapman, William K. Cummings & Gerard A. Postiglione

Publishers: Comparative Education Research Centre and Springer
ISBN 978-962-8093-98-4
June 2010; 388 pages
Price: HK$250/US$38

This book examines issues that have emerged as higher education systems and individual institutions across East Asia confront and adapt to the changing economic, social, and educational environments in which they now operate. The book's focus is on how higher education systems learn from each other and on the ways in which they collaborate to address new challenges. The sub-theme that runs through this volume concerns the changing nature of cross-border sharing. In particular, the provision of technical assistance by more industrialized countries to lower and middle income countries has given way to collaborations that place the latter's participating institutions on a more equal footing. At the same time, there is a greater number of partnerships that link higher education systems in the East Asian region to one another. Even as boundaries become more porous and permeable, there is growing acceptance of the view that cross border collaboration, if done well, can offer mutually beneficial advantages on multiple levels. There is a new recognition that the intensified international sharing of ideas, strategies of learning, and students is not only of enormous value to systems and institutions but essential to their long term survival. To this end, the chapters in this volume examine various motivations, goals, mechanisms, outcomes and challenges associated with cross-border collaboration in higher education.

David W. CHAPMAN is the Birkmaier Professor of Educational Leadership in the Department of Organizational Leadership, Policy, and Development in the College of Education and Human Development at the University of Minnesota. **William K. CUMMINGS** is Professor of International Education and International Affairs at George Washington University. **Gerard A. POSTIGLIONE** is Professor and Head, Division of Policy, Administration and Social Sciences, and Director of the Wah Ching Centre of Research on Education in China, Faculty of Education, the University of Hong Kong.

More details: www.hku.hk/cerc/Publications/publications.htm